Introduction

to

MAMMALOGY

E. LENDELL COCKRUM

UNIVERSITY OF ARIZONA
TUCSON

THE RONALD PRESS COMPANY · NEW YORK

Preface

The material in this book has been prepared to meet the needs of a college-level course in mammalogy and wildlife management and to serve naturalists, wildlife technicians, and others interested in mammals. Over a period of several years it was tested in classroom usage.

A scanning of the contents will show that the material is divided into two parts: the first discusses basic principles, including characteristics, classification, distribution, reproduction, development, behavior, populations, and economic relationships of mammals. The second part presents in systematic order each of the 123 families of living mammals. Since mammals are world-wide in distribution, examples, especially in the first part, have been drawn from both Old World and New World species.

Necessary limitations of space to fit this text to the introductory course have meant that at times discussions have been abbreviated or various aspects of a topic have been omitted. In many cases alternate (and often highly controversial) theories have had to be introduced with little or no comment.

The accounts of the families in the second section of the book have been designed to demonstrate the great morphological, distributional, and behavioral diversity found among the mammals of the world. To achieve this, almost as much space has been allotted to some rare and little-known groups as to those that are common and widespread. For the dual purpose of indicating the diversity within each family, and as a reference useful in further reading, a list of Recent genera is provided at the end of each account of a family.

The reference system used (giving the author's name and year of publication in place of some system employing numbers) was adopted as a technique for exposing the students to the names of the various workers, both past and present, in the field of mammalogy. References are divided into two major types: General Bibliography and Literature Cited. The General Bibliography consists of a selected group of references of special interest and includes a number of references that have been most helpful in writing the book. This bibliography will lead the reader to additional information about the common mammals in his own region, while the Literature Cited contains references to the items actually referred to in the text.

A large number of persons have assisted, in one way or another, with the preparation of this manuscript. For many helpful suggestions, comments, and criticisms, I wish to thank the undergraduate and graduate students who have used and read the various versions of this manuscript; Lyle Sowls and Roger Hungerford of the Arizona Cooperative Wildlife Research Unit and Joseph T. Bagnara of the Department of Zoology at the University of Arizona; William H. Burt of the University of Michigan, W. Frank Blair of the University of Texas, E. Raymond Hall of the University of Kansas, and Donald F. Hoffmeister of the University of Illinois. For the use of photographs, I wish to thank Ernest P. Walker, formerly Associate Director of the United States National Zoological Gardens, who took most of the photographs used here; Bruce J. Hayward of New Mexico Western State College; and John N. Hamlet. For the preparation of illustrations, I acknowledge with deep appreciation the efforts of Betty Bradshaw (who prepared all but two of the illustrations), Jane Eppinga, and Bernard Maza. Donald Sayner, Scientific Illustrator in the Department of Zoology at the University of Arizona, offered constructive criticisms of these drawings.

For help in the mechanics of manuscript preparation, I am grateful to several persons, especially Jane Eppinga, who typed the final draft of the manuscript, and Clark Cubley, who prepared the distribution maps.

E. LENDELL COCKRUM

Tucson, Arizona
  May, 1962

Contents

Part I
BIOLOGY OF MAMMALS

Part II
MAMMALIAN ORDERS AND FAMILIES

v

Part I
BIOLOGY OF MAMMALS

1
Characteristics of Mammals

INTRODUCTION

Mammals are usually considered to be the pinnacle of vertebrate development and today form the dominant animal feature in the ecology of the world. This is all the more true when we consider man and his effect on the environment.

Mammals have all of the characteristics of the vertebrates, including the dorsal hollow nerve cord, a notochord (present in embryonic stages and replaced by the backbone), and pharyngeal clefts (during embryonic development). The presence of an amnion and an allantois in the fetal membranes separates the mammals from the fish and amphibians, as does the absence of gills. Mammals differ from reptiles and resemble birds in that they are warm-blooded (possibly some extinct mammal-like reptiles were also warm-blooded), have a four-chambered heart, and have a complete, double circulatory system. Mammals are more highly evolved than birds in method of reproduction, in paternal care and suckling of young, and in the greater development of intelligence.

A number of external and internal features are characteristic of mammals. Several of these are listed below and some of the more important characteristics are discussed in detail in the following pages.

LIST OF CHARACTERISTICS

External Characteristics
1. Size, in general, is larger than in other living vertebrates.
2. Pelage, or hair, is present in at least some stage of development of all mammals. A Pterosaurian reptile is known to have had hairlike structures, otherwise hair is unique with mammals
3. An external ear opening, surrounded by a well-developed pinna or conch, is present in most mammals. The pinna is reduced or absent in certain fossorial and aquatic species.

Internal Characteristics
  I. Features of the soft anatomy
    1. Mammary glands (milk glands) are present in all females of this class.

3

2. The young are born alive in all mammals except the egg-laying monotremes and, possibly, some of the extinct groups.
3. The cerebral hemispheres of the brain (the part associated with memory and reason) are highly variable in size within the order but, in general, are greatly enlarged in comparison with other vertebrates. The early mammals, however, were little advanced over mammal-like reptiles in this feature.
4. A muscular diaphragm separates the lungs from the posterior body cavity. Birds, the only other vertebrate with a diaphragm, have a non-muscular diaphragm.
5. Facial muscles are usually well developed.
6. The red blood cells are non-nucleated when fully developed (except in the camels).

II. Osteological features
    1. Skull
       a. A double occipital condyle (formed by the exoccipital bones) is found in all mammals.
       b. The zygomatic arch is an appendage of the skull instead of a part of the skull.
       c. Each ramus of the mandible is composed of a single bone, the dentary.
       d. The jaw articulates directly with the squamosal. This is the most diagnostic osteological feature of the class Mammalia.
       e. Three ear ossicles are present. To the stapes of the primitive tetrapod vertebrate are added the articular (malleus) and the quadrate (incus).
       f. The tympanic bone, originating from the reptilian angular bone, surrounds and protects the inner ear.
       g. There is a single external nareal opening (the opening in the skull for the nasal passages).
       h. A secondary hard palate is formed from the premaxilla and maxilla and, occasionally, the palatines.
       i. Teeth are present in the jaw. These teeth are not diagnostically different from those of the mammal-like reptiles.
    2. Postcranial elements
       a. There is a marked distinction between the series of vertebrae; the following groups are recognized: cervical, thoracic, lumbar, sacral, and caudal.
       b. The limbs are rotated forward with marked angulation. This type of leg suspension is not diagnostic but is certainly characteristic.
       c. The ankle joint is between the tibia and the tarsus; in reptiles and birds, it is between the tarsal elements.

EXTERNAL FEATURES

Externally, mammals show considerable variation. This variation can be seen in over-all size, in the development of the pinnae of the ears, in the amount and distribution of hair, and in the external expression of differences in internal structures which result in various types of limbs and tails. Some of these differences are discussed below.

SIZE

There appears to be some question as to which is the smallest living mammal. The pygmy shrew (*Microsorex hoyi*) of North America, which has a body length of 50 to 65 mm., a tail length of 25 to 30 mm., and a skull that is 13.0 to 15.8 mm. in length, has been listed as the smallest living mammal by some authors. Weights of this small shrew range from 2.8 to 3.5 grams (28.3 grams to one ounce). The dwarf shrew (*Suncus gracilis*) of South Africa appears to be about equally small. It has a head and body length of from 42 to 62 mm. and a tail length of from 24 to 31 mm. The greatest length of the skull varies from 14.1 to 15.2 mm. The writer has not been able to locate any records of weight for this species. The little yellow bat (*Rhogeëssa parvula*) of Mexico has a head and body length of approximately 46 mm. and a tail length of 30 mm. The greatest length of skull ranges from 11.2 to 12.2 mm. Again, weights are not available.

The largest living terrestrial mammal is the elephant. Some elephants are over 3.3 m. (11 feet) tall and weigh up to 6590 kg. (14,500 pounds). The largest living mammal is the blue whale (*Balaenoptera musculus*). It reaches a length of 302 m. (105 feet) and weights of up to 107,272 kg. (236,000 pounds; as much as 1,573 average men). This whale is the largest of all animals, living or extinct, and exceeds several times the bulk of the largest dinosaurs. Most species of mammals are comparatively small, the average size being about that of a small house cat.

HAIR

One of the most obvious external features of mammals is the presence of hair; it completely covers the bodies of most species, although it may be restricted to specific areas in some kinds. Marine mammals in general have the hair reduced, and in whales (Cetacea) it is almost entirely absent, with only a few vibrissae about the lips or else present only in the young.

Hairs are specialized outgrowths of the epidermis, just as are the horn coverings of cows and sheep, and the claws, nails, hooves, and horny pads of the feet of other mammals. An individual hair develops first as a thickening of the epidermis. This thickening pushes downward into the dermis. At the base of this developing hair follicle an upcupping of dermal tissues forms the hair papilla. The dermal papilla is richly supplied with blood vessels that furnish food for the growth of the hair (see Fig. 1–1). The hair is forced out of the skin by growth from below.

A hair is a multicellular structure that, after being pushed out by the skin, is dead. A single hair follicle may produce several hairs by budding and usually has one or more sebaceous (oil) glands associated with it. The oily secretions of the sebaceous glands make the

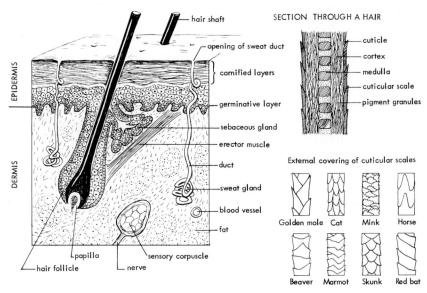

Fig. 1–1. A generalized section through a mammalian hair, indicating relationships with associated structures. Hairs show great variations both in internal structure and in the nature of their external surface.

dead hair less brittle. When a follicle finally ceases to proliferate cells, the growth of the hair ceases. Muscles (sometimes voluntary, usually involuntary) and nerves (sometimes) are connected to the base of the hair.

In cross-section, a typical hair is made up of three layers: the inner medulla, the outer cuticle, and the intermediate cortex. The medulla contains shrunken cells of dried epithelial structures and may contain pigments. Hairs can be classified as to the structure of the medulla: (a) absent—no medulla present; (b) discontinuous —air spaces separate the parts of the medulla; (c) intermediate— several separate air spaces of the discontinuous type arranged in a regular pattern; (d) continuous—the air spaces are arranged to form a column; and (e) fragmental—with air spaces arranged in irregular groups and forming no pattern. There is a close correlation between the type of medulla and the diameter of the hair, with the smallest hairs having the medulla absent and the largest hairs having a fragmental medulla. These air spaces add greatly to the insulation properties of hair.

The cortex, between the medulla and the outer cuticle, makes up the bulk of the hair and usually is transparent but may contain pigments. The cuticle is a thin outer layer of scales. It does not contain pigment, but the scales may be smooth, shingled, spined, spiraled or otherwise adorned. The arrangement of the scales of the cuticle is often characteristic of a species and has been used as a means of identifying loose hairs from dens or from scats.

A hair may be circular or elliptical in cross-section. Flattened hairs are curly while circular hairs are usually straight or only slightly curved. The pelage of mammals falls into the following major categories (after Noback, 1951):

I. Vibrissae are hairs with specialized follicles that contain erectile tissues. They are large stiff hairs that are primarily sensory in function and have been called feelers, whiskers, sensory hairs, sinus hairs, and tactile hairs. Two subdivisions are recognized: (a) *active tactile hairs*, which are under voluntary control, and (b) *passive tactile hairs*, which are not under voluntary control.

II. Body hairs are those with follicles that do not contain erectile tissue. They are of various sizes and are more or less defensive or protective in function. In many cases, the follicle has a good nerve supply, thus the hair serves a passive sensory function. Two subdivisions are recognized: guard hairs and underhairs.

A. *Guard hairs* are more or less stiffened hairs that are variously called overhair, top hair, and cover hair. Three subtypes are recognized: (a) *Spines* are greatly modified and enlarged hairs that are defensive in function. Porcupine quills are examples of spines. (b) *Bristles* are firm hairs, usually pigmented and scattered over the body's surface. They have been called transitional hairs, protective hairs, primary hairs, and overhair. This group includes the mane hairs of horses and lions. (c) *Awns* are hairs with a firm tip and a weaker, softer base.

B. *Underhairs* are the uniformly soft hairs that have been called underwool, ground hair, and underfur. Three subtypes are recognized: (a) *Wool* is made up of long, soft, usually curly hairs. (b) *Fur* is made up of thickly spaced, fine, relatively short hairs. (c) *Velli* are the finest and shortest of hairs and have often been called down, wool, or fuzz. Velli are often seen on foetal or newly born mammals and, in this classifiction, include lanugo (embryonic) hair.

The color of a mammal is the result of color of the skin (due to skin capillaries and to pigments in the skin), or the color of the pelage, or both. Color of the hair is determined by the amount and distribution of pigments present plus the structure of the hair. Any pigment in the hair is laid down while it is still growing in the follicle. Once the hair grows out (and thus is no longer a living structure), the pigments cannot be removed by the body. Due to the sun's action, or to the action of foreign materials on the hair, some bleaching may occur over a long period of time. This bleaching is accomplished by the breaking down of part of the pigment by chemical action. The oft-repeated tale of the man whose hair turned white overnight, as the result of some severe fright (or perhaps an electric shock), appears to have no valid basis in fact. Conceivably the mechanism which causes pigment to be laid down in growing hairs might break down and, from a given instant in time onward, additional pigments might not be deposited. The pigment already present in the hair that has grown out would remain, however. Thus, some time later when the person has a haircut that removed all of the older hair with pigment present, the hair could "turn white overnight."

Two pigments are normally found in mammalian hairs, melanin and xanthophyll. Melanin results in black or brown hair. It may occur in longitudinal striae or rows in the cortex and as clumps of granules in the medulla. Xanthophyll, resulting in reddish or yellowish colors, occurs only in the medulla, as a subterminal band near the end of the hair. The normal hair found on mammals such as the rabbit or the mouse contains a terminal band of melanin (black or blackish), a subterminal band of xanthophyll (red or yellowish), and a basal area of melanin. Such a hair is called *agouti*. Color patterns result from genetically controlled variations in the amounts and distribution of pigments present in the hair.

It has recently been discovered that certain mammalian furs fluoresce under ultraviolet light. Much additional data is needed on this point before any conclusions can be drawn; but from the small amount of data available, this does not appear to have any phylogenetic significance. In fact, one personal observation leads to the conclusion that, at least in some species, this characteristic is subject to age variation (and perhaps individual variation?). On the other hand, Latham (1953) found that this technique could be used to separate the pelts of the least weasel (*Mustela rixosa*) from those of *M. frenata* and *M. erminea*. The pelts of the least weasel fluoresce while the others do not.

From laboratory studies of the genetics of coat color in the house mouse, Norway and black rats, domestic rabbit and guinea pigs, a number of parallel coat color mutations have been discovered. Storer and Gregory (1934) reviewed some of these findings and correlated the known mutations with mutations in the coat colors of feral pocket gophers (Family Geomyidae). The color mutations include the albino allelomorph series (containing seven mutations from the normal presence of color), the extension allelomorph series (containing three mutations affecting the amounts and area of deposition of melanin), and the agouti allelomorph series (containing four mutations concerned with the expression of yellow pigments). In addition, a number of single genes controlling coat color are known.

Dichromatism is the condition of two well-marked color phases occurring in different individuals of the same species. As far as is known, the occurrence of these color phases is genetically controlled. Often it consists of a black phase (melanism) as contrasted to the normal wild type. Such is the case in the silver fox (a melanistic red fox), the black fox squirrel (*Sciurus niger,*) the black red-backed mouse (*Clethrionomys*), and the black gray squirrel (*Sciurus carolinensis*). In each of these cases it is possible for the black phase and the normal phase to occur in the same litter. Often the incidence of the two phases varies geographically; usually the darker phase becomes more prevalent in the northern part of the range of the species. In some of the deer mice (*Peromyscus*) there is a dichromatic condition consisting of buff individuals as contrasted to the normally darker individuals. Variable colors, a condition in which the animal changes color with the season, is a result of molting and is discussed under that heading.

INTERNAL FEATURES

When compared with such vertebrate groups as the fishes and reptiles, mammals are notably stable in most of their morphological features. This stability is probably the result of the long period of evolution in the mammal-like reptile group (the direct ancestors of mammals) wherein much of the variability was eliminated. A dynamic example of this stability is evident in the number of cervical vertebrae in the vertebral column. In one family of the Class Reptilia (Order Sauropterygia, Family Pliosauridae) the number of cervical vertebrae varies from 13 to as many as 76 in number. In the Class Mammalia, in contrast, all but two or three minor exceptions have 7 cervical vertebrae.

OSTEOLOGICAL FEATURES

The mammalian skeleton is internal, is made up primarily of bone, and serves three major functions: It supports the body, serves as points of attachment for muscles, and protects certain vital organs such as the brain, nerve cord, heart, and lungs.

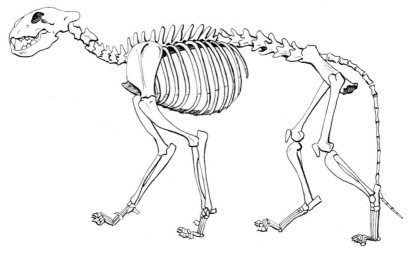

Fig. 1–2. The skeleton of a typical mammal. The major subdivisions of the mammalian skeleton, as outlined in the text, are evident in this drawing.

The following outline indicates the major subdivisions of the mammalian skeleton (see Fig. 1–2):

I. Axial skeleton (medially situated)
   A. Skull
      1. Cranium (brain case)
      2. Sense capsules (around nose, eyes, and ears)
      3. Visceral arches
         a. Jaws
         b. Hyoid
         c. Larynx
   B. Vertebral column
      1. Cervical (neck) vertebrae
      2. Thoracic (chest) vertebrae
      3. Lumbar (lower back) vertebrae
      4. Sacral (hip) vertebrae
      5. Caudal (tail) vertebrae
   C. Thoracic basket
      1. Ribs (paired)
      2. Sternum (breast bone)

II. Appendicular skeleton (lateral and paired)
    A. Pectoral (anterior) elements
        1. Pectoral (shoulder) girdle
           a. Scapula
           b. Clavicle
           c. Coracoid
        2. Pectoral (fore) limb
           a. Humerus (upper arm)
           b. Radius and ulna (forearm)
           c. Carpals (wrist)
           d. Metacarpals (palm)
           e. Phalanges (fingers)
    B. Pelvic (hind) elements
        1. Pelvic (hip) girdle
           a. Ilium (dorsal)
           b. Pubis (anterior)
           c. Ischium (posterior)
        2. Pelvic (hind) limb
           a. Femur (thigh)
           b. Tibia and fibula (shank)
           c. Tarsals (ankle)
           d. Metatarsals (sole)
           e. Phalanges (toes)

SKULL

As is shown in the above outline, the mammalian skull is a composite structure. Although not strictly correct ontogenetically, it is usually referred to as being made up of a cranium (composed of the braincase or cranium proper, the sense capsules, and the upper jaws, all of which are fused into a single, solid structure) and the mandibles (or lower jaw). The hyoid elements and cartilagenous elements in the larynx are usually ignored. The bones which make up the mammalian skull are shown in Fig. 1–3.

TEETH

Although teeth are not characteristic of mammals, they are extremely useful in any study of mammalian relationships, since they (1) reflect the food habits of the mammal, (2) are preformed before they break through the gum, thus reflecting genetic relationships rather than environmental effects, and (3) are usually well preserved as fossils.

Mammalian teeth are composite structures that are *thecodont;* that is, they are set in sockets in the jaw. A typical tooth is made up of the following parts: *Enamel* is the hard white material usually covering the exposed part of the tooth. This enamel is the hardest

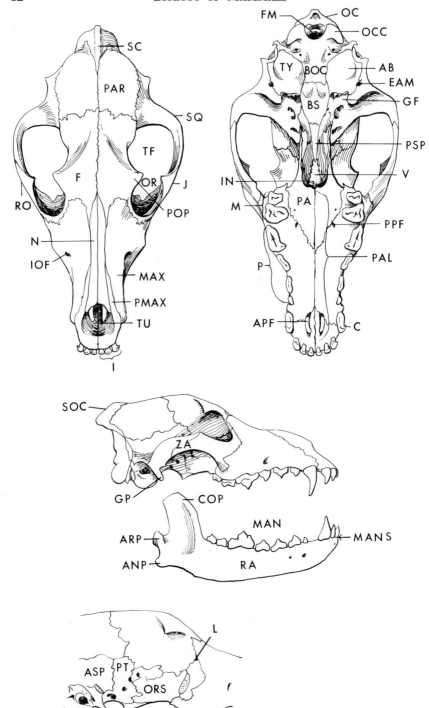

tissue in the mammalian body. It may be asbent in the teeth of some mammals such as the Edentates. *Dentine* is the bonelike material that makes up most of the bulk of the tooth. *Cement* is the bony material that replaces the enamel as the covering of the dentine on the roots of the tooth. On most teeth this is a thin inconspicuous layer, but in the advanced plant-feeding mammals it becomes an important part of the tooth. In such mammals, the teeth may have deep enamel folds and the cement may grow over the whole tooth, even filling in the depressions in the crown. *Pulp* is the central living portion of the tooth. In young animals, the pulp is widely open at the base and is in communication with the blood system. In most adults, this opening is reduced to a small foramen. Such teeth are termed "rooted." In some mammals the pulp cavity does not constrict and the tooth continues to grow throughout life. Such teeth are known as "rootless" and are considered to have persistent pulp.

Dentition in mammals is generally heterodont; that is, the teeth are modified in shape and size to serve specialized functions in the toothrow. Four types of teeth are generally recognized. *Incisors* are the teeth on the premaxillary bone of the upper jaw and the corresponding teeth in the lower jaw. Primitively, incisors were nipping in function and, as a group, have remained relatively unspecialized. The primitive placental mammal has three incisors in each half of the jaw, above and below. In marsupials and more primitive mammals there may be as many as five incisors above and four below, on each side. *Canines* generally have a simple, conical crown

Fig. 1–3. A coyote skull. The various regions, bones and cavities are indicated by the following abbreviations:

AB—auditory bulla	IOF—infraorbital foramen	PMAX—premaxillary
ANP—angular process	J—jugal	POP—postorbital process
APF—anterior palatine foramen	L—lacrimal bone	PPF—posterior palatine
ARP—articular process	M—molar teeth	foramen
(condyle)	MAN—mandible	PSP—presphenoid
ASP—alisphenoid bone	MANS—mandibular symphysis	PT—pterygoid
BOC—basioccipital	MAX—maxilla	RA—ramus of maxilla
BS—basisphenoid	N—nasal	RO—rostrum
C—canine tooth	OC—occiput	SC—saggital crest
COP—coronoid process	OCC—occipital condyle	SOC—supraoccipital crest
EAM—external auditory meatus	OR—orbit	SQ—squamosal
F—frontal	ORS—orbitosphenoid	TF—temporal fossa
FM—foramen magnum	P—premolar teeth	TU—turbinals
GF—glenoid fossa	PA—palatine	TY—tympanics
GP—glenoid process	PAL—palate	V—vomes
I—incisors	PAR—parietal	ZA—zygomatic arch
IN—internal nares		

and are long teeth used for holding and piercing. Canines are always one on each side above and below. The upper canine is borne on the maxillary bone. Some primitive placental mammals have double-rooted canines, but all modern forms have a single-rooted canine (if present). *Premolars*, used for shearing, cutting, and slicing, are unspecialized and usually contain only one main cusp in generalized dentition. In most of the advanced plant feeders, the premolars have been greatly modified. The maximum number of premolars in eutherian mammals is four on each side above and below. In marsupials and older types of mammals, the number of premolars is varied and is as great as 5/4 in Mesozoic mammals. *Molars*, primarily intended for crushing, are three in number on each side above and below in primitive placentals. In some Mesozoic mammals there are eight molars on each side. Molars are distinguished from all other teeth by never having milk predecessors. This has led to the opinion that molars are actually delayed milk teeth.

In general usage among mammalogists is a system of expressing the number and position of teeth present in a given mammal. This is called the *dental formula.* Since mammals are normally bilaterally symmetrical, it is necessary to mention the teeth of only one side of the jaw. The following is the dental formula of a primitive placental:

$$\frac{\text{Incisors } 1, 2, 3. \quad \text{Canine } 1. \quad \text{Premolars } 1, 2, 3, 4. \quad \text{Molars } 1, 2, 3.}{\text{Incisors } 1, 2, 3. \quad \text{Canine } 1. \quad \text{Premolars } 1, 2, 3, 4. \quad \text{Molars } 1, 2, 3.} = 44 \text{ total}$$

The numbers above the line represent the teeth on one side of the upper jaw; those below the line represent the teeth of the lower jaw. This formula is often abbreviated to:

$$\text{I } 3/3, \text{ C } 1/1, \text{ P } 4/4, \text{ M } 3/3 = 44$$

Among the placental mammals, departures from this general formula are usually by reduction. In the extended formula above, a zero can be substituted for any given number to indicate a missing tooth. The dental formula for a house mouse (*Mus*) would be:

$$\frac{\text{Incisors } 1, 0, 0. \quad \text{Canine } 0. \quad \text{Premolars } 0, 0, 0, 0. \quad \text{Molars } 1, 2, 3.}{\text{Incisors } 1, 0, 0. \quad \text{Canine } 0. \quad \text{Premolars } 0, 0, 0, 0. \quad \text{Molars } 1, 2, 3.} = 16 \text{ total}$$

In general, loss of molars is from back to front while loss of premolars is from front to back. The dental formula for the house cat (*Felis*), for example, is:

$$\frac{\text{Incisors } 1, 2, 3. \quad \text{Canine } 1. \quad \text{Premolars } 0, 2, 3, 4. \quad \text{Molars } 1, 0, 0.}{\text{Incisors } 1, 2, 3. \quad \text{Canine } 1. \quad \text{Premolars } 0, 2, 3, 4. \quad \text{Molars } 1, 0, 0.} = 32 \text{ total}$$

Most mammals are diphodont (that is, they have two sets of teeth), with the milk teeth consisting only of incisors, canines, and premolars, while the permanent teeth consist of incisors, canines, premolars, and molars. Apparently, there are some marsupials that have no milk dentition and, among the placentals, the milk dentition may be lost in the uterus before birth.

ADAPTATION OF THE TEETH

In general, adaptations of mammalian teeth are closely correlated with the food habits of the mammal. These adaptations are evident

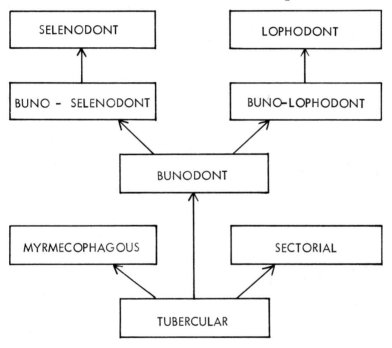

Fig. 1–4. The probable evolution of the various types of mammalian molar teeth.

in the crown patterns of many of the placental mammals. The major types of crown patterns are as follows (their relationships are shown in Fig. 1–4):

The *tubercular* type is the primitive molar crown pattern of the Eocene marsupials and placentals. In these primitive mammals, the tooth was low-crowned (*brachyodont*) and had three simple cusps (or tubercles) arranged in a triangle (termed tritubercular), an adaptation for a diet of insects. In modern insectivores, these three primitive cones (called protocone, paracone, and metacone in the upper molar) are usually retained; modifications consist primarily in the addition of cusps. This type of tooth, for crushing and cutting, is found in shrews and in some of the primitive carnivores.

The *sectorial* type is a modification of the tubercular type of molar crown pattern used for cutting and shearing of food. Examples of sectorial teeth are the cheek teeth (molars and premolars) of members of the cat family (Felidae). An intermediate stage (*tuberculo-sectorial*) for crushing and cutting is found in such animals as the coyote and the dog.

The *bunodont* type is a modification of the tubercular type of molar for crushing and is usually associated with an omnivorous diet. A tooth with this modification is usually brachyodont, quadrate in shape, and has low, rounded cusps. The cheek teeth of pigs, javelina, and man are examples of bunodont crowns.

The *selenodont* molar pattern is a modification of the bunodont type in which the individual cusps of a bunodont tooth become converted into crescents. These crescents wear down, forming enamel ridges on a flat surface. This is a grinding tooth associated with a herbivorous diet. The selenodont tooth, in its extreme development (e.g., the cow) is high-crowned (*hypsodont*) to compensate for the great wear on the teeth resulting from a herbivorous diet. Several structural stages are evident in the molars of the ungulates. The pig, for example, has a typical bunodont tooth that is brachyodont. *Anthracotherium*, an extinct piglike Artiodactyla, has bunodont outer cusps and selenodont inner cusps on the same tooth (*buno-selenodont*), and the tooth is short-crowned. The deer has a selenodont tooth that is brachyodont while the cow has a selenodont tooth that is hypsodont.

The *lophodont* molar pattern is a second modification of the bunodont type in which the cusps are fused into transverse lophs or ridges with intervening valleys. This, too, is a grinding tooth for a herbivorous diet. In its extreme development the lophodont tooth is hypsodont, again compensating for the additional wear of a grinding tooth. Several structural stages are evident in the molars of the ungulates. The first in the series might well be the pig, with its bunodont, brachyodont molars. The mastodon, an extinct proboscidian, had a brachyodont molar with bunodont outer cusps and lophodont inner cusps (*buno-lophodont*). The living tapir has a brachyodont, lophodont molar while the elephants have hypsodont, lophodont molars. The lophodont-like cheek teeth of rabbits, incidentally, are not considered typical.

The *myrmecophagous* mammalian molar is a degeneration of the tubercular type of molar teeth. In this modification, the teeth become simple peglike structures without an enamel covering (sloths and armadillos) or completely disappear (anteaters).

ORIGIN OF THE MAMMALIAN MOLAR

A number of theories have been advanced to account for the complex molar teeth found in mammals. For the ultimate ancestor of the complex mammalian molar, most workers refer to the simple,

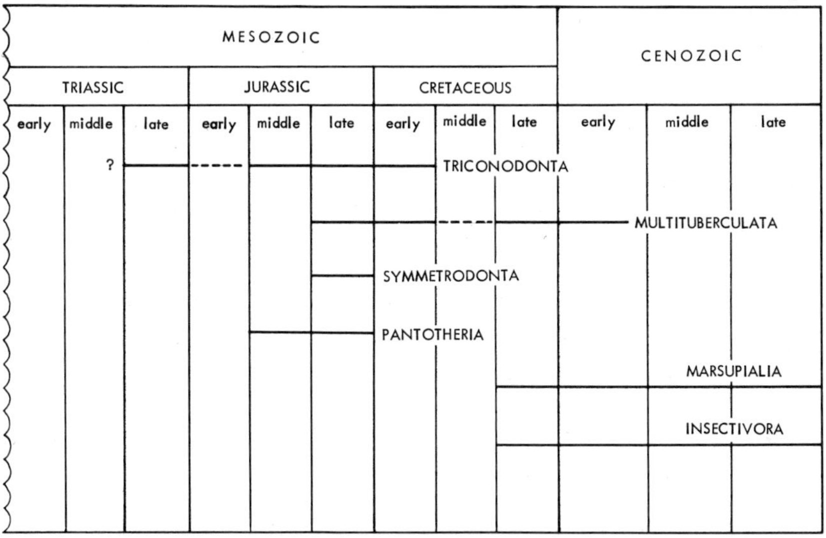

MESOZOIC									CENOZOIC		
TRIASSIC			JURASSIC			CRETACEOUS					
early	middle	late	early	middle	late	early	middle	late	early	middle	late
	?						TRICONODONTA				
								MULTITUBERCULATA			
					SYMMETRODONTA						
					PANTOTHERIA						
										MARSUPIALIA	
										INSECTIVORA	

Fig. 1–5. Geologic distribution of the primitive groups of mammals.

single-cusped haplodont tooth found in some of the later mammal-like reptiles. The actual details of how this type of tooth evolved into the complex molar have been the subject of much disagreement.

Since the tubercular molar was already present in marsupials and placentals at the close of the Mesozoic Era, obviously an examination of fossils from later times would not give any information bearing on the origin of the tubercular molar. Thus the earlier part of the paleontological record is the only part that will yield pertinent information. Unfortunately, the earlier part of the record is far from complete. The distribution in time of the primitive mammals is given in Fig. 1–5; the morphology of their teeth is indicated in Fig. 1–6.

Briefly the fossil record is as follows: From the Upper Triassic is known one "dubious possible ally" of members of the Order Triconodonta. If this is in fact a mammal, it is the earliest known mammal. No mammalian fossils are known from the Early Jurassic. From Middle Jurassic are known members of the Order Triconodonta (a few teeth and jaws) and the Order Pantotheria, both of which have

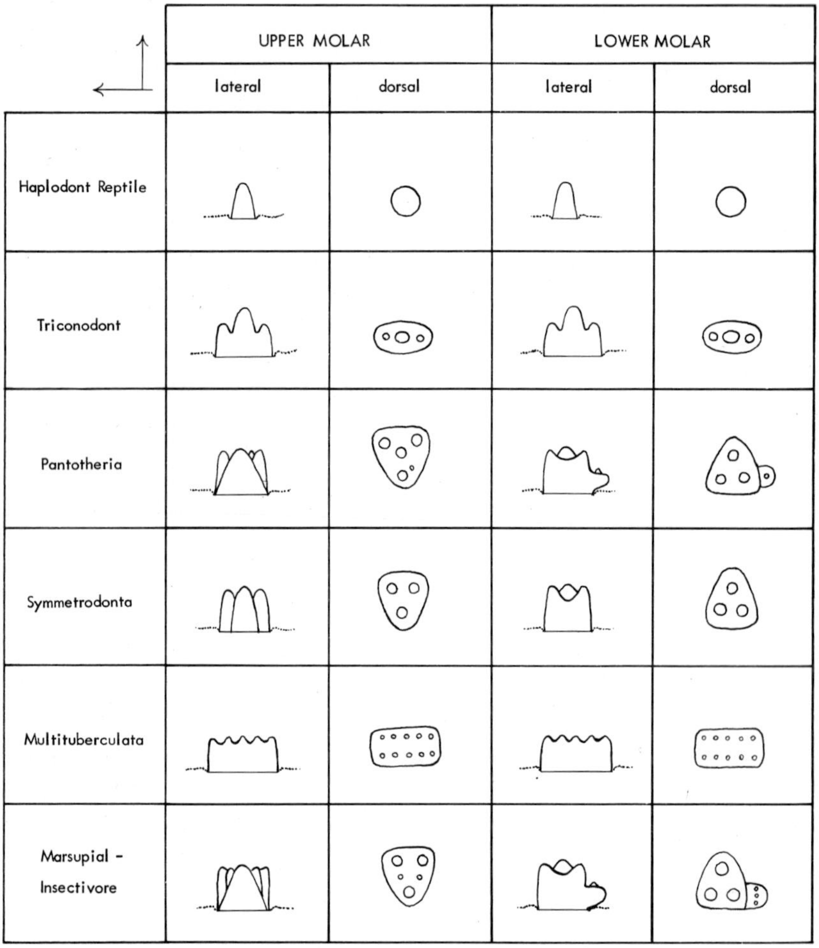

	UPPER MOLAR		LOWER MOLAR	
	lateral	dorsal	lateral	dorsal
Haplodont Reptile				
Triconodont				
Pantotheria				
Symmetrodonta				
Multituberculata				
Marsupial – Insectivore				

Fig. 1–6. The morphology of the molars of the primitive mammals.

clearly defined tuberculate teeth (Fig. 1–6) and show no intermediate stages between them and the supposed ancestral haplodont (or single-crowned) reptilian molar. In the Late Jurassic, representatives of four mammalian orders are known: Order Triconodontia; Order Pantotheria (not known from later time); Order Multituberculata (first appearance in the fossil record); and Order Symmetrodonta (first and last appearance in the fossil record). Few mammalian fossils are known from the Early Cretaceous. In fact, only six specimens are known and only one of these has any teeth. These belong to the Orders Multituberculata and Triconodonta. No mammalian fossils are known from the Middle Cretaceous. By Late Cretaceous both the Order Marsupalia and the Order Insectivora (the most primitive placental mammal), with their tubercular molars, are known. Also persisting through the Late Cretaceous and into Early Cenozoic were the Multituberculates.

Theories as to the origin and development of the tritubercular molar of marsupials and primitive placentals fall into two categories, those which hold that the molar develops from the fusion of two or more single-crowned teeth and those which hold that it developed from a modification of the crown of a single tooth.

The earlier theories concerning the origin of the multituberculate molars appear to fall into the first category, that the molar developed from the fusion of two or more teeth. The *concrescence theory* of Gervais (1854) held that there was a coalescence of two or more simple tooth germs in the formation of teeth with multiple cusps, with two separate tooth germs for a bicuspid, three for a tricuspid, etc. Variants of this theory have been supported by several later workers. Kukenthal (1891), for example, contended that the molar teeth, with their outer and inner rows of cusps, resulted from the lateral fusion of one milk tooth with one or more of the permanent series. Rose (1892) proposed the fusion hypothesis, based on his embryological studies of teeth in the opossum, *Didelphis*, and man, *Homo*. According to his hypothesis, the lower molars go through a sequence of embryological stages that approximately repeat their ancestral history but such does not occur in the embryology of the upper molars. Further, according to Rose, the complex mammalian molar is the result of the fusion of two reptilian triconodont teeth, one buccal and one lingual. Thus, according to Rose, every human tooth has a potential of six cusps and incompleteness in the developing tooth buds keep this from occurring.

There are three objections to the concrescence theory. (1) It does not explain the complex ungulate molars nor the increase in lophs in the molar of the elephant, both of which have arisen by the addition of new material to a less complex ancestral tooth. (2) There is no embryological or morphological evidence that the styles, lophs, and cones of the mammalian molar ever existed as separate elements. (3) If the complication of teeth results from the fusion of separate teeth, then those with complex teeth should show a reduction in the number of teeth. Actually, when there is a reduction in the number of cheek teeth in the higher placentals, it results from the failure of tooth germs to produce teeth, not through coalescence of tooth germs.

Theories in the second group (modification of a single tooth) fall into two major classes. One class holds that the primitive mammalian molar was not a simple haplodont cusp but was a tooth with a number of tubercules such as occurs in the Order Multituberculata. In fact, these theories are often grouped together as the "multituberculate theory." In some theories, the origin of this multituberculate tooth is given as a result of concrescence (see above) while others make no attempt to explain its origin. Bolk's (1921–22) dimer theory, the plexidont or progressive simplification theory of Ameghino (1899) and Friant's functional theory appear to be examples of this group. The second class of theories derives the mammalian molar from the complication of the crown of a simple haplodont tooth. The Cope-Osborn tritubercular theory falls into this class, as does the supporting premolar analogy theory.

Bolk's dimer theory is in part a concrescence theory and in part a simplification theory. It holds that the primitive reptilian molar was triconodont and that the haplodont reptile tooth resulted from the lateral compression and union of two triconodont tooth germs. Further, according to this theory, all mammalian teeth are morphologically equivalent to and could become six-cuspate if it were not for incomplete development of the tooth germs. Objections to this theory include the fact that there is no evidence that primitive reptilian teeth were triconodont. In fact, just the reverse is true, for all known primitive reptilian teeth had only a single cusp and the triconodont tooth did not appear until some of the higher reptile groups were developed. Further, in mammals, only the postcanine teeth assume a triconodont form. If *all* mammalian teeth were potentially six-cusped, surely some incisors and canines would show this characteristic, even if only in an occasional aberrant tooth. Finally, there is no embryological evidence of a concentration of germ buds to form the incisors and canines.

The plexidont or progressive simplification theory of Ameghino (1899) holds a view similar to that of Bolk's dimer theory. According to this view, the primitive mammalian molar was a result of the fusion of several tooth buds, and the tritubercular, triconodont, and haplodont stages are secondary simplifications. In other words, the teeth of the descendants are less complex than are teeth of their ancestors.

The functional stimulus theory, proposed by Friant (1933), holds that the ancestral mammalian molar was complex, as in the multituberculates, and that the more simple teeth of higher mammals result from the wearing down of cusps in the embryo by a vertical motion of the jaws.

The trituberculate theory (or the so-called Cope-Osborn Theory) was first proposed by E. D. Cope (1878) and elaborated by Henry Fairfield Osborn (1907). As first proposed by Cope, the theory held that the molar of the placental mammal, no matter what its present simplicity or complexity, is the genetic descendant of a tritubercular molar such as occurred in the primitive insectivores of the Late Cretaceous.

Osborn elaborated on the original theory by arranging the Mesozoic mammals in a series supposed to represent structural stages of development and presumably genetic descent. Further, Osborn proposed a system of nomenclature for the mammalian molar cusps. These structural stages and the nomenclature are illustrated in Fig. 1–7. Unfortunately, Osborn made a number of errors, as has been demonstrated by later findings. First, Osborn had only a few worn upper molars of the Pantotheres available and thus failed to see and properly interpret the various cusps present (see Fig. 1–7). Second, he supposed that the triconodonts evolved into the symmetrodonts. More recent findings do not support this conclusion. In fact, it is now thought that the triconodonts are not closely related to the other mammals, but represent a group with ancestry directly from another group of mammal-like reptiles. Third, on the grounds of homology, Osborn used the protocone as being equivalent to the old reptilian single crown. However, from the premolar analogy theory (see below) and from embryological evidence, it appears that the paracone is probably equivalent to the original crown. Thus it appears that the symmetrodont and the triconodont stages are not logically structurally intermediate stages.

In résumé, Cope's contribution, that the higher placentals evolved from a primitive tritubercular placental ancestor, still stands. For the most part, Osborn's contributions to the theory have been discredited. However, he is credited with two contributions: a system of nomenclature and for recognizing that the pantothere stage is ancestral to the trituberculate stage.

The premolar analogy theory of Scott (1892) holds that the progressive molarization of premolars evident in various mammals is analogous to the sequence of development of a single molar. Since neither the fossil record nor embryology gives any real clue to the development of the tritubercular molar, such observations are useful in understanding how the trituberculate teeth may have arisen. As illustrated in Fig. 1–8, the primitive single cusp appears to be

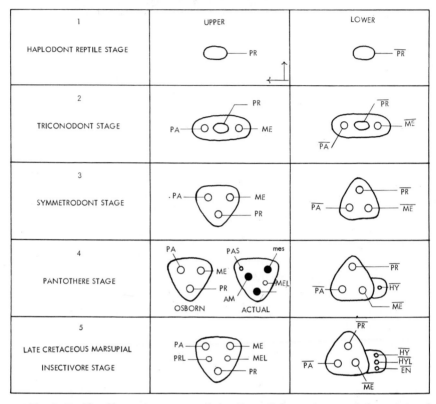

Fig. 1–7. The five major stages of the Cope-Osborn theory of the origin of the mammalian molar. The following abbreviations are used for the names of the cones:

Upper molars
pr—protocone
pa—paracone
me—metacone
pas—parastyle
mes—metastyle
mel—metaconule
prl—protoconule
am—amphistyle

Lower molars
pr—protonid
pa—paraconid
me—metaconid
hy—hypoconid
hyl—hypoconulid
en—entoconid

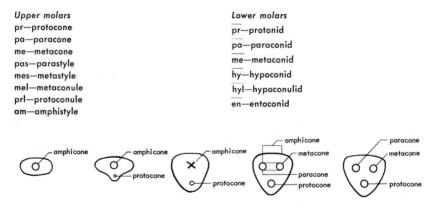

Fig. 1–8. The progressive molarization of a series of premolars, the basis of Scott's premolar analogy theory.

homologous with the paracone and not with the protocone, as thought by Osborn.

VERTEBRAL COLUMN AND THORACIC BASKET

The vertebral column is made up of a series of intersegmentally arranged vertebrae. The vertebrae, which serve as the central support (or backbone), also protect the nerve cord from injury. A vertebra is made up of a centrum or cylindrical body from which bony plates arise and fuse dorsally to form a neural arch. Extensions of the neural arches, zygapophyses, overlap to give additional firmness to the backbone. Most vertebrae also have lateral growths from the centrum (transverse processes). The vertebrae of mammals are differentiated into five regions, with the typical vertebrae of each region being so well differentiated that they can be identified, even when isolated.

The cervical vertebrae (those of the neck) are characteristically seven in number, regardless of the length of the neck of the mammal. Exceptions are the sloths, which have either six or nine, and the Sirenia, which have six cervical vertebrae. In whales, dolphins, and armadillos, the centra of the cervical vertebrae are often fused together, making identification of single vertebrae difficult. Cervical vertebrae typically have well-developed neural arches and spines, pre- and postzygapophyses, and transverse processes.

The two anterior vertebrae are differentiated as the atlas and the axis. The ring-shaped atlas has no centrum and has wide transverse processes. Anteriorly, it has two deeply concave surfaces which articulate with the base of the skull. The axis has a centrum that is elongated anteriorly as an odontoid process (actually the centrum of the atlas fused to that of the axis) and a large neural spine which overlaps that of the axis. It is these arrangements that permit the typical up and down movement (the "yes" movement) and the side to side movement (the "no" movement) of the head.

The thoracic vertebrae bear long ribs which are articulated to smooth areas at the outer edges of the short, stout transverse processes and in a facet that is half in one centrum and half in the adjacent one. Most thoracic vertebrae have short centra, tall posteriorly directed neural spines, and small zygapophyses. The number of thoracic vertebrae (and of ribs) varies from species to species and even occasionally within one species. The total number of thoracic and lumbar vertebrae, however, is a constant number in a given species and even in larger groups. In bats, for example, this total is seventeen while in carnivores it is twenty or twenty-one. The anterior ribs are attached ventrally to a sternum, or breast bone, while the posterior ribs are joined to each other and to the sternum by cartilaginous rods.

The lumbar vertebrae are usually four to seven in number but may be as few as two (some monotremes) or as many as twenty-one (Cetacea). Typically, they are large, stout, and have long neural spines and long transverse processes which project forward.

The sacral vertebrae, typically three to five in number (but six to eight in some Perissodactyla and up to thirteen in some Edentates) are fused into a single structure, the sacrum, which serves as a point of attachment for the pelvic girdle.

The caudal vertebrae are extemely varied in number, ranging from only a few in some "tailless" forms (man, for example, has three to five fused into a single bone, the coccyx) to as many as fifty.

APPENDICULAR SKELETON

The pelvic girdle of mammals consists of an innominate or hip bone on each side, each of which embryologically consists of three elements, a larger dorsal ilium, a posterior ischium, and an anterior pubis. These three elements are still evident in many immature mammals. The dorsal part of the innominate bones articulates with the sacrum and laterally each has a large acetabulum which serves as the articulation point for the upper element of the leg, the femur. The hind limb consists of the typical elements given above.

The pectoral girdle varies considerably among the various species of mammals. In all, the scapula (shoulder blade) is the most important element. In those kinds wherein the motion of the forelimb is restricted to only a fore-and-aft plane, such as the horse, only the scapula is present. In those with a wide range of possible movement, such as in most primates, a well-developed clavicle (collar bone) is also present. In the monotremes, the reptilian elements of the coracoid and precoracoid remain in the pectoral girdle, but in all the placental mammals these are reduced to a coracoid process on the scapula. The forelimbs typically consist of the elements indicated above.

MODIFICATIONS OF THE APPENDAGES

The shape, length, and even the number of skeletal elements in the appendages have evolved as primitive mammals developed specialized locomotive techniques in their terrestrial environment. Further modifications have occurred, associated with the occupation of subterrestrial, arboreal, aquatic, and aerial habitats.

TERRESTRIAL LOCOMOTION

Many different types of terrestrial locomotion are encountered among the terrestrial mammals. Several specific mechanisms are difficult to classify, but most of them fall into one of the following categories.

Ambulatory (or walking) locomotion was characteristic of the primitive mammal. Among living mammals, raccoons and bears are ambulatory. Such animals are plantigrade, that is, the wrist, metacarpals, ankles, metatarsals, and digits are on the ground as the animal walks. They have five digits on each of the front and rear appendages; the metacarpals and metatarsals are unmodified; the upper and lower arm (and leg) are approximately the same length; and the joints of the limbs provide a moderate amount of movement in all directions.

Cursorial (or running) locomotion was probably the first modification from the plantigrade type. Cursorial modifications in their extreme are seen in such animals as the deer, giraffe, and horse. Such animals have a reduction in the number of digits as well as in the number of metacarpals and metatarsals; in addition, the weight is borne on the tips of the digits. The ends of the digits usually form hooves. Such animals are termed ungualigrade. The upper arm (and leg) is shortened and intensely muscular. Usually the radius fuses with the ulna and the tibia with the fibula. Little lateral motion is possible in the limbs. The neck is elongated to permit the head to reach the ground.

Several living mammals are intermediate between the plantigrade and the ungualigrade forms listed above. Many carnivores, for example, walk chiefly on the digits, metacarpals, and metatarsals, and have the ankle and the wrist elevated and the thumb and big toes reduced or even lost. Such animals are termed digitigrade.

Graviportal (carrying great weight) locomotion is illustrated by the elephants. Animals of this type have the five digits present on the fore and hind limbs. These digits are distributed in a circle around the edge of the foot. Most of the weight is borne by the digits and by the pads of elastic tissue under the foot. Such an arrangement is termed subungualigrade or rectigrade. The upper sections of the limbs are longer than the lower sections. The fibula and the radius are enlarged, almost as large as the ulna and the tibia. The joints in the appendage are flat-surfaced and the limbs are straight and heavy.

Saltatorial (jumping) locomotion is another modification of the primitive ambulatory type. It is found in such mammals as jumping mice, kangaroo rats, and kangaroos. Modifications include a shortening of the front legs, a tremendous elongation of the hind feet and legs, and an elongation of the tail. The elongated tail apparently serves as a balancing organ.

FUNCTIONAL TYPES OF TERRESTRIAL LOCOMOTION

Normally, terrestrial mammals employ all four limbs in their movements (quadrupedal locomotion). The mechanical sequence of placing the feet on the ground shows considerable variation.

The *walk* is the normal quadrupedal motion of most cats, dogs, and ungulates (hooved mammals). In this the animal raises diagonally opposite feet and moves them forward while the weight of the body is being supported by the two opposite appendages. The two feet that have been advanced are placed on the ground and the other two are raised and advanced.

The *pace* is the result of a different coordination of limb movements. The giraffe, bear, and camel normally pace. They raise the legs of the same side and advance them simultaneously while the weight is supported by the legs of the opposite side.

The *trot* occurs in many animals that normally walk when they move at a faster rate. In the trot, diagonally opposite limbs throw the body simultaneously, and between the instants of support by one diagonal set of legs or the other, there is a period of suspension.

The *gallop* occurs when many quadrupeds exert a maximum effort for rapid locomotion. It consists of a succession of leaps. In a simple gallop the animal leaps forward by means of its hind feet, stretches its body as far forward as possible, and lands on the two forefeet. Immediately the hind feet are pulled forward so that they land near the forefeet, thus supporting the body and beginning the cycle again. In more complex gallops such as occurs in rabbits, the forefeet do not touch the ground simultaneously, and the hind feet may be placed down in front of the forefeet. This characteristic of the rabbit's gallop causes many inexperienced trackers actually to track rabbits backward.

Several normally quadrupedal mammals occasionally employ only the hind limbs in locomotion (bipedal locomotion). This attitude can be maintained for a few steps in such animals as the gazelle, the Old World stag, and the armadillo. Bipedal locomotion is best developed in the higher primates. The lar gibbon, chimpanzees, and gorilla are bipedal, but man is the only completely bipedal mammal.

Leaping is a means of locomotion employed by a number of mammals showing saltitorial modifications. In these leaps the tail is usually employed to help support and balance the body.

SUBTERRESTRIAL LOCOMOTION

One of the habitats available to primitive terrestrial mammals was to burrow underground. Modifications for moving and living in this habitat are termed *fossorial* adaptations. These adaptations include a reduction in the length of the limbs; the development of deep grooves in the limb joints; the development of heavy-limb muscles with large areas for attachments on the bones; the development of a thick, short neck; the elongation of the skull; the development of forefeet that are larger than the hind feet; a reduction or disappearance of the eyes, external ears, and tail; and the development of tactile hairs on the nose and tail. A number of mammals show tendencies toward these fossorial adaptations but such forms as the moles, the golden moles, and the marsupial moles illustrate these adaptations in their extreme form.

A mole (Family Talpidae) burrows through soft earth simply by forcing the body forward through the soil. It holds on to the sides of the burrow with the enlarged hands and forces its head forward by means of powerful arm muscles. Powerful neck muscles then raise the head, thus pushing the dirt aside and opening the burrow. In compact or hard soils the forefeet are used to scrape away earth from the front of the tunnel. This loose dirt is then pushed back down the length of the tunnel and to the surface through a short vertical tunnel.

The golden mole (Family Chrysochloridae) of Africa appears to burrow in a manner similar to that of the talpids. The marsupial moles (Family Notoryctidae) of the Australian region have the snout covered with a horny shield and have no eyes or eyelids. They burrow through the loose sandy soil (and sand) of the interior of Australia without leaving a permanent tunnel behind them.

ARBOREAL LOCOMOTION

A number of mammals, especially primates, show adaptations fitting them for movement among the limbs of trees. These adaptations include the elongation of all parts (particularly the limbs and tail); the development of opposable digits; a tendency for the tail to become prehensile; the presence of generalized limb joints, permitting a wide range of movement; and an increase in the size of the eyes.

A number of different devices are employed in climbing and holding onto tree branches. Most arboreal primates have prehensile fingers and many New World monkeys have a prehensile tail that aids in arboreal locomotion. The tarsiers have adhesive disks on their paws. Some mammals, such as the squirrels and sloths, have well-developed nails for clinging to the bark of trees.

Brachiation is a special type of arboreal locomotion developed in some of the primates such as the lar gibbon. These animals hang suspended from a branch by one arm and reach out and grasp a second branch with the other hand. They can progress quite rapidly through the trees with this hand-over-hand motion.

AQUATIC LOCOMOTION

With the reinvasion of aquatic habitats came a whole series of modifications for life and locomotion in the water. Obviously not all groups solved the problems of living in this habitat in the same way. In fact, among living mammals, all grades of adaptations are found, ranging from those that have no special adaptations to the extreme adaptations found in whales. General features found in many aquatic mammals include the development of fusiform shape (torpedo shape), shortening or complete loss of hind limbs, increase in the number of digital bones in the hand, loss of the tail or modification into flippers (flukes), shortening of the neck, the addition of a thick layer of fat under the skin, and the loss of hair.

Most terrestrial mammals can swim, if the need arises. Even such desert-dwelling forms as the kangaroo rat and the pocket mouse have been observed to swim. Such species as rabbits, hedgehogs, and armadillos will readily take to water and even swim across small streams to avoid enemies. Most ungulates and carnivores, including cats, are excellent swimmers. A black bear (*Ursus americanus*), for example, has been observed to swim five miles. Most, if not all, species of bats can swim if, by chance, they accidentally fall into the water. Some, especially certain wide-winged vespertilionids, can actually take off from the surface of the water.

A series of mammals might well be classified as amphibious since they appear to be equally at home and in the water. Such animals as the water shrews (*Sorex palustris*), the giant water shrew (Family Potamogalidae), beavers, muskrats, water rats, and otters (*Lutra*) seem to be equally adept at movements on land and in the water. When swimming, the beaver keeps most of the body submerged and keeps its front legs folded back under its chest. Swimming is accomplished by the hind feet and legs. The hind feet, with the webbed toes somewhat spread, move together, pushing the beaver through water.

Sea otters (*Enhydra*) are more aquatic than the amphibious forms listed above. They rarely come to shore and when they do, they move very awkwardly on land. In the sea they usually float on their backs, with the feet in the air, and move by slow lateral movements of the tail. Only when they move extremely rapidly do they turn over on their stomachs.

Even more aquatic are the seals and sea lions. In this group are almost all stages of terrestrial locomotion from normal quadrupedal to an awkward "hitching" in which the rudimentary limbs are not used but motion is accomplished by contortions of the whole body. In the water these rudimentary limbs are used in locomotion. The eared seals (Family Otaridae) and the walrus (Family Odobenidae) are not so modified for aquatic life as are the earless seals (Family Phocidae). In the Otaridae and Odobenidae, the hind legs turn forward in the normal quadrupedal manner when the animal is on land but turn backward for swimming when in the water.

When on land the sea lion uses all four limbs in a normal quadrupedal manner, but, because of the short length of the free hind limbs, the hind quarters of the body are swung forward to accomplish locomotion. At slow speeds in the water only the forelimbs are used. For more rapid speeds both the fore- and hind limbs are employed.

In the earless seals (Family Phocidae) the hind limbs are permanently turned backward for swimming. On land the forelimbs support the body while the hind quarters hitch forward. All the toes are connected by a web that almost reaches the ends of the digits. In swimming, the hind feet usually stroke alternately, with the web spread on the stroke and folded on the return. Occasionally both limbs are employed simultaneously. The forelimbs are kept pressed against the body when swimming.

The strictly aquatic mammals of the orders Cetacea and Sirenia (whales and sea cows) move through the water by oscillations of the horizontally flattened tail and flukes in a vertical plane. The oscillations of the tail and flukes are not synchronous; rather, the flukes lead the tail by a quarter of a stroke.

AERIAL LOCOMOTION

Several arboreal mammals jump or leap through the air from one branch to another. However, two major adaptations have occurred in some mammals that enable them to move longer distances through the air.

Volant, or gliding, adaptations have occurred in a number of unrelated groups, including flying phalangers (Marsupialia), flying lemurs (Dermoptera), and flying squirrels (Rodentia). These modifications include the development of a patagium (or gliding membrane) of skin that connects the fore- and hind limbs (and often

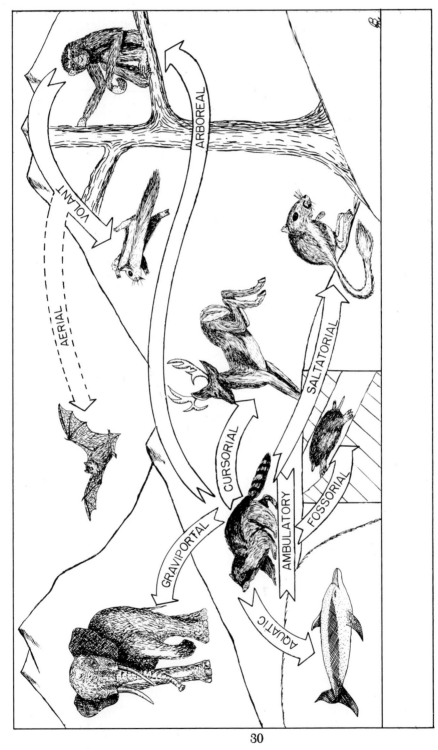

Fig. 1–9. Types of locomotion. Adaptive radiation probably resulted from modifications into various specializations from the primitive ambulatory type of locomotion (diagram by Bernard Maza).

the forelimbs with the sides of the neck and the hind limbs with the tail). The joints of the limbs are limited to one plane of action, and the tail is usually flattened for use as a rudder.

True flight has been developed in only one mammalian order, the Chiroptera, or bats. Adaptations include modification of the hand into a wing, an enlargement of the breast muscles, and a reduction of the size and importance of the tail. Digits two through five, inclusive, of the hand become greatly elongated and support a membrane that serves as the wing.

EVOLUTIONARY SEQUENCE OF LOCOMOTIVE ADAPTATIONS

As is indicated in Fig. 1–9, ambulatory locomotion is the primitive type in mammals. Radial adaptations from this primitive type permitted the development of cursorial, arboreal, saltatorial, graviportal, aquatic, and fossorial types of locomotion. The volant or gliding type of locomotion probably developed from forms with arboreal adaptations. Just which type was ancestral to true flight has been the subject of much debate. One view is that it resulted from extreme cursorial adaptations, while another view holds that it developed from volant ancestors.

SPEED OF LOCOMOTION

Some of the variation that exists in the speed of locomotion of the various kinds of mammals is indicated in Table 1–1. These speeds, in general, represent maxima attained over short courses and can rarely be maintained for extended periods of time. A race horse, for example, has reached speeds of 42.3 miles per hour over a course of 440 yards but, over a 100-mile course, the record is an average of 11.2 miles per hour. Examination of the table reveals that, in general, the fastest mammals are those with the cursorial type of locomotion. Further, faster locomotion is possible on land than in aquatic habitats.

The fastest mammal is either the cheetah (*Aciononyx jubatus*) which, over short courses, has been clocked at speeds approaching 70 miles per hour, or the pronghorn (*Antilocapra americana*) which also reaches a maximum of 70 miles per hour for short bursts. The sloth may well be the slowest mammal. When extremely pressed, it can move over short distances at a maximum rate of one-half mile per hour.

ADAPTATIONS FOR SPECIAL HABITATS

Many radial adaptations from the typical mammal have occurred which are associated with life in specific habitats.

TABLE 1–1

Speeds of Various Species of Mammals, Grouped According to Their Types of Locomotion

	Miles Per Hour	Remarks
Terrestrial Mammals		
Order Marsupialia		
Great kangaroo (*Macropus*)............	25	Pressed
Virginia opossum (*Didelphis marsupialis*)	4.2 (4.1–4.3)	2 trials
Order Insectivora		
Short-tailed shrew (*Blarina brevicauda*)..	1.8 (1.4–2.2)	2 trials
Order Primates		
Langur monkey (*Presbytis aquaticus*)....	23+	On ground, 70 yd.
Order Rodentia		
Kangaroo rat (*Dipodomys heermanni*)...	5.4–12	Pressed, 16–52 ft.
Woodchuck (*Marmota monax*)	10	For max. of 1 min.
Chipmunk (*Eutamias* sp.)	10	Pressed, 50 yd.
Eastern chipmunk (*Tamias striatus*).....	7.6 (6.2–10)	8 trials
Red squirrel (*Tamiasciurus hudsonicus*)..	8.5 (7.9–9.0)	2 trials
Gray squirrel (*Sciurus carolinensis*).....	12.9 (9.0–17)	6 trials
Deer mouse (*Peromyscus maniculatus*)...	4.9 (4.2–5.6)	4 trials
Deer mouse (*Peromyscus leucopus*)	5.7 (4.7–6.8)	2 trials
Order Lagomorpha		
Wild rabbit (*Oryctolagus*)	20–25	
White-tailed jackrabbit (*Lepus townsendii*)	34	50 yd.
Arctic hare (*Lepus arcticus*)	30–40	Pressed, 3 mi.
Order Carnivora		
Family Canidae		
Wolf (*Canis lupus*)..................	28–40	200 yd.
Coyotes (*Canis latrans*)	28–43 24	Max., short dash Average, 1 mi.
Jackal (*Canis aureus*)	35	
Gray fox (*Urocyon cinereoargenteus*)....	40	Pressed, 0.75 mi.
Family Hyaenidae		
Spotted hyaena (*Crocuta crocuta*)	40	
Family Felidae		
Lion (*Felis leo*)	50	
Cheetah (*Acinonyx jubatus*)	65–70	Max., 440 yd.
Order Proboscidea		
African elephant (*Loxodonta africana*)...	15–25	
Order Perissodactyla		
Indian wild ass (*Equus hemionus*)	30	Average, 16 mi.
Mountain zebra (*Equus zebra*)	40	
Domestic horse (*Equus caballus*)........	42.3 11.2	440 yd. Trotting, 100 mi.
Black rhinoceros (*Diceros bicornis*)	28	Max., short bursts
Order Artiodactyla		
Family Suidae		
Wart hog (*Phacochoerus aethiopicus*) ...	30	
Family Camelidae		
Camel (*Camelus dromedarius*)..........	9–10	Racing
Family Giraffidae		
Giraffe (*Giraffa camelopardalis*)	28–32	Pressed

TABLE 1-1 *(Continued)*

Speeds of Various Species of Mammals, Grouped According to Their Types of Locomotion

	Miles Per Hour	Remarks
Family Antilocapridae		
Pronghorn antelope (*Antilocapra*	70	Max., short bursts
americana)	20–36	Normal gait
Family Cervidae		
Elk (*Cervus canadensis*)	18	Unhurried, 1 mi.
White-tailed deer (*Odocoileus*		
virginianus)	49	Max., pressed
Barren ground caribou (*Rangifer arcticus*).	25	Average max.
Moose (*Alces alces*)	35	Pressed, 0.25 mi.
Family Bovidae		
Bighorn sheep (*Ovis canadensis*)	30	Pressed, 0.25 mi.
Wildebeest (*Connochaetes* sp.)	50+	Max., 0.25 mi.
Grant's gazelle (*Gazella granti*)	50+	Max., 0.5 mi.
FOSSORIAL MAMMALS		
Order Insectivora		
Eastern mole (*Scalopus aquaticus*)	1.5	On surface
AERIAL MAMMALS		
Order Chiroptera		
Big brown bat (*Eptesicus fuscus*)	10.0 (8.2–15.0)	7 trials
VOLANT MAMMALS		
Order Rodentia		
Flying squirrel (*Glaucomys volans*)	4–5	
AQUATIC MAMMALS		
Order Rodentia		
Beaver (*Castor canadensis*)	2	Max.
Muskrat (*Ondatra zibethicus*)	3	Max.
Order Cetacea		
Dolphins (unspecified)	35–37	
Bottle-nosed dolphin (*Tursiops truncatus*).	21	Max.
Blue whale (*Sibbaldus musculus*)	23	Max., 10 min.
	16	Average, 2 hr.

SOURCE: These data are from a number of sources, primarily Bourlière (1954), Layne and Benton (1954), and Spector (1956).

In mammals living in hot climates, the hair is often sparse, either as a result of a general loss of hair or as a result of thinning of the underhair. The skin, when the hair is lost, becomes much thicker, probably as an aid in preventing dehydration of the body tissues and for better protection from the external environment. Generally, mammals living in hot climates accumulate little fat. Since one of the problems facing mammals in a hot climate is the elimination of excess heat from the body, there is a general increase in the total body surface as compared to its volume. This increased surface area is accomplished by enlargement of the extremities; that is, the limbs, ears, and tail. The increased surface area permits a greater heat loss. Further, most mammals in hot climates are active only at twilight or at night.

In mammals living in cold climates, retention of body heat is often a severe problem. In general, cold-dwelling mammals have a much thickened pelage and often a high fat storage, especially under the skin. These both tend to serve as insulators in conserving body heat. Further, the extremities are extremely reduced and often the ears and tail are practically lost, thus reducing the total body surface in relation to its volume and further conserving body heat. The large accumulations of fat are often associated with hibernation during the coldest part of the year. The pelage of cold-dwelling mammals tends to turn white in the winter (or to be white throughout the year), and many species grow large claws which serve as ice picks. Finally, most species in this habitat are active during the daytime, thus taking advantage of whatever heat from the sun may be available.

Mammals living in desert habitats exhibit many of the modifications of those living in hot climates. The pelage tends to be sparse and activity is usually nocturnal. Some of the larger forms, such as the antelopes, have the individual hairs coarse, thick, and frequently with a hollow core—all of which serve as a more efficient insulating device. Further, many forms undergo aestivation (periods of inactivity) when food is not available or when especially high temperatures exist. Several rodents have developed the ability to live without drinking water. Their water needs are met by a series of physiological adaptations, including the ability to secrete highly concentrated urine (and thus resorbing much water otherwise lost), and, in some forms, to form free water as a by-product from the breakdown of carbohydrates in their food.

Mammals living at high elevations show, in general, the same adaptations as those living in cold climates. Further, because of the lower oxygen concentrations at high elevations, there is an increase in lung capacity and an increase in the number of red blood corpuscles per unit volume of blood.

Mammals living in marine environments have undergone a number of modifications. As is clearly shown in Table 1–2, amphibious and aquatic mammals are able to stay submerged for much longer periods of time than are terrestrial mammals. Apparently this ability to remain submerged is not accomplished by a larger lung capacity nor by an increased oxygen-carrying ability of the blood. The relative lung capacities of the seals and manatees, for example, are about the same or only slightly larger than in man, and that of some whales is only one-half that of man. Further, probably most of the

TABLE 1–2

Maximum Duration of Submersion in Various Mammals

	Time (minutes)
Order Primates	
Family Hominidae	
Man (*Homo sapiens*)	2.5
Order Rodentia	
Family Castoridae	
Beaver (*Castor canadensis*)	15.0
Family Cricetidae	
Muskrat (*Ondatra zibethicus*)	12.0
Family Muridae	
White rat (*Rattus rattus*)	3.1
Order Carnivora	
Family Canidae	
Dog (*Canis familiaris*)	4.5
Order Pinnipedia	
Family Phocidae	
Common seal (*Phoca vitulina*)	15.0
Gray seal (*Halichoerus grypus*)	20.0
Elephant seal (*Mirounga angustirostris*)	30.0
Order Sirenia	
Family Trichechidae	
Manatee (*Trichechus manatus*)	16.0
Order Cetacea	
Family Physeteridae	
Sperm whale (*Physeter catodon*)	75
Family Ziphiidae	
Bottle-nosed whale (*Hyperoodon rostratis*)	120
Family Balaenopteridae	
Fin-backed whale (*Balaenoptera borealis*)	30
Blue whale (*Sibbaldus musculus*)	49

Source: These data are from various sources, primarily Bourlière (1954) and Spector (1956).

air of animals such as the seal is exhaled before they submerge, perhaps to make the body less buoyant (Fig. 1–10).

Three main factors enable the diving mammal to remain submerged for such long periods of time: a more complete renewal of the air in the lungs at each inhalation; a decrease in the sensitivity of the respiration center to an increased amount of carbon dioxide in the blood; and a series of physiological adaptations restricting the use of oxygen to only the most essential body functions during the dive.

As far as the renewal of air in the lungs is concerned, only 15 to 20 per cent is renewed in man with each inhalation, while as much as 90 per cent is renewed in one inhalation by some whales. The physiological adaptations for remaining underwater for extended periods of time are many. Some examples of these adaptations (Scholander, 1940) are described below.

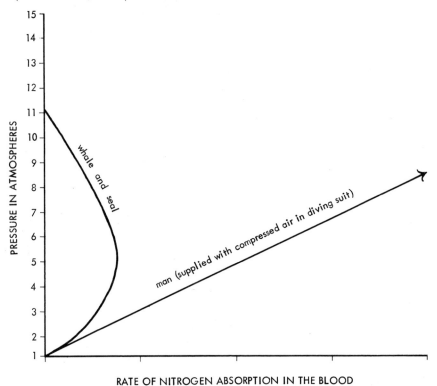

RATE OF NITROGEN ABSORPTION IN THE BLOOD

Fig. 1–10. The comparative rates of nitrogen absorption in man, wearing a diving suit, and a whale or seal.

Although there is a reduction of volume of air in the lungs at the beginning of a dive, especially as compared to that of a typical terrestrial mammal, other adaptations compensate for this. Proportionally, there is a greater volume of blood in aquatic than in terrestrial mammals. Thus, at the beginning of a dive, more oxygen is available from the blood. Further, the muscles of aquatic mammals contain a large quantity of myoglobin, a substance related to the haemoglobin of the blood, which has the ability to store oxygen. The presence of myoglobin gives the characteristic dark color to the flesh of aquatic mammals. In the sperm whale and others which have the ability to remain submerged for extended periods of time (up to two hours), the color of the flesh is almost black. Estimates for the fin whale indicate that at the beginning of a dive the total available oxygen is stored as followed: in the blood, 42 per cent; in the muscles, 42 per cent; the lungs, 9 per cent; and in the tissue fluids, 7 per cent.

In seals the heart rate slows down as the dive begins and there is a constriction of blood vessels to the less critical organs. Immediately after a seal starts to dive, the heart beat drops from 150 per minute to only 10 per minute. The blood pressure appears to remain normal in the large arteries and in the brain but drops drastically in the muscles and the visceral organs.

There is no evidence so far that the heart rate of the whale decreases during the dive; although, for many obvious reasons, data on this subject are sparse. If this is true, then it is postulated that extensive submersion is permitted by two interacting conditions: the muscles continue to operate by building up a larger oxygen debt than is possible in terrestrial mammals, and the respiratory center of the brain is less stimulated by increased carbon dioxide concentrations. In terrestrial mammals, when respiration ceases (such as occurs when a man holds his breath), the resultant higher levels of carbon dioxide which accumulate in the blood stimulate the respiratory center of the brain, causing breathing to begin again. In aquatic mammals, much higher concentrations of carbon dioxide are required to stimulate the respiratory center; resultantly, they can "hold their breath" longer than can terrestrial mammals.

2
Distribution and Classification

CLASSIFICATION

One uniform feature of all animal life is the occurrence of differences between individuals (variations). Often the variations are minute and are not readily evident. Such is exemplified by human identical twins. More variation is evident between brothers and sisters or, for that matter, between individuals in a litter of dogs. Progressively greater differences are evident between a dog and a cat; a dog and a rabbit; and a dog and a bat. However, even these animals have a large number of features in common (e.g., hair, teeth, bear living young, etc.) and differ from other animals such as birds, snakes, and fish. The differences between animals, then, ranges from the minute variations to be seen between identical twins to major evolutionary differences such as those found between such groups as dogs and fish.

The classification of animals is an attempt to group animals of common origin into distinct categories, in other words, according to "blood relationships." Distinction must be made between various levels of differences. Individual differences must be eliminated from consideration and features characteristic of populations must be used as the basis of forming groups.

If we had a complete record of the ancestors of all living animals, we could easily arrange them with respect to blood relationship. The problem of dividing them into groups would be difficult, if not impossible, as few morphological gaps would exist in such a series. However, only a poor record exists of the past history of animals (the paleontological record is notoriously incomplete for many). As a result, the classification of animals is based primarily upon the presence of differences between groups of living animals and the presence of features common to the population (likenesses).

TAXONOMIC CHARACTERS

The features of an animal that serve to illustrate likenesses and differences (morphology, embryology, ecology, reproduction, habits, etc.) are called characters. Many of these characters are of such a nature that they are not readily evident to the person interested in classification. Call notes, habits, and physiological features, for instance, are not a part of the data usually preserved with an animal. Thus, for practical purposes, such characters are not available for purposes of classification. Those characters that are used in classification are often called *taxonomic characters*. These are usually readily discernable, morphological in nature, and concern size, proportions, structure, coloration, and color pattern.

The classification of animals is based on the proper evaluation of taxonomic characters. All taxonomic characters vary. This variation falls into the following categories:

A. Individual variation
   1. Nongenetic variation
      a. Phenotypic variation
      b. Age variation
      c. Seasonal variation
   2. Genetic variation
      a. Sexual
      b. Individual
B. Population variation

In classification we are interested in the variation of populations. When an animal is described it is (or should be) described in terms of the population it represents. However, in order properly to evaluate such variation, we must be able to recognize individual variations of all types. Obviously a classification that places a kitten and its parents in two (or three) different taxonomic categories would not be of much use. However, it was not too long ago that melanistic fox squirrels, *Sciurus niger* (that may show up in the same litter as normally colored squirrels) were thought to be either hybrids or, perhaps, a distinct species.

Population variations are used as bases for arranging animals in a taxonomic hierarchy. The resultant arrangement is an attempt to express the "blood relationships" and the "genealogical tree" of the animals concerned. The following is an example of the various conventional and generally accepted taxonomic categories employed in the classification of mammals (Simpson, 1945). Those marked with an asterisk (*) are considered obligatory in the formal classification of a mammal.

*Kingdom—Animal
 *Phylum—Chordata
   Subphylum—Vertebrata
   Superclass—Tetrapoda

*Class—Mammalia
  Subclass—Theria
    Infraclass—Eutheria
      Cohort—Ferungulata
        Superorder—Paraxonia
          *Order—Artiodactyla
            Suborder—Ruminantia
              Superfamily—Cervoidea
                *Family—Cervidae
                  Subfamily—Odocoileinae
                    Tribe—Odocoileini
                    Subtribe
                      *Genus—*Odocoileus*
                        Subgenus—*Eucervus*
                        *Species—*hemionus*
                          Subspecies—*eremicus*

Ordinal Characters. The various orders of mammals are based on taxonomic differences judged by competent authority to be of major significance. These are usually concerned with differences in limbs (modifications for flying, running, aquatic life, etc.), digits (reductions and modifications), and the nature of the ends of the digits (nails, claws, hooves). These characters are associated with major differences in the dentition (presence or absence of canines, major modifications in types of molars and premolars) as well as characters of the soft anatomy, such as the structural complexity of the brain (Fig. 2–1).

Family Characters. Family characters in mammals are concerned with differences judged to be of a lower grade of significance. Such features are often associated with internal modifications of the body, such as the presence or absence of skull characters and modifications of the teeth (especially molars and premolars) and modifications of the external body form often correlated with adaptations to a particular environment. Such modifications as quills, horns, and antlers usually fall into this category (Fig. 2–2).

Generic Characters. Generic characters are less marked and often have to do with differences in the skull and teeth. Often, but not always, these differences are associated with obvious external features. For example, differences between most genera in the Sciuridae are rather evident externally; however, in the family Cricetidae, the differences between certain genera are not at all obvious externally and resort must be made to cranial examination.

Specific Characters. Specific characters usually have to do with differences in size, color and markings, ear shape and size, and other prominent external features. Variations in skulls at the species level

Fig. 2–1. The order of mammals is based on major differences in limbs, digits, and cranial modifications.

are usually concerned only with size and proportions. As a result, it is difficult to recognize species differences in fossil mammals where external features are not available to confirm or deny conclusions.

A species is usually defined in terms of reproductive isolation or lack of interbreeding (see Mayr, 1942). In general, speciation or

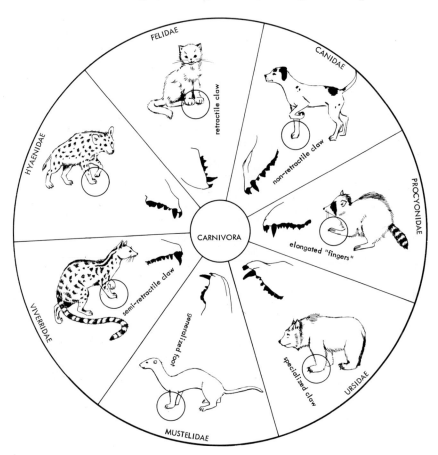

Fig. 2–2. The *family* of mammals is based on lesser differences in limbs, digits, and cranial modifications.

species formation in the class Mammalia is a population phenomenon. It results from the separation, either in time or in space, of a population from the parent population, and differentiation and reproductive isolation of these groups by natural selection or random fixation (Wright, 1931, and elsewhere) of mutations that occur or are already available in the population as stored variability (Mather and Harrison, 1949).

In actual practice, the data necessary to show the presence or absence of reproductive isolation for a given population sample are usually lacking; thus the degree of morphological difference must be used as a basis for judging whether or not differences between two population samples are the result of individual variation, geographic variation within one species, or species differences.

Subspecies Characters. A subspecies or geographic race is usually defined in terms of minor morphological differences (size, shades of coloration, pattern, etc.) evident between population samples of a species from two (or more) parts of the range of the species. This is often associated with obvious differences in the environment.

NOMENCLATURE

Nomenclature is concerned with the application of a name to a given kind of animal. Common or vernacular names are applied to most of the well-known mammals. Unfortunately, however, such names are not uniform. Even among the larger mammals, there is some confusion (the American elk is closely related to the Old World red deer while the elk of the Old World is the same genus as the North American moose); among the smaller mammals common names have little meaning. "Field mice" is a categorical term that includes uncounted dozens of species of at least two orders (Insectivora and Rodentia), and the term "gopher" is applied to a varied assortment of animals. While "gopher" generally refers to rodents of the family Geomyidae, the term is also applied to several different ground squirrels of the family Sciuridae and, in the southeastern United States, to a tortoise (Class Reptilia).

To avoid the confusion inherent in vernacular names, zoologists have a system of binominal nomenclature wherein two Latin or latinized words are used as the scientific name of an animal. (In those cases where the species is divided into subspecies or geographical races, a third Latin or latinized word is appended to the name.) By mutual agreement at the International Congress of Zoologists in 1898, a permanent Commission on Nomenclature was created to prepare an International Code of Nomenclature. Under this code a name once properly published as a generic name for any animal is not available as a generic name of any other animal. Further, no two species (or subspecies) in one genus can bear the same name. If a genus, species, or subspecies has been described more than once, the earliest name and author is recognized under the law of priority and duplicate names are termed synonyms (see Schenk and McMasters, 1936, and Mayr, Linsley, and Usinger, 1953, for a discussion of the International Code of Nomenclature).

MAJOR DIVISION OF MAMMALS

Man has not always recognized that all of the mammals, as we know them today, comprise a group of closely related individuals warranting being placed in the same major category. In 1693, John Ray, an Englishman, in his book *Synopsis Methodica Animalium Quadrupedum et Serpentine Genesis*, first bracketed the terrestrial and aquatic mammals (as known today) as Vivipara. Before this, the aquatic mammals had been grouped with the fish. Even Linnaeus, in the first nine editions of *Systema Naturae*, continued to join the aquatic mammals with the fish. In the tenth edition (1758) Linnaeus first separated the aquatic mammals from the fish and placed them with the other mammals.

Mammals arose in the Mesozoic Age from mammal-like reptiles. Based on the fragmentary paleontological evidence, a generalized primitive mammal is thought to have been small, about the size of a chipmunk, to have been plantigrade (flat-footed) and ambulatory, and to have had a small brain with the cerebral hemispheres practically smooth. Of course nothing can be said with certainty about either the soft anatomy or the reproductive processes in this hypothetical ancestral mammal. Like the living monotremes, it may well have been an egg-laying animal. The teeth were probably already heterodont. From this primitive form, progressive evolution has occurred in the reproductive and nervous system and radial adaptations have occurred in the appendages and teeth.

Living members of the class Mammalia are readily divisible into three groups are the monotremes, the duck-billed platypus and the of the reproductive system, and the method of reproduction. These three groups are the monotremes   the duck-billed platypus and the spiny "anteater" of Australia, which are egg-laying types; the marsupials (the opossum and a number of Australian forms), which give birth to their young in an embryonic condition; and the placentals (including all other living orders of mammals), in which the young are retained for a longer time in their mother's body and which have a highly developed placenta. These subdivisions have been given various names and accorded various taxonomic ranks by different students of mammalian taxonomy. We shall refer to them as Prototheria (= first mammals), Metatheria (= middle mammals) and Eutheria (= typical mammals).

When one attempts to fit the various extinct kinds of primitive mammals into the classification outlined above, many difficulties are encountered. The monotremes (Prototheria) are almost unknown as fossils. Early marsupials and placentals (Metatheria and Eutheria) are rare. Many of the fossil forms are not closely related to any living group and, obviously, nothing is known of their soft anatomy or mode of reproduction, so that their relationships to living forms are obscure. The following classification of the major subdivisions of the Class Mammalia is based upon meager evidence available for the fossil forms plus the evidence of living mammals (modified from Simpson, 1945). In this classification the mammals are divided into three subclasses: Prototheria, Allotheria, and Theria.

The subclass Prototheria is considered to be the most primitive group, although they are not known from any old fossil remains. The prototheres show a mixture of primitive characteristics, mixed with several specialized characteristics. The primitive characteristics include the presence of coracoid and precoracoid elements in the shoulder girdle, the absence of an external conch on the ear, and the fact that the females lay eggs. Specialized characteristics include the fact that teeth are present only in young animals. Members of this subclass are known from the Pleistocene and Recent of Australia and includes only the Order Monotremata.

The Subclass Allotheria (= other mammals) includes only forms long extinct. Not much is known about these mammals since not a single postcranial skeleton is known. They probably were rodent-like in habits, and certainly in size. Based on the evidence furnished by their teeth, the allotheres probably were not ancestral to the therian mammals; rather, they represent a separate branch of mammalian forms that arose from the mammal-like reptiles. The Order Multituberculata and perhaps the Order Triconodonta belong to this subclass. Multituberculates are known from the Upper Jurassic through the Lower Eocene while the Triconodonts are known only from the Upper Jurassic.

The Subclass Theria is known from the Late Cretaceous to the Recent. Characteristics include a greatly reduced coracoid element in the shoulder girdle, usually represented only as a process on the scapula; the ear usually has an external conch; teeth are present in both young and adults; and the females produce living young. This subclass is divided into three infraclasses, Pantotheria, Metatheria, and Eutheria. The Infraclass Pantotheria (real mammals) are possible ancestors of the higher mammals. They are known from the Upper Jurassic and Lower Cretaceous. This infraclass includes two orders, Pantotheria and Symmetrodonta.

The Infraclass Metatheria is known from the Upper Cretaceous to the Recent. It includes only the Order Marsupialia. The metatheres have a very small or no placental attachment for the embryos. The embryos stay in the uteri for only a short time and finish their development in a marsupium.

The Infraclass Eutheria is known from the Upper Cretaceous to recent and includes most of the living kinds of mammals. Members of this infraclass have a well-developed placenta and do not have a marsupium.

A CLASSIFICATION OF MAMMALS

A simplified classification of the known mammals, living and fossil, is given below. Many of the steps in the taxonomic hierarchy are omitted and no families containing only fossil forms are listed. Following the names of the families is a common name of the family or the common names of the best-known members of the family. The following abbreviations indicate the continents on which the family occurs.

*—Extinct	M.—Malagasy
A.—America	N.—North
Af.—Africa	E.—East
As.—Asia	S.—South
Au.—Australia	W.—West
Eu.—Europe	

Class MAMMALIA

Subclass Prototheria
    Order Monotremata—monotremes
        Family Tachyglossidae—spiny echidna, Au.
        Family Ornithorhynchidae—duckbilled platypus, Au.
*Subclass Allotheria
    *Order Multituberculata, N.A., As., Eu.
    *Order Triconodonta, N.A.
Subclass Theria
*Infraclass Pantotheria
    *Order Pantotheria, N.A., Eu., Af.
    *Order Symmetrodonta, N.A., Eu.
Infraclass Metatheria
    Order Marsupialia—marsupials
        Family Didelphidae—opossums, N.A., S.A.
        Family Dasyuridae—Australian meat- and insect-eating marsupials, Au.
        Family Notoryctidae—marsupial mole, Au.
        Family Peramelidae—bandicoots, Au.
        Family Caenolestidae—mouse opossums, S.A.
        Family Phalangeridae—possums and phalangers, Au.
        Family Phascolomidae—wombats, Au.
        Family Macropodidae—wallabies, kangaroos, Au.

Infraclass Eutheria
   Order Insectivora—insectivores.
      Family Solenodontidae—solenodons, W. Indies.
      Family Tenrecidae—tenrecs, M.
      Family Potamogalidae—otter-shrew, Af.
      Family Chrysochloridae—golden "mole," Af.
      Family Erinaceidae—hedgehog, E., As., Af.
      Family Macroscelididae—"elephant shrew," Af.
      Family Soricidae—shrews, E., As., Af., N.A.
      Family Talpidae—moles, Eu., As., N.A.
   Order Dermoptera
      Family Cynocephalidae—"flying lemur," As.
   Order Chiroptera—bats
    Suborder Megachiroptera
      Family Pteropidae—fruit-eating bats, As., Af., Au.
    Suborder Microchiroptera
      Family Rhinopomidae—mouse-tailed bats, As., Af.
      Family Emballonuridae—sheath-tailed bats, tropics except Au.
      Family Noctilionidae—bulldog bats, tropical A.
      Family Nycteridae—hispid bats, Af., Malaya
      Family Megadermidae—large-winged bats, tropical Af., As., Au.
      Family Rhinolophidae—horseshoe bats, Eu., As., Au.
      Family Hipposideridae—Old World leaf-nosed bats, tropical Old World
      Family Phyllostomatidae—American leaf-nosed bats, N.A., S.A.
      Family Desmodontidae—vampires, tropical A.
      Family Natalidae—funnel-eared bats, tropical A.
      Family Furipteridae—smoky bats, S.A.
      Family Thyropteridae—disk-winged bats, tropical A.
      Family Myzopodidae—golden bat, M.
      Family Vespertilionidae—vespertilionid bats, worldwide
      Family Mystacinidae—short-tailed bats, New Zealand
      Family Molossidae—free-tailed bats, worldwide in tropics and subtropics
   Order Primates
    Suborder Prosimii
      Family Tupaiidae—tree "shrews," S.As.
      Family Lemuridae—lemurs, M.
      Family Indridae—woolly "lemurs," M.
      Family Daubentoniidae—aye-aye, M.
      Family Lorisidae—slow loris, bush babies, As., Af.
      Family Galagidae—galago, east equatorial Africa
      Family Tarsiidae—tarsier, East Indies to Philippines
    Suborder Anthropoidea
      Family Cebidae—New World monkeys, tropical A.
      Family Callithricidae—marmosets, tropical A.
      Family Cercopithecidae—Old World monkeys, Eu., As., Af.
      Family Pongidae—gibbon, orangutan, and relatives, Af., As.
      Family Hominidae—man, worldwide.
  *Order Tillodontia
  *Order Taeniodontia

Order Edentata
  Family Myrmecophagidae—anteaters, S.A., Central A.
  Family Bradypodidae—tree sloths, S.A., Central A.
  Family Dasypodidae—armadillos, S. A., N.A.
Order Pholidota
  Family Manidae—pangolins, scaly anteater, As., Af.
Order Lagomorpha
  Family Ochotonidae—pikas, Eu., As., N.A.
  Family Leporidae—hares and rabbits, Eu., As., Af., N.A., S.A.
Order Rodentia—rodents
  Suborder Sciuromorpha
    Family Aplodontidae—mountain "beaver," N.A.
    Family Sciuridae—squirrels, Eu., As., Af., N.A., S.A.
    Family Geomyidae—pocket gophers, N.A.
    Family Heteromyidae—"kangaroo" rats, N.A., northern S.A.
    Family Castoridae—beavers, N.A., Eu., As.
  Suborder Myomorpha
    Family Anomaluridae—scaly-tailed squirrels, Af.
    Family Pedetidae—spring haas, Af.
    Family Cricetidae—cricetid mice, E.As., M., N.A., S.A.
    Family Spalacidae—"mole" rat, Eu., As., Af.
    Family Rhizomyidae—bamboo rat, As., Af.
    Family Muridae—Old World rats and mice, native in Eu., As., Af.,
      A., introduced worldwide.
    Family Gliridae—dormice, Eu., As., Af.
    Family Platacanthomyidae—spiny dormice, As.
    Family Seleviniidae—Selvin's mice, As.
    Family Zapodidae—jumping mice, Eu., As., N.A.
    Family Dipodidae—jerboas, Eu., As., Af.
  Suborder Hystricomorpha
    Family Hystricidae—Old World porcupines, As., Af.
    Family Erethizontidae—New World porcupines, N.A., S.A.
    Family Caviidae—guinea pigs, cavies, S.A.
    Family Hydrochoeridae—capybara, tropical A.
    Family Dinomyidae—false paca, S.A.
    Family Dasyproctidae—pacas, tropical A.
    Family Chinchillidae—chinchilla, S.A.
    Family Capromyidae—hutias, West Indies.
    Family Myocastoridae—nutria, C.A., S.A.
    Family Octodontidae—octodonts or hedge rats, S.A., W. Indies.
    Family Ctenomyidae—tucu-tucu, S.A.
    Family Abrocomidae—chinchilla rat, S.A.
    Family Echimyidae—spiny "rat," Central and S.A.
    Family Thryonomyidae—cane rats, Af.
    Family Petromyidae—rock rat, Af.
    Family Bathyergidae—"mole rat," Af.
    Family Ctenodactylidae—gundis, Af.
Order Cetacea
  Suborder Odontoceti—toothed whales
    Family Platanistidae—Ganges River dolphin, rivers of India.
    Family Iniidae—Amazon and white flag dolphin, rivers of S.A. and
      China.

Family Physeteridae—sperm whales, all oceans.
Family Ziphiidae—beaked whales, all oceans.
Family Kogiidae—pygmy sperm whale, Atlantic, Pacific and Indian oceans.
Family Monodontidae—white whale, narwhal, south polar oceans.
Family Delphinidae—dolphins and porpoises, all oceans and large rivers.
    Suborder Mysteceti—whale-bone whales.
Family Eschrichtiidae—gray whales, northern Pacific Ocean.
Family Balaenopteridae—fin-backed whale, all oceans.
Family Balaenidae—right whales, all oceans.
Order Carnivora—carnivores
Family Canidae—dogs, foxes, etc., worldwide.
Family Ursidae—bears, Eu., As., N.A., S.A.
Family Procyonidae—raccoons, etc., As., N.A., S.A.
Family Mustelidae—skunks, weasels, etc., Eu., As., Af., N.A., S.A.
Family Viverridae—civets and allies, Eu., As., Af., M.
Family Hyaenidae—Hyaena, As., Af.
Family Felidae—cats, Eu., As., N.A., S.A.
Order Pinnipedia
Family Otariidae—eared seals, primarily Pacific and southern Atlantic oceans.
Family Odobenidae—walrus, north polar regions.
Family Phocidae—true seals, all oceans, many larger rivers
*Order Condylarthra
*Order Litopterna
*Order Notoungulata
*Order Astrapotheria
Order Tubulidentata
Family Orycteropodidae—aardvark, Af.
*Order Pantodonta
*Order Dinocerata
*Order Pyrotheria
Order Proboscidea
Family Elephantidae—elephants, As., Af.
*Order Embrithopoda
Order Hyracoidea
Family Procaviidae—conies, Af., As.
Order Sirenia
Family Dugongidae—sea cow, Pacific Ocean
Family Trichechidae—manatee, NA., S.A., Af.
Order Perissodactyla
Family Equidae—horses, E., Af., As., now worldwide.
Family Tapiridae—tapirs, As., S.A.
Family Rhinocerotidae—rhinoceros, As., Af.
Order Artiodactyla
    Suborder Suiformes
Family Suidae—pigs, Eu., As., Af., now worldwide.
Family Tayassuidae—peccaries, N.A., S.A.
Family Hippopotamidae—hippootamus, Af.
    Suborder Tylopoda
Family Camelidae—camels, S.A., As.

Suborder Ruminantia
    Family Tragulidae—chevrotain, As., Af.
    Family Cervidae—deer, elk, Eu., As., N.A., S.A.
    Family Giraffidae—giraffe, Af.
    Family Antilocapridae—pronghorn, N.A.
    Family Bovidae—cows, bison, Eu., As., Af., N.A.

DISTRIBUTION OF MAMMALS

Mammals vary in abundance, both as to numbers of kinds and numbers of individuals, in the various parts of the world. In the United States, for instance, the number of species in the various states show considerable variation. In general, states east of the Mississippi River have very few species of mammals; states in the mountainous parts of the West have more, and those in the Southwest have the most. This difference in numbers of species can be correlated, in part, with the number of different types of habitat available in the state. Table 2–1 shows the number of kinds of mammals from various states in the United States. It adequately demonstrates the great variations present within the United States.

From such data it is evident that no one species of mammal occurs uniformly over the whole world; rather, each is restricted to a definite range or area of distribution. As one examines the records of occurrence of any given animal, it is immediately evident that distribution is not unidimensional; rather, it occupies both time and space. Further, even at a given time, animals are not uniformly distributed in space; a given kind is usually restricted to a particular kind of environment. Certain kinds, for example, occur only in water while others occur only in the desert. We can therefore list three distinct aspects of distribution of any given mammal. These are *geographical distribution,* or distribution in space; *geological distribution,* or distribution in time; and *ecological distributon,* or the special habitats within a given time and space that are occupied by the mammal.

GEOGRAPHICAL DISTRIBUTION

Some mammalian species have a wide geographical range. The deer mouse (*Peromyscus maniculatus*) is a species with a wide distribution. Its geographical range extends from central Alaska and all of Canada from the tree line southward throughout all of the western United States and southward in the mountains of central Mexico to a point south of Mexico City. It is absent in the southeastern United States. This is a geographical range in excess of five million square miles. In contrast to the large geographical range of the deer mouse is that of the Florida mouse (*Peromyscus floridanus*) of

TABLE 2–1

Number of Kinds of Terrestrial Mammals in Selected States in the United States

The numbers indicate the number of families and, in parentheses, the number of genera, followed by the number of species.

	California(1)	Arizona(2)	Nevada(3)	Utah(4)	Idaho(5)	Kansas(6)	Ohio(7)	Tennessee(8)	Florida(9)
Order									
Marsupialia	1(1)1	1(1)1	0	0	0	1(1)1	1(1)1	1(1)1	1(1)1
Insectivora	2(4)16	1(2)5	2(3)8	1(1)5	1(1)4	2(3)3	2(6)7	2(6)8	2(4)4
Chiroptera	3(11)23	3(14)27	3(18)22	2(9)17	1(6)11	2(9)13	1(6)9	1(7)12	2(10)13
Edentata	0	0	0	0	0	1(1)1	0	0	1(1)1
Lagomorpha	2(3)8	1(2)5	2(3)7	2(3)7	2(3)6	1(2)5	1(2)2	1(2)4	1(1)2
Rodentia	9(25)90	8(22)70	9(23)56	8(25)61	8(22)41	8(23)34	6(21)24	6(21)31	6(13)18
Carnivora	5(16)32	5(16)22	5(14)18	5(15)23	5(13)20	5(12)17	4(9)13	5(12)15	5(10)12
Artiodactyla	3(5)6	4(5)6	3(4)6	3(6)6	3(8)9	3(4)5	2(3)3	2(3)3	2(2)2
Totals									
Orders	7	7	6	6	6	8	7	7	8
Families	25	23	24	21	20	23	17	18	20
Genera	65	63	57	59	53	55	48	52	42
Species	166	135	111	118	91	80	69	74	53
Forms	432	290	232	247	137	119	71	85	104

SOURCES: (1) Grinnell, 1933; (2) Cockrum, 1960; (3) Hall, 1946; (4) Durrant, 1952; (5) Davis, 1939; (6) Cockrum, 1952; (7) Bole and Moulthrop, 1942; (8) Kellogg, 1939; (9) Sherman, 1952.

peninsular Florida, with a geographical range of less than 40,000 square miles, and that of the Suisun shrew (*Sorex sinuosus*), known only from Grizzly Island near Suisun, Solano County, California.

The causes of such differences in size of geographical ranges are not simple. Every species produces offspring in excess of the number that can survive within the normal range. This results in a "population pressure" which in turn causes an expansion of the ecological and geographical range of the species. Operating against this population pressure are a number of diverse factors which, acting together, tend to set the limits of a given species of mammal at any given time. These factors and their interactions, however, are dynamic; thus the range is subject to change. Some of the factors influencing the distribution of mammals are briefly indicated below.

PHYSIOGRAPHIC FACTORS INFLUENCING DISTRIBUTION

A number of physiographic factors, such as latitude, topography, weathering, and edaphic factors have an influence on the distribution of a given species of mammal. Fig. 2–3 indicates the relationship between altitude and latitude.

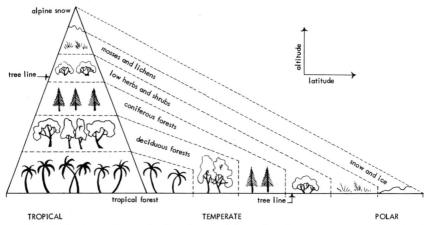

Fig. 2–3. Latitude and altitude are interrelated, with various latitudinal zones having their counterparts at various elevations.

Latitude, with its associated climatic and biological differences, has a definite influence on mammalian distribution. Few species of mammals range from the tropics to the polar regions. In the Far North there are few species of mammals. Each species, however, is usually represented by a large number of individuals. In the tropics, on the other hand, there is a large diversity of species and relatively few individuals of each species. Table 2–2 gives a comparison of

TABLE 2–2

Number of Kinds of Non-Marine Mammals in Northern Alaska, Arizona, and Costa Rica

F = number of families; G = number of genera; and S = number of species. The columns labeled "common" indicate those mammals that occur in the two regions being compared.

Orders	Alaska(1)			Common Alaska-Arizona			Arizona(2)			Common Arizona-Costa Rica			Costa Rica(3)			Common Costa Rica-Alaska		
	F	G	S	F	G	S	F	G	S	F	G	S	F	G	S	F	G	S
Marsupialia	0	0	0	–	–	–	1	1	1	1	1	1	1	6	7	–	–	–
Insectivora	1	1	3	1	1	1	1	2	4	1	0	0	1	1	5	1	0	0
Chiroptera	0	0	0	–	–	–	3	14	27	3	8	6	8	59	86	–	–	–
Primates	0	0	0	–	–	–	0	0	0	–	–	–	3	4	4	–	–	–
Edentata	0	0	0	–	–	–	0	0	0	–	–	–	4	7	7	–	–	–
Lagomorpha	1	1	1	1	1	0	1	2	5	1	1	1	1	1	3	1	0	0
Rodentia	3	7	8	3	4	1	8	22	70	6	6	3	9	23	54	3	3	0
Carnivora	4	9	13	4	7	5	5	16	22	4	9	10	5	13	24	3	3	1
Perissodactyla	0	0	0	–	–	–	0	0	0	–	–	–	1	2	2	0	0	0
Artiodactyla	2	4	4	2	1	0	4	5	6	2	2	2	2	3	4	1	0	0
Totals	11	22	29	11	14	7	23	62	135	18	27	23	35	119	196	9	3	1

SOURCES: (1) Bee and Hall, 1956; (2) Cockrum, 1960; (3) Goodwin, 1946.

the number of species in northern Alaska with the number of species in Costa Rica, Central America.

Topography, and its components of altitude (Fig. 2–3), drainage, and exposure, also affects the distribution of mammals, even in localities of the same latitude. In general, the fauna of the higher elevations of mountains in the north temperate parts of the world show relationships with northern faunas. There is usually a decrease in the number of species at the higher elevations. An excellent example of altitude as a barrier is illustrated by the bats. Ryberg (1950) found that, on a worldwide basis, only 10 percent of the species of bats occur at elevations in excess of 2,000 feet; that less than 5 percent occur at elevations in excess of 6,000 feet; and that only 19 species (less than 1 percent) are known to occur at elevations of more than 10,000 feet, and then only at a restricted time of year.

The drainage of an area affects both plants and animals, for the type of vegetation varies considerably with drainage. A poorly drained area is often a swamp, an ideal habitat for many kinds of mammals, including muskrats and beavers. Conversely, these swamps are barriers to certain species of dry land. Larger rivers and lakes are barriers to the distribution of many kinds of mammals. Much of the Colorado River in the southwestern United States acts as a barrier to many small terrestrial mammals (Goldman, 1937; Durrant, 1952).

In the Northern Hemisphere south-facing slopes receive more sunlight than north-facing slopes. This difference in exposure also affects the fauna and flora. In general, at localities in the same general latitude and elevation, north-facing slopes show faunal and floral relationships with localities at higher elevations or more northerly latitudes.

Weathering, as such, probably does not have much effect on mammalian distribution. However, the long-term effects of weathering (soil formation, mountain erosion) do cause differences in distribution patterns.

Edaphic factors (or factors pertaining to the state or condition of the soil) are a major influence on the local distribution of mammals (see Hardy, 1945). Further, the nature of the soil can influence the body form of burrowing rodents such as pocket gophers (see Davis, 1938; and Davis, Ramsey and Arendale, 1938). Finally the soil can be a barrier to mammalian distribution. In the southwestern United States the desert kangaroo rat, *Dipodomys deserti*, is found only in soft sands, commonly in sand dunes. It is restricted in its eastern and northern distribution in Arizona, in part by areas of hard soils and rocks. In the same area the rock pocket mouse,

Perognathus intermedius, is found only on rocky slopes and old lava flows.

To mammals that depend upon caves, rock crevices, and similar features of the physical environment for shelters, the absence of such shelters can prove to be a barrier to distribution.

CLIMATIC FACTORS INFLUENCING DISTRIBUTION

A number of climatic factors, especially temperature and moisture, have a direct or an indirect influence in mammalian distribution. The temperature of the environment, in its various aspects, includes air temperature, water temperature, and soil temperature. This effect is best seen at the edges of the ranges where seasons of unusually hot or unusually cold weather result in the reduction or elimination of the species (see Taylor, 1934).

The amount of available *moisture* determines, to a great extent, the type of vegetation of a given area. This results in the development of different habitats which determine the type of mammals present. The moisture of an area is determined by precipitation (snow, rain, dew, etc.), humidity, soil moisture, and flooding. Many mammals, such as the pocket mice (*Perognathus*) and the kangaroo rats (*Dipodomys*) of the southwestern United States, are adapted to regions of low precipitation. A few examples of lack of moisture having a dramatic effect on the occurrence of mammals have been published. One such example is how, during an extended dry period in western Kansas, the lack of moisture, interacting with other environmental factors (primarily the killing off of food and cover plants), resulted in the almost complete elimination of the prairie vole (*Microtus ochrogaster*).

Grinnell (1939) has pointed out some of the effects of a wet year on mammalian populations, and a rather dramatic example of the effect of increased rainfall has been pointed out by Huey (1941). A strip of soil along each side of a highway across a desert in southern California receives more moisture than the adjacent area because of the runoff of water from the pavement. As a result the types of vegetation in these strips has changed. The adjacent desert is not a suitable habitat for pocket gophers, yet these rodents can live in the area along the highway and have extended their range some distance along these narrow strips.

The humidity of a region is usually associated with the amount of sunlight, precipitation, and the amount of winds. Regions with differing humidities usually contain vastly different associations of plants and animals. The direct effect of humidity, alone, however, is difficult to measure.

The amount of moisture in the soil is usually associated with the amount of local precipitation but is influenced by the slope and soil type of the region. Occasionally local areas have a high soil-moisture content resulting from underground seepage. Soil moisture has a direct bearing on the vegetation type in the area, and thus influences the kinds of terrestrial mammals present. Certain burrowing species are directly influenced by soil moisture.

Flooding is usually restricted to stream valleys. It usually results from a particular topographic conformation plus excessive precipitation, although unusually high temperatures resulting in a rapid melting of snow have often caused floods. A flood can cause the complete elimination of most small mammals from the area flooded. Scheffer (1908) reported that, in one year of high water in the Kansas River and its tributaries in eastern Kansas, pocket gophers (*Geomys*) were practically exterminated on the flood plains of the river. In successive years the area was repopulated by individuals from adjacent, unflooded areas. Blair (1939) has published observations on the effects of stream valley flooding in eastern Oklahoma.

BIOLOGICAL FACTORS INFLUENCING DISTRIBUTION

Biological factors (plants and other animals) can be just as effective barriers to mammalian distribution as any physical factor. The absence of food, the absence of vegetation for shelters, the presence of parasites, diseases, and enemies—all can serve as effective barriers.

That plants are necessary for the existence of mammals is obvious. All mammals depend upon plants directly or indirectly for food. The type of plants present influences the type of mammals present; arboreal species do not occur in a grassland nor do grassland forms occur in a forest.

Animals in general interact with mammalian species in many different ways. Some species are used as food, others are predators on the mammals present. While the presence of predators in an area usually is not a barrier to distribution, it certainly influences the population levels present in the region. The artificial elimination by man of predators in a given region often results in an unbalanced situation wherein a given species of mammal reaches population levels in excess of the available food and shelter. The result is usually a crash in population levels, often to a point below the original level.

Apparently the very existence of certain species of mammals is dependent upon the presence of a second species. Such appears to be the case with the black-footed ferret (*Mustela nigripes*) in North

America. The black-footed ferret has almost invariably been taken in or around prairie-dog towns where it feeds on these rodents and uses their burrows for shelters. With man's constant warfare against the prairie dogs the black-footed ferret has become almost extinct.

GEOLOGICAL DISTRIBUTION

Mammals arose some 150 to 175 million years ago from a group of mammal-like reptiles, the Synapsida. In this long period of time it is not surprising that the geographical distribution of mammals has varied and that even major groups of mammals have arisen and become extinct. Our knowledge of the geological history of mammals is based on fossil remains. A fossil is an organic relic preserved in the rocks or other sediments that gives evidence as to the character of the original organism. In the case of mammals, these evidences are usually in the form of unaltered hard parts such as teeth and skeletal parts. Unusual cases are the mammoths and woolly rhinoceros found frozen in Siberia and Northern Alaska, the skeletons of mammals from peat bogs and tar pits, and the dried skin and hair of ground sloths in some caves in Nevada, New Mexico, and Arizona.

The chronological sequence of the fossils is determined by a combination of many techniques. In an ideal situation, the fossils are laid down in beds or layers, the newer layers being on top. By correlating partial series of beds, a sequence of events (and faunas) can be determined. In the more recent deposits, fossils of mammals are common, but in progressively older deposits few fossils (of any kind) are preserved. Thus our knowledge of the primitive mammals is very limited. The geological column and time chart (Fig. 2–4) shows the relation of the origin and development to that of the other animals and gives the names of the pertinent geological eras, periods, and epochs.

At the close of the Paleozoic era the Synapsida (the mammal-like reptile group from which mammals arose) was morphologically very close to the main line of reptile development. During the Mesozoic era members of the reptilian subclass became divergent and modified. Probably at least five large groups of Synapsida developed mammal-like characters. These five divergent lines were mammalian in at least 50 percent of their osteological features. Animals included in the Class Mammalia probably arose from different groups of the Subclass Synapsida, thus the Class Mammalia is probably polyphyletic in origin. The mammalian Subclass Prototheria (the monotremes) may have had an independent origin in the mammal-like reptiles, as may have had the Subclass Allotheria.

Era and Per Cent of Time	Periods and Epochs and Estimated Years Since Each Began			Events
Cenozoic 4%	Age of Man	Quaternary	Recent 20,000	Rise of modern man.
			Pleistocene 1,000,000	Primitive man; primitive mammals mostly extinct by close of epoch.
	Age of Mammals	Tertiary	Pliocene	Some decline in mammals.
			Miocene	Mammals at maximum; rise of modern carnivores.
			Oligocene	Rise of higher mammals.
			Eocene	Archaic mammals disappear: modern mammals appear.
			Paleocene 60,000,000	Rise of archaic placentals.
Mesozoic 9%	Age of Reptiles		Cretaceous 120,000,000	Small marsupial mammals and insectivores; great reptiles specialized, then disappear.
			Jurassic 155,000,000	First toothed birds.
			Triassic 190,000,000	First mammals (?)
Paleozoic 24%	Age of Amphibians Age of Fishes Age of Invertebrates 550,000,000			First marine fossils; rise of primitive vertebrates.
Proterozoic 25%	925,000,000			Soft-bodied invertebrates (?); worm casts; sponge spicules.
Archeozoic 38%	1,500,000,000			Probably unicellular plants and animals; no fossils.

Fig. 2–4. The geologic time chart.

The marsupials and the placentals (in the Subclass Theria) probably had a common origin within the Class Mammalia. Figure 2–5 illustrates the probable relationships of the major groups of mammals.

PAST DISTRIBUTION OF NORTH AMERICAN MAMMALS

Mesozoic. TRIASSIC. The oldest deposits in North America are from the close of the Triassic. Almost all known specimens are from one small pocket. Members of the four orders present included Multituberculata, Symmetrodonta, Triconodonta, and Pantotheria. The pantotheres are believed to be the ancestors of both the mar-

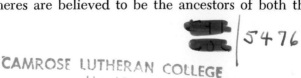

supials and the placentals. At this time the large reptilian dinosaurs were still common.

CRETACEOUS. 1. *Early.* Until recently mammalian fossils of this
age were unknown in North America. In 1949 two specimens
referable to the order Triconodonta were found.

2. *Late.* Three orders, Multituberculata, Marsupialia, and Insectivora, are known from this time. The marsupials were much like
the living opossum and are referable to the same family (Didelphidae).

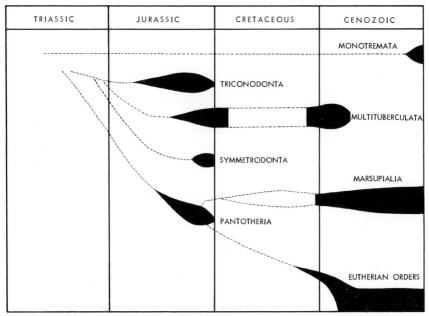

Fig. 2–5. The geologic distribution and probable relations of the major
groups of mammals.

Cenozoic. The Cenozoic is known as the "Age of Mammals."
With the close of the Mesozoic, the large dinosaurs became extinct.
The first period of the Cenozoic, Paleocene, was the first appearance
in the fossil record of most orders of mammals. Many of the common orders of this period are extinct today; others are greatly
reduced in number. With the exception of the marsupial Family
Didelphidae, no families were represented that are living today.

Mammals became more diversified in the Eocene and Oligocene.
Forty families are known from the North American Oligocene, only

eighteen of which are living today. The Miocene has been called the "Golden Age of Mammals" because of the great diversification of kinds present. The Pliocene, Pleistocene, and Recent have been times of a progressive decrease in diversity and extinction of mammals. The following is a list of the families now found in North America, north of Mexico, with an indication of their geological history in North America. Indications of earlier records elsewhere are given.

MARSUPIALIA
    Didelphidae—Late Cretaceous to Recent
INSECTIVORA
    Soricidae—Early Oligocene in Europe; mid-Oligocene to Recent in North America.
    Talpidae—Mid-Oligocene to Recent.
CHIROPTERA
    Phyllostomatidae—no fossils known
    Vespertilionidae—Lower Oligocene of Europe; Lower Pliocene to Recent in North America.
    Molossidae—Lower Oligocene of Europe; Pleistocene to Recent in N.A.
EDENTATA
    Dasypodidae—Paleocene of South America; Pleistocene to Recent in North America.
LAGOMORPHA
    Ochotonidae—Upper Oligocene, Asia; mid-Miocene to Recent, North America.
    Leporidae—Upper Eocene to Recent, North America.
RODENTIA
    Aplodontidae—Upper Eocene to Recent.
    Sciuridae—Miocene to Recent.
    Geomyidae—Mid-Oligocene to Recent.
    Heteromyidae—Mid-Oligocene to Recent.
    Castoridae—Early Oligocene to Recent.
    Cricetidae—Oligocene to Recent.
    Muridae—Pliocene, Europe and Asia; Recent in North America.
    Zapodidae—Oligocene, Europe; mid-Pliocene to Recent, North America.
    Erethizontidae—Oligocene, South America; Upper Pliocene to Recent, North America.
    Capromyidae—Miocene, South America; recent, North America.
CARNIVORA
    Canidae—Upper Eocene to Recent.
    Ursidae—Mid-Miocene, Europe; Lower Pliocene to Recent, North America.
    Procyonidae—Lower Miocene to Recent.

Mustelidae—Lower Oligocene to Recent.

Felidae—Lower Pliocene, Europe; Pliocene to Recent, North America.

ARTIODACTYLA

Tayassuidae—Lower Oligocene to Recent.

Cervidae—Lower Oligocene, Asia; Lower Miocene to Recent, North America.

Antilocapridae—Mid-Miocene to Recent.

Bovidae—Lower Miocene, Europe; Pleistocene to Recent, North America.

THE RELATIVE UNIFORMITY OF MAMMALS

As compared to several other classes of vertebrates, members of the Class Mammalia are uniform in many features. The vertebrate skeleton, for example, had become highly specialized even before mammals as such existed. One group of mammal-like reptiles (Synapsida, Order Therasida) had the following characteristics often considered to be characteristic of mammals: The dentary bone was very large, making up almost all of the lower jaw. The teeth were thecodont and probably diphyodont, and perhaps some of these reptiles were warm-blooded.

This long history of specialization has resulted in great stability in mammals. An example of this is seen in the number of cervical vertebrae. In the Class Reptilia, for example, the number of cervical vertebrae varies considerably. In one minor group, the Plesiosaurs, the number of cervical vertebrae varied from 10 to 60 or 70. All mammals, with only two or three minor exceptions, have only seven cervical vertebrae. Even the giraffe has only seven cervical vertebrae. This stability is repeated throughout the mammalian skeleton.

The chief variations of the mammalian skeleton that occurred in the Cenozoic are adaptive in nature. The teeth and limbs are the two main parts of the skeleton showing this variation. Variations in the teeth appear to be associated with diet, and variations in locomotion tend to be reflected in the distal segments of the limbs. Two other general changes occurred in mammals in the Cenozoic which do not appear to be adaptive, or, at the most, only slightly so. There was a great enlargement in the forebrain, especially in the cerebral hemispheres. The second general change in the Cenozoic was an increase in the size of the body. This did not occur in some groups, such as the rabbits, and in certain other lines of descent there was an actual decrease in size. As a general rule, however, the average size of mammals increased throughout the Cenozoic.

The geological distribution of the living orders of mammals is indicated in Fig. 2–6.

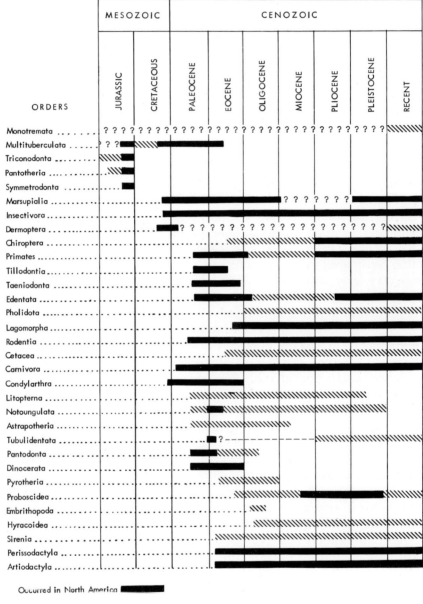

Fig. 2–6. Distribution, in time, of the order of mammals.

ECOLOGICAL DISTRIBUTION

Types of environment normally inhabited by a species of mammal make up its ecological range. The most obvious major divisions of mammalian environments are salt water, fresh water, and land. Such groups as the whales and porpoises spend their entire life in salt water. In all cases mammals are dependent upon oxygen secured from air, thus aquatic mammals must surface at rather regular intervals to secure needed air. Otherwise their life processes are carried on only in the water. A few species, such as the manatees, live in both salt water and fresh water, but most aquatic mammals are restricted by food sources to a marine habitat. There are few strictly aquatic fresh-water mammals; most are more properly termed amphibious, spending a greater or lesser part of their life on land.

The land, through the interactions of the many physical, climatic, and biological factors outlined above, has a larger number of different habitats. Some of the more obvious major types of terrestrial habitats are grasslands, desert, forests, and plains. Each of these can be subdivided into a number of recognizable units, each of which might be the unique habitat of one or more species of mammals. Several different systems of classifying these land habitats have been proposed.

THE CLASSIFICATION OF TERRESTRIAL HABITATS

Several different factors or combinations of factors have been used as bases for arranging the multitude of terrestrial habitats into meaningful groupings. Climate, plants, animals, and plants and animals have all been used to set up such classifications, as outlined below.

The various aspects of *climate* (temperature, rainfall, humidity) have been used separately, in combination, and in combination with plants and/or animals as bases for classifying various habitats. The *life zone* system of C. Hart Merriam (1894: 209–213) is based primarily on temperature. Merriam thought that certain temperatures were of critical importance to the distribution of plants and animals, especially during the season of growth and reproduction. He stated that "while it is not for a moment supposed that the subject has been disposed of in all its details, it is confidently believed that the principles controlling the geographic distribution of terrestrial animals and plants have been discovered and they may be expressed as follows: In *northward* distribution terrestrial animals are restricted by the sum of the positive temperatures for the entire season of growth and reproduction. In *southward* distribution they are restricted by the mean temperature of a brief period during the hottest part of the year." Merriam divided North America into seven "life zones." From north to south (and from mountaintop to sea level) these seven life zones are Arctic-alpine, Hudsonian, Canadian, Transition, Upper Sonoran, and Tropical. Today the life zone system is based on the actual distribution of plants and animals rather than on climatic factors. For a fuller discussion of the life zone system, see Kendeigh (1932).

Humidity was used by Grinnell and Swarth (1913: 217) as the basis of *faunal areas*. According to them: "In the restricted sense in which we believe the term best employed, a fauna is a subdivision of a Life Zone, based upon conditions of atmospheric humidity." Grinnell (1914: 63) expanded the theory and applied it to the lower Colorado River valley. He wrote: "Every animal is believed to be limited in distribution zonally by greater or lesser degree of temperature . . . Many species are kept within geographic bounds in certain directions only by an increasing or decreasing degree of atmospheric *humidity* . . . By the plotting of the ranges of many animals as well as plants, coincidence in this regard is found in so many cases as to warrant the recognition of a number of 'faunal areas,' on the causative bases of relative uniformity in humidity."

Plants. The characteristic assemblages of terrestrial plants (presumably the result of climatic factors such as temperature, humidity, and moisture) have been used as the basis of one system of classification. The divisions in this classification are termed plant formations. The major formations occurring in North America are tundra, coniferous (evergreen) forest, broad-leaved deciduous forest, grassland, sagebrush, desert, and tropical rain forest. Each of these can be divided into subdivisions of lesser geographic extent (Weaver and Clements, 1938).

Animals. Just as the characteristic assemblage of plants has been used as the basis of ecologic classifications of land habitats, the presence or absence of a given kind of animal in an area has also been used as the basis of setting up *faunal areas*. A faunal area, then, is characterized by a particular assemblage of animal species. The causative factors of this assemblage are usually assumed to be the interaction of edaphic, topographic, climatic, and biotic factors. A special type of faunal area, termed *distributional areas,* has likewise been set up, based upon particular assemblages of animal species of one taxonomic group such as the Class Mammalia (see Cockrum, 1952; Durrant, 1952).

Plants and Animals. The characteristic association of certain plants or plant types with certain animals has also been used as a basis of at least three modern systems of classification.

LIFE ZONE. The original concepts of Merriam are discussed above. Today the life zone system is based on the actual distribution of plants and animals, with certain species of plants and animals used as life zone indicators. Whereas the life zone system is readily applicable in the western United States, it is not as readily applicable, if at all, in the eastern United States and in North America in general. For this reason it is not in widespread use today among biologists (see Merriam, 1890, 1899a, 1899b; Bailey, 1913; Hall and Grinnell, 1919; Daubenmire, 1938).

BIOME. A biome is a major biotic (= plant-animal) community. While supposedly based on both plants and animals, the biomes have been mapped on the basis of vegetation alone, but important animals in the biomes of North America have been proposed (see Shelford, 1932; Clements and Shelford, 1939; Kendeigh, 1932; Pitelka, 1941). Biomes on a worldwide basis are termed "biome-type" (see Allee *et al.*, 1949).

1. *Biotic communities.* These correspond to biomes (by definition) or subdivisions of biomes (see Pitelka, 1941; Hesse, Allee, and Schmidt, 1951).
2. *Biotic areas.* These are subdivisions of biotic communities, assemblages of plants and animals of a given area which are recognizably distinct from assemblages in adjoining areas as a result of the interaction of climatic, geographic, edaphic, and biotic factors (Clark, 1937; Davis, 1939).

BIOTIC PROVINCES. This system is set up for North America supposedly on the basis of the distribution of plants, animals, and physical factors of the environment. Dice, who first proposed this system wrote (1943: 3): "Each *biotic province* . . . covers a considerable and continuous geographic area and is characterized by the occurrence of one or more important ecologic associations that differ, at least in proportional area covered, from the associations of adjacent provinces. In general, biotic provinces are characterized also by peculiarities of vegetation type, ecological climax, flora, fauna, climate, physiography, and soil." A biotic district according to Dice (*op. cit.*) is: "a subdivision covering a definite and continuous part of the geographic area of a biotic province. Biotic districts are distinguished by ecologic differences of less importance than those that separate biotic provinces."

3

Reproduction and Development

INTRODUCTION

Reproduction is the mechanism by which a species is maintained from generation to generation. In mammals the process of reproduction is sexual. All mammals are dioecious; that is, the sexes are separate, and normally a given individual has the sex organs and secondary sexual characteristics of only one sex. A few cases of abnormalities of both primary and secondary sexual characteristics have been noted. These abnormalities usually fall into one of the following categories: true hermaphroditism, gynandromorphism, and false hermaphroditism.

True *hermaphroditism* (from Hermaphroditus, the son of Hermes and Aphrodite of Greek mythology) exists when both ovaries and testes occur in the same individual. Such cases are extremely rare. According to Arey (1952), only 42 cases of true hermaphroditism have been authenticated in humans. A single case of true hermaphroditism has been reported in each of three rodents, the house mouse (*Mus musculus*), the meadow mouse (*Microtus pennsylvanicus*), and the guinea pig (*Cavia porcellus*) (see Asdell, 1946).

Gynandromorphism exists when a female gonad and duct exists on one side and a male gonad and duct on the other side of the same individual. The external genitalia show characteristics intermediate between male and female and the secondary sexual characteristics are usually mixed. Twenty cases of this nature have been reported in the cow (*Bos taurus*) and the pig (*Sus scrofa*).

False hermaphroditism exists when the gonads are of one sex, either male or female, and the secondary sexual characteristics and external genitalia are intermediate or approximate those of the opposite sex. According to Asdell (1946), many cases of pseudohermaphroditism are actually the result of sex reversal.

Considering only the normal aspects of sexual reproduction in mammals, reproduction can be conveniently divided into five phases or parts: gamete formation, fertilization, implantation, gestation, and parturition. For detailed information on mammalian reproduction, see Nelsen (1953), Arey (1952), and Asdell (1946).

GAMETE FORMATION

The reproductive cells, or gametes, of mammals are the ova or eggs and the spermatozoa. These are produced in separate animals, the ova by the ovaries in the female and the sperm by the testes in the male. Associated with the ovary and the testes are a number of accessory reproductive organs. The male reproductive organs are illustrated in Fig. 3–1. Spermatozoa are produced in the testes. From a testis they pass into a network of small convoluted tubules, the epididymis, and thence through a *vas deferens* (plural, vasa deferentia) to the *urethra,* where they are joined by spermatozoa from the other vas deferens. Near here secretions from the *vesicular glands* (also known as seminal vesicles) and from the *prostate gland* are added to the spermatozoa. The spermatozoa and the glandular secretions then pass through the urethra to the base of the penis, where secretions from the *bulbourethral gland* (Cowper's gland) are added. The resultant mixture of spermatozoa and glandular secretions is called *semen.* The semen then passes out of the male body through the *penis* or copulatory organ.

The amount and composition of semen produced at any one time varies within the individual and within the species of mammal. In man two to five per cent of the semen originates in the testes; 15 to 30 percent in the prostate; and 40 to 80 percent in the vesicular glands. Some examples of the volume of semen produced are: Fox, 0.2 to 4.0 ml.; man, 2 to 6 ml.; dog, 2 to 4 ml.; bull, 2 to 10 ml.; stallion, 30 to 300 ml.; and boar, 150 to 500 ml. The volume reduces with age in most mammals.

The position of the testes in the various species of mammals is varied. Most kinds have a *scrotum* or saclike structure as an external attachment of the body. During the breeding season, at least, the testes are descended into this integumental sac. In some, such as the Artiodactyla, and most Perissodactyla and Primates, the testes are scrotal, i.e., descended into the scrotum, throughout adult life. In most rodents the testes are in the body cavity (abdominal) except during the breeding season, when they are scrotal. Most insectivores and bats and whales do not have a scrotum. In these mammals, the testes distend the abdominal wall during the breeding season, thus coming to lie near the surface of the body. Some mammals, such as the marine forms (whales and seals), elephants, and the rhinoceros, do not have scrota but retain the testes in the body cavity at all times. *Crytorchism* exists when testes normally scrotal

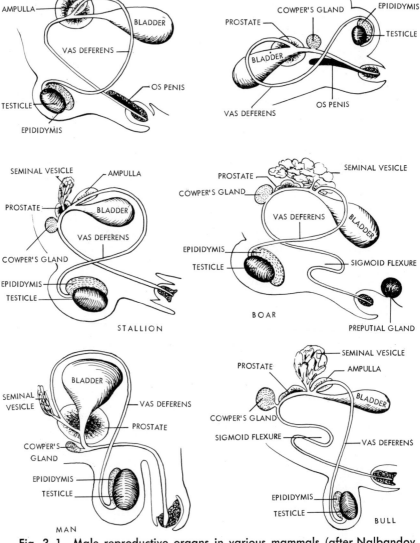

Fig. 3–1. Male reproductive organs in various mammals (after Nalbandov, 1958).

in position fail to descend from the body cavity into the scrotum. In man, at least, the higher temperatures in the body cavity affect the developing spermatozoa and usually cause sterility.

A bone, called the *os penis*, or baculum, is found in the penis of several kinds of mammals. It occurs in many bats, most rodents, and most carnivores. The degree of development of this bone is extremely varied; yet, for any one species, it appears to be fairly constant. The *os penis* has been used as an aid in the identification of closely related species (White, 1953) and as an aid in determining the approximate age of an individual animal. Elder (1951) and Lechleitner (1954) applied this technique to mink; Wright (1950) applied it to the long-tailed weasels.

The female reproductive organs are illustrated in Fig. 3–2. Typically, they consist of a pair of *ovaries* (which produce the ova), a

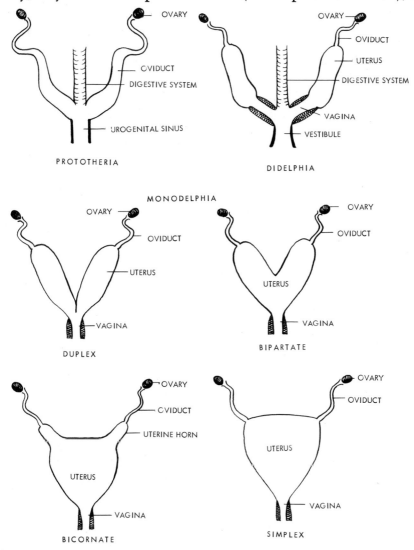

Fig. 3–2. Female reproductive organs in various mammals.

pair of *oviducts* (Fallopian tubes), which conduct the ova from the ovary to the enlarged *uteri* (paired) where, in most mammals, embryonic development occurs, and a single *vagina* opening to the outside of the body. The terminal portions of the female reproductive tract show various degrees of separation from the digestive system and the uteri vary in the degree to which they are fused into one structure. The following classification and Fig. 3–2 illustrate these variations.

Prototheria. In this arrangement the oviducts and the uteri are separate and enter a urogenital sinus (which serves both in the reproductive system and in the urinary sytem) which, in turn, empties into the cloaca (which also serves in the elimination of wastes from the digestive system). In animals of this type, the ova are not retained in the uterus; rather, they are laid and then hatched externally. This arrangement is found in most reptiles and, among mammals, in the monotremes.

Didelphia. This arrangement, found in the marsupials, shows advancement over the Prototheria type in that the digestive system opening is completely separate from the urogenital opening. The urinary and reproductive systems retain a common external opening called the vestibule. The vagina, uterus, and oviduct are all paired.

Monodelphia. This arrangement, found in all eutherian mammals, has only a single vagina opening to the outside. This opening is usually more separated from the urinary opening than is the case in the Didelphia. Four subgroups, based upon the relationships between the uteri, are usually recognized.

1. *Duplex.* In this arrangement, the uteri are completely separate, each with a separate cervix or opening from the vagina, but are joined to a single vagina. This arrangement occurs in rodents and rabbits.
2. *Bipartite.* In this arrangement there is but a single cervix, and the lower portions of the two uteri are fused; but in the major part of their length the uteri are still separate. Implantation of embryos usually occurs in the unfused portions of the uteri. This type occurs in most carnivores and in some ruminants.
3. *Bicornuate.* In this arrangement, the lower two-thirds of the two uteri are fused into a single structure while the upper third of each uterus remains separate. Implantation of embryos usually occurs in the lower portion. This condition exists in many ungulates.
4. *Simplex.* The uteri are fused into a single structure so that, functionally, there is but a single uterus. This arrangement occurs in the higher primates, including man.

Mossman (1953) has discussed the uses of the morphology of the genital system and of the fetal membranes as criteria for taxonomy and phylogeny. He points out that these systems are practically isolated from any direct selective effects of the external environment and thus are not subject to convergence as a result of similar habitats.

SEXUAL PERIODICITY AND REPRODUCTIVE SEASONS

As has been admirably presented by A. V. Nalbandov (1958), the reproductive cycle of mammals, in its broadest sense, including the maturation and functioning of the gonads, the associated sexual organs, and the secondary sexual characteristics, is controlled by the interaction of a series of hormones. Each of these hormones is specific in its activities, starting (or stopping) specific functional activities of specific organs. Optimal reproductive performance does not occur, however, unless the whole endocrine system is in the necessary proper balance. Thus, while not mentioned herein, the adrenal and other ductless glands do have an important effect on reproductive activities.

The anterior lobe of the pituitary produces the gonadotropic hormone complex which maintains primary control over the reproductive organs and processes. This hormone complex is divisible into at least two distinct hormones, a follicle-stimulating hormone (abbreviated FSH) and a lutenizing hormone (abbreviated LH). These hormones were named from experiments done on female rats, but later experiments demonstrated that identical hormones were produced in male animals. This discovery led to renaming the LH in males as the "interstitial-cell" stimulating hormone or ISCH. The use of this second name, however, is not universal. Most endocrinologists tend to use LH, whether the hormone is produced in male or female animals.

Most kinds of mammals have breeding seasons restricted to a definite time of year. This breeding season is usually at a time most advantageous for the pregnant female and the newborn young. Even in those kinds of mammals that breed at all times of the year, there is usually some period of lesser activity associated with periods of environmental stress. From the limited information available, it appears that tropical species have longer breeding seasons than do species living in temperate regions.

Mammals having definite breeding seasons may have one or two seasons each year separated by periods of complete sexual inactivity during which the gonads of the females, and in some cases, of the males, undergo involution, reducing size and ceasing gamete formation. In males with normally scrotal testes, the testes are retracted into the body cavity. Most of the accessory and secondary sex structures also undergo involution during this period of sexual inactivity.

Light appears to have an important bearing on the establishment of breeding seasons in many mammals. The short-tailed vole, *Microtus agrestis*, of Europe breeds during those months that normally have more than 100 hours of sunlight but not during months with less sunlight. Thus, in England, the breeding season is from February or early March to September (Matthews, 1952). A number of species, such as ferrets or goats, become reproductively active if, during their reproductively inactive season, they are placed in a situation with an artificially increased length of day. Such mammals have been termed "long-day" breeders. Other species, such as the domestic sheep, apparently react to a decrease in the length of day and are termed "short-day" breeders.

The presence or absence of the proper amounts of gonadotropic hormones, FSH and LH, determines whether or not the individual is reproductively active. For many species it is thought that an increase in the amount of light in the spring influences the hypothalamus, either directly through the eye or indirectly through the orbital tissues and the eye stalk. The hypothalamus in turn causes the anterior lobe of the pituitary to secrete increased amounts of gonadotropic hormones and initiates the breeding cycle. The amounts of gonadotropic hormones necessary to stimulate gamete formation are apparently specific characteristics (with the usual individual variations present) and either too low or too high a level will cause a cessation of gamete production. The sheep, a "short-day" breeder, normally has a much higher concentration of gonadotropic hormones present in the blood stream during the summer (or non-breeding) period than it does in the fall, during the breeding season.

Light alone, however, does not explain seasonal breeding. As Nalbandov (1958) points out: "Light, temperature, adequacy of food supply, neural stimuli (such as the presence of males or other animals), time of feeding, and probably a host of other factors, singly or, more probably in combination, are responsible for the reproductive rhythm of birds and mammals."

Further, it is not unusual to find geographic variations in the sexual periodicity of a single species. In England, for example, the European field vole, *Microtus agrestis*, breeds from February to October but in southern France it breeds the year around (Bourlière, 1954). In North America, several small rodents, including the

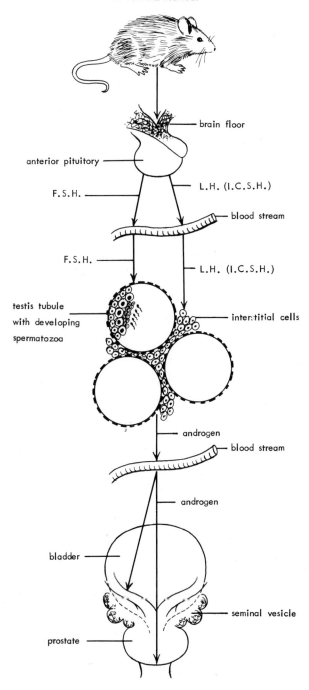

EXTERNAL STIMULI

brain floor

anterior pituitary

F.S.H.

L.H. (I.C.S.H.)

blood stream

F.S.H.

L.H. (I.C.S.H.)

testis tubule
with developing
spermatozoa

interstitial cells

androgen

blood stream

androgen

bladder

seminal vesicle

prostate

Fig. 3–3. The sequence of events in the hormonal control of spermatogenesis in a seasonally reproductively active male mammal.

wood mouse (*Peromyscus leucopus*), the deer mouse (*Peromyscus maniculatus*), and the cotton rat (*Sigmodon hispidus*), have a restricted breeding season in the northern part of their range and breed practically the year around in the southern part of their range.

In male animals, spermatogenesis is initiated by action of the follicle stimulating hormone, FSH. Completion of spermatogenesis, however, does not occur without the action of the lutenizing hormone, LH. LH acts on the interstitial cells, causing the production of a hormone, androgen (sometimes called testosterone). It is unclear as to which of three possibilities complete spermatogenesis: (1) LH acts directly on the seminiferous tubules of the testes to complete spermatogenesis; (2) androgen acts to complete spermatogenesis; or (3) both LH and androgen are necessary to complete spermatogenesis. In any case, androgen does develop and control the activity of the male accessory sex organs and the secondary sexual characteristics. Figure 3–3 illustrates these relationships.

In most female mammals there is a recurrent *estrus*, or "heat," cycle, caused by the interaction of two ovarian hormones and resulting in cellular changes in the uterus and vagina as well as in behavioral differences. Under the influence of the gonadotropic hormone FSH, ova begin development in the ovary. These developing ova and associated cells, known as follicles, produce a hormone,

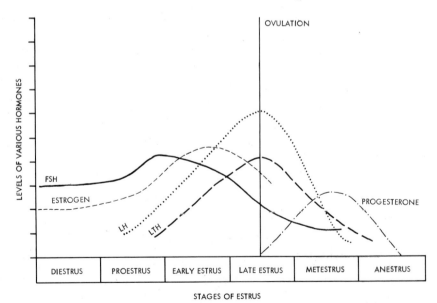

Fig. 3–4. The relative level of concentration in the bloodstream of the various hormones during the course of the estrus cycle in the female.

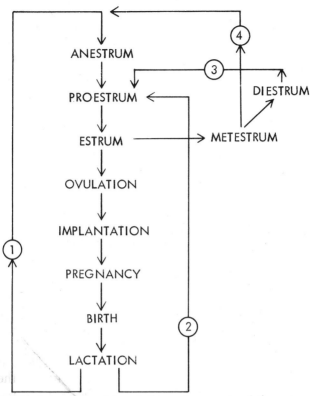

Fig. 3–5. The interrelationships of the various parts of the estrus cycle. A monestrus female producing young would follow cycle 1; a non-gravid monestrus female, cycle 4. A polyestrus female producing young would follow cycle 2; a nongravid polyestrus female would follow cycle 3.

estrogen. Continued growth of the follicle produces higher levels of estrogen, which causes a decrease in the production of FSH and an increase of LH.

The estrus cycle, then, consists of the successive interactions of two groups of ovarian hormones, estrogen and progesterone (Fig. 3–4). These cause gross morphological changes in the female reproductive tract. These changes have led to the recognition of several pronounced stages in the estrus cycle (Heape, 1930). The relative length and intensity of the various phases of the cycle are dependent upon (1) species threshold, (2) amounts of hormone circulating in the blood, and (3), in some species, reaction of the central nervous system to the hormones. The cycle length and duration of their parts are not constant but may be expressed in averages for each species. The stages in the estrus cycle usually recognized are as follows (see Fig. 3–5).

Anestrus. During this stage the female reproductive organs are quiescent; this is the non-breeding season. The uterus is normal and somewhat anaemic and the female shows no disposition to mate. In many mammals this period covers the greater part of the year.

Proestrus. During this period the uterus becomes swollen, the vagina enlarges and becomes turgid, and the animal "comes into heat." In the ovary the follicles are growing rapidly. A small flow of blood from the vagina often occurs at the close of this period.

Estrus. During this period the female is receptive to the male and fruitful coition is possible. The ova are usually discharged from the ovary late in this period. If conception takes place at this time, pregnancy normally occurs. Lactation follows gestation, and at the end of the breeding period anestrum recurs. Lactation, according to some authors, prevents the start of another estrus cycle; yet, in certain mammals, parturition is followed immediately by another estrus cycle. The cricetid rodent *Microtus*, for example, may have fruitful coition within one hour after parturition.

Metestrus. This period follows estrus if fruitful mating has not occurred. The female reproductive tract resumes the normal condition and anestrus results.

These are the phases that normally occur in a *monestrus* mammal; that is, a mammal with only one breeding season each year. However, in some mammals, especially rodents of the families Cricetidae and Muridae, and certain of the cervids, metestrus is followed by only a short period of quiescence before proestrus resumes. Such mammals are termed *polyestrus* and the short quiescent period is called the *diestrus.*

COPULATION

After various types of preliminary courtships such as are discussed in the chapter on behavior, copulation occurs. The length of time in *coitus,* that is the length of time the sexes are together, varies with the kind of mammal. The usual position of copulation is dorsoventral with the male astride the female. Ventral copulation, in which the sexes unite belly to belly, has been observed in the hamster and in the two-toed sloth. According to Asdell (1946), Slijper has studied the structure of the penis in its relation to the duration of coitus and developed the following classification of morphological types of peni.

1. *Indifferent type.* This type occurs in the Rodentia, Lagomorpha, and Edentata. In these groups coitus is described as being mod-

erately long in duration. In some, such as the golden hamster, copulation is brief but repeated many times (65 to 75). In Shaw's jird (*Meriones shawi*), copulation has been repeated as many as 224 times in two hours. In the American Porcupine (*Erethizon dorsatum*) the number of copulations is small but each act consumes one to five minutes.

2. *Fibroelastic type.* This type occurs in the Solenodontia, Cetacea, Cervidae, Antilocapridae, and Bovidae. In these groups coitus is very brief. In the domestic bull and ram it consumes but a few seconds (Dukes, 1955).

3. *Vascular type.* This type occurs in several insectivores, Chiroptera, Primates, Carnivora, Pinnipedia, and Perissodactyla. In this group coitus is moderate to very long in duration. In the dog, for example, coitus may take 15 to 30 minutes (Dukes, 1955). In the short-tailed shrew (*Blarina brevicauda*) the male mounts the female from behind, holding her with his front legs.

4. *Intermediate type.* This type of penis occurs in the Sirenia, Proboscidea, Suidae, Tayassuidae, and Hippopotamidae. In these mammals coitus is intermediate in length. In the domestic boar, for example, coitus usually consumes several minutes (Dukes, 1955).

IMPLANTATION

Usually fertilization occurs shortly after ovulation. This is followed by cleavage of the zygote or fertilized ovum, as it passes into the uterus. At the blastocyst stage of development, some of the cells are concerned with the development of the embryo while others form a series of three membranes around the embryo; an amnion forms and fills with fluid, thus bringing the embryonic blood vessels of the allantois into close contact with the surface of the uterus. This is the process of implantation. Processes of the chorion, called villi, become imbedded in depressions in the surface of the uterus. The composite structure of the maternal and embryonic tissues is called the placenta.

The degree of intimacy between the maternal and embryonic parts of the placenta, as well as the form of the placenta, varies in the different mammals. The relationships between the maternal and embryonic parts of the placenta have been classified as follows (see Nelsen, 1953):

1. *Epitheliochorial type.* In this type of implantation, the embryonic tissue merely forms an intimate contact with the epithelian cells of the uterine wall. This relationship is found in the pig.

2. *Endotheliochorial type.* In this type of implantation, the embryonic tissue erodes the epithelium of the uterine wall, resulting in contact

of the embryonic epithelium with the endothelium of the maternal blood vessels. This relationship is found in most carnivores.

3. *Endotheliochorial plus syndesmochorial type.* In this type of implantation, the attachment between the embryonic and maternal tissues occurs in certain areas known as cotyledons. In parts of these cotyledons, the association of the embryonic and maternal tissues is of the endotheliochorial type (see above) but in other areas, only the epithelium of the uterus is eroded, leaving the embryonic epidermis in contact with the connective tissues of the uterine wall, a condition known as syndesmochorial. This relationship is found in the bovids (cows, sheep, and goats).

4. *Hemochorial type.* In this type of implantation, the epithelium, the connective tissues, and the endothelium of the blood vessels in the wall of the uterus are eroded by the embryonic tissues, permitting the chorionic epidermis to be in direct contact with the maternal blood supply. This relationship is found in insectivores, bats, primates, and rodents.

5. *Hemoendothelial type.* In this type of implantation, the early stages of embryonic attachment are of the epitheliochorial type. As pregnancy progresses, there is an erosion of maternal tissues resulting in associations of the hemochorial type. Finally, in advanced pregnancy, even the embryonic epithelium disappears, leaving the endothelium of the embryonic blood vessels in contact with the maternal blood. This relationship is found in the lagomorphs (rabbits).

The placentas of mammals are of two general types, deciduate and non-deciduate. The term deciduate was given to indicate the loss, at birth, of the lining of the uterus. Although the loss is insignificant in some of the so-called deciduous types, the terminology has been retained. The form of the placenta as well as the degree of intimacy between the maternal and embryonic membranes is associated with the deciduous nature of the placenta. Following is a classification of placental types:

Non-deciduate. In this group the allantois enlarges and occupies the length of the trophoblast. In the simplest condition the villi fit into depressions in the uterine wall and at birth are drawn out without damage to uterine wall. The villi may be more complex and branched. There are four subdivisions of this group: (1) The *diffuse* type in which the villi are scattered over the surface of the trophoblast and the villi are either simple or branched; (2) the *cotyledonary* type in which the villi are grouped together as cotyledons and there are several cotyledons scattered over the trophoblast; (3) the *intermediate* type in which both cotyledons and simple villi are present; and (4) the *zonary* type in which the villi are branched and are arranged in cotyledons. The cotyledons are arranged in a band or zone around the trophoblast.

Deciduate. In this group the uterine epithelium is always destroyed by the trophoblast. The fetal and maternal blood are in close relation. There are two subdivisions of this group, the first of which is the *zonary* type, in which the villi of the placenta are arranged in a band around the embryo. When birth occurs, some blood vessels and connective tissues of the uterine wall are shed with the placenta. This type is found only in carnivores. The second type is the *discoidal* type, in which the relationship between maternal and embryonic circulatory systems is even closer. The spaces in which the maternal blood circulates are not maternal capillaries but are broad lucunar spaces formed by the walls of trophoblast. The shape of this attachment is usually discoidal but it may be oval, bell-shaped, saucer-shaped, or concave.

Normally, implantation occurs shortly after fertilization, but in some kinds of mammals it does not occur for several weeks or months later. Such a condition is termed *delayed implantation* and occurs in such mammals as the marten, fisher, badger, weasel, armadillo, and possibly the black bear. In delayed implantation, cleavage of the fertilized ovum or zygote is normal until the blastocyst stage is reached. At that time cleavage and growth cease and the resumption of development and implantation may not occur for weeks or months.

GESTATION

Gestation is the period of time that the developing embryo is carried in the body of the mother. Much variation exists in the length of the gestation period. In fact, the major subdivisions of the Class Mammalia illustrate this diversity. In the Subclass Prototheria, gestation in the usual sense does not occur in that members of this subclass are oviparous; that is, they lay eggs which hatch outside the body.

Members of the Subclass Theria, however, are viviparous; that is, they retain the embryo within the body, and thus have a gestation period. Two infraclasses of this subclass have living representatives and these two show marked differences in length of gestation. In the Infraclass Metatheria (the marsupials), the period of gestation is very short and the young are born in an extremely undeveloped condition. The young opossum (*Didelphis* of eastern North America), for example, spends only twelve and one-half days in the uterus. At birth it is so small that eighteen of them may rest in a teaspoon. At birth young opossums have the forelegs and feet well

TABLE 3–1

The Types of Uteri and Placentation Found in the Various Orders of Mammals

Order	Uterus	Placentation	Os Penis
Monotremata	Prototherous	None; oviparous	(?)
Marsupialia	Didelphous	None in all but a few genera	Absent
Insectivora	Duplex(?)	Discoidal deciduate usually concave hemochorial	Absent
Dermoptera	Duplex	Discoidal deciduate	(?)
Chiroptera	Duplex	Discoidal deciduate, saucer- or bell-shaped. Hemochorial	Present in some
Primates			Absent in most
Prosimii	Bicornuate	Non-deciduate, diffuse	
Anthropoidea	Simplex	Deciduate, discoidal hemochorial	
Edentata	Duplex	Deciduate, discoidal often dome-shaped	(?)
Pholidota	Bicornuate	(?)	(?)
Lagomorpha	Duplex	Deciduate, discoidal hemoendothelial	Absent
Rodentia	Duplex or bicornuate	Deciduate, discoidal hemochorial	Present in most
Cetacea	Bicornuate	Non-deciduate, diffused branched villi	(?)
Carnivora	Duplex or bicornuate	Deciduate, zonal endotheliochorial	Present
Tubulidentata	(?)	(?)	(?)
Proboscidea	Bicornuate	Non-deciduate(?) zonary	(?)
Hyracoidea		Non-deciduate(?) zonary	(?)
Sirenia	Bicornuate	Non-deciduate(?) zonary	(?)
Perissodactyla	Bicornuate	Non-deciduate, diffuse	(?)
Artiodactyla	Bicornuate	Non-deciduate	Absent
Suidae		Diffuse, unbranched villi	
Tayassuidae		Epitheliochorial	
Hippopotamidae		Intermediate	
Camelidae		Intermediate	
Tragulidae		(?)	
Cervidae		Intermediate	
Giraffidae		Intermediate	
Antilocapridae		(?)	
Bovidae		Cotyledons numerous, endotheliochorial plus syndesmochorial	

developed (the forefeet have sharp, hooked claws), while the hind limbs are mere buds. There is enough neuromuscular coordination and sensory response to enable the young to climb from the vaginal opening to the marsupial pouch. In the marsupial pouch the young attaches to a nipple and continues development for almost two additional months.

In the second subdivision of the Subclass Theria, that is, in Infra-class Eutheria, the period of gestation is influenced by three main factors: (1) size of the mother, (2) condition of the young at birth, and (3) number of young per litter. Many of the small mice have a gestation period of only 17 days, while none of the smaller kinds have a gestation period much longer than three weeks. Table 3–2

TABLE 3–2

The Relation Between the Size of the Female and the Length of Gestation in Eutherian Mammals

Species of Mammal	Length of Gestation in Days
Hamster (*Cricetus auratus*)	16.5
Cottontail rabbit (*Sylvilagus floridanus*)	30
Domestic rabbit (*Oryctolagus cuniculus*)	30–32
House cat (*Felis domesticus*)	63
Lion (*Felis leo*)	108
Spotted hyaena (*Crocuta crocuta*)	110
Swine (*Sus scrofa*)	112–115
Sheep (*Ovis aries*)	150
Goat (*Capra hircus*)	146–151
Elk (*Cervus canadensis*)	255
Moose (*Alces alces*)	240–250
Cow (*Bos taurus*)	280
Marten (*Martes caurina*)*	261–276
Fisher (*Martes pennanti*)*	338–358
Horse (*Equus caballus*)	328–345
Many whales	365
Black rhinoceros (*Rhinoceros bicornis*)	530–550
Indian elephant (*Elephas maximus*)	607–641

* Note how the marten (261–276 days) and the fisher (338–358 days) are out of place, relative to their size. This is the result of delayed implantation.

clearly shows the relationship of size and length of gestation period. The effect of delayed implantation is clearly evident in the case of the marten and the fisher.

Based upon the relative advancement of development at birth, young mammals are divisible into two groups, altricial and preco-cial. *Altricial* young are born naked, blind, and helpless, as in rab-bits, most rodents, and most carnivores. *Precocial* young are born fully haired, the eyes are open, and the young are able to move at once, as in hares, jackrabbits, deer, and domestic livestock. As a general rule, mammals with precocial young tend to have a longer gestation period than those with altricial young.

The number of young in each litter tends to influence the length of gestation. The gestation period tends to be slightly shorter in those species with only one or two young at a birth than in those of similar size that produce large litters. The correlation is not so great, however, as in the size relationship pointed out above.

REPRODUCTIVE CAPACITY

As can be seen by an inspection of Table 3–3, the reproductive capacity of mammals varies greatly. On the one extreme, the elephant, after a maturation period ranging from 8 to 16 years and after a gestation period of 624 days, has a single young. This is in contrast to some of the smaller mammals that have high reproductive potentials. The house mouse (*Mus musculus*), after a maturation period of 35 days followed by a gestation period of 19 days, has a litter of young ranging to twelve in number. A single female may have as many as six litters in one year. Other rodents, such as the Norway rat (*Rattus norvegicus*), are known to have as many as twenty young in one litter.

Large litters are not necessarily restricted to rodents. The Virginia opossum (*Didelphis marsupialis*) has up to twelve young at a time; the domestic dog, up to twenty-two; and the domestic pig, fifteen or more. Conversely, not all small litters are restricted to large mammals. Many small bats have only one young per litter and one litter per year. Some rodents, such as the spring haas (*Pedetes caffer*), normally have only one young per litter (occasionally two) and only one litter per year.

PARTURITION

Parturition, or birth, occurs when the foetus has completed its growth in the uterus. Most female mammals retreat to some den or nest previously prepared for the birth of the young. Such is the case in most kinds of mammals with altricial young. Often those with precocial young merely retreat to some hiding place for the process. In any case, after the maternal vagina dilates, slow rhythmic contractions of the uterus gradually force the foetus through the vagina to the outside. Either this process ruptures the foetal membranes or else the mother tears the membranes from the young, thus permitting the young animal to breathe. The umbilical cord is soon severed by the mother and generally the placental membranes are eaten by the female.

The most common position of the female during parturition is lying down, but some give birth while standing up. In the whale and in the hippopotamus, birth occurs in the water. In these cases the young surfaces within a few seconds after birth to breathe.

TABLE 3-3

Summary of Reproductive Data for Selected Types of Mammals

	Age at Puberty	Breeding Season	Sexual Cycle Type[1]	Sexual Cycle Duration, Days	Gestation Period, Days	Litter Size	Litter No./Yr.	Mating Habits[2]	Maximum Life Span, Years
Order Monotremata									
Family Ornithorhynchidae									
Platypus (Ornithorhynchus paradoxus)	1–2 yr.	July–Oct.	Me	60		1.9 (1–3)			10
Family Tachyglossidae									
Spiny echidna (Tachyglossus aculeata)		June–Sept.	Me			1			50(?)
Order Marsupialia									
Family Didelphidae									
Virginia opossum (Didelphis marsupialis)	8 mo.	Jan.–Oct.	Pe	28	12.5	10 (8–12)	2		7
Family Dasyuridae									
Marsupial cat (Dasyurus viverrinus)		June–Aug.	Me		8–14	6	1		
Family Phalangeridae									
Common phalanger (Trichosurus vulpecula) ..	1 yr.	Mar. & Apr.	Pe		16	1	2		
Family Macropodicae									
Rat-kangaroo (Bettongia cuniculus)		Mar.–Dec.	Pe		42	1			
Kangaroo (Macropus rufus)		Once a yr.	Me		30–40	1	1		16.3
Order Insectivora									
Family Erinaceidae									
Hedgehog (Erinaceus europaeus)	2 yr.	Mar.–Sept.	Me		34–49	5 (3–7)	1		4
Long-eared hedgehog (Hemiechinus auritus) .		July–Sept.				3(1–4)			

TABLE 3–3 (Continued)

Summary of Reproductive Data for Selected Types of Mammals

	Age at Puberty	Sexual Cycle			Gestation Period, Days	Litter		Mating Habits[2]	Maximum Life Span, Years
		Breeding Season	Type[1]	Duration, Days		Size	No./Yr.		
Family Macroscelidae									
Elephant shrew (*Elephantulus myurus*)		Sept.–May	Pe			1–2			3.4
Family Soricidae									
Short-tailed shrew (*Blarina brevicauda*)	50–80 days	Feb.–Sept.	Pe		17–20	4.5 (3–8)	2		2.5
European common shrew (*Sorex araneus*)	2 yr.	May–Sept.	Me		13–19	5 (3–7)	1		
Family Talpidae									
European mole (*Talpa europaea*)	2 yr.	Mar.–May	Me		28–42	3.7 (1–7)	1(2)(?)		
Eastern mole (*Scalopus aquaticus*)		Mar. & June			42	2–5			
Order Dermoptera									
Family Cynocephalidae									
Flying lemur (*Cynocephalus volans*)					60	1	1		
Order Chiroptera									
Family Pteropidae									
Flying fox (*Pteropus giganteus*)		Jan.–Apr.				1	1		19
Family Desmodontidae									
Vampire bat (*Desmodus rotundus*).........		All yr.	Pe	5+ mo.		1	1+	Po	12
Family Vespertilionidae									
Big brown bat (*Eptesicus fuscus*)		Fall	Me	150	35	2 (1–4)	1	Pr	15

	No. young	Gestation (days)	Estrous cycle (days)		Breeding season	Sexual maturity	Longevity (yr)
Order Primates							
Family Lemuridae							
Lemur (*Lemur fulvus*)..							
Lemur (*Lemur macaco*)..	1-2	146			Births in spring		25.5
Family Daubentoniidae							
Aye-aye (*Daubentonia madagascarensis*)	1						7.5
Family Lorisidae							
Slow loris (*Nycticebus coucang*)		90					10
Family Galagidae							
Grand galago (*Galago crassicaudatus*)	1-2	120			Sept.	20 mo.	13
Family Tarsiidae							
Spectral tarsier (*Tarsius spectrum*)	1		23.5	Pe	All yr.		
Family Callithricidae							
Marmoset (*Callithrix jacchus*)	2 (1-3)	146 (140-150)				Female, 14 mo.	16
Family Cercopithecidae							
Grivet monkey (*Cercopithecus aethiops*)	1-2	210	31	Pe	All yr.		24
Barbary ape (*Macaca sylvanus*)	1	210	27-33	Pe	All yr.		18+
Chacma baboon (*Chaeropithecus porcarius*)	1-2	210	29-42	Pe	All yr.	4 yr.	17+
Rhesus monkey (*Macaca mulatta*)	1	164 (155-180)	28	Pe	All yr.	3 yr.	29
Sacred baboon (*Chaeropithecus hamadryas*) ..	1 (2)	183	31-36	Pe	All yr.		24
Family Pongidae							
Chimpanzee (*Pan satyrus*)	1	237 (216-261)	34-35	Pe	All yr.	8-9 yr.	40
Orangutan (*Pongo pygmus*)		240-270	29	Pe			26.5

TABLE 3-3 (Continued)

Summary of Reproductive Data for Selected Types of Mammals

	Age at Puberty	Breeding Season	Sexual Cycle		Gestation Period, Days	Litter		Mating Habits[2]	Maximum Life Span, Years
			Type[1]	Duration, Days		Size	No./Yr.		
Lar gibbon (Hylobates lar)	8–10 yr.	All yr.	Pe	29–30	210	1			23
Family Hominidae Man (Homo sapiens) ...	12–15 yr.	All yr.	Pe	27–28	267	1			
Order Edentata Family Myrmecophagidae Giant anteater (Myrmecophaga tridactyla) ...					190	1			
Family Bradypodidae Two-toed sloth (Choloepus didactylus) ...					263	1	1		11
Three-toed sloth (Bradypus cuculliger)		Mar.–Apr.			120–180	1	1		
Family Dasypodidae Armadillo (Dasypus novemcinctus)	1 yr.	Born Jan.–Mar.	Me		150–240	4	1		
Order Pholidota Family Manidae Indian pangolin (Manis pentadactyla)		Born Jan.–Mar.				1–2			
Order Lagomorpha Family Ochotonidae Pika (Ochotona princeps)		May–July			30	2 (2–5)	2		

86

Family Leporidae								
Snowshoe hare (*Lepus americanus*)	1 yr.	Mar.–Aug.	Pe	30 (30–38)	3 (1–7)	1	Pr	8
European rabbit (*Oryctolagus cuniculus*)	5–8 mo.	All yr.	Pe	31 (30–35)	8 (1–13)			13
Eastern cottontail (*Sylvilagus floridanus*)	40 wk.	Jan.–Aug.	Pe	26.5–30	4.5 (2–7)	2–3		10
Order Rodentia								
Family Sciuridae								
Fox squirrel (*Sciurus niger*)	11 mo.	Dec.–Aug.		45	3 (1–6)	2		7.5
Gray squirrel (*Sciurus carolinensis*)	1–2 yr.	Dec.–Aug.		44	4 (1–6)	1–2	Pr	14.5
Antelope ground squirrel (*Citellus nelsoni*)								6
Chipmunk (*Tamias striatus*)	2.5–3 mo.	Mar.–July	Pe	31	(3–6)	2		7
Woodchuck (*Marmota monax*)	1 yr.	Mar.–Apr.		28	4			9
Alpine marmot (*Marmota marmota*)		Apr.		35–42	2–5			13
Prairie dog (*Cynomys leucurus*)	1 yr.	Mar.–Apr.	Pe	28–32	5.5 (2–10)			
Family Geomyidae								
Pocket gopher (*Geomys bursarius*)	3 mo.	Feb.–Aug.	Pe	40–50	3 (1–9)	1–3		
Pocket gopher (*Thomomys bottae*)				19	4 (1–11)	2		
Family Heteromyidae								
Pocket mouse (*Perognathus flavus*)			Pe					5
Kangaroo rat (*Dipodomys merriami*)			Pe					5.5
Family Castoridae								
Beaver (*Castor canadensis*)	2 yr.	Jan.–Feb.		120 (42–128)	4 (1–6)	1		19

TABLE 3–3 (Continued)

Summary of Reproductive Data for Selected Types of Mammals

	Age at Puberty	Breeding Season	Sexual Cycle Type[1]	Sexual Cycle Duration, Days	Gestation Period, Days	Litter Size	Litter No./Yr.	Mating Habits[2]	Maximum Life Span, Years
Family Pedetidae									
Spring haas (*Pedetes caffer*)		Once a yr.				1 (2)	1		7.5
Family Cricetidae									
Deer mouse (*Peromyscus maniculatus*)	50 days	All yr.	Pe	4–5	23.5 (22–27)	5 (2–8)			7–8
Hamster (*Mesocricetus auratus*)	5–8 wk.	All yr.	Pe	4	16 (15–18)	1–12	3		1.8
Muskrat (*Ondatra zibethicus*)	1 yr.	Apr.–Oct.	Pe		30 (19–42)	7 (1–11)	2	Mo, Pr	
Vole (*Microtus agrestis*) .	Male, 6–8 wk.; female, 3 wk.	Feb.–Oct.	Pe		21 (21–29)	4		Pr	
Woodrat (*Neotoma micropus*)		Apr.–Dec.	Pe		33	2 (2–3)			
Family Muridae									
Harvest mouse (*Micromys minutus*)		Summer	Pe		21	6 (5–9)			2.5
House mouse (*Mus musculus*)	35 days	All yr.	Pe	4	19 (19–31)	6 (1–12)	(4–6)		3
Norway rat (*Rattus norvegicus*)	37–67 days	All yr.	Pe	4–5	21 (21–30)	12 (4–20)	2	Pr	4
Family Gliridae									
Garden dormouse (*Eliomys quercinus*) ..		May–June	Pe		22	2–6	1		5.5

Family Zapodidae								
Jumping mouse (*Zapus hudsonius*)		May–July	Pe		18	7 (5–8)	1–2	
Family Hystricidae								
Porcupine (*Hystrix cristata*)					63–112	2	2	20
Family Erethizontidae								
Porcupine (*Erethizon dorsatum*)	3 yr.	Nov.–Dec.	Me		112	1 (1–4)		
Family Caviidae								
Guinea pig (*Cavia porcellus*)	55–70 days	All yr.	Pe	16	68 (58–75)	3 (1–8)	3–4	6
Family Hydrochoeridae								
Capybara (*Hydrochoerus capybara*)					104–126	3–8	1	8.5
Family Dasyproctidae								
Agouti (*Dasyprocta mexicana*)		All yr.						13
Agouti (*Dasyprocta agouti*)		All yr.			104	2 (2–4)		10
Family Chinchillidae								
Chinchilla (*Chinchilla laniger*)	4 mo.	All yr.	Pe	28	105–115	2 (1–6)	1–8	7
Family Myocastoridae								
Nutria (*Myocastor coypus*)	8 mo.	All yr.	Pe	24–29	120–150	2–10	2	
Order Cetacea								
Family Delphinidae								
Dolphin (*Delphinus delphis*)					276			
Harbor porpoise (*Phocoena phoccena*)		July–Oct.			183	1		
Family Balaenopteridae								
Sei whale (*Balaenoptera borealis*)	2 yr.	May–Aug.	Pe		360	1		25–30

89

TABLE 3–3 (Continued)

Summary of Reproductive Data for Selected Types of Mammals

	Age at Puberty	Breeding Season	Sexual Cycle Type[1]	Sexual Cycle Duration, Days	Gestation Period, Days	Litter Size	Litter No./Yr.	Mating Habits[2]	Maximum Life Span, Years
Order Carnivora									
Family Canidae									
Wolf (*Canis lupus*)	2 yr.	Dec.–Apr.	Me		63	3–9			14
Coyote (*Canis latrans*)	2 yr.	Dec.–Apr.	Me		60–65	6.2	2		15
Dog (*Canis familiaris*)	6–8 mo.	Spring–fall	Me	9	63 (53–71)	7 (1–22)		Pr	34
Red fox (*Vulpes fulva*)	10 mo.	Dec.–Mar.	Me	2–4	52 (49–56)	4–9		Po	12
Arctic fox (*Alopex lagopus*)					60				14
Family Ursidae									
Grizzly bear (*Ursus horribilis*)	2–3 yr.	June–July	Me		208 (180–225)	2 (1–4)		Mo	31
Brown bear (*Ursus arctos*)	6 yr.	Apr.–June	Me		210	2 (1–2)			34
Polar bear (*Thalarctos maritimus*)		Feb.–Mar.	Me		240	2			33
Family Procyonidae									
Kinkajou (*Potos flavus*)		Apr.				1			19.5
Raccoon (*Procyon lotor*)	1 yr.	Jan.–June	Pe		63 (60–73)	4 (1–6)			13
Family Mustelidae									
Honey badger (*Mellivora ratel*)					180	2			23.5
Marten (*Martes martes*)	2 yr.	July–Aug.	Me		255–285	3–5			15
Otter (*Lutra lutra*)		Winter	Pe	26	61–63	4			11
Otter (*Lutra canadensis*)		Feb.	Me		60–288	1–4			15
Badger (*Taxidea taxus*)	Male, 2 yr.; female, 4 yr.	Aug.–Sept.	Me		183–265	3 (1–7)			13
Ferret (*Mustela putorius*)		Mar.–Aug.	Pe		42–45	8.5 (5–13)			

90

Species	Age at maturity	Breeding season			Gestation (days)	Number of young		Longevity (yr)
Sable (*Martes zibellina*)	2 yr.	June–Aug.	Pe	9–12	270–285	1–4		
Striped skunk (*Mephitis mephitis*)		Mar.		9–10	62	3–8		6
Family Viverridae								
Civet (*Viverra zibetha*)		May–June				3–4		15.5
African civet (*Civettictis civetta*)		Mar.–Oct.				2–5	2	13.5
Family Hyaenidae								
Spotted hyaena (*Crocuta crocuta*)		All yr.	Pe	14	91–110	1 (2)		25
Family Felidae								
Bengal tiger (*Felis tigris*)	1.5 yr.	All yr.			105–112	3 (1–6)		19
Lion (*Felis leo*)	2 yr.	All yr.	Pe	21	105–113	1–6		30
Mountain lion (*Felis concolor*)	2 yr.	All yr.			90–93	3 (1–5)	Every 2d yr.	16
Bobcat (*Lynx rufus*)		Late Feb.			50	3 (1–4)		25
House cat (*Felis cattus*)	6–15 mo.	Feb.–July	Pe	15–28	63 (52–69)	4	Pr	27
Order Pinnipedia								
Family Otariidae								
Sea lion (*Zalophus californianus*)		June–July	Me		348–365	1		23
Northern fur seal (*Callorhinus ursinus*)	2 yr.	July	Me		360	1		
Southern seal (*Arctocephalus pusillus*)	2 yr.	Oct.–Dec.			330–360	2 (1–2)		20
Family Odobenidae								
Walrus (*Odobenus rosmarus*)	4–5 yr.	Apr.–July			365 (330–370)			
Family Phocidae								
Gray seal (*Halichoerus grypus*)						1		41
Order Tubulidentata								
Family Orycteropodidae								
Aardvark (*Orycteropus afer*)		Born May–July				1		

TABLE 3–3 (Continued)

Summary of Reproductive Data for Selected Types of Mammals

	Age at Puberty	Breeding Season	Sexual Cycle		Gestation Period, Days	Litter		Mating Habits[2]	Maximum Life Span, Years
			Type[1]	Duration, Days		Size	No./Yr.		
Order Proboscidea									
Family Elephantidae									
Indian elephant (*Elephas maximus*)	8–16 yr.		Pe	3–4	624 (510–720)	1			69
African elephant (*Loxodonta africanus*)		Jan.–Feb.			(630–660)	1			36
Order Hyracoidea									
Family Procaviidae									
Rock dassie (*Procavia capensis*)		June–July			225	2 (1–6)	1		
Order Sirenia									
Family Dugongidae									
Dugong (*Dugong dugong*)		Winter			365	1	1		
Order Perissodactyla									
Family Equidae									
Domestic horse (*Equus caballus*)	1 yr.	All yr.	Pe	10–37	336 (264–420)	1			62
Burchell's zebra (*Equus quagga*)		Mar.–Nov.			340–365	1			25
Ass (*Equus asinus*)	1 yr.	Mar.–Aug.	Pe	22	365 (340–385)	1			19.3
Family Tapiridae									
Brazilian tapir (*Tapirus terrestris*)					397 (392–405)	1			30.5
Family Rhinocerotidae									
Two-horned rhinoceros (*Didermocerus sumatrensis*)	20 yr.	July–Oct.	Me		210	1			47

Order Artiodactyla
Family Suidae

	Age at maturity	Breeding season		No.	Gestation	Litter		Wt.
Wart hog (*Phacochoerus aethiopicus*)		June–July			171–175	4	Po	15
Swine (*Sus scrofa*)	7 (5–8) mo.	All yr.	Pe	21	114 (101–130)	9 (6–15)		27
Family Tayassuidae								
Collared peccary (*Tayassu tajacu*)					144 (142–148)			
Family Hippopotamidae								
Nile hippopotamus (*Hippopotamus amphibius*)	3 yr.	All yr.	Pe	30	231 (210–250)	1		49.5
Family Camelidae								
Llama (*Lama glama*)	1 yr.	Summer & fall			330	1		21
Camel (*Camelus bactrianus*)		All yr.	Pe	10–20	315–410	1		25.5
Camel (*Camelus dromedarius*)					265–380	1		25
Family Tragulidae								
Indian chevrotain (*Tragulus minima*)		June–July			120	2		
Family Cervidae								
Sambar deer (*Cervus unicolor*)		Oct.–Nov.			240	1–2		26.5
Wapiti (*Cervus canadensis*)	3 yr.	All yr.	Pe	21	255 (249–262)	1	Po	22
Red deer (*Cervus elaphus*)	Male, 3.5 yr.; female, 2.5 yr.	Sept.–Oct.	Pe		234 (225–246)	1	Po, Pr	19
European elk (*Alces alces*)		Sept.–Oct.	Me	14	240–250	1	Po	25
Reindeer (*Rangifer tarandus*)	1.5 yr.	Sept.–Oct.			230 (210–246)	1		12

TABLE 3-3 *(Continued)*

Summary of Reproductive Data for Selected Types of Mammals

	Age at Puberty	Breeding Season	Sexual Cycle Type[1]	Sexual Cycle Duration, Days	Gestation Period, Days	Litter Size	Litter No./Yr.	Mating Habits[2]	Maximum Life Span, Years
Family Giraffidae									
Giraffe (*Giraffa camelopardclis*)	3 yr.	July–Sept.	Pe		400–480	1			28
Family Antilocapridae									
Pronghorn (*Antilocapra americana*)		Sept.–Oct.				1–2			15
Family Bovidae									
Domestic cow (*Bos taurus*)	6–14 mo.	All yr.	Pe	14–23	281 (210–335)	1	1	Po, Pr	39
Antelope (*Hippotragus niger*)		All yr.			270–281				
Bison (*Bison bison*)	3 yr.	All yr.	Pe	21	275 (270–285)	1 (1–2)	1	Po	Fe 22
Eland (*Taurctragus onyx*)		All yr.	Pe	21	260 (255–270)	1			
Brindled gnu (*Connochaetes taurinus*)	Female 2 yr.	June	Pe		240–270				16
Goat (*Capra hircus*)	8 mo.	Sept.–winter	Pe	21	148 (135–160)	1–5		Pr	18

[1] Types of sexual cycle are: Me = monestrus; Pe = polyestrus.

[2] Types of mating habits are: Mo = monogamous, mates with only one male in a lifetime; Po = polygamous, mates with a different male each season; Pr = promiscuous, mates with two or more different males in any one breeding season.

SOURCES: Aldous, 1930, 1937; Asdell, 1946; Bourlière, 1954; Brown, 1925; Carter, 1955; Comfort, 1956; Dice, 1953; Fouch, 1958; Hawbecker, 1958; Hooper, 1956; Liers, 1958; Manville, 1953, 1957; Matheson, 1957; Prakash, 1960; Reuther, 1961; Schramm, 1961; Sowls, 1961; Spector, 1956; Wharton, 1950.

GROWTH AND DEVELOPMENT

As indicated above, there is a correlation between the length of gestation period and the developmental condition of the newly born young mammal; those having short gestation periods have altricial young, while those with long gestation periods have precocial young. The newly born altricial young of many rodents, lagomorphs, and carnivores are dependent upon their mothers for more or less prolonged periods of time. Young bears, for example, are completely blind, naked, and helpless at birth. The young black bear (*Ursus americanus*) weighs less than a pound at birth, although a large adult female may weigh in excess of 300 pounds.

Conaway (1958) has described the development of young least shrews (*Cryptotis parva*). At birth they are naked and have the eyes closed. During the first two days there is little change in appearance. On the third day the dorsal surface begins to darken and crawling movements can be observed. Pigmentation of the nose and chin becomes evident on the fourth day, and by the sixth day hair is visible on the dorsum. During the next few days the young become fully haired. At the end of 14 days the eyes are open and the young appear similar to the adults, except that they are smaller and have the characteristic silvery immature pelage. Conaway (*op. cit.*) obtained a weight-growth curve of this shrew (see Fig. 3–6). Growth is extremely rapid, with the birth weight being doubled by the end of the fourth day. The maximum growth weight occurred between the sixth and tenth day. Between the tenth and seventeenth day the growth weight declined. It appears probable that during this time the metabolic rates of the young increased rapidly and that the young were not securing enough nourishment from nursing. The total mass of a litter of five young is approximately three times that of the mother on the eighteenth day. Between the eighteenth and the twenty-fourth day, the growth rate again increases. It is during this time that the young begin to take meat; they are weaned by the twenty-first day.

Morrison *et al.* (1954: 376–386) found a linear relation between age in days and weight in the early growth of several small rodents (see Table 3 4 und Fig. 3–0). Young precocial mammals are very different. In the case of the black-tailed deer (*Odocoileus hemionus*), for example, Golley (1957) observed the birth of twin fawns. "Closer observation revealed that she had given birth to one fawn and was licking the afterbirth from its back and legs. At 7:34 A.M. she rose to her feet and walked about the newborn fawn. The legs of a second fawn could be seen protruding from her vagina at this

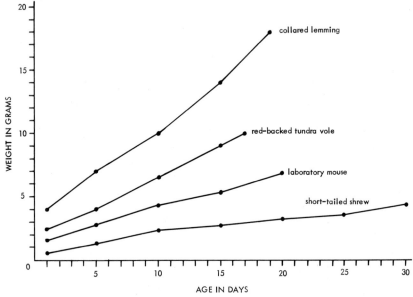

Fig. 3–6. Growth curves for selected small mammals (drawn from data by Conway, 1958, and Morrison *et al.*, 1954).

TABLE 3–4

Early Growth Constants for Several Species of Mice

The initial growth rate is the average for the first 20 days except those marked +, which are based on an average for first 12 days.

Species	Adult Weight, Grams	Initial Growth Rate	
		Gram/Day	Per Cent/Day
White mouse (*Mus musculus*)	22	0.30+	1.4
Peromyscus maniculatus	20	0.33	1.7
Peromyscus maniculatus	22	0.40	1.8
Peromyscus leucopus	25	0.43	1.7
Peromyscus truei	28	0.40	1.4
Peromyscus gossypinus	29	0.53	1.8
Peromyscus californicus	40	0.60	1.5
Clethrionomys rutilus	26	0.49	1.9
Microtus guentheri	43	0.70	1.6
Microtus oeconomus	45	0.79	1.8
Microtus pennsylvanicus	48	0.80+	1.7
Microtus californicus	62	0.98+	1.6
Dicrostonyx rubricatus	50	0.76	1.5

SOURCE: Compiled by Morrison *et al.* (1954).

TABLE 3–5

Chemical Composition of the Milk of Various Mammals

	Grams per 100 gm. of Whole Milk					No. of Days Needed To Double Birth Weight
	Water	Protein	Fat	Lactose	Ash	
Primates						
Monkey	88.4	2.2	2.7	6.4	0.18	
Orangutan	88.5	1.4	3.5	6.0	0.24	
Man	88.0	1.2	3.8	7.0	0.21	180
Edentata						
Anteater	63.0	11.0	20.0	0.3	0.8	
Lagomorpha						
Rabbit	71.3	12.3	13.1	1.9	2.3	
Rodentia						
Guinea pig	81.9	7.4	7.2	2.7	0.85	
Rat	72.9	9.2	12.6	3.3	1.4	
Carnivora						
Cat	81.6	10.1	6.3	4.4	0.75	9
Dog	76.3	9.3	9.5	3.0	1.2	8
Fox	81.6	6.6	5.9	4.9	0.93	
Pinnipedia						
Seal	46.4	9.7	42.0	(?)	0.85	14
Harp seal	43.8	11.9	42.8	0	0.9	5
Hooded seal	49.9	6.7	40.4	0	0.9	
Cetacea						
Whale	64.8	11.1	21.2	1.6	1.7	
Dolphin	44.9	10.6	34.9	0.9	0.53	
Blue whale	47.2	12.8	38.1	(?)	1.4	
Fin-backed whale .	54.1	13.1	30.6	(?)	1.5	
Proboscidea						
Elephant	70.7	3.6	17.6	5.6	0.63	
Perissodactyla						
Donkey	90.3	1.7	1.4	6.2	0.4	
Horse	90.1	2.6	1.0	6.9	0.35	60
Mule	90.0	2.0	1.8	5.5	0.47	
Zebra	86.2	3.0	4.8	5.3	0.7	
Artiodactyla						
Suidae						
Pig	82.8	7.1	5.1	3.7	1.1	18
Camelidae						
Camel	87.7	3.5	3.4	4.8	0.71	
Llama	86.5	3.9	3.2	5.6	0.8	
Cervidae						
Deer	65.9	10.4	19.7	2.6	1.4	
Reindeer ....,,	64.8	10.7	20.3	2.5	1.4	
Hippopotamidae						
Hippopotamus .	90.4	0.6	1.5	4.4	0.1	
Bovidae						
Bison	86.9	4.8	1.7	5.7	0.9	
Cow	87.0	3.3	3.7	4.8	0.72	47
Goat	87.0	3.3	4.1	4.7	0.77	
Buffalo	82.1	5.9	7.9	4.7	0.78	
Sheep	82.0	5.6	6.4	4.7	0.91	10

SOURCES: Spector (1956); Bourlière (1954); and Sowls *et al.* (1961).

time. She then lay down and at 7:40 gave birth to the second fawn. By 7:47 she had licked the second fawn clean and had eaten the afterbirth. At 8:20 A.M. the fawns were seen taking a few steps."

At first young mammals are more or less dependent upon the milk of the mother for nourishment. The length of time that the young depend upon the mother for food is not known, since the length of the lactation period of the female is unknown for most wild mammals and the young often continue to nurse for some time after they begin to take other food. The least shrew (*Cryptotis parva*) weans its young within three weeks after their birth, while the young walrus continues to nurse for as long as 18 months (Chapskiy, 1936).

The milk of several kinds of mammals has been analyzed and found to vary. Table 3–5 presents some of these analyses. There appears to be a correlation between the amount of protein in the milk and the growth rate of the young. For example, in man where it takes, on the average, 180 days for the young to double its birth weight, the milk contains only 1.2 parts per hundred of protein. In the harp seal, which doubles its birth weight in five days, on the other hand, the milk contains 11.9 parts per hundred. However, much of the rapid weight gain in seals is due to fat deposition and not to increase in size.

The southern elephant seal (*Mirounga leonina*) has a spectacular weight increase. The average young female weighs 101 pounds at birth; its weight is doubled in 11 days, tripled in 17 days, and quadrupled in 21 days (Laws, 1953:33). Young elephant seals are born on land and do not have blubber enough to provide insulation and buoyancy until they are several weeks old. Thus the high fat content of seal milk is obviously of adaptive advantage.

SEXUAL MATURITY

In general, sexual maturity occurs before growth has ceased. The data presented in Table 3–3 illustrate the great variation in age at which sexual maturity is attained. In general, sexual maturity is reached quite early in the small cricetid and murid rodents. The female short-tailed vole (*Microtus agrestis*) of Europe reaches sexual maturity in 21 days and the male in 6 to 8 weeks. The house mouse (*Mus musculus*) reaches maturity in 35 days. Some rodents take considerably longer to reach sexual maturity. In the prairie dog (*Cynomys leucurus*) it takes one year; the beaver (*Castor canadensis*) and the pocupine (*Erethizon dorsatum*) usually breed in the third year, although Bradt (1938) reported some beaver breeding in the second year.

Among the Artiodactyla, sexual maturity is reached quite early, relative to their large size. As a result of selective breeding, domestic sheep and goats reach sexual maturity in 7 to 8 months, the domestic cow in 6 to 14 months. Wild species apparently take somewhat longer: reindeer, 18 months; bison and wapiti, 3 years. The Indian elephant (order Proboscidea) reaches sexual maturity between 8 and 16 years. The two-horned rhinoceros (*Didermocerus sumatrensis*) reportedly does not reach sexual maturity until it is 20 years old. The higher primates, relative to their size, appear to take the longest time to reach sexual maturity. The Rhesus monkey takes 3 years; the Chacma baboon, 4 years; and the chimpanzee and lar gibbon, 8 to 10 years. In man, sexual maturity is reached between the 12th and the 15th year, usually earlier in females than in males.

MOLTING

At birth the young mammal may have a coat of fur or it may be naked, not developing fur until the first few days of life. The same hairs are not present throughout the life of the individual but are lost and replaced at intervals. In most mammals the individual hairs reach a given stage of development and then growth ceases. After a period of time a new hair develops, either from the same dermal papilla or from another developing in the same area. The new hair either pushes out the old or it drops out at a later time. The result is a process called molting. Molting is often an orderly process that begins at a given point and proceeds, in a definite pattern, until complete. The place of origin and pattern of molt vary with the kind and age of mammal concerned. Some kinds of mammals have no definite periods of molt but rather seem to be continually losing a few hairs as a few new ones develop.

In most mammals there are three major pelages: the juvenal, the subadult, and the adult, although a nestling pelage is recognized in some animals. A definitive molt occurs between each of these pelages.

The pelages of the cottontail rabbit (*Sylvilagus floridanus*) have been described by Negus (1958:246–252). He correlated the various pelages with the age and weight. Young cottontails are born naked and the first pelage, the nestling fur, is attained by the end of the first two weeks of life. It is fine and downy in texture, dense and grayish in color. This *nestling pelage* is retained until the rabbit is 5.5 weeks old. At this time the young cottontail weighs between 114 and 241 gm. (4 and 8.5 ounces). This first molt occurs between 5.5 and 7 weeks, when the weight range is 241 to 284 gm. (8.5 to 10 ounces). During this molt the nestling fur is replaced by the *juvenal pelage.* The juvenal pelage is retained from age 7.5 to 10.5 weeks (weight range 298–497 gm. or 10.5–17.5 ounces) and is characterized by the thinness of the hair, a salt-and-pepper appearance, and a generally dark coloration. Between ages 11 and 14.5 weeks (weight 511–767 gm. or 18–27 ounces) this pelage is replaced by the subadult pelage. The *subadult pelage* is retained from age 15 to 30+ weeks (weight 795–1250+ gm. or 28–44+ ounces); this fur is characterized dorsally by a lighter, buff color and ventrally by a lighter gray color than occurs in the adult summer pelage. The dark outer long hairs are sparse. *Adult summer pelage* is darker than the subadult pelage and is glossy in appearance as a result of a greater density of long hairs. In the fall this pelage is replaced by the winter pelage. Young cottontails still in juvenal pelage at the time of the fall molt apparently omit subadult pelage and molt directly into the winter pelage.

Ecke and Kinney (1956:249–254) described two preadult and an adult pelage in the meadow mouse, *Microtus californicus.* A juvenal pelage, which is molted between the 23rd and 45th day of life, is replaced by the postjuvenal (=subadult?) pelage. A second molt starts almost immediately, and by the 60th day of life, adult pelage is present. Most adult mammals undergo at least one seasonal molt while some have several. These molts have a very definite economic value to a fur trapper. The open season for trapping must so be regulated that only prime furs are taken. Prime furs are those in which the molt to the longer winter pelage is complete and the new pelage has reached its complete growth. Unprime furs are those in which the molt is not complete or the growth of the new hairs is not complete.

In the Barrow ground squirrel (*Citellus undulatus*) of northern Alaska, which is active only during five months of the year, two molts occur during the short summer. A spring molt, to a summer pelage almost lacking in underfur, occurs in June or July; a fall molt to a winter pelage containing a thick underfur and long silky guard hairs occurs in August or September.

Some kinds of adult mammals molt only once each year. Constantine (1957:461–466), for example, found that the Brazilian free-tailed bat (*Tadarida brasiliensis*) and the cave myotis (*Myotis velifer*) had only one molt per year, with the males molting earlier than the females.

The time of molting in some adult mammals is very highly irregular. In the porcupine (*Erethizon dorsatum*) Po-Chedley and Shadle (1955:84–94) found the time of molting of adults to be so varied as to be an individual affair. Ecke and Kinney (1956:249–254) found molting in adult meadow mice (*Microtus californicus*) to be highly irregular. The long-tailed weasel is an example of a mammal with two molts each year. In the southern part of its range this weasel remains brown throughout the year. In the northern part of its range, however, it turns white in winter. Once observers thought that this white resulted from the bleaching of the brown hairs (or by the migration of pigments from the hair back into the body). It is now known that this results from a molt in which the new hairs do not contain pigment.

Several quite unrelated mammals in the north have a white winter pelage, as is shown in Table 3–6. The time sequence of such color molts is probably dependent upon the length of daily illumination, irrespective of the environment or temperature. Light enters

TABLE 3–6

Mammals Exhibiting Variable Colors (White Winter Pelage, Dark Summer Pelage) in Some Part of Their Range

The asterisk (°) indicates that members of the species inhabiting the southern part of their range do not turn white in winter.

Lagomorpha
  Leporidae
    White-tailed jackrabbit, *Lepus townsendi* °
    Snowshoe hare, *Lepus americana* °
    Arctic hare, *Lepus arcticus*
    Varying hare, *Lepus timidus* °
Rodentia
  Cricetidae
    Collared lemming, *Dicrostonyx hudsonius* °
    Collared lemming, *Dicrostonyx groenlandicus*
Carnivora
  Canidae
    Arctic fox, *Alopex lagopus* °
  Mustelidae
    Short-tailed weasel, *Mustela erminea* °
    Long-tailed weasel, *Mustela frenata* °
    Least weasel, *Mustela rixosa* °
    Weasel, *Mustela nivalis* °

the eyes and probably affects the pituitary gland. This gland, in turn, affects the secretion of the gonadotropic hormones. An increase in the amount of gonadotropic hormones causes the animal to assume its summer pelage. The fall molt is often completed long before the first snow has fallen, and the spring molt may be completed while there is still a foot of snow in the woods. Lyman (1943) has reported on an excellent set of experiments indicating how light is the controlling factor in the molting cycle in the snowshoe rabbit.

It has been adequately demonstrated by Lyman and others (Bisonette and Bailey 1944:221–260 on weasels and by Novikov and Blagodatskia 1948:577–580 on the varying hare, *Lepus timidus*) that the amount of light controls the time of molting in variable-colored mammals (as it probably does in all mammals that molt seasonally). The basic cause of white winter pelage, however, appears to be much more complex and, perhaps, controlled by different mechanisms in different mammals. In general, there appears to be a direct relation between the duration of snow in an area and the duration of white pelage. In the Arctic hare, *Lepus arcticus*, this geographic variation is well developed. The northern subspecies, *Lepus arcticus monstrabilis*, from Ellesmere and Devon Islands at 80 degrees north latitude, remains white the whole year, while in the Hudson Bay region, *L. a. labradorius* has a dark summer pelage from late June to late August. Altitude as well as latitude has an effect on the time of molting. Smith (1940) reported that in the Green Mountain area of Vermont in mid-June, individuals at 2800 feet were in summer pelage while those at 4000 feet (where snow lasts into May) were just losing the white winter pelage.

Degerbøl and Mohl-Hansen (1943:1–40) found that Greenland collared lemmings (*Dicrostonyx groenlandicus*) reared in captivity near Copenhagen did not turn white in winter (except very transiently) after the first winter. Even during the first winter the pelage was acquired quite late—January–February instead of late September or early October, as occurs in their natural habitat.

In other species of variable-colored mammals that have been transplanted to areas farther south, ths cessation of a white winter pelage has not occurred. The arctic foxes (*Alopex*) in the London Zoo continued to turn white in winter, even though the climate there is quite mild (Cott, 1940). Hall (1951) reported that long-tailed weasels (*Mustela frenata*) from populations that turned white in winter, when placed in captivity in areas where winter did not occur, continued to turn white in winter while those in a reverse experiment did not change into winter pelage.

These cases indicate that the development of a white winter pelage is genetically fixed. Presumably it has resulted from natural selection of those individuals which best fit into their immediate environment. Obviously a white mammal in an area with little or no snow would be more readily seen than one in a brownish pelage. The reverse would be equally true. Presumably those individuals whose color was in striking contrast to that of their surroundings would be subject to higher predation and eventually the genes producing this situation would be eliminated from the population.

Some laboratory experiments have been conducted which tend to confirm this viewpoint.

Dice (1947) exposed variously colored races of *Peromyscus* to predation by owls. Even at very low light intensities individuals in marked contrast to their background were subject to greater predation than those that more nearly matched the background color.

A more natural experiment appears to have occurred in the case of the varying hare (*Lepus timidus*) that inhabits the Faroe Islands. Degerbøl (1940) has recorded this experiment in some detail. In 1854 or 1855 a pair of varying hares was introduced into the Faroe Islands from Norway. During the first several years following this introduction, these hares and their descendants turned white in winter even though snow was rare or absent. By 1875, only half of the population turned white in the winter; by 1885, only one-fourth; and by 1890, only a small fraction of the population became white in winter. By the late 1930's, when Degerbøl made his study, none of the population became white in winter. Here, the obvious implication is that a genetic trait for white winter pelage was selected against and eliminated from the population in a spectacularly short period of time.

OLD AGE

In nature it is rare that an individual reaches old age. In a study of a selected sample (almost all were in adult pelage) of deer mice (*Peromyscus leucopus*) in a museum collection, all taken from a restricted locality in eastern Kansas, none showed signs of thin pelage and other features characteristic of old age in captivity (Cockrum, 1954: 373). Few longevity records are available of marked individuals in nature, but those available indicate that potential longevity is greater in captivity than is known for any wild animal taken. For example, the fox squirrel in the wild is known to live 7.5 years, but it has been kept in captivity for almost 15 years.

Some measure of potential longevity can be secured from animals in captivity. Here, however, we find that some species do not do as well in captivity and probably do not live as long as they might in nature. Table 3-7 records some of the information from animals in captivity. In general, small rodents and insectivores live only a few years. The maximum age in captivity of the deer mouse, *Peromyscus maniculatus*, is less than 7 years (Dice, 1933: 147). Among the small insectivores, the short-tailed shew, *Blarina brevicauda,* lives only 2.5 years in captivity. Jackrabbits live somewhat longer, with one record of the European rabbit, *Oryctolagus cuniculus,* living to an age of 13 years. The potential longevity of carnivores is even greater:

coyote, 15 years; dog, 34 years; brown bear, 34 years; honey badger, 23.5 years; house cat, 27 years; and lion, 30 years. Some artiodactyls live even longer in captivity: domestic hog, 27 years; camel, 25.5 years; European elk, 25 years; giraffe, 28 years; pigmy buffalo, 28 years; domestic cow, 39 years; and Nile hippopotamus, 49.5 years.

The perissodactyls (horses and allies) live even longer: tapir, 30.5 years; rhinoceros, 47 years; domestic horse, 62 years. The oldest known elephant reached an age of 69 years.

From these observations it is obvious that man, who occasionally reaches ages slightly in excess of 100 years, has the greatest potential longevity of any known mammal.

4

Behavior

DAILY ACTIVITIES

In the normal life of a mammal, at least some effort is devoted to the following types of activities: securing food and water, rest, play, defense of territory, and sanitation. The percentage of time devoted to each of these activities varies with the season, local conditions, and species of mammal studied. Seasonally, nest building and reproductive activities, including courtship, breeding behavior, and care of young, account for much of the daily activity. Mammals show great variations in the daily pattern of activity, not only as to the time of the day in which these activities occur but also as to the duration of the activity. Animals like the shrews are active almost all of the time, day and night, but their active periods are interrupted by periods of rest. Species such as the squirrels, which are active only during the daylight hours, are termed diurnal. Species such as many rabbits, which are active in the early evening and early morning, are termed crepuscular. Species such as most bats and many rodents, which are active only at night, are termed nocturnal.

Three aspects of normal daily activity that warrant further consideration are home range, territory, and homing behavior.

HOME RANGE

The concept of home range in vertebrate populations has been recognized for some years. Seton (1909) expressed this concept in the following statement: "No wild animal roams at random over the country: each has a home region, even if it has not an actual home." A more recent writer defines home range as "that area about its established home which is traversed by the animal in its normal activities of food gathering, mating, and caring for young. Occasional sallies outside the area, perhaps exploratory in nature, should not be considered as in part of the home range" (Burt, 1940). A simpler and more inclusive definition is: "The home range is the area over which an individual travels in its normal, daily activities" (Blair, 1953).

METHODS OF DETERMINING HOME RANGE

A number of techniques have been utilized in determining the size of the home range of mammals: tracking in snow (Scott, 1943); direct observations of diurnal species (Burt, 1930); live-trapping, marking and releasing, and subsequent recapturing and marking animals with an automatic device that, at a given station, colors the individual with a dye characteristic of that location. New (1958) developed a system of bait stations, each with food containing a characteristic dye. Diurnal species can be marked so that they can be recognized without the necessity of recapture. Various stains and dyes and colored plastic ear tags have been used in this manner (Manville, 1949). Most of the available data on home ranges have been accumulated from the live-trapping, marking and releasing, and recapture of individuals. Such studies are usually based upon the results of live traps set in a grid pattern over the study area.

The live-trapping, marking, and releasing technique is based upon the assumption that an animal will be trapped at least in the biologically important parts of its home range (Hayne, 1949). Standardization of the interpretation of the resultant data remains to be worked out. The distance between traps has an influence on the results (Mohr, 1947; Hayne, 1950), and the difference in intensity of the use of the various parts of the home range, although usually ignored, should be considered (Blair, 1942; Hayne, 1949). Finally, various methods of calculating the size of the home range are available for interpreting the data accumulated. Most of the methods fall into one of the following classifications.

The *minimum home range* method consists of computing the area of a polygon resulting from connecting the outside points of capture of an individual animal (see Fig. 4–1a). The resultant figure represents the absolute minimum known area of the home range of the individual concerned and is usually less than the actual home range.

The *minimum home range plus estimate* method consists of utilizing the data necessary for determining minimum home range and extending the home range beyond the known points of capture. Several methods for such estimates have been used, most of which involve the addition of a boundary strip one-half the distance to the next trap. One system consists of drawing the line about the points of capture in such a manner as to exclude, so far as possible, traps where the animal was not taken and computing the resultant area (Fig. 4–1b). A second system consists of drawing the line about the points in accordance with an arbitrary set of rules and computing the resulting area. This system accepts the presence within the

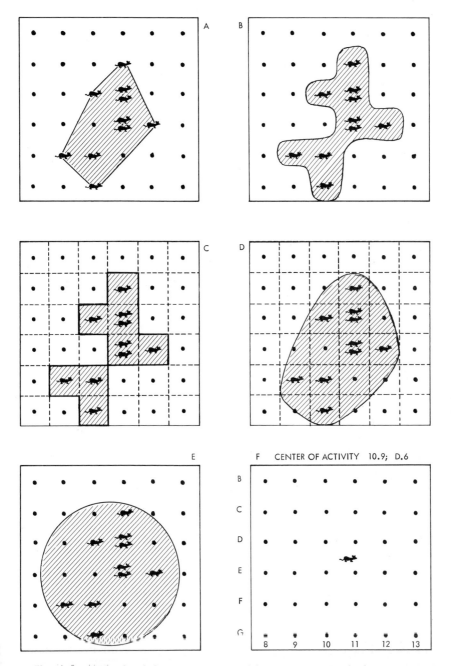

Fig. 4–1. Methods of determining size of home range. Each dot represents a live trap from which a small rodent might be recovered. The small mice represent one or two recaptures of the same individual. Fig. 4–1 A–E represents different ways of utilizing the same information to arrive at an estimate of the home range. In Fig. 4–1F, the single mouse represents the center of activity as computed from the same data.

home range of traps which the animal may not visit during the relatively short trapping periods usually used (Fig. 4–1c, d).

The *greatest distance between captures* method consists of using the greatest distance between points of capture of an individual as the diameter of a circle or as the major axis of an ellipse. The area so enclosed is assumed to be the home range (Fig. 4–1e). As has been pointed out by Hayne (1950), each of these methods of calculating the size of the home range has inherent limitations. In general, the accuracy and completeness of the results is dependent upon trap density and upon the duration of trapping.

Two other measures of home range have been devised. One is the *frequencies of distances between points of consecutive capture.* This method illustrates, in part, that the frequency of capture is less toward the periphery than it is toward the center of the individual's activities. However, the tabular results are difficult to interpret. Certainly the tendency to interpret such figures as distances traveled is not correct. Further, the presence of traps between the home of the animal and periphery of the actual home range would have an effect on the probability of capture toward the periphery.

The second is the *distribution of the points of capture about a center of activity.* This system, proposed by Hayne (1949), mathematically defines the "center of activity." According to Hayne, "The center of activity may be computed in the following manner. First, a system of rectangular coordinates must be set up on the map showing the location of the traps. Numerical values are assigned to positions along these coordinates. The position of each point of capture of an animal, then, may be defined according to its location in relation to each of the two axes of the coordinate system. The center of activity may be located by averaging all the locations along the vertical axis and all the locations along the horizontal axis. The two values resulting from this procedure and the two coordinates of the point are here termed the center of activity. This point may be viewed as a two-dimensional average of a group of points." This system is illustrated in Fig. 4–1f. Once the center of activity has been determined, it may be used in several ways. Two applications are: (1) to determine effects on centers of activity of climatic or seasonal changes or changes in population concentrations, and (2) to determine average distance of points of capture from the center of activity.

SIZE OF HOME RANGE

As can be seen in Table 4–1, the available information on the size of home range shows great variation. Some of this variation is the result of the differences in techniques of the various investigators. However, as discussed by Blair (1953: 7–21), a number of other factors affect the size of the home range. A discussion of several of these factors follows:

Size of Animal. In general, the size of the home range is roughly correlated with the size of the individual. Murie (1944) estimated the home range of the Alaskan grizzly bear, *Ursus horribilis,* to be approximately 9 miles in diameter while the raccoon, *Procyon lotor,* has a home range approximately 1 mile in diameter (Stuewer, 1943). Smaller mammals have even smaller home ranges. The male eastern cottontail, *Sylvilagus floridanus,* for example, may range over 100 acres (Haugen, 1942), while small rodents normally range over only a fraction to 4 or 5 acres (see Table 4–1).

Mobility. The type of locomotive adaptations of a species influences the size of the home range. No home range studies are available for the highly motile, aerial bats, but limited observations indicate that their home range is probably measured in miles and not in a few acres, as in the case of small terrestrial rodents. There is some indication that the saltatorial zapodids have larger home ranges than do similar-sized non-saltatorial rodents in the same habitat (Table 4–1 and Blair, 1953: 20). Fossorial forms, such as moles and pocket gophers, have much smaller home ranges than terrestrial mammals of similar size.

Food Habits. As a general rule, the herbivores have a much smaller home range than do the carnivores. The wolf, *Canis lupus,* for example, is known to have a home range up to 50 miles in diameter (Murie, 1944), while the white-tailed deer, *Odocoileus virginianus,* in a more or less uniform habitat in central Missouri, has a home range varying in size from 0.5 to slightly over 2 square miles (Progulske and Baskett, 1958).

In a mesquite area in southern New Mexico, Blair (1943) found that the grasshopper mice (*Onychomys torridus* and *Onychomys leucogaster*), which feed mainly on insects, had a greater home range than did the similar-sized seed-eating deer mice (*Peromyscus maniculatus* and *Peromyscus leucopus*) in the same area. The short tailed shrew (*Blarina brevicauda*), another species feeding on insects and other invertebrates, has a home range as large as or larger than the larger vegetarian species in the same habitat (specifically deer mice, *Peromyscus,* and meadow voles, *Microtus;* see Table 4–1).

Habitat. The food and cover available in an area likewise influence the size of the home range. In many cases in the smaller mam-

TABLE 4–1

Size of Home Range and Population Densities of Selected Species of Small Mammals

Species	Habitat and Season	Population Density [1]	Home Range in Acres [2] Males	Females
Order Marsupialia				
Family Didelphidae				
Opossum (*Didelphis marsupialis*)	U.S.		X 11.5 (2–58)	
Order Insectivora				
Family Soricidae				
Blarina brevicauda	U.S., forest, summer	0.8–2.2	1.2 (1.1–1.4)	0.6 (0.5–1.5)
Cryptotis parva	U.S., forest	2	0.4	0.6
Order Lagomorpha				
Family Leporidae				
Swamp rabbit (*Sylvilagus palustris*)	U.S., swamp, winter	0.056	18.9 (11.0–27.5)	
Cottontail (*Sylvilagus floridanus*)	U.S.		14.0 (8–22.5)	
Order Rodentia				
Family Sciuridae				
Fox squirrel (*Sciurus niger*)	Calif.		X 154 yd.	X 130 yd.
Chipmunk (*Eutamias quadrimaculatus*)..	Ore., forest, fall	1.4–3.8	2.2	1.2
Chipmunk (*Eutamias townsendi*)	Mich., summer, forest	0.8–15.0	–	–
Chipmunk (*Tamias striatus*)	Calif., low desert, early spring	15–20/sq. mi.	2.3 (0.9–4.7)	2.1 (0.6–7.3)
Ground squirrel (*Citellus mohavensis*)	Calif.		X 106 yd.	
Ground squirrel (*Citellus beecheyi*)	Mich., forest, summer	1–2	0.36	0.59
Flying squirrel (*Glaucomys volans*)			3.7+	3.7+
Family Heteromyidae				
Kangaroo rat (*Dipodomys ordii*)	N. M., mesquite, late spring	0.3–1.2	3.41 ± 0.25	3.29 ± 0.47
Kangaroo rat (*Dipodomys merriami*)	N. M., mesquite, late spring	0.6–1.1	4.07 ± 0.24	3.88 ± 0.51
Pocket mouse (*Perognathus penicillatus*)..	N. M., mesquite, late spring	0.3–0.9	2.72 ± 0.48	1.09 ± 0.14
Family Cricetidae				
Oldfield mouse (*Peromyscus polionotus*)..	Fla., sandy island, fall	0.8–1.4	(1.97–10.66)	
Golden mouse (*Peromyscus nutalli*)	Tex., flood plain	0.3–2.2	1.46 ± 0.17	1.40 ± 0.22

Species	Location and season	Range		
White-footed mouse (*Peromyscus leucopus*)	N. M., mesquite, spring	0.05–0.2	3.1	4.1
	Mich., forest		0.28	0.21
Deer mouse (*Peromyscus maniculatus*) ..	N. M.	0.3–0.7	4.66 ± 0.33	4.10 ± 0.39
	Mich.		0.77 ± 0.06	0.63 ± 0.07
Grasshopper mouse (*Onychomys leuco-gaster*)	N. M., mesquite, spring	0.1–0.4	3.8–4.8	1.5–2.1
Grasshopper mouse (*Onychomys torridus*)	N. M., mesquite, spring	0.1–0.2	3.1–12.4	3.6–7.8
Cottonrat (*Sigmodon hispidus*)	U.S., grassland, summer	7.5	0.85	0.44
Meadow mouse (*Microtus pennsylvanicus*)	Mich., moist bluegrass, summer	5.8–14.6	0.31 ± 0.02	0.19 ± 0.03
	dry bluegrass, summer	0.6–2.6	0.50 ± 0.07	0.28 ± 0.03
Meadow mouse (*Microtus montebelli*) ...	Japan	34–43	0.35	0.35
Meadow mouse (*Synaptomys cooperi*) ..	U.S., forest			0.8–1.0
Red-back mouse (*Clethrionomys gapperi*)	U.S., forest, late summer		1.89	0.57
Family Muridae				
Woodmouse (*Apodemus sylvaticus*)	England	3–11	0.72	0.24
Woodmouse (*Apodemus peninsulae*)	Korea, forest	1	1.88 ± 0.30	
Striped field mouse (*Apodemus agrarius*)	Korea, forest	4.9	1.70 ± 0.25	1.09 ± 0.14
Family Zapodidae				
Jumping mouse (*Zapus hudsonicus*)	Mich., forest, summer	0.2–5.0	0.89 ± 0.11	0.92 ± 0.11
Woodland jumping mouse (*Napaeozapus insignis*)	Mich., forest, fall		3.05	2.36
Order Carnivora				
Family Mustelidae				
Marten (*Martes americana*)	Mont., year round		X̄ 588	X̄ 172

SOURCE: Data in this table were compiled from Baumgartner (1943); Blair (1936, 1940a and b, 1941b, 1942, 1943, 1951); Buckner (1957); Burt (1930, 1940, 1943); Edwards (1946); Erickson (1949); Evans and Holdenreid (1943); Gashwiler (1959); Hawbecker (1958); Hawley and Newby (1957); Howell (1954); Jones and Barber (1957); Jordan (1948); Lowe (1958); McCarley (1958); Miller (1958); Morris (1955); Stickel and Stickel (1949); Storer, Evans, and Palmer (1944); Tamaka and Teramura (1953); Tappe (1941); Yerger (1953); Youngman (1956).

[1] Figures for population density are given in animals per acre unless otherwise noted.

[2] X̄ indicates average value.

mals it is difficult to separate the effects of food and cover in the habitat. Blair (1940) found that in a dry, sparse bluegrass habitat meadow voles (*Microtus pennsylvanicus*) had a larger home range than those in a nearby moist, heavy bluegrass habitat (males averaged 0.50 acres in contrast to 0.31 acres; females 0.28 versus 0.19 acres). Blair (1943) found that deer mice (*Peromyscus maniculatus* and *Peromyscus leucopus*) living in a relatively open mesquite habitat in southern New Mexico had larger home ranges than the same species have in the more heavily vegetated areas of Michigan.

The striped field mouse (*Apodemus agrarius*) of Korea apparently has a larger home range in grass and shrub areas than in forest areas. Youngman (1956) found that males had a home range averaging approximately 0.71 acres in a brush area while Jones and Barber (1957) found the home ranges of males to average 1.7 acres in a forest area. This is probably another example of the fact that subclimax situations usually have more food available than do climax forests.

The location of the home site in the habitat as well as the size of the specific habitat in which the species live has been indicated as influencing the size of the home range (Blair, 1953). Baumgartner (1943) found that fox squirrels (*Sciurus niger*) living in small woodlots had smaller home ranges than those living in large areas. This smaller home range might also be the result of a greater population density in the small woodlots.

Population Density. Blair (1953) thought that there was no evidence that population density had any influence on the size of the individual home ranges. A later study made by Frank (1957) reported that in times of high populations in the field vole (*Microtus arvalis*) of Germany, a high "condensation potential," based particularly on social mechanisms, resulted in a reduction in the home range size, the formation of "great families," the formation of overwintering communities, the communal nesting of females, and a reduction in the number of males in the population. Additional studies of this nature are needed to determine the over-all effects of population density on home range.

Sex. In general, males have a larger home range than do females. Presumably this is the result of a greater attachment to the nest and young on the part of the female, but no data are available to substantiate this viewpoint. As can be seen in Table 4–1, the larger home range in males has been demonstrated in most species studied.

Age. In general, young altricial mammals, when they first venture from the nest, remain closer to the nest than do the adults, thus occupying a smaller home range. Blair (1942), for example, found that the average size of the home range of seventeen immature female deer mice (*Peromyscus leucopus*) was 1.07 acres, while that of fourteen adult females was 1.4 acres. Precocial animals, on the other hand, usually remain with the adult female continually; thus they have the same home range that the adult female occupies during this time.

Season of Year. Not many studies now available give information as to seasonal variations in home range. Much additional work is needed in this area before any clear-cut conclusions can be reached. Blair (1943) found that in southern New Mexico a significant difference existed between sizes of the home ranges of female Ord kangaroo rats, *Dipodomys ordi,* and Merriam kangaroo rats, *Dipodomys merriami,* as determined for March and compared with April and May. In March the home ranges of female *D. ordi* averaged 1.09 ± 0.36 acres, while in April and May the average was 3.29 ± 0.47 acres, a difference between the means of 3.7 times its standard error. A female had a range of 0.32 acres in March, 2.27 acres in April, and 3.38 acres in May. No immatures were taken on the study plots in March but were taken in April and May.

SOCIAL BEHAVIOR

The activities and behavioral traits that occur only when animals are living in groups and that are not shown when the animal lives as a solitary individual are known as social behavior. Social behavior in mammals is an area that has barely been explored and in which much remains to be done before any general statements can safely be made. Even a basic classification of society types is impracticable at the present time.

Some of the outstanding behavioral studies that have been made are Darling (1937) on the red deer of Scotland, Carpenter (1934, 1935, 1940) on various primates, and King (1955) on the black-tailed prairie dog.

Some types of social behavior that have been studied in several species and in which some meaningful conclusions can be drawn are territorial behavior, communication, and social hierarchy.

TERRITORIAL BEHAVIOR

A territory is that part of the home range that is protected from other individuals of the same species (Burt, 1943), whether it includes all the home range or only the nest site. Thus two or more individuals may include the same area as part of their home range, but, in those kinds showing territorial behavior, part of the home range is protected from invasion by other individuals (Fig. 4–2). Territorial behavior is well known in diurnal birds, especially during the mating season. These territories vary in size from as much as 2.5 acres in some of the smaller passerine birds to such small areas as the immediate vicinity of the nests in colonial species such as English sparrows.

The size of the territory, or even if a territory exists, is not known for most mammals. The only certain approach to the study of the

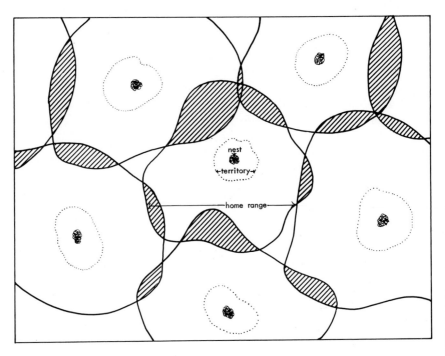

Fig. 4–2. The relationship between home range and territory.

problem appears to be by direct observation. This, however, is no easy matter in nocturnal mammals.

Territorial behavior has been reported for the European wild rabbit (*Oryctolagus cuniculus*), at least for females during the breeding season. At this time a female will actually chase away any intruders of the same species, even engaging in combat if necessary to accomplish her aims (Southern, 1948). In the eastern cottontail (*Sylvilagus floridanus*) Haugen (1942) found no overlap in the home ranges of females and thought this evidence of territorial behavior. In the pikas (*Ochotona princeps*) Kilham (1958: 307) found territorial behavior. He reported that pikas have a "caack" call which advertises ownership and that the territories are marked by scent.

Similar territorial behavior has been indicated for several members of the squirrel family, Sciuridae. Rice (1957: 129) observed a male tassel-eared squirred, *Sciurus aberti*, defending a tree from intrusions by seven other males. In the protected tree was a female in heat. Copulation was observed, but it was interrupted by an attempted reinvasion of the tree by other males. Kilham (1954: 252) observed territorial behavior in the red squirrel, *Tamiasciurus hudsonicus*, during the season of collecting and storing pine cones. Such behavior at feeding stations was reported by Gordon (1936). Additional sciurids in which territorial behavior has been indicated include the eastern chipmunk, *Tamias striatus* (Burt, 1940; Blair, 1941); long-eared chipmunk, *Eutamias quadrimaculatus* (Storer, Evans and Palmer, 1940); chickaree, *Tamiasciurus douglasi* (Gordon, 1936); golden-mantled ground squirrel, *Citellus lateralis* (Gordon, 1936); Mexican ground squirred, *Citellus mexicanus* (Edwards, 1946); and fox squirrel, *Sciurus niger* (Allen, 1943). In the criceted rodents, territorial behavior is rare or absent (Blair, 1953: 24), although it has occasionally been reported on insufficient data.

In certain polygamous mammals, the males defend their harem against other males of the same species. This is not necessarily a territorial defense in the usual sense of the word, for the actual area defended shifts with the location of the harem. Such harems are apparently formed in all the eared seals (Family Otariidae), the walruses (Family Odobenidae), and by the grey seal, *Halichoreus grypus*, and the southern elephant seal, *Mirounga leonina*, both in the family Phocidae. Harem formation is also known in several of the artiodactyls, such as the American elk (*Cervus canadensis*), the European red deer (*Cervus elaphus*), and in some of the bovids.

Koford (1957) made an intensive study of the vicuna (*Vicugna vicugna*, Family Camelidae) which lives high in the central Andes of South America. He found that the individuals were grouped into family bands and male troops. The family bands consist of one adult male, one to nine adult females, one or more immature females, and the young of the year. The male troops consist of all male vicunas that are not members of family groups and often consist of forty or more members. The male with the family group actively defends territory, principally against other males, both from adjacent families and from male troops. The defense of the territory consists primarily of aggressive display, rarely direct attack.

Some mammals normally live in a family or some other type of social group and that group will defend a given territory against other individuals and groups of the same species. Languars of India (*Presbytis entellus*) live in troops, and one troop will actively defend its territory from another troop. The howling monkeys (*Alouatta palliata*) of Central America also unite into clans, each with its own defended territory (Carpenter, 1934, 1935, 1940, 1942, 1950). Similar group behavior has been reported for the muskrat (*Ondatra zibethicus*) during at least part of the year (Sather, 1958).

On the other hand, little or no evidence of territorial behavior has been found in a long list of mammals. Fitch (1948: 513) could not find any evidence of territorial defense in the California ground squirrel (*Citellus beecheyi*). Murie (1944) observed two female wolves raising their young at the same time in the same den. Crabb (1948) found that, in Iowa, the dens and connecting trails were not defended by any one individual or group of spotted skunks (*Spilogale gracilis*), rather they were used by the whole population of the area.

Graf (1956) suggested that territorialism normally exists in deer (especially the elk, *Cervus canadensis*), but has not been recognized because the territories are not defended by antagonistic behavior of display; rather, the territories are marked by the placement of "sign posts," such as saplings that have the bark scraped off and then rubbed by the muzzle. These "sign posts" identify the territory in the absence of the owner. Ueckermann (1956) explained the peeling of bark from saplings by the European red deer (*Cervus elaphus*) as a means of securing food and not as a territorial "sign post." Again, more data are needed for proper interpretation of this behavior.

COMMUNICATION

Communication behavior in animals is usually defined as those actions of an individual that influence another individual. Such communicative behavior usually falls into one of the following categories: acoustic, visual, olfactory, or tactile signals. In general, the mammals that live in social groups have the more highly developed set of communication signals.

Acoustic Signals. Mammals vary greatly in their abilities to make and utilize acoustic signals. As far as vocal signals proper are concerned, mammals appear to range from near-mutes that rarely make vocal sounds to men, who are capable of using highly complex languages.

Darling (1937), in his famous study of the Scottish red deer (*Cervus elaphus*), has discussed the age, sexual, and seasonal variations in voice. The young have one set of calls, the adult females a second, and the adult males a third. Some of these serve as alarms to alert the herd, others appear to be directed only toward the young.

King (1955) recognized a "vocabulary" of 10 different calls in the prairie dog, ranging from a commonly used warning bark to a chuckle, a fear scream, and a fighting snarl. Each call is the result of a specific stimulus, and results in a characteristic action from other individuals. Carpenter (1935) reported a vocabulary of fifteen to twenty calls in the howling monkeys of Panama.

The moose in Ontario, Canada, call throughout the year, and De Vos (1958) recognized three distinct calls: an alarm call used by both sexes, a whine used by the calves and yearlings to attract their mother, and a short grunt used by the females to attract their young.

Mammals utilize a number of acoustic signals other than vocal signals. Probably one of the best known is the slapping of the tail on the water in the case of the beaver. This danger signal, which can be heard at distances up to a half-mile on a quiet night, is extremely effective. Many fossorial rodents, such as the kangaroo rat of the western United States, and jirds and jerboas of the Old World drum on the ground with the hind feet. Tail rattling is used by other rodents including the wood rats (*Neotoma*) and the Old World porcupines (*Hystrix*). A number of mammals including the prairie dog utilize tooth chattering as a means of acoustic communication, often when two individuals are in dispute.

Visual Signals. A number of visual signals are utilized by mammals, including stance, facial expression, and position of tail, ears or other body parts. The use of white tail patches, exposed when the tail is elevated, is well known in the rabbits and hares, in various deer, and in the pronghorn (*Antilocapra americana*). Schenkel (1947) has made an intensive study of expression in wolves, wherein he illustrates the meaning of various facial expressions and tail positions.

Olfactory Signals. The detection of olfactory signals in a natural population of mammals is usually difficult. The scent glands used are almost invariably some type of cutaneous gland. Depending upon their location, they are known as pedal (on the foot as in the muntjac), preorbital (in the bushbuck), inguinal, gular (in the mastiff bat, *Eumops*), preputial, or anal (especially in the carnivores).

Some of these glands are obviously correlated with sexual behavior, while others appear to be used primarily in territorial defense. A few are obviously defense mechanisms.

King (1955) found that in the prairie dog anal scent glands emit a strong, musky odor, especially when the individual is fighting or irritated. The sense of smell is most conspicuously employed during territorial-defense behavior. In territorial disputes, both mammals alternate in smelling the scent glands of the other.

Tactile Signals. King (1955) found that in the prairie dog tactile stimulation plays an important role in recognition of individuals, group cohesion, sexual behavior, play, and fighting. The most frequently used of the tactile signals was an identification kiss, used to identify individuals of a coterie (a closed social group within the prairie dog town).

SOCIAL HIERARCHY

The presence of a hierarchy among social mammals has long been recognized. The details of this hierarchy, however, have not been worked out in most species. Two aspects of this phenomenon are discussed here: leadership behavior and dominance-subordination behavior.

Leadership Behavior. The presence of leadership behavior is readily evident in many of the gregarious ungulates. In the red deer (*Cervus elaphus*) studied by Darling (1937) the organization is a matriarchy, with the hind (female) being the leader of the herd. Here the female is throughout the year the leader of a herd of adult females and of young of both sexes. During the breeding season males join the herds and fight among themselves as they attempt to establish harems of females which they dominate. As soon as danger appears, however, the females again come together under the leadership of the dominant female. Similar social organizations are found among many other Cervidae and some of the Bovidae.

Dominance-Subordination Behavior. "Peck-order" behavior, in which social rank is dependent upon the number of "pecks" given or received, is well known in flocks of hens. Similar behavior has recently been found to occur in social mammals. Katz (1949), for example, has studied the social behavior in a herd of twelve Barbary sheep living in a fenced-in plot of about two acres, in the Bronx Zoo in New York. In this herd of four males, four females, and four young, he found a straight-line dominance from the top of-the-list male, through the males, through the females, and thence through the young to the most subordinate individual of the herd.

ORIENTATION AND HOMING ABILITY

This is another area of mammalogy wherein much still remains to be done. In fact, so little has been done that only preliminary conclusions can be reached at this time and additional findings may show these conclusions to be wrong.

It is usually assumed that, at least in diurnal terrestrial mammals, visual landmarks are utilized when an animal moves around in its normal home range. For nocturnal forms, it is generally assumed that visual cues are supplemented by tactile and olfactory cues. In fossorial forms with reduced or degenerated eyes, it is generally assumed that orientation cues are primarily tactile and olfactory in nature. In recent years it has been shown that the European mole (*Talpa europea*) can orient itself, without the aid of either olfactory or tactile landmarks, as to the relations between its burrow and its hunting territory (Krizat and Godet, 1952). Eloff (1951) has reported on the sense of direction in the blind fossorial rodents of South Africa, the mole-rats (*Bathyergus maritimu* and *Cryptomys hottentotus*).

The ability of bats to move about in the total darkness of caves, as well as their ability to capture small insects at night, remained a complete mystery until relatively recently. Many earlier writers supposed that bats had some mysterious "sixth sense" which enabled them to avoid obstacles. Persons unfamiliar with the details of the sonar mechanism utilized by bats will find Donald Griffin's recent book, *Listening in the Dark*, a fascinating review of the subject. In oversimplified terms, a bat emits a supersonic vocal call and, by listening to the echo of this call, determines his orientation in the environment. This system is so sensitive that a bat can (while in flight) detect, locate, and capture insects as small as the fruit fly (*Drosophila*). The various kinds of bats show considerable variation in the details of the sonar mechanism, with some actually using FM (frequency modulation).

The tendency for an animal to return to the point of original capture (presumed to be the home) after being released at a distance has been known for some years. Such action is usually termed homing and often has been reported as resulting from a "homing instinct." This activity has been investigated in considerable detail in birds, especially in homing pigeons.

When one examines the mass of data available from hundreds of homing experiments accidentally or deliberately conducted with mammals, three interpretations appear possible: (1) a confusion of individuals occurred, in which case the experiment was not valid; (2) the individuals were actually released in their normal home range, thereby invalidating the experiment; or (3) the individuals were released beyond their home range and a valid homing experiment was actually performed.

The first possibility, a confusion of individuals, may well explain many of the tales about cats and dogs that have returned from excessive distances. This is illustrated by the following case. A family moved from Tucson, Arizona, to Los Angeles, California (airline distance of approximately 500 miles) taking their pet collie dog with them. Within a few days the dog disappeared from their new home in Los Angeles. A week later a collie, thought to be the same dog, appeared at their old home in Tucson. The owner of the dog made a trip from Los Angeles to Tucson, only to discover it was not the same dog.

The second possibility, releasing within the normal home range, certainly has occurred in many so-called homing experiments. Unfortunately, in many cases, the size of the home range of the experimental animal has not been known. However, the release of bats just outside the entrance to the cave where they were taken does not constitute a homing experiment. Many cases of this type can be cited from the literature. Blair (1953: 25) listed several "homing experiments" which apparently fall into this category. The list includes the experiment published by Stickel (1949) concerning homing in the deer mouse (*Peromyscus leucopus*) that Bourlière (1954) recounted in his book, *The Natural History of Mammals*.

With respect to the third possibility, releasing outside the normal home range, several explanations are logically possible: (a) Individuals return home as a result of an innate instinct or "homing sense"; (b) the individual is familiar with a larger area than his normal home range and was released within the familiar area; (c) the individual, in being transported to the unknown area, obtained orientation information enabling it to follow a return route to its home; (d) by random dispersal from a release point, individuals, by chance, return to familiar territory and home; (e) individuals by habitat selection (food, cover, terrain, elevation, vegetation, etc.) restrict the area of random dispersal and, by chance, return to familiar territory and home; (f) individuals follow a search pattern in attempting to return home, thus increasing the chances of homing.

Just which of these explanations is applicable to homing in mammals is unclear but, as will be seen in the following discussion, it appears obvious that not all species react in the same way.

No clear-cut case can be presented for a "homing instinct" which guides the individual home. Most cases which appeal to a "homing instinct" could probably be explained in other terms if the facts of the case were better known. In several cases the return to the home site may have been the result of the individual being familiar with an area larger than his normal home range. This is a major problem in interpreting the results of homing experiments made with migratory mammals such as some bats.

Some cases of homing appear to have been the result of the individual obtaining orientation information as he was being taken from the home area, and this information furnished the cues which made the return trip possible. It is well known that dogs and horses can return from unfamiliar territory (at least from distances of a few miles) if they can see where they are going. A pertinent experiment was performed by Grzimek (1943) with horses. He took five blindfolded mares (on foot or in vehicles) for distances varying from 3 to 10 miles from their home into unfamiliar territory. None of these were able to return home. That visual cues are not totally responsible for homing behavior is well illustrated by a recent experiment with bats conducted by Mueller and Emlen (1957). They released 25 blindfolded bats at a distance of 25 miles from the point of capture and 18 of these returned the same night, 10 with the blindfolds still intact.

In the carnivores of the family Canidae, dogs have returned home from distances as great as 20 miles, presumably by means of visual landmarks (Bourlière, 1954); and the kit fox (*Vulpes macrotis*) was found to have homed from a distance of 20 miles in Utah (Egoscus, 1956).

Keith and Waring (1956) released a total of 54 marked snowshoe hares (*Lepus americanus*) at varying distances up to 12 miles from the place of capture and 12 were later retaken, 9 within their original home ranges. The 3 that had not returned "came originally from areas separated from the release point by sections of a large lake, and thus were denied a direct route of return." Fitch (1947) reported returns of 3 cottontail rabbits (*Sylvilagus auduboni*) from distances of 3150 to 4400 feet, but 20 others that were moved about 0.75 mile did not return. It is probable that when these rabbits were moved beyond familiar territory, they did not return.

Among sciurids, homing has been reported in the eastern chipmunk, *Tamias striatus* (Layne, 1957; 7 of 18 from 430 to 1200 feet, average 650 feet).

SEASONAL ACTIVITIES

Many of the activities of mammals are influenced by the season of the year, some of which have already been discussed (e.g., breeding, molting, size of home range). The following three types of activities, hibernation, aestivation, and migration, are classically seasonal in occurrence but, as we shall see, are not always so.

HIBERNATION

Classically, birds and mammals have been considered to be warm-blooded, or homoiothermic, while the lower vertebrates and the invertebrates have been considered to be cold-blooded, or poikilothermic. In warm-blooded animals the body temperature is held at a constant temperature, while in cold-blooded animals the body temperature adjusts passively to the surrounding temperature. More recently, however, animals have been divided into three groups, based upon their relationships to the temperature of their surroundings (see Cowles, 1940). These three groups are: (1) Ectothermal (poikilothermal) animals adjust passively to the surrounding temperature; this group includes all "cold-blooded" animals. (2) Endothermal (homoiothermal) animals are those which regulate and maintain an almost uniform body temperature by various methods. Most birds and mammals are in this group of "warm-blooded" animals. (3) Heterothermal animals do not completely control the body temperature. Newly hatched birds, many newly born mammals, the monotremes (the duck-billed platypus and the echidna), the sloth and other edentates, many bats, and others are members of this group. All animals that have true hibernation are placed in this group.

The two major sources of heat in an animal's body are the products of metabolism and the absorption of heat. The losses of heat by an animal are mainly through radiation, conduction and convection, vaporization of water, and circulation of heat from internal areas to external surfaces.

For a given species of animal, there are three cardinal temperatures: the minimum, the optimum, and the maximum. The optimum temperature is usually nearer the maximum than the minimum temperature. The lethal high temperature for animal life is usually between 40° C. and 50° C. (104°–122° F.). This lethal high temperature kills by multiple causes, including enzyme inactivation, enzyme destruction, and irreversible protein coagulation. In addition, the cell membrane becomes more permeable, toxins are liberated, and haemoglobin loses most of its affinity for oxygen at high temperatures.

In ectothermic animals, the factors favoring the loss of heat are almost equal to the factors generating heat. Thus the minimum temperature for ectothermic animals is determined by the freezing temperature of protoplasm (a few degrees below 0° C.). The minimum temperature is associated with the water balance of the animal. Usually 70 to 90 percent of the protoplasm of an animal cell is water. A high percentage of this water is not free but is chemically bound to various organic components of the cell. This bound water resists freezing. Thus a partially dehydrated animal can better withstand freezing.

In all probability, freezing kills an animal by the formation of ice crystals in the protoplasm which, in turn, mechanically damages the cell structure and the cell membrane. Three types of evidence support this view. (1) If cooling is fast, then no ice crystals are formed. Then, if the animal is warmed rapidly, it survives. For example, vinegar "eels" reduced to minus 1.7° C. in liquid air, then warmed in hot water, survive; but if cooled slowly or warmed slowly, ice crystals form in the protoplasm and death results. (2) Many insects freeze during the winter months, yet survive. It is improbable that crystals form, but there is no evidence for this. (3) When freezing occurs slowly, dehydration occurs and many invertebrates encyst, thus avoiding freezing by reduction of the water content of the protoplasm.

Many ectothermic animals that live in areas with cold seasons avoid freezing by burrowing into the ground or under leaf mold, fallen trees, etc., thus escaping freezing temperatures. Aquatic animals, as long as they remain in water, do not freeze (but will freeze if in ice!).

Many heterothermic mammals also avoid freezing temperatures by retreating into a burrow or a cave. There the cold parts of the year are spent in hibernation. Hibernation is an inactive state involving (1) a lowering of all metabolic activities, and (2) a lessening of ability to regulate body temperature. Some idea of this can be obtained by comparing the usual conditions in the human with those that would probably exist if man hibernated. The normal rate of heart beat is 72 times per minute, but in hibernation it would beat 2 or 3 times per minute. The normal body temperature is 98.6° F.; in hibernation it would be 40° F. The normal respiratory rate is 12 to 14 per minute; in hibernation it would be only 1 every 4 minutes. Some indication of the variation in metabolic rates is given in Table 4–2.

CHARACTERISTICS OF HIBERNATION

The following characteristics of hibernating mammals serve to illustrate the great physiological differences between them and active mammals.

Body Temperature. The body temperature of a hibernating mammal approaches that of the surroundings, often within 1° C.

TABLE 4-2

Metabolic Rates of Various Mammals in Hibernation

Mammal	Temperature Air °C	Temperature Rectal °C	Heart Rate[1]	Respiration Rate[2]	Oxygen Consumption[3]	CO_2 Production[3]	R.Q.[6]
Order Marsupialia							
Family Didelphidae							
Opossum (*Didelphis marsupialis*)[5]	2–8	33					
Order Insectivora							
Family Erinaceidae							
Hedgehog (*Erinaceus europaeus*)	2–3	6.2–7.7	18–24		0.013–0.033		
	3.5	5			0.88	0.83	0.68
	6				0.40	0.29	0.73
	9.7	12.0			0.126	0.056	
Family Rhinolophidae							
Greater horseshoe bat (*Rhinolophus ferrumequinum*)	13	13			0.150	0.089	
	19	19			0.425	0.366	0.77
Lesser horseshoe bat (*R. hipposideros*) .	15	15			2.23	1.80	0.80
Family Vespertilionidae							
Little brown bat (*Myotis lucifugus*) ...	23	23.2		72–89	0.45		
	0.5				0.113		
					0.022–0.039		
Keen's bat (*Myotis keenii*)	21.5	2	7–10		0.85	0.009	0.65
Mouse-eared bat (*Myotis myotis*)	1.7	22.7		140–168	0.020	0.033	0.71
	2.5	–			0.051	0.175	0.72
Pipistrelle (*Pipistrellus pipistrellus*) ...	–	–			0.247	0.038	
	5	5			0.053		
	–	–					
Noctule (*Nyctalus noctula*)	4.3				0.51	0.38	0.75
	12.5				3.49	2.58	0.74
As awakening from hibernation ...	20				0.403	0.314	0.78
	30				0.682	0.484	0.71

Species							
Big brown bat (*Eptesicus fuscus*)	8 22–26	9		3–10	0.8		
Parti-colored bat (*Vespertilio murinus*)	7.05	7.05	50–55		0.037		
Long-eared bat (*Plecotus auritus*)	8 0 5 10	6.5 10.7			0.020 0.037 0.069 0.094	0.049 0.079	0.71 0.84
Order Rodentia **Family Sciuridae** European marmot (*Marmota marmota*)	10	10.5 4–7 8	4–5	0.35	0.018 0.008–0.034	0.012	0.68
Woodchuck (*Marmota monax*)	8	6 7.2 11.7 15.5	5	6	0.320 0.015	0.230	0.72
Suslik (*Citellus citellus*)	7 11 13				0.034		
Thirteen-lined ground squirrel (*Citellus tridecemlineatus*)	4.0 8.6 12.5	3–10[4] 5.7 10.2 13.6	5–20	1 1.6 1.8	0.081–0.191 0.081 0.125 0.197		
Arctic ground squirrel (*C. undulatus*)..	5.9	5.2 5.9	68	10 6			
Family Cricetidae Golden hamster (*Mesocricetus auratus*)	5 5.5 5.8 5	5–6 5.5[4] 6.4[4] 5	4–15		0.183 0.032 0.06 0.060–0.080	0.132	0.72
Family Gliridae Fat dormouse (*Myoxus glis*)	6 11.8				0.029 0.024	0.021	0.72
Common dormouse (*Muscardinus avellanarius*)	6 10.1 11.6	10–12	9–10		0.80	0.57	0.71

TABLE 4–2 (Continued)

Metabolic Rates of Various Mammals in Hibernation

Mammal	Temperature		Heart Rate [1]	Respiration Rate [2]	Oxygen Consumption [3]	CO_2 Production [3]	R.Q. [6]
	Air °C	Rectal °C					
Order Carnivora							
Family Ursidae							
Black bear (*Ursus americanus*) [5]	−3.5	31.2		2–3			
	4.4	35.5					
Family Procyonidae							
Raccoon (*Procyon lotor*) [5]							
Family Mustelidae							
Badger (*Taxidea taxidea*) [5]							
Skunk (*Mephitis mephitis*) [5]							

SOURCE: Prosser, 1956.

[1] Heart rates in beats per minute.

[2] Respiration rates are given in respirations per minute. However, respiration rates are highly irregular in hibernation. There may be several minutes with no respiration followed by several respirations, all within a single minute.

[3] In milliliters per gram of body weight per hour.

[4] Oral temperature.

[5] These mammals exhibit a "winter sleep" but do not show the typical reductions of metabolic rates characteristic of true hibernation. They respond to external stimuli immediately and show little or no drop in body temperature.

[6] Respiratory quotient.

It has been reported that normally, if the temperature of the surroundings approaches freezing, the hibernating mammal usually awakens, thus avoiding freezing. Svihla (1958), however, reported that the Arctic ground squirrel, *Citellus undulatus*, at Fairbanks, Alaska, was recorded with a cheek pouch temperature below freezing, and awakening did not occur. Mammals that hibernate usually have a lower body temperature, even when not hibernating, than do other mammals.

Respiration. The rate of respiration varies greatly in non-hibernating mammals. In the ground squirrel, where the average is 187 inspirations per minute in active individuals, rates in excess of 200 per minute have been recorded. In hibernation, the rate is greatly reduced, being ½ to 4 per minute in the hibernating thirteen-lined ground squirrel, *Citellus tridecemlineatus*. Inspirations in the hibernating woodchuck, *Marmota monax*, may occur as infrequently as once each 4 to 6 minutes. A hibernating big brown bat, *Eptesicus fuscus*, has periods of 3 to 8 minutes without evident respiration, followed by periods of 3 minutes or less with respiration at the rate of 25 to 50 per minute. Upon being aroused, this bat has a respiration rate of 200 per minute (Evans, 1938).

Circulation. Slow circulation is characteristic of hibernating mammals. In the thirteen-lined ground squirrel, the heart normally beats at the rate of 225 times per minute. The rate is as high as 400 beats per minute in frightened individuals. In hibernations the rate averages 17 beats per minute and may be as low as 5. Not only does the rate of the heart beat slow down, but there is also a decrease in the volume of blood in the blood vessels. A limb can be amputated from an animal that has been hibernating for some time and almost no bleeding results. In addition, the spleen is greatly enlarged with stored red blood corpuscles (Johnson, 1931).

Irritability. Animals in hibernation respond very slowly to external stimuli. At temperatures intermediate between those of hibernation and those of normal activity, the animals usually move in a dazed manner and, at hibernating temperatures, stimuli result in almost no movement. Such is not true in the case of the bears, raccoons, skunks, badgers, and opossums, where the touch of a hand or the sound of a voice results in immediate reactions of the usual type.

CAUSES OF HIBERNATION

Rasmussen (1916) and Johnson (1931) summarized most of the available information concerning hibernation, and neither they nor any recent worker has arrived at any single, clear-cut statement as to the cause of hibernation. The following factors have been proposed as causes of hibernation, and most are probably at least contributory.

Temperature. Many workers have considered low temperature as a cause of hibernation. Certainly cold weather is contributory, but a sudden severe cold wave may kill the animal before it even enters hibernation. Mammals show much variation in time of hibernation, as related to temperature. The eastern woodchuck, *Marmota monax,* and adult western jumping mice, *Zapus princeps,* often hibernate before the first killing frost. Chipmunks, certain bats, and certain carnivores such as skunks and bears, remain active for a much longer period of time. In fact, it is questionable whether the "winter sleep" of bears, skunks, raccoons, badgers, and opossums are properly termed hibernation. These mammals, although they become dormant for several weeks at a time during the coldest part of the year, usually arouse immediately upon being stimulated. Apparently there is no significant lowering of the metabolic rate during the "winter sleep."

Food. Scarcity or lack of proper foods and perhaps the moisture content of available food at least influence the beginning of hibernation in many kinds of mammals. The lack of food is obvious in the case of the insectivorous bats, for insects are rarely encountered during cold weather. As a result, bats must migrate to a warmer area, hibernate, or starve during the cold season. The case is not so clear, however, with certain herbivorous mammals, such as certain of the ground squirrels, *Citellus,* and the marmots, *Marmota,* for vegetation of some type is available in most habitats throughout the year. Further investigations show some pertinent differences between the diet of these mammals and other herbivores.

Mammals can be divided into two major groups on the basis of their food habits. The first group consists of those which feed on a given type of food throughout the year, and that type of food is available throughout the year. No mammals in this group hibernate. The second group contains those which feed on a given type of food during the spring, summer, and early fall, and this type of food is not available during other seasons. Bats, for example, feed on flying insects and ground squirrels and marmots feed on green vegetation, neither of which is available during the cold season. All hibernating mammals and others fall into this second group.

In the little pocket mouse, *Perognathus longimembris,* Bartholomew and Cade (1947) found a relation between the presence or absence of food, the temperature, and entering hibernation. When no food was available to captive pocket mice, the body temperature dropped almost to the ambient temperature, even when the animal was in a warm environment. When food was available and the air temperature was low (0° to 9° C.), some would enter hibernation while some remained active. As soon as no food was available, all entered hibernation at these temperatures. Lyman (1954: 545) found a great difference between the reactions of the thirteen-lined ground squirrel and the golden hamster, *Mesocricetus auratus,* to temperature and food differences. If obese thirteen-lined ground squirrels were placed in the cold, with or without food and water, they entered hibernation within 24 hours. Golden hamsters, when placed in a cold environment, increased their intake of food and water (but showed no increase in exercise), and began to store food. A denial of the ability to hoard food caused a delay in the onset of hibernation.

Obesity. The storage of a large amount of fat is necessary for successful hibernation. In general, old, fat individuals enter hibernation earlier than do young individuals; also, males hibernate before females (the females had to raise the young before fat could be accumulated). Individuals in the lowlands enter hibernation before members of the same species living at high elevations, perhaps because they have had more time to acquire a layer of fat.

One-third of the weight of bats just before entering hibernation in fall may be fatty tissues, while one-seventh of the weight of a woodchuck may be fat.

Confined Air. An increase in the amount of carbon dioxide in the air of the den was an early explanation given for hibernation. Proponents of this viewpoint contended that the increased carbon dioxide caused autonarcosis. Later studies have indicated that this is not causative, yet it may hasten hibernation. In one experiment ground squirrels placed in half-gallon cans with only four small nail holes for ventilation entered hibernation before ground squirrels placed in well-ventilated cans (Johnson, 1930).

AESTIVATION

Aestivation, or summer sleep, occurs in a great many different kinds of mammals. In general, aestivation occurs during periods of great environmental stresses, such as extreme heat, drought, or lack of food. In many forms, aestivation consists of merely long periods of little or no activity, with no decrease in the metabolic rate below the normal resting rate. In heterothermic mammals, the body temperature approaches the ambient temperatures, and aestivation appears to be the same physiological mechanism that is operative during hibernation. However, since ambient temperatures are not so low during the summer as they are during the winter months, the metabolic rate is not so reduced as it is during hibernation.

Many bats lack thermoregulation, thus resting temperatures and metabolic rates are dependent upon ambient temperatures. Nevertheless, when active, they can maintain body temperatures of 40° C. or above. Hock (1951), in a study of the metabolic rates and body temperatures of bats, concluded that the normal lowering of the body temperature to near the ambient temperature in inactive bats was not physiologically different from that found in hibernation, except in degree.

MIGRATION

The term *migration,* in its classical definition, implies the periodic departure from and return to a given region by a given individual. Associated with, and often confused with, migration are the phenomena of emigration (one-way movement outward from a given area), immigration (one-way movement into a given area), and nomadism (unpredictable wandering based upon the presence or absence of food and/or water). Based upon the incentives, migration has been divided into three categories (Heape, 1931). (1) *Climatic migration.* These are movements undertaken to secure more suitable conditions for a period of time and are always followed by a return journey. (2) *Alimental migration.* These are movements undertaken in search of food when food supplies temporarily fail in the home area and are always followed by a return journey. (3) *Gametic migration.* These are movements undertaken for the production or feeding of young. Such movements, thought by Heape to be largely governed by a factor in the reproductive system, serve for the preservation of the species. Climatic and alimental migrations, in contrast, serve for the preservation of the individual. Actually, gametic migrations are concerned with only one-half of the trip. The return to the original area may well be due to climatic or alimental causes.

Migrations, however, can also be classified as to the time involved and the nature of the movements. Most usages of the term *migration* fall into one of the following categories:

Megatemporal Migrations. Paleontologists and biogeographers use the term *migrations* to apply to the movements of certain groups or species of animals from one continent to another, or from one area to another. The term is applied to the species, the animal group, the animal community, or even to the total biotic community. Such movements, often only in one direction (emigration or immigration), involve long periods of time, often thousands or even millions of years. When classified on the basis of the causative agent, these migrations may have been climatic or alimental in nature but probably resulted from a combination of the two factors.

The term *migration* has also been used to describe movements such as the expansion of range of the armadillo (Fitch, Goodrum, and Newman, 1952). Such movements are probably best classified as emigrations (or immigrations, depending upon the point of view).

Seasonal Migrations. In this classification fall most of the classical examples. Less is known about seasonal migrations of mammals than is known about those of the birds. Seasonal migration of mammals fall into three categories: (1) latitudinal migrations, (2) altitudinal migrations, and (3) local migrations.

1. *Latitudinal migrations, or north-south movements.* Numerous examples of this type of migration are to be found among mammals (Fig. 4-3). Bats of the temperate zone of North America can be divided into two groups according to the places where they spend the day. One group, the tree bats, spend the day hanging among the leaves of plants. The other group, the cave bats, usually spend the day in a cave, rock crevice, attic of a building, a hollow tree, or some similar place. The tree bats, *Lasiurus* and perhaps *Lasionycteris,* are presumed to undergo latitudinal migrations. Allen (1939) has summarized the evidence for this view. It has long been assumed that the cave bats did not show extensive latitudinal migrations. However, recent studies indicate that some species, at least, do undergo latitudinal migrations (Bourlière, 1954).

Latitudinal migrations have been demonstrated in several whales and seals. The northern fur seals, *Callorhinus ursinus,* for example, migrate from the Pribilof Islands during October, November, and December (some stay the year around) to distances as great as 3000 miles to the south. The adult females and the young of both sexes travel the greatest distances; the adult males usually stay in northern waters (Kenyon and Wilke, 1953).

In the Far North the caribou (Banfield, 1951) spends the summer months on the barrens, moving to the tree line (usually to the south) where the winter is spent. Hamilton (1939) and Bourlière (1954) give some of the details of these migrations and furnish additional basic references.

2. *Altitudinal migrations.* Several kinds of mammals move down mountain sides to valleys and other relatively snow-free areas to

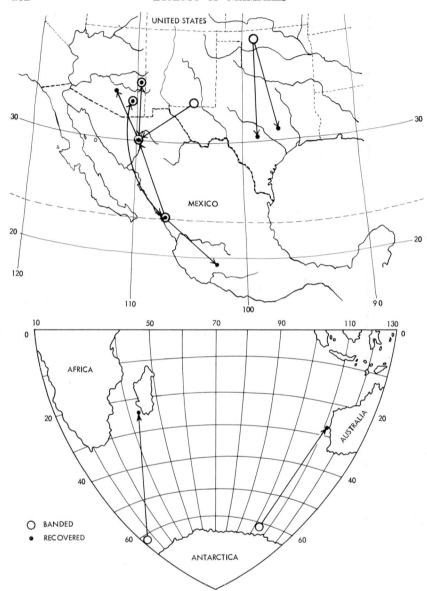

Fig. 4–3. Migration routes in mammals. The upper figure shows some of the seasonal movements recorded for the Brazilian free-tailed bat (*Tadarida brasiliensis*) in southwestern North America (based on data from Glass, 1958, and Villa and Cockrum, 1962). The lower figure illustrates seasonal movements of the humpbacked whale in the southern Pacific Ocean (based on data from Rayner, 1940).

spend the winter months. Such migrations vary in length from 10 to 60 or 70 miles. Edwards and Rotcey (1955) reported that a moose herd in British Columbia moved from a summer range in the mountains at elevations between 5000 and 7000 feet to a lowland winter range, at elevations of 2500 to 4000 feet; they sometimes move a distance of 40 miles to accomplish this change of habitat. Additional cases af altitudinal migration have been reported for elk (Murie, 1951), mule deer (Einarsen, 1956; Russell, 1932), and bighorn sheep (Hamilton, 1939).

3. *Local migrations.* Certain mammals show seasonal migrations that do not clearly fall into either of the two previous categories. Such movements usually involve changes in habitat associated with seasonal differences in habitats. Examples of this type of migration include the movements of Norway rats and house mice and the movements of many bats. In the case of the Norway rats and house mice, many individuals leave the protection of buildings during the spring and summer and move out into the surrounding fields and gardens. In the fall, as cold weather returns, the rats and mice again seek the shelter of buildings. In the case of many cave bats of temperate areas, the winter months are spent in hibernation in suitable caves. In the spring these bats move out to summer colonies, often at considerable distances from the winter hibernals.

The Pacific white-sided dolphins, *Lagenorhynchus obliquidens*, spend the winter and spring months near shore feeding on anchovy. During the summer and fall, however, the dolphins move to offshore waters where they feed on saury (Brown and Norris, 1956).

Diurnal Movements. Movements from an area where periods of rest are accomplished to an area where feeding activities are carried on fall into the classification of daily, or diurnal, migrations. Several good examples of this are to be seen among the invertebrates and birds. Perhaps the activities of certain mammals, especially bats, may fall into this classification when their habits are better understood.

Irruptive Migrations. Movements which occur at no regular intervals are usually the result of failures in food or water supplies and can be properly classified as irruptive migrations. Such migrations are always followed by a return trip when conditions have improved. Few examples among mammals are available. Usually the factors influencing food and water supplies are seasonal, and the resulting movements are classified as seasonal migrations. The so-called "irruptive migrations" of lemmings are actually emigrations, since the individuals never return.

EMIGRATION AND IMMIGRATION

Emigration and immigration are the same phenomenon, and the term used depends upon the viewpoint of the one making the report. Emigration is a one-way movement outward *from* a given area, while immigration is a one-way movement *into* a given area. Lampio (1957) reported on the "migration" of the European red squirrel, *Sciurus vulgaris*, in Finland. These movements have been going on for ages and are still strong today. These movements are usually, but not always, associated with poor food conditions. The movements, which often involve large populations, are slow, with scattered groups moving about the speed of a man's walking, and are usually in a westward direction, but in some areas the direction of movement is toward the south or east. Most of the moving individuals are lost and no clear explanation is yet available as to the cause of the movements.

BURROWING BEHAVIOR

The fossorial habitat has been successfully occupied by both herbivores and insectivores and, to some extent, by carnivores. Some of these mammals are so modified for their subterranean life that they never turn around in their burrow. Fossorial mammals that back up, rather than turn around, in their burrows have short, reversible pelage or are naked. Backing up, as compared with turning around, makes the accomplishment of certain activities such as searching, defense, nest building, and defecation rather complicated. Watson (1961) found that the behavior of the mole rat, even on the surface of the ground, was rather stereotyped and that the animal backed up on the surface for the same activities that it did in that manner in the tunnel.

Fossorial Herbivores. Rodents adapted for a fossorial root-eating habitat occur on all the major continents except Australia. All are remarkably similar in structure and habits, although they belong to several different families; all are about the same size; all dig extensive burrows with characteristic mounds of earth at their entrances; all secure their food and water requirements from the roots of plants; and none venture far, if at all, from their burrows. All of these forms, several of which are listed in Table 4–3, are the result of convergent evolution.

Fossorial Insectivores. A fossorial insect-feeding habitat also has been utilized by highly unrelated mammals that, as a result of convergent evolution, resemble each other greatly. All live primarily in underground tunnels, and all have reduced ears and eyes and a short, tactile tail. These include the marsupial mole (*Notoryctidae*) of Australia, the golden moles (*Chrysochloridae*) of Africa, and the moles (*Talpidae*) of Eurasia and North America.

Fossorial Carnivores. No carnivore is strictly fossorial, although some are semifossorial. Balph (1961) has described an unusual method of predation by the semifossorial badger (*Taxidea taxus*). Normally these badgers secure their prey, often ground squirrel, by excavating the burrows of both active and hibernating individuals.

TABLE 4–3

Ecological Equivalents of Fossorial Herbivorous Rodents in Various Parts of the World

Continent	Area	Animals		
		Genera	Family	Suborder
Eurasia	Mediterranean Region	*Spalax*	Spalacidae	Myomorpha
Eurasia	China	*Myospalax*	Cricetidae (sometimes considered to be a separate family)	Myomorpha
North America	Mainly eastern	*Geomys, Thomomys,* and others	Geomyidae	Sciuromorpha
South America	Peru	*Ctenomys*	Ctenomyidae	Hystricomorpha
Africa	Eastern Africa	*Heterocephalus, Bathyergus,* and *Tachyoryctes*	Rhizomyidae	Myomorpha

During June and July, in the area studied (Utah), ground squirrels relax their normal defense of the territory and, when disturbed, dash into the nearest burrow. During this season badgers were found to dig into a burrow system, construct a tunnel to another opening, and, without disturbing this opening on the surface, remain underground waiting for a ground squirrel to dash into the opening to "safety." Indirect evidence indicated that this technique was successful.

REINGESTION

Reingestion (the taking in of material that has already passed through the digestive tract) is a behavioral trait that may eventually be found to be widespread among mammals. In recent years reingestion has been reported in the shrews (*Sorex,* Crowcroft, 1957), the white-toothed shrews (*Crocidura,* Booth, 1956), many hares and rabbits (summarized by Lechleitner, 1957), the mountain beaver (*Aplodontia,* Ingles, 1961), and various other rodents. The function of reingestion is still unknown. Suggested reasons include cellulose digestion and the conservation of vitamins, proteins, and trace elements.

DEFENSE

A large variety of defense behaviors is evident in mammals. One of the most curious methods of defense involves the habit of rolling into a ball. This behavior occurs in a number of unrelated mammals. Mammals employing this ruse are covered either by a hard tough exoskeleton (such as the dermal plates in the armadillos, Order Edentata, or the epidermal scales of the pangolin, Order Pholidata) or a dorsal pelage of quills or spines (such as in the hedgehogs and porcupines, families Hystricidae and Erethizontidae, respectively). Gupta (1961) has described in detail the osteological and myological modifications that enable the Indian hedgehog (*Paraechinus micropus*) to assume this protective position.

5
Populations

INTRODUCTION

The population of a given species of mammal (or, for that matter, of any living organism) has been expressed as a formula: $P = BP - ER$, where P is the population, BP is the breeding potential and ER is the environmental resistance. The breeding potential of most mammals is much greater than the region they occupy will support. Two examples of the great breeding potential of small rodents will serve to demonstrate this point.

The meadow mouse, *Microtus*, has a gestation period of 21 days and has six to eight young per litter. One female, in captivity, gave birth to 17 litters in one year and a second female gave birth to 13 litters before she was one year old. If we assume that we have an adult pair of meadow mice, that all young produced live, and that the sex ratio of young is one to one, then, using the above figures, we find that in one year, 1,000,000 individuals could result from the original pair.

The barn or Norway rat, *Rattus*, has a gestation period of 21 to 22 days. It has three to six young per litter and an average of ten litters per year. It is mathematically possible for one pair to produce a total of 359,709,482 descendants in three years and, at the end of ten years, a total of 48,319,698,843,030,344,720 descendants if $P = BP$.

Of course such large numbers do not occur in nature because the second portion of the formula is operative—the environmental resistance. Some of the factors included in environmental resistance are restricted food supply, restricted space (including restricted numbers of shelters), adverse climatic conditions (including calamities such as floods), intra- and interspecific competition, predators, parasites, and diseases.

The actual size of most mammalian populations is not known for several reasons. The habits of most mammals are secretive, thus visual counts of numbers cannot be easily made. Further, the habitats of many kinds are inaccessible to persons making the census.

Since it is not usually possible for the census taker physically to "count heads," he must resort to various sampling techniques and formulae in an effort to secure a reliable estimate of the actual population size. As is evident, this procedure is beset by many pitfalls. Finally, even if the exact population size of a given species were known for a given area, this population is subject to rather rapid fluctuations. Because of these difficulties, population density estimates of mammals have been called "educated guesses."

Although the actual size of the population is usually not determinable, it is often desirable to have data concerning the estimate of probable population size and structure. This is especially true for game and fur-bearing mammals where such data are mandatory for logical game management procedures. In such cases estimates of population size based on actual data are much more useful than "guesses."

METHODS OF ESTIMATING POPULATION SIZE

Several different techniques have been used to arrive at some idea of the size of populations of various kinds of mammals. They are divisible into two general categories, direct counts and indirect estimates.

Direct Counts. In a few cases an actual *census*, or count of all individuals present, has been attempted. Actual counts of various big game species have been made from vantage points and from airplanes and helicopters. Aerial photographs have been used as an aid in such censuses. Obviously such counts are most accurate on species that live in open grasslands and in tundra areas. Even here, however, many individuals often escape notice, thus making the census inaccurate to some indeterminable degree. Certain species of bats gather in caves where they hibernate in winter months. Often rather accurate counts can be made of the number of individuals of a given species in a given cave at a given time. Uncertainty as to how many individuals of a given species are hibernating in some unfound crack or crevice in the same cave, and how many are hibernating in some undiscovered hibernal in the general region, plus an almost complete lack of knowledge as to the summer ranges of the individuals counted make such counts of limited usefulness.

Tanaka (1958) has found that *corpse recovery* after a poisoning campaign aimed at control of the brown rat (*Rattus*) is a reliable index to population size. He found that poisoning killed, on an average, 50 percent of the population. Further, this percentage of kill remained constant even though several different types of poison were used.

Indirect Methods. The habits and habitats of most mammals do not permit a direct count over a large area. For some of the species of this type, indirect methods of estimating the total population have been attempted. Four general methods of indirect estimates have been developed. These are the counting of sign, the use of sample areas, removal methods, and capture-recapture methods.

COUNTING OF SIGN

Several techniques have been developed which utilize the counting of sign left by a mammal's activity, either as a basis of estimating total population or for obtaining indices for comparative purposes. The number of beaver dams, gopher mounds, mole runways, pack rat nests, muskrat houses—all of these and others have been used to estimate the population of an area. The number of scats or pellets found in a given area has been the basis of several attempts to estimate total population. Tracks of mammals, in snow, dust, or mud, have been used as indices of population density, as have signs of feeding on vegetation. Obviously all of these counts leave much to be desired, for it is usually impossible to demonstrate a reliable correlation between the frequency of sign and the actual size of the population.

SAMPLE AREAS

The counting of individuals in a given sample area and using this as the basis of estimates for a larger area is a type of indirect estimate that has been used on several diurnal species. The strip census is often used. This method consists of actually counting the number of individuals seen in a given strip through an area (too often along a road), computing the number observed per unit area, and applying this figure to a similar larger area. Many inherent limitations of such a technique are immediately evident. The size, shape, and habitats represented in the sample area may have a considerable influence on the results. Further, the time of day (or year) as well as the visual acuity and experience of the observer are factors that must be considered in interpreting results. Finally, the number of individuals in a place where they can be seen may have little or no correlation with the actual number present in the sample area.

REMOVAL METHOD

The removal method relies on counting individuals actually removed from a population. Data from removal trapping and bag counts are the basis of several techniques of estimating population size. The simplest uses of such data make no pretense of arriving at the actual number of individuals in the population; rather, they merely give figures that can be used to express the relative size of the population on one area in relation to another. Two such methods are trap nights and hunting-hours per kill. One trap set for one night is one trap night. One hundred traps set for one night or one trap set for one hundred nights would both be recorded as 100 trap nights. The number of individuals of a given species captured in a given area in a given number of trap nights can be compared directly with similar data from another area or from another season. Similarly, the average number of hours spent by each hunter for each game mammal in his bag furnishes a figure that can be compared directly with similar data from another area or another season. Obviously such figures may bear little or no relationship to the actual size of population in the area.

In the case of snap traps, Beer and others (1958) found a difference between sexes in susceptibility to traps and found, further, that this difference varied with habitat and species. For example, these workers found that, on small islands in Minnesota, female deer mice (*Peromyscus*) were more susceptible to trapping than were males, while on the mainland the males were more susceptible to trapping.

More complicated formulas have been derived which attempt to relate the number of individuals removed from a population to the actual size of a population. Almost all such methods make two basic assumptions which may or may not be true: (1) The size of the population in the area being sampled remains constant (except for the individuals removed) during the study period, and (2) no one individual is more likely to be removed from the population than any other individual. This second assumption implies that the population is randomly distributed throughout the area for which the population estimate is being made and that the method of removal is strictly random. Intuitively one suspects that these assumptions are not always true. The population size of an area is always subject to fluctuation; birth, death, emigration, and immigration all influence the population of a given area. Further, family groups, colonial behavior, and habitat selection all tend to make the distribution of individuals in even a small area far from random.

Finally, Zippin (1956) has shown on strictly theoretical grounds that even when these two basic assumptions are true, removal methods are not reliable when the sample size does not exceed 200 individuals. With these limitations in mind, let us examine some of the uses that have been made of removal data.

Saturation trapping is one of the sources of removal data. This method involves intensive trapping of a quadrat of a given size (usually one acre in the case of small mammals) for three successive nights and the direct expression of results as individuals per acre

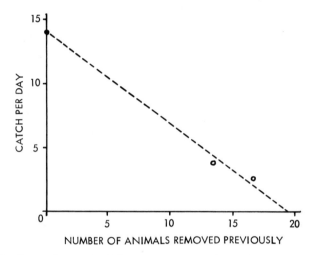

Fig. 5–1. A graphic method for estimating total populations of small mammals. This method, developed by Hayne (1949), is based on the results of three or more consecutive periods of trapping and consists of plotting the catch per day (the vertical axis) against the total number previously removed from the population (the horizontal axis). A straight line is fitted to the points and extended to the horizontal axis. The value at the point of intersection is the estimate of the total population.

(see Bole, 1939; Stickel, 1946). A *graphic method* of estimating total population from the results of three or more consecutive nights of trapping has been developed by Hayne (1949). The method consists of plotting the catch per night on the vertical axis against the total number previously removed from the population on the horizontal axis. A straight line is fitted to the points and extended to the horizontal axis. The value at the point of intersection is the estimate of total population (Fig. 5–1).

Since it has been adequately demonstrated that once an individual has been removed from a population other individuals tend to move into the area left vacant (see Stickel, 1946, 1954). Tamaka (1958) developed a mathematical formula that attempts to compensate for this immigration. Unfortunately, however, this does not adequately compensate for the other variables mentioned above.

Ratios are the basis of several formulas that have been developed to utilize data from bag counts in conjunction with data secured from some other source. The data required, in addition to the bag count, is in the nature of a ratio determined before and after the hunting season. These techniques have been applied primarily to big game, and the ratios used are the male : female ratio and the adult : juvenile ratio. One of these formulas is:

$$P = \frac{f''(K - K^*)}{f'' - f'}$$

where P is the total population before the hunting season, f' is the preseason proportion (of females or of juveniles), f'' is the post-season proportion (of females or juveniles), K is the total number killed, and K^* is the number of females (or juveniles) killed (see Petrides, 1949). This system has two obvious sources of error: (1) It is uncertain that the proportions used are the ratios actually present in the population. Differential habits of age groups and sex groups in a population make this difficult to determine. (2) This method assumes that the kills were made at random over the whole area. This is probably far from the case in most hunts, for hunters tend to remain close to roads or to concentrate in areas where hunting is reported to be "good."

CAPTURE-RECAPTURE METHODS

These methods are based upon the capture, marking, and release of individuals and the subsequent recapture of marked individuals. Assumptions in the utilization of these data are usually (1) the population is uniform during the study period, (2) the sampling and the distribution of the population is random, and (3) marked and unmarked individuals have an equal chance of being caught.

Leslie and Chitty (1951) have shown by mathematical means that the precision of this method is very good when the assumptions are known to be true. However, in nature, these assumptions are rarely true. The population size is rarely uniform for even a short period of time. From the standpoint of the capture-recapture method, the death rate (actual deaths and losses from the area by emigration) is not important, for it is assumed that the death rate is equal for both marked and unmarked individuals. The dilution rate (that is, the number of unmarked individuals entering the area, either by birth or by immigration) does, however, have an important effect on the results. Further, the distribution of a population is seldom random, even in a small area of uniform habitat, and random trapping is hard to achieve, for many kinds of mammals have definite home ranges. Also there may be age, sexual, or seasonal differences in bait acceptance (assuming the samples are secured from baited live traps) and in activity in general. For example, Gentry and Odum (1957) found, while trapping small rodents in Georgia, that weather conditions had a great effect on trapping success, with significantly greater success on cloudy, warm nights than on clear cool nights. In working with a wood mouse (*Apodemus sylvaticus*) population in England, Miller (1958) found that males moved around more between May and September than they did in other parts of the year. Finally, marked and unmarked individuals may not have equal chances of being caught. The marking techniques may be detrimental to the individual; the individual, once marked, may leave the study area as a result of its disturbance; or the marked individual may learn that a live trap is a ready source of food and return time after time.

The *Peterson* or *Lincoln Index* (Lincoln, 1930) is one of the best-known formulae based on capture-recapture data. It is expressed by the ratio: $P : S :: M : R$, where P is the population, S is the size of a given sample, R is the number of recoveries in the sample, and M is the total number of marked individuals that have been released in the area. A simple mathematical manipulation transforms this ratio into a working formula: $P = SM/R$. For example, assume that we wish to determine the size of the population of meadow mice in a given field. First we set a series of live traps at random in the field, marking and releasing the individuals caught. Next we take another sample, again at random, and determine the number of marked individuals recovered. Assume that the number originally marked was 200 (that is, $M = 200$) and that the total number taken in the second sample was 200 (that is, $S = 200$) and included 50 marked individuals ($R = 50$). Using these values in the above formula we have

$$P = \frac{(200) \times (200)}{50} = 800$$

Our estimate of the population, then, would be 800 individuals.

Home range computations, based on the capture-recapture method, have been used to estimate total population. Once the average size of the home range of a mammal has been determined, this information can be used to estimate the number of individuals in a larger area. Of course such factors as age, sexual and seasonal differences in the size of home range, as well as the effect of differences in habitats must be considered when such estimates are made.

POPULATION COMPOSITION

Often it is of little significance merely to know how many animals are in a given region. To understand the biology of the population, information is needed as to the sex ratios, age distribution, and reproductive status of its members. Such data are even harder to secure than are estimates of population size.

It is usually simple to determine the sex of an individual animal if it is in captivity where it can be examined. Newborn and sexually immature individuals of certain species, however, do not have the secondary sexual characteristics at all well developed, and an autopsy is often necessary to confirm the sex of a given individual.

Age, even in cases where the individual can be examined closely, is often impossible to determine. The ages of non-captive individuals, observed only from a distance, are usually impossible to determine. In many species, only two age groups can be readily recognized, adults and immatures. In certain species, however, morphological features can be correlated with age. At least some of the bovids appear to have definite growth rings evident on their horns. In these forms the growth of the horn is retarded or halted during one season of the year, usually a cold or a dry season, resulting in a distinct transverse streak with loosened edges. In general, the horns grow rapidly during the first two or three years and, thereafter, at a much slower rate. Thus the rings are far apart near the tip of the horns and often very close together at its base. Such growth rings have been observed in the chamois, *Rupicapra*, ibex, *Capra*, and bighorn, *Ovis* (Cowan, 1940).

In the cervids the antlers are shed annually, thus they do not show growth rings. Further, although older cervids often have larger antlers with more points, no clear correlation can be made between size of antler or number of points on the antler and age.

Teeth have been the basis of several attempts to determine age in mammals. The sequence of the loss of the milk dentition and the appearance of the permanent dentition is apparently rather constant in some species. By observing this sequence in animals of known age, a criterion can be set up for estimating the age of animals of unknown age. Unfortunately the full permanent dentition is acquired by most mammals by the time they reach adulthood, thus this technique has only limited application in determining the age composition of a given population.

Severinghaus (1949) has worked out a technique of determining the age of deer (*Odocoileus*) based on tooth development and degree of wear of teeth (see Fig. 5–2). Similar techniques have been worked out for the roebuck, moose (*Alces alces*) (Peterson, 1955, and Baumann, 1949); the stag, *Cervus elaphus* (Baumann, 1949); the javelina, *Tayassu angulatus* (Sowls, 1961); the elk, *Cervus canadensis* (Quimby and Gaab, 1957); and the pronghorn, *Antilocapra americana* (Dow, 1952).

For older mammals, in which the permanent teeth are all present, the amount of wear evident on the various teeth has been used as a basis of dividing the adult population into various age groups. That the amount of wear on the teeth is roughly correlated with age is usually accepted. However, just what relation this wear has to actual age is somewhat obscure. Certainly variations in the types of foods available to a given species could result in differences in wear.

A typical example of the problems encountered in attempting to correlate tooth wear with supposed age can be seen in the case of bats of the genus *Myotis*. In the eastern United States these bats are always born in June or early July. On strictly a priori grounds it should be possible to divide a given population sample into groups that would indicate wear of 1, 2, 3, etc., years' duration.

Annual rings of growth have been reported in the teeth of some kinds of mammals. Scheffer (1950) indicates that the rings that occur in the canine teeth of pinnipeds are formed each year and result from a lack of growth during the summer, when the animal usually eats little or nothing while in the harems. Laws (1952) has found such growth rings in the teeth of the elephant seal (*Mirounga leonina*). Christian (1953) has reported that in hibernating bats, such as the big brown bat (*Eptesicus fuscus*), growth rings also occur in the canine teeth. Fisher and Mackenzie (1954) have reported a technique for the rapid preparation of tooth sections for age determinations.

Other morphological features have been used to estimate the age of an individual. Some of these measures include weight, size, and degree of development of some specified organ or bone. Some examples follow. The size, weight, or structure of the baculum has been used to estimate the age of the muskrat, beaver, raccoon, and many mustelids, such as the otter, weasel, and mink (Friley, 1949; Popov, 1943). The structure of the baleen plates has been used to estimate the age of the mysticeti whales (Ruud, 1940, 1945). The weight of the lower jaw has been used to estimate the age in the Levant vole, *Microtus guentheri* (Bodenheimer, 1949). The degree

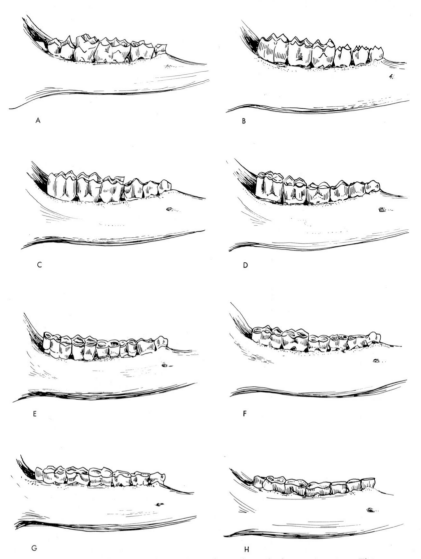

Fig. 5–2. The estimation of age based on dental characteristics. This system was originally worked out by Severinghaus (1949) and has been refined by others. The above drawings are based on a series of mandibles from known-aged white-tailed deer (*Odocoileus virginianus*) in the collection of the Arizona Cooperative Wildlife Research Unit at the University of Arizona. (A) Age, 6 months; the deciduous premolars are still in place and only the first molar has erupted. (B) Age, 18 months; permanent premolars present and all molars erupted. (C) Age, 2½ years; slight wear on the first molar. (D) Age, 3½ years; some wear on both the first and second molars. (E) Age, 4½ years; some wear on all molars. (F) Age, 5½ years; further wear. The degree of flattening of the crowns of the cheek teeth is the basis of (F), (G), and (H). (G) Age, 7–8 years; further wear. (H) Age, 10 or more years; extreme wear, especially on the premolars and first molar.

of ossification of the tail vertebrae has been used as an estimate of age in *Microtus arvalis* (Hagen, 1955). The length of the lower tooth row has been used to estimate the age in still other *Microtus* (Sperber, 1948). The growth of various bones has been used in the cottontail, *Sylvilagus floridanus* (Hale, 1949). Tail pelage characteristics have been used to determine age in the gray squirrel, *Sciurus carolinensis* (Sharp, 1958).

Some of these techniques can only be correlated with age in a very rough way. For example, the baculum merely indicates if the individual is a young of the year, an immature, a young adult, or an adult. Others give a more exact indication of age. In all cases, however, the use of these techniques is restricted to the period of growth and development, which in most species ceases when adulthood is reached. Further, all have inherent restrictions in that two individuals of the same species rarely develop at exactly the same rate, for the rate of development is influenced by many factors, including the amount and types of food available, environmental conditions, diseases and parasites, and genetic makeup. Finally the known-age animals used as standards in these techniques are usually animals that have been raised in captivity. Captivity, in itself, may have a great influence on the rate of development of an animal.

SEXUAL COMPOSITION

For wild animals, little is known concerning the sex ratios at birth and in the adult population. It has been generally assumed that the sex ratio of a given population is one male to one female. The available studies indicate that this assumption may not be true in many species. Unfortunately, many of the studies that have been made probably do not reflect the actual sex ratios, since the probability of capture is usually not the same for the two sexes. Beer *et al.* (1958), for example, found that on small islands female deer mice (*Peromyscus maniculatus*) were more susceptible to capture than were males, while on the mainland the males were more susceptible to capture. These authors also supposed that males on the mainland were more vulnerable to predation and to accidents than were the females. They found the highest percentage of males in the population in late summer and early fall; the lowest percentages were found in the spring months.

In many kinds of mammals there appear to be more males than females at birth; yet in many of these same species, the females are more abundant later in life (Table 5–1). Robinette *et al.* (1957) have collected all of the data available to them concerning the differential mortality by age and sex among mule deer (*Odocoileus*

TABLE 5–1

Sex Ratios of Various Mammals at Different Ages

These ratios are expressed in terms of 100 males to the number of females; the sample size on which the ratio was computed appears in parentheses.

	Embryonic	Birth	Immature	Adult
Order Marsupialia				
Family Didelphidae				
Opossum (*Didelphis marsupialis*)	100:129(48)			100:70(3874)
Order Chiroptera				
Family Vespertilionidae				
Little brown bat (*Myotis lucifugus*) ..		100.98		
Order Primates				
Family Hominidae				
Man (*Homo sapiens*)		100:94.7		
Order Rodentia				
Family Cricetidae				
Muskrat (*Ondatra zibethicus*)		100:72		
Family Muridae				
Rat (*Rattus norvegicus*)	100:95(1044)		100:75(1325)	100:133(3937)
Family Chinchillidae				
Vizcacha (*Lagidium peruanum*)				100:96
Order Carnivora				
Family Procyonidae				
Racoon (*Procyon lotor*)				100:71(277)
Family Mustelidae				
Mink (*Mustela vison*)				100:42(174)
Order Artiodactyla				
Family Cervidae				
Mule deer (*Cdocoileus hemionus*)	100:90(2299)	100:83(808)	100:88(13046)	

SOURCES: Based on data from Dozier and Allen (1942); Errington (1951); Griffin (1940); Pearson (1951); Petrides (1949b, 1950); Robinette *et al.* (1957; Schein (1950).

hemionus). For 2,299 fetuses they found a sex ratio of 111 males to 100 females; at birth 808 young had a sex ratio of 121 : 100; and for 13,046 hunter-killed fawns, 114 : 100. Among older deer the males suffer disproportionately heavier losses.

A similar situation exists in the European red deer (*Cervus elaphus*). Miller (1932) found, in Scotland, 162 males to 109 females among the unborn young; at birth a smaller percentage of males (but still exceeding the females in number); and, as adults, 35.6 percent males as against 64.4 percent females.

Apparently even within the gestation period there is often a variation in the sex ratio. Chapman *et al.* (1938) examined 2,044 fetuses from butchered cows. In young embryos (5–10 cm. in length), 126 of which were examined, 65 percent were males, while in older embryos (81–90 cm.), the sex ratio was at most even.

Various factors have been found to influence the sex ratio of embryonic and young animals. Inadequate nutrition of the adult female apparently causes a decline in the number of surviving male offspring (Bernstein, 1948, in humans; Parkes, 1924, in mice; Robinette, 1957, in mule deer). The age of the mother also has an influence, for a higher percentage of males exists among the first born than in later births (Schoenfeld, 1943, in humans; Robinette, 1957, in mule deer).

AGE COMPOSITION

Few data are available concerning the longevity of wild animals and even less is available concerning the age composition of a given population. Such information, however, is of prime importance in determining the effective breeding population for game management purposes or for understanding population genetics.

Most studies of age composition have been concerned with determining the percentage of young animals in the population. Table 5–2, from Petrides (1951), shows the juvenile : adult ratios for the cottontail rabbit (*Sylvilagus floridanus*) in eastern United States.

In the muskrat (*Ondatra zibethicus*) a total of 14,199 animals were examined during various trapping seasons in the United States. Of these, 10,118 were young animals, or in other words, a ratio of 248 young animals for each adult. Thus it is obvious that the life expectancy of the muskrat is extremely short.

Among most of the smaller rodents, life expectancy is even less. A spectacular indication of this is shown by Bodenheimer's (1949) study of the Levant vole (*Microtus guentheri*) in Palestine. He compiled the age-class distribution of a series of 550 skulls taken from a series of owl pellets and found the distribution shown in Table 5–3.

TABLE 5–2

Age Composition of Various Population Samples of the Cottontail Rabbit (Sylvilagus floridanus)

	Ohio–Live Trapping		Pennsylvania –Hunting 1 Month, Nov., 1947
	21-Month Period	1 Month, Nov., 1947	
Males			
Total	107	17	138
Adults	7	2	14
Juveniles	100	15	124
Young per adult	14.3	7.5	8.9
Females			
Total	85	17	102
Adults	7	3	17
Juveniles	78	14	85
Young per adult	11.1	4.7	5.0
Totals			
samples taken	192	34	240
adults	14	5	31
juveniles	178	29	209
young per adult	12.7	5.8	6.7
young per female	25.4	9.7	12.3

SOURCE: Based on data from Petrides, 1951.

TABLE 5–3

Age Composition of a Population of Levant Voles (Microtus guentheri)
(Based on an analysis of the age of 550 skulls taken from owl pellets.)

Age in Days	Number	Per Cent of Total
25 or less	11	2
26 to 35	52	9
36 to 50	129	23
51 to 70	170	31
71 to 100	98	18
101 to 150	60	11
More than 150	30	6
Total	550	100

SOURCE: After Bodenheimer (1949).

From these figures it is evident that less than 6 percent of the population reached an age of more than 5 months. In a study of the wood mouse population in England, Miller (1958) found that individuals seldom live longer than a year in the field.

One intensive study was made of the age structure of a gray fox
(*Urocyon cinereoargenteus*) population in the southeastern United
States by John Wood (1958). Using a number of age-estimating
techniques (amount of tooth wear, degree of calcification of cranial
sutures, development of the vomer, the weight of the baculum, and
body weight) as cross-checks, he found the following age structure
to exist:

Less than one year old	61.1%
One year old	28.3%
Two years old	7.1%
Three years old	1.8%
Four years or older	1.6%

Adolph Murie (1944) collected all the skulls and skull fragments
of bighorn sheep (*Ovis canadensis*) that he could find in Mt. Mc-
Kinley National Park in Alaska. Of the 829 skulls he found, he was
able, by using rings on the horns and dental characteristics, to determine the age at death of 655 individuals. These had the age distribution shown in Table 5–4.

TABLE 5–4

Age Distribution of a Series of Skulls of Bighorn Sheep (*Ovis canadensis*)
Found in Mount McKinley National Park, Alaska

Age in Years	Number	Per Cent
Lambs	41	6
1	117	18
2	10	2
3	9	1
4	9	1
5	23	4
6	34	5
7	37	6
8	48	7
9	79	12
10	92	14
11	88	14
12	64	10
13	1	Less than .05
14	3	Less than .05
Total	655	100

SOURCE: Murie (1944).

From these figures it is evident that the young and the old
animals are especially vulnerable to diseases and predation, while
animals between 2 and 5 years of age suffer little from these factors.

The series of 32 skulls of male bighorns, all taken in 1889 from Mount Chopaka, Washington, probably represents the largest number of specimens available from any one locality (Table 5–5). Dal-

TABLE 5–5

Age Distribution of a Series of Male Bighorn Sheep (*Ovis canadensis*) Killed in One Season on Mount Chopaka, Washington

Age	Number	Per Cent
3	2	6
4	1	3
5	3	9
6	8	25
7	6	19
8	3	9
9	3	9
10	5	16
11	1	3
Total	32	

SOURCE: Based on Dalquest and Hoffmeister (1948).

quest and Hoffmeister (1948) studied this series in some detail. The ages of these individuals appear to supplement the information found by Murie, when one assumes that young animals were not taken because they lacked large horns.

FACTORS INFLUENCING BIRTH RATE

Birth rates of wild animal populations are affected by a large number of interacting factors; thus, the resultant situation is such that it is usually impossible to isolate controlling factors in a given situation. Some of the influencing factors have been isolated: (1) nutrition, (2) age of female, and (3) environmental factors.

Nutrition. The nutrition of the individual female has an influence on the age of puberty, the frequency of birth during the life of the individual, the number of ova shed at each ovulation, and the number (and sex) of embryos retained to parturition.

Bodenheimer (1949) has demonstrated the effects of various diets on Levant voles (*Microtus guentheri*) in captivity. He kept adult, mated females on a given diet for 100 days and counted the number of young resulting from each female. Females maintained on a standard laboratory mouse diet averaged 73 young; wheat, barley, and carrots, 75 young; wheat and water, 18; carrots alone, 18; wheat, meat, and water, 0; meat alone, 0.

Apparently certain foods contain materials with gonadotropic effects such that fertility can be increased. Alfalfa, corn, and oats have such an effect on rabbits but not on laboratory rats (Friedman, 1934). Bourlière (1954) reported that Mendelsohn found that flax-seed added to the diet of captive Levant voles (*Microtus guentheri*) increased summer fertility. Unpublished experiments by R. A. Loomis and others at the University of Kansas revealed that the cotton rat, *Sigmodon hispidus*, rarely bred in captivity until wheat germ was added to its diet.

In nature, low food supplies often influence the reproductive cycle rather drastically. The musk ox, after a very hard winter, is reported to omit the following breeding season (Peterson, 1956).

The Age of the Female. This factor has a definite bearing on the number of young produced. Using captive field mice (*Microtus agrestis*), Leslie and Ranson (1940) found considerable individual variation in the time of onset of reproductive activity with several females being fertilized as early as 4 weeks of age. Litter size of young females was significantly lower than in females that were 12 to 28 weeks old at the time of fertilization. From 36 weeks of age on, fewer became pregnant and, in those that did, the average litter size was greatly reduced.

Environmental Factors. Various environmental factors also influence birth rates. In the European wild rabbit, it has been fairly clearly demonstrated that control measures stimulate breeding (Bull, 1956).

Heavy population densities also cause a decrease in birth rates. Working with confined colonies of house mice (*Mus musculus*), Crowcroft and Rowe (1957) obtained some interesting results. They started with four confined colonies, each consisting of one male and two females, and, in each colony, a constant excess of food and water. These populations were allowed to grow, undisturbed by human interference, for 18 months. Each population varied in the rate of increase but, at the end of 18 months, the populations were comparable in size. The main factor that controlled population size was the low fecundity of the females. Many of the adult females had inactive ovaries and, in one population, reproduction ceased entirely at the end of 10 months. Curiously enough, the survival rates of both the young and adults were not affected by population size.

In the nutria, Harris (1956) found that in periods of population highs there was an increased resorption rate of embryos, and thus, a lower birth rate.

Kalela (1957) found that population size influenced the age of puberty on voles (*Clethrionomys rufocanus*) in Finland. During a population low (1954) nearly all the young, both males and females, born early in the year were sexually mature by fall; yet the following year (1955), when the population was high, nearly all the males and most of the females were still sexually immature by fall. Population levels of European hares (*Lepus europaeus*) in a given hunting season in southwestern Finland are apparently associated with the amount of snow (and not the temperature) of the preceding season (Siivonen, 1956). Shelford (1954) has related the fecundity and milk production of antelope with the total amount of solar radiation. More work must be done to determine the extent and importance of this factor.

Microhabitat may also influence the birth rate of mammals. A study made in England by Laurie (1946) of the number of litters of house mice produced each year by house mice in various habitats showed considerable variation. Laurie's findings are shown in Table 5–6.

TABLE 5–6

Differences in the Birth Rates and Productivity of House Mice *(Mus musculus)* Associated with Differences in Microhabitat

Microhabitat	Average Number of Litters per Year	Average Number of Young per Litter	Total Average Yearly Offspring
Corn ricks	10.22	5.6	57.2
Flour warehouses	7.97	5.6	46.7
Cold storage plants	6.68	6.37	42.6
Human habitations	5.52	5.6	30.9

SOURCE: Based on Laurie (1946).

POPULATION DENSITIES

The number of individuals per unit area varies not only within the species (population fluctuations) but also between two species (species differences). The population densities of a given species have been classified as follows (Mohr, 1947):

1. Economic density. The trait characteristic of the species, or optimal.
2. Highest density. Unusual concentrations, or maximal.
3. Minimum density. The low point in population fluctuations, or minimal.

The variation of densities of individuals of different species is greatly influenced by the relative sizes of the species being compared. Obviously, all other factors being equal, more mice than deer can live on an acre of ground. To avoid this situation, population densities can be expressed in unit weight per unit area, such as grams per acre instead of individuals per acre. Table 5–7 is adapted from Mohr (1947). Population density is expressed in grams per acre; species are grouped according to food habits.

TABLE 5–7

Population Densities of Mammals Associated with Differences in Food Habits

To make direct comparison between large and small animals possible, densities are expressed in grams per acre.

HERBIVOROUS DIET

Pocket gopher (*Thomomys talpoides*)	Up to 1400
Pocket gopher (*Geomys bursarius*)	Up to 5250
Eastern cottontail (*Sylvilagus floridanus*)	Up to 5600
Ground hog (*Marmota monax*)	Up to 8850
Meadow mouse (*Microtus pennsylvanicus*)	Up to 9600
Ground squirrel (*Citellus tridecemlineatus*)	Up to 9650
Prairie dog (*Cynomys leucurus*)	Up to 28,375
Belding's ground squirrel (*Citellus beldingi*)	Up to 49,895

SPERMIVOROUS DIET

White-footed mouse (*Peromyscus leucopus*)	Up to 165
Deer mouse (*Peromyscus maniculatus*)	Up to 190
Kangaroo rat (*Dipodomys spectabilis*)	Up to 275
Kangaroo rat (*Dipodomys merriami*)	Up to 540
Chipmunk (*Tamias striatus*)	Up to 740
Red squirrel (*Tamiasciurus hudsonicus*)	Up to 2290
Fox squirrel (*Sciurus niger*)	Up to 4070

OMNIVOROUS DIET

Raccoon (*Procyon lotor*)	Up to 980
Opossum (*Didelphis marsupialis*)	Up to 1250
Armadillo (*Dasypus novemcinctus*)	Up to 4355

INSECTIVOROUS DIET

Masked shrew (*Sorex cinereus*)	20–45
Striped skunk (*Mephitis mephitis*)	180–285
Smoky shrew (*Sorex fumeus*)	40–470
Star-nosed mole (*Condylura cristata*)	310–830
Brewer's mole (*Parascalops breweri*)	50–1225

CARNIVOROUS DIET

Bobcat (*Lynx rufus*)	10
Badger (*Taxidea taxus*)	12
Arctic fox (*Alopex lagopus*)	30
Red fox (*Vulpes fulva*)	30
Gray fox (*Urocyon*)	40
Coyote (*Canis latrans*)	Up to 50
Mink (*Mustela vison*)	50
Long-tailed weasel (*Mustela frenata*)	Up to 60

SOURCE: Adapted from Mohr, 1947.

POPULATION FLUCTUATIONS

The number of individuals per unit area is not constant but is subject to variation both in space and in time. These two variants can be termed (1) temporal fluctuations and (2) geographical fluctuations.

TEMPORAL FLUCTUATIONS

As time passes, the population density of a given species in a given area is subject to fluctuation. These are of three main types: (1) seasonal fluctuations, (2) multiannual fluctuations, and (3) irruptions. In addition, geological or megatemporal fluctuations occur, and in the past these occasionally resulted in extinction of species.

Seasonal Fluctuations. Most mammalian populations show a seasonal fluctuation in size. This fluctuation is most marked in species with high breeding potentials and with marked reproductive seasons. Population densities of most small rodents, for instance, are usually several times greater in the fall (just after cessation of the reproductive season) than they are in the spring. This seasonal fluctuation is also recognized in most big game populations. In addition to seasonal fluctuations in population densities, there is usually a marked seasonal fluctuation in adult-juvenile ratios.

Multiannual Fluctuations. In addition to seasonal fluctuations of population densities, many species show marked variations over a period of years. These fluctuations have often been incorrectly referred to as "cycles." Fluctuations are properly termed "cycles" only when the peaks and low points are regularly placed, a situation that rarely exists in biological systems. Multiannual fluctuations are much more marked in northern latitudes or, in mountainous areas, at higher elevations. Such fluctuations are well known in the Old World lemming and in the lemmings, snowshoe rabbits, foxes, and other carnivores in northern North America. An excellent description of the rise and fall in snowshoe rabbit population is given by Soper (1921).

There is no general agreement as to the causes of multiannual fluctuations. Of the many supposed causes that have been proposed, the following are listed to give the student some idea as to their diversity:

Food. The abundance of food causes population build-ups; on the other hand, the exhaustion of food supplies by a large population causes death by starvation to most of the individuals.

Predators, parasites, and diseases. The absence of these factors causes a build-up in population levels; their presence causes crashes and resultant low population intensities.

Sunspots. The presence of sunspots (and the supposed associated meteorological phenomena) causes high mammal populations; the reduction or absence results in low populations (see Elton, 1942).

Weather. Favorable climatic conditions over extended periods cause population build-ups; adverse conditions cause crashes and resultant lows.

Reproductive rate. Changes in reproductive rates (accounted for in a number of different ways) regulate the build-up and break-down in population levels.

Diet. Periodic changes in the vitamin and mineral content of available food cause nutritional situations which contribute to the build-up or collapse of population cycles.

Hormones. Population-wide exhaustion of certain hormone systems (such as the pituitary—see Christian, 1950) causes drastic decline of populations. Since this theory was first·proposed, a large mass of data has been amassed which seems to support it. Dawson (1956) reported that stress situations produce spleenic enlargement in the vole, *Microtus agrestis.* Christian and Davis (1956) found that "there is a density-dependent stimulus to the pituitary-adreno-cortical system of wild Norway rats that operates independently of season or supplies of the usual environmental necessities." Davis and Christian (1957) found, in artificial populations of mice (*Mus musculus*), that socially high-ranking mice had smaller adrenals than low-ranking mice. Louch (1958) used blood eosinophil levels and adrenal weights to compare the relation between the adreno-cortical activity and population size in two different populations of meadow voles (*Microtus*). He found that drought conditions made for higher levels in both high and low populations and that high populations increased these levels even more.

Randomness. A recent proposal is that multiannual fluctuations are not cyclic (many authors of recent years have implied that multiannual fluctuations are strictly cyclic and attempt to explain the nonconformity of the data to the theory) but, rather, are strictly random in the distribution of highs and lows. These random fluctuations are an expression of the fact that the influence of the environment is not simple (see Cole, 1951). Pedersen (1957) presented data on fluctuations in the populations of the Danish voles for the period of 1875–1953. The fluctuations, often but not always on a three-year cycle, were thought to be due to chance and not to climatic conditions.

Irruptions. Occasionally the environment of a mammalian species is unusually favorable for reproduction. If the breeding potential of the species is high and the environmental resistance is low, then, in a relatively short period of time, even in one reproductive season, the species becomes extremely abundant over rather extensive areas. Irruptions have been recorded several times in the Old World. Two spectacular irruptions in North America have also been recorded.

In the Humboldt Valley of Nevada, ranchmen noted an abundance of field mice (*Microtus montanus*) in the early spring of 1906. The numbers increased rapidly during the summer and by November, 1906, the high point was reached. At that time it was estimated that on several large ranches there were 8000 to 12,000 mice to each acre. This is the equivalent of one mouse for each 4 square feet, or 27 mice on the area covered by a 9- by 12-foot rug. This is approximately equivalent to 60,480 grams per acre, or 133 pounds per acre (see Piper, 1909).

An irruption of house mice occurred in Kern County, California, in January, 1927. At the source of this irruption in the dry bed of Buena Vista Lake, there were 82,880 mice per acre (204 in an area covered by a 9- by 12-foot rug; 1,119,008 grams per acre). In one grain bin 20 feet square, there were 3520 mice in sight at one time and around another grainery, two tons of mice were killed in one day (see Hall, 1927).

The meadow mice (*Microtus montanus*) of the western United States underwent a widespread irruption starting in the winter of 1956–57 (Spencer, 1958). In 1957 especially, from Colorado to the Pacific Coast, there was exceptionally lush vegetation, and the meadow mice spread into many habitats. In many areas cultivation forced the voles to concentrate in restricted areas and by January, 1958, several areas had as many as 800 individuals per acre, while a few areas may have had as many as 3000 per acre. In this irruption the sex ratio apparently was not unbalanced, as had been reported in some irruptions. Much agricultural damage was reported as resulting from this outbreak.

GEOGRAPHICAL FLUCTUATIONS

The simplest pattern of distribution of a given species would be one in which a species would be found in equal numbers throughout all the habitats of its range (*x* density) and absent beyond the geographical limits of its range (*o* density) (Blair, 1951).

The usual pattern of mammalian distribution is mosaic in respect to population densities. Within the geographic range of the species, the population density may vary from high to low, or it may even be zero. This type of population fluctuation is well known. Obviously it is the basis of preferred hunting areas, and is usually correlated with ecological differences between areas. However, not all geographical fluctuations can be correlated with measurable ecological factors.

Few studies have been made of the geographic variations of population densities, primarily because the data on population densities for various areas in the geographic range of a species are not comparable. Further, published figures on population densities often represent populations in ideal habitats or of unusual densities.

FACTORS INFLUENCING MORTALITY RATES

The main factors that influence mortality rates are divisible into two groups: (1) those that are dependent upon population density (such as diseases, predation, intraspecific competition), and (2) those that are independent of population density (such as accidents, fires, and climatic mishaps). The role of these factors in abnormal situations has been recorded so many times that further repetition seems unnecessary. However, few observations of the effect of these factors under normal conditions have been recorded and their effect is not understood. For example, it is generally known that diseases, under unusual conditions, do great damage to mammalian populations; yet, in most populations, the disease rate is apparently quite low.

Bourlière (1954) has described how an epidemic of bovine plague spread from northern to southern Africa in 10 years (1887–1897), killing, as it did so, several hundred thousand native buffalos and antelopes, in addition to six million head of cattle.

Elton and others (1931) made an intensive investigation of the health and parasites of a natural population of the wood mouse, *Apodemus sylvaticus*. Table 5–8 shows the results of these examinations.

TABLE 5–8

Health Conditions of a Population of Wood Mice (*Apodemus sylvaticus*)

	Number Examined	Number Diseased	Percentage Diseased
Blood cultures	468	0	0
Liver	989	25	2.6
Lungs	475	2	0.4
Alimentary canal	719	2	0.3
Spleen	719	1	0.1
Skin of legs (scab mites)	924	102	11.1
Skin (lesions)	1156	1	0.1

SOURCE: Based on data from Elton, Ford, Baker, and Gardner (1931).

From this table it is evident that the wood mouse population, as a whole, was very healthy.

The paratyphoid group of viruses (*Salmonella*) has been observed as prevalent in some populations at certain times and has been proposed as a possible course of extensive mortality in mammalian populations. Dalmat (1944) reported *S. typhosa* from 19 deer mice (*Peromyscus*) caught in the central United States. Myer and Matsumura (1927) isolated 58 cultures from 775 wild rats (*Rattus*) taken in San Francisco. Bradshaw (1956), on the other hand, cultured tissues from 260 small rodents from central Kansas without isolating *Salmonella* sp.

During the vole outbreak of 1957–58 in the northwestern United States, mentioned above, United States Public Health Service personnel studied disease conditions in living and dead animals from various areas (Kartman *et al.*, 1958). They found that a tularemia epizootic accompanied the vole outbreak and that from 20 percent to 35 percent of the *Microtus* taken alive died of tularemia. However, although tularemia decimated some populations, it did not eliminate them.

McKeever *et al.* (1958) tested sera from 2004 mammals from the southeastern United States to determine if agglutinating antibodies of tularemia were present. They secured the results shown in Table 5–9. Further, they examined 80 spleens in an attempt to isolate *Pasteurella tularensis*. They were successful in only one case.

TABLE 5–9

Incidence of Positive Agglutinating Antibodies Tests for Tularemia in 2004 Mammals from Southeastern United States

	Per Cent Positive
Opossum (*Didelphis marsupialis*)	11.9
Cottontail (*Sylvilagus floridanus*)	0.5
Fox squirrel (*Sciurus niger*)	2.5
Red fox (*Vulpes fulva*)	11.5
Gray fox (*Urocyon cinereoargenteus*)	24.3
Raccoon (*Procyon lotor*)	24.9
Striped skunk (*Mephitis mephitis*)	21.5
Spotted skunk (*Spilogale putorius*)	12.5
Bobcat (*Lynx rufus*)	22.0
House cat (feral)	6.2

Bradshaw (1956), using a hemagglutination inhibition test on 320 small rodents from central Kansas, found no evidence of tularemia.

Leptospirosis organisms have been found in several species of wild mammals. Table 5–10 presents the results of a survey of blood samples from 906 mammals from Ohio that were tested for *Leptospira pomona* (Anon., 1958).

TABLE 5–10

Incidence of Positive Diagnosis for *Leptospira pomona* in 906 Mammals from Ohio

	Number Tested	Per Cent Positive
Opossum, *Didelphis*	43	2.0
Rabbit, *Sylvilagus*	150	0.0
Muskrat, *Ondatra*	37	0.0
"Mice"	142	0.7
"Rats"	165	0.6
Foxes, *Urocyon* and *Vulpes*	55	25.0
Raccoon, *Procyon*	70	23.0
Skunks, *Mephitis*	11	55.0
House cats, feral	9	0.0
Deer, *Odocoileus*	224	19.0

McKeever *et al.* (1959) examined 2501 wild mammals from Georgia to determine the incidence of leptospirosis.

6
Economic Relationships

Introduction. Mammals are so interwoven with man's economy that it is practically impossible to arrive at any concise statement concerning their monetary worth in either a positive or a negative sense. Henderson and Craig (1932) compiled a book filled with facts and figures concerning their economic relationships. The first half of this book treats the various aspects of economic mammalogy, while the last half of the book discusses the past and present economic relationships of each order and of many families of mammals.

This chapter makes no attempt to list all the possible implications of mammals; rather, it is an attempt, by the use of selected examples, to indicate the multiplicity and diversity of the interrelations between mammals and man's economy. These are presented under two major headings: (1) influences on the environment and (2) relationships with man.

INFLUENCES ON THE ENVIRONMENT

Effects on the Physical Environment. Since the whole environment of the earth is important to man, any change in this environment has an effect, either positive or negative, on man's economy. Environmental influences can be divided into two categories: (a) influences on the physical environment and (b) influences on the biological environment.

Mammals have multiple effects on the physical environment. One of the more obvious effects is that resulting from digging in the soil. The cumulative effects of such fossorial rodents as pocket gophers (*Geomys*) is great. Grinnell (1923) estimated that in one year, Yosemite Park, California, pocket gophers raised 8,000 tons of earth an average of 8 inches. Scheffer (1940) found that a single female *Geomys* dug 510 feet of tunnel and built 105 mounds in one season. Buechner (1942) found that pocket gophers were much more numerous in overgrazed areas than in areas that had not been grazed for a number of years.

162

This digging in the soil is a mixed blessing to man. In cultivated areas fossorial animals often destroy crops, especially such root crops as potatoes and onions. Further, in irrigated regions such digging often does great damage to earthen irrigation canals. On the other side of the ledger, however, this digging is often of immeasurable value in aerating the soil, loosening soil for the growth of grasses, and, especially in areas of low rainfall, in making holes to help absorb runoff water. Hawbecker (1944) attributed a large increase in available food in parts of the western United States to the cultivation activities of the giant kangaroo rat, *Dipodomys*. Eloff (1953), for example, found that an opening of the runway system of the free state mole, *Cryptomys*, absorbed 1155 gallons of water poured in at the rate of 4.4 gallons per minute.

Grazing by large numbers of herbivores results in a packing of the soil. This soil packing is often of such a magnitude that it influences the dominant vegetation over wide areas. As has been pointed out elsewhere (Cockrum, 1952), grazing by domestic ungulates and, earlier, by wild ungulates including *Bison*, has resulted in a dis-climax of short grasses in large sections of the Great Plains of the United States.

In study plots of this region protected from grazing, the climax vegetation is a mixture of short grasses and grasses of mid-height. Overgrazing of these grasslands and packing of the soil by the hooves of bison resulted in ideal conditions for the prairie dog. Before the bison were killed off, certain areas were continuous colonies for miles. Without tramping of the soil, grasses and weeds took over and prairie dogs became much reduced in numbers. By the end of the nineteenth century, however, cattle grazing reached such an intensity in parts of western Kansas that prairie dogs were again numerous and widespread. In recent years, however, their numbers have become greatly reduced as a result of poisoning and trapping campaigns.

Dam-building by beavers is another activity that affects the physical environment. In addition to the mere impoundment of water to form ponds, the runoff rates of the area are greatly affected and, in and around the beaver ponds, new habitats are created for various aquatic and marsh-dwelling plants and animals.

Another mammalian activity influencing soils is the habit among many animals of collecting materials for nests and the subsequent decay of these nest materials. A number of rodents, such as pack rats (*Neotoma*) of North America, the house-building "jerboas" (*Conilurus*) of Australia, and the shelter-building *Rattus* of Africa, accumulate large piles of organic debris around their nests, further adding to the physical changes in the soil in that spot. Some of the pack rat dens are 3 to 4 feet in height and may cover an area up to 12 feet in diameter.

All such activities, as well as the underground storage of foods and the production of body wastes, affect the physical environment in ways that would not occur if mammals were absent from the region.

Effects on the Biological Environment. The influence of mammals on the biological environment can be considered under two categories: (a) influences on plants and (b) influences on other animals.

The total effect of mammals on plants is hard to evaluate. Certainly many kinds of mammals depend entirely on plants for food, shelter, and nesting sites. Some of these activities are highly destructive to the plants while others apparently have little or no effect. Foresters concerned with reseeding cut or burned-over areas are well aware of the high toll taken of seeds and seedlings by a number of small rodents, even under normal population levels. At times of population highs, rodent activites can be extremely detrimental. For example, Charles (1956) reported that during periods of high populations, voles (*Microtus*) in Scotland damaged or killed up to 75 per cent, and locally 100 per cent, of plantation trees that were up to 15 years old.

Conversely, mammals often serve as disseminating agents in the spread of various plants. In the southwestern United States, for example, the spread of mesquite brush into former grassy areas has been attributed to the activities of the kangaroo rat (*Dipodomys merriami*). The spread of various seeds has also been attributed to frugivorous mammals wherein the seeds have been ingested along with fruit pulp and later excreted in the feces. In recent years the importance of various nectivorous bats in the pollination of certain plants has been the subject of increased study.

Mammals affect other animals in numerous ways, some harmful and some beneficial. The activities of predators, insectivores, piscivores, and animals with similar carnivorous diets certainly influence other animals just as directly as does the removal of vegetation by herbivores. Further, competition for food, living space, nest and den sites, as well as serving as agents for scattering parasites and diseases of other animals, are important aspects of environmental influence.

Just one example of the extremely complicated interactions of animals was recently reported (Anon., 1958b) in the Klamath Basin of Oregon. There, as a result of a population irruption of meadow mice (*Microtus*), food for waterfowl was destroyed and a mass migration resulted, the ducks and geese moving on to where food was available.

RELATIONSHIP WITH MAN

Just as there are many interrelations between mammals and the environment as a whole, there is also a multitude of interrelations between man and other mammals. Various aspects outlined here include (a) competition with man, (b) competition with domestic animals, (c) as food, fur, and game, (d) as domestic animals, (e) as enemies, and (f) in relation to public health.

Competition of Mammals with Man. Like any other animal, man is in competition with others of his own species as well as with other species of animals for food and shelter. This competition is not always as evident as it is in the case of other animals, yet it is just as real. Some aspects of this competition include competition for agricultural and forestry products, competition for stored foods, and competition for wild fruits, nuts, and berries.

With respect to man's competition with other animals, the effect of rabbits and small rodents on grain crops is well known. The damage to growing and stored crops runs into uncounted billions of dollars each year in the United States alone.

A number of fossorial rodents feed on tuberous crops. Watson (1961) reported that the mole rat (*Spalax*) not only feeds on but also stores onions and potatoes in its burrow system.

Even more spectacular, however, is the damage done by some of the larger mammals. The hippopotamus, for example, does considerable damage to crops, especially rice, in parts of Africa (Clarke, 1953). Current preventative measures utilized by the natives include low fences and leaving marginal swamp strips between the rivers and crop areas.

Competition of Mammals with Domestic Animals. Mammals also affect man's interests in that they are often in competition with domestic animals for forage and water as well as being implicated as predators.

Food, Fur, and Game. The place of wild animals as a source of meat is not nearly so important today as it was as recently as one hundred years ago. Historically, the exploration and early development of the United States was dependent upon native herbivores as sources of fresh meat. Early government survey groups had professional hunters assigned specifically to secure fresh meats from the surrounding areas. Even today there are still a few groups of people that depend on wild animals for food.

Currently, in the United States alone, wild mammals are the sources of several million pounds of meat annually. In addition to the big game species, rabbits and squirrels are important in this respect. In the 1960 "National Survey of Fishing and Hunting" in the United States, it was estimated that slightly more than 12 million persons hunted small game in the United States during that year and that an average of almost $60 was spent by each hunter. The total expenditures of sports hunters and fishermen during the same year was in excess of $3.8 billion in the United States alone.

Counts of the numbers of small game animals taken are difficult to determine. Some estimates of small game bags are available for restricted areas. In North Carolina, in the 1949–50 season, for example, Stains and Barkalow (1951) estimated the total kill and approximate poundages taken by licensed hunters as follows: squirrels, 2,486,696 (1,486,696 pounds); rabbits, 2,149,048 (5,480,072 pounds); opossum 195,432 (781,729 pounds); and raccoon 83,306 (449,836 pounds).

Estimates of big game bags are more readily available. The Fish and Wildlife Service of the United States Department of the Interior estimated the hunter kill in 1959 as follows: moose, 5,125; elk, 67,766; white-tailed deer, 981,865; mule deer, 926,224; pronghorn, 56,751; black bear, 21,246; and grizzly bear, 214.

In the past, fur trapping has been extremely important economically. The impact of the activities of the early fur trappers on North America alone cannot be determined. Large portions of the New World were explored and settled as a direct result of the activities of trappers.

Even today fur trapping is an important industry in many parts of the world. According to Ashbrook (1952), between 25 and 30 million mammal skins were taken as fur in the United States and Alaska in 1951. In the same year the United States imported raw furs valued at 109 million dollars and exported furs valued at 32 million dollars. The estimated retail value of the garments manufactured from these furs ranged from 300 to 400 million dollars.

Domestic Mammals. A clear, concise definition of a domestic animal is practically impossible to compose. Henderson and Craig (1932) restricted the term to those animals that have become adapted to life in close association with man, and living about human habitations with the approval of man. Clearly, ordinary dogs, cats, horses, cows, goats, pigs, and such animals are domesticated. Wild or feral dogs, horses, and burros, although derived from domestic stocks, are probably best considered to be semidomesticated. Table 6–1 provides a list of the more common domesticated mammals. To be successfully domesticated, a mammal must be gregarious by nature and must have a moderate degree of intelligence.

TABLE 6–1

The Classification and Probable Place of Origin of Domestic Mammals

Order and Family	Domestic Stocks	Ancestral Wild Stocks	Place of Origin
Lagomorpha			
Leporidae	All breeds domestic rabbits	*Oryctolagus cuniculus,* European rabbit	Europe
Rodentia			
Cricetidae	Golden hamster	*Mesocricetus auratus*	Eastern Mediterranean
Muridae	White and colored mice	*Mus musculus,* house mice	Asia or Europe
	White rat	*Rattus norvegicus,* Norway rat	Western Asia
Caviidae	Guinea pig	*Cavia porcellus*	South America
Chinchillidae	Chinchilla		South America
Carnivora			
Canidae	Domestic dogs (*Canis familiaris*)		
	Spitz and chow	*Canis aureus,* jackal	Western Asia
	Pariah dogs	*Canis aureus,* jackal	Northeastern Africa
	Collie and poodle	*Canis lupus,* wolf	India
	St. Bernard, Newfoundland, and bulldog	*Canis lupus,* wolf	Tibet
	Deerhounds, wolfhounds, and dachshund (= badgerhound)	*Canis lupus,* wolf	Northeastern Africa
	Black and silver foxes	*Vulpes fulva,* American red fox	Northeastern North America
Mustelidae	Ranch, platinum, and blue mink	*Mustela vison,* mink	Northeastern North America
Felidae	Domestic cats (*Felis domesticus*)	*Felis silvestris,* European wildcat	Europe
Proboscidea			
Elephantidae	Elephant	*Elephas maximus,* Indian elephant	India

TABLE 6–1 (Continued)

The Classification and Probable Place of Origin of Domestic Mammals

Order and Family	Domestic Stocks	Ancestral Wild Stocks	Place of Origin
Perissodactyla			
Equidae	Domestic horses		
	Draft types	*Equus caballus*	Europe
	Race types	*Equus przewalski*	Western Asia
	Gray asses	*Equus hemionus*	Western Asia
	White asses	*Equus asinus*	Northern Africa
Artiodactyla			
Suidae	Swine	*Sus scrofa,* wild boar	Europe and Southeastern Asia
Camelidae	Dromedary, camel (one-humped)	*Camelus dromedarius*	Mongolia
	Bactrian camel (two-humped)	*Camelus bactrianus*	Mongolia
	Llama	*Llama glama*	South America
	Alpaca	*Llama peruana*	South America
Cervidae	Reindeer	*Rangifer tarandus*	North Europe
	Père David's deer	*Elaphurus davidianus*	China
Bovidae	European cattle	*Bos primigenius*	Europe
	Asiatic cattle	*Bos banteng*	Southeastern Asia
	Yak	*Bos grunniens*	Central Asia
	Water buffalo	*Bubalus bubalis*	Southern Asia
	Goats		
	Ordinary breeds	*Capra hircus*	Western Asia
	Angora and Kashmir	*Capra falconeri*	Western Asia
	Sheep		
	Ordinary breeds	*Ovis musimon*	Southern Europe
	Merino and fat-tailed	*Ovis ammon*	Western Asia

The economic importance of domestic mammals cannot be under-rated. Much of the protein in man's diet comes directly from do-mestic mammals. In addition, they are the source of many impor-tant products, including milk, wool, leather, fur, and fats. Further, even in this age of the internal combustion engine, domestic mam-mals are important as draft animals and as beasts of burden. As shown in Table 6–2, mammals were widely used in World War II.

As Enemies of Man. Mammals as enemies of man is not the important factor that it may have been during the past. One reason for this is that most of the larger predators have been eliminated from large areas of the earth's surface. But even today in the United States, an occasional human is killed by a mammal and records of attack by wild mammals are not at all unusual. Almost invariably, however, such attacks occur when the mammal is wounded, cornered, or is trying to protect its young.

TABLE 6–2

Estimates of the Number of Domestic Mammals in the World

Mammal	World Population, 1917 [1] (thousands)	Used in World War II [2] (thousands)	World Population, 1957–58 [3] (thousands)
Horses	100,000	2,500	69,900
Donkeys	10,000	–	–
Camels	3,000	50	10.4 (excl. U.S.S.R.)
Water buffalos	20,000	–	–
Elephants	–	6.4	–
Reindeer	–	100	–
Dogs	–	150	–
Cattle	–	–	868,000
Pigs	–	–	453,700
Sheep	–	–	939,000
Goats	–	–	328,200

[1] Craig and Henderson (1932).
[2] Burns (1957).
[3] Erus (1959).

Public Health Implications. Mammals are often involved in the harborage or transmission of parasites and diseases that affect the health of man. Both domestic and feral mammals are involved. Bubonic plague, tularemia, Rocky Mountain spotted fever, and rabies are among the epidemic diseases that often occur in feral mammals and occasionally are transmitted directly or indirectly to man. The dollar value of economic losses to man and livestock through these diseases is beyond estimate.

The *Yearbook of Agriculture, 1956,* issued by the United States Department of Agriculture, was concerned primarily with animal diseases. The annual losses to agriculture through animal diseases was set at an excess of 2 billion dollars per year. This book should be consulted by anyone interested in further information concerning this complex subject.

Part II
MAMMALIAN ORDERS
AND FAMILIES

7

Order Monotremata

Monotremes

The monotremes are a small group of primitive, egg-laying mammals known only from the Australian region. The ordinal name is derived from *mono* (= single) and *trema* (= hole) and refers to the single external opening for the reproductive, urinary, and digestive systems. Nothing is known of the past history of the monotremes, but the morphology and habits of the few living forms, as well as their isolated distribution, indicate that they are the modern descendants of a primitive stock. The egg-laying habits, the structure of the female reproductive tract and the shoulder girdle—these and other features are reptilian in nature. One group of the living forms is specialized for an aquatic existence while the other group is specialized for a diet of ants. Both groups have lost all traces of teeth in the adult stages.

CHARACTERISTICS

The limbs are specialized, showing modifications for aquatic environment (platypus) or for digging (echidna). The skull differs from the usual placental mammals in that the lacrymal and jugal bones are absent, the auditory bullae are absent, a prevomer bone is present, and the cochlea of the inner ear is only slightly coiled. The teeth are present only in very young animals and are replaced in adults by a horny beak or plates. Postcranial features include a large coracoid and precoracoid element in the pectoral girdle, epipubic (marsupial) bones on the pelvic girdle, two heads on the cervical ribs, and only one on the thoracic ribs. Features of the soft anatomy include the absence of external pinna on the ear; brain reptile-like, cerebral hemispheres smooth; cloaca present, with two oviducts (no uteri or vaginae) opening separately into the dorsal wall of the cloaca; mammary glands without nipples; testes abdominal, penis conducting only sperm. The females are oviparous, laying leathery-shelled eggs whose development is more reptile-like than birdlike.

The monotremes are not fully homoiothermic in that the body temperature varies from 27.6° to 32.6° C.

RANGE

Geographically the monotremes are known only from the Australian region, being reported from Australia and the associated islands of Tasmania and New Guinea (Fig. 7–1). Geologically they are known only from the Pleistocene and Recent.

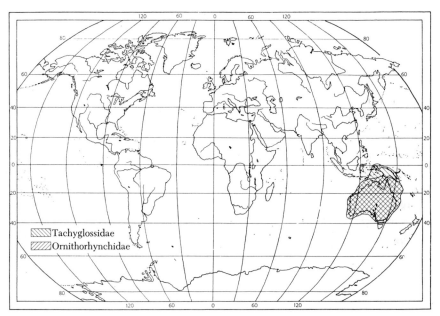

Tachyglossidae
Ornithorhynchidae

Fig. 7–1. The distribution of families Tachyglossidae and Ornithorhynchidae.

RELATIONSHIPS

The relationship of the monotremes to the other mammals is unknown, but it has been supposed by some that they represent the specialized descendants of a line of mammals that arose from the mammal-like reptiles independently of the other known kinds of mammals.

Family TACHYGLOSSIDAE
Spiny Echidna

STRUCTURE

The spiny anteaters are adapted for burrowing and for a diet of small insects. They have reduced ears and an elongated snout.

They are small, with a total length of up to 30 inches (*Zaglossus*) and with a very short tail. An adult male spiny echidna may weigh as much as 9 pounds. An adult long-beaked echidna kept in captivity at the London Zoological Gardens weighed approximately 35 pounds. The snout is elongated and cylindrical and contains a long, sticky, extensile tongue that is as much as 12 inches in length. The salivary glands are usually greatly enlarged. No teeth are known even in embryonic forms. The lower jaws are just two thin bones. The limbs are short and powerful, and the toes have extremely strong, wide claws used for digging. The middle claw may be longer, for preening. The body is covered with coarse hairs and spines. The females have an egg pouch or marsupium on the stomach. This marsupium appears morphologically to be a depressed teat.

NATURAL HISTORY

Spiny echidnas (Fig. 7–2) generally inhabit open forests in rough, rocky areas. They are crepuscular, being active mainly in the late afternoon and evening after spending the daytime in a hole under a rock or in a hollow log. They feed by moving and turning over stones and quickly gathering the exposed ants and small insects with the long sticky tongue. In captivity they eat bread, milk, diced meat, hard-boiled eggs, and are especially fond of raw eggs. Reportedly they can go without food for at least a month.

The female lays a single egg early in September. The egg is thought by LeSouf and Burrell (1926) to be deposited directly from the cloaca into the marsupial pouch, although others report that the female places the egg in the pouch with her mouth. The young hatches from the egg with the aid of an egg-tooth.

The young echidna is carried in the pouch for several weeks. When too large to be carried, and when it has grown a coat of hair, it is left in a dry, warm place while the mother is out feeding.

In the colder parts of its range, the echidna hibernates during the cold season. Sutherland (1897) reported that the average body temperature of the echidna is 29.4° C., that on a cold morning it may be as low as 22° C. and, when exposed to the midday sun, may rise to 36.6° C. He further reported that the echidna hibernates for four months in the cold season.

RECENT GENERA

Total, 2.

Tachyglossus Illiger. Au., Tasmania, New Guinea.
Zaglossus Gill. New Guinea, Papua.

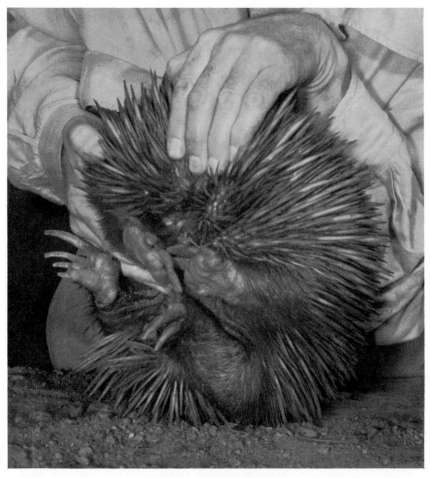

Fig. 7–2. The echidna or spiny anteater (*Tachyglossus aculeatus*). (Ernest P. Walker.)

Family ORNITHORHYNCHIDAE

Duckbilled Platypus

STRUCTURE

This family contains only one member, the duckbilled platypus. The common name, duckbilled platypus, is derived from the curious structure of the face of the animal. The rostrum projects forward and is covered with a soft, rubbery layer of skin, thus forming the duck-like bill that is approximately 65 mm. (2.5 inches) long and 50 mm.

(2 inches) wide. The external nares are on the dorsal surface of the bill. The jaws do not contain teeth, thus making the appearance even more birdlike. The eyes and ears are sunken in a slitlike depression on the side of the rostrum. Teeth are formed in the embryo but are absorbed prior to hatching. At hatching the young have a hard, sharp process on the muzzle that may serve the same function as the "egg-tooth" in birds. The embryonic teeth are replaced in the adults by two horny plates.

Males are larger than the females, being approximately 610 mm. (24 inches) in total length, while the females rarely reach more than 460 mm. (18 inches) in length. Approximately one-fourth of the total length is made up by the tail. The maximum adult weight is approximately 900 grams (2 pounds).

The duckbill is primarily aquatic, but is able to move about on land. The feet are webbed for swimming, and on land it walks on the knuckles of the forefoot and the hind foot is turned backward. The fur is close set and glossy, a dark grayish brown in color. The eyes are set high on the head and maximum visibility is about 30 degrees above the horizontal, thus making land perception difficult. Both the eyes and the ears are in a single fold that closes when the animal submerges.

Both adult and young males, as well as young females, have a movable horny spur on the hind foot. In the adult male this spur is associated with a gland that is supposed to secrete a poison. The tail is flattened dorsoventrally.

NATURAL HISTORY

The habitat of the platypus is similar to that of the muskrat. It occurs in association in water ranging from swift mountain streams, lakes, turbid creeks, and mudholes. It probably hibernates, at least for short periods of time, during the cold season (Holmes, 1939). Most of the time is spent in the water where it feeds on various aquatic life, including insects, worms, snails, and crayfish. It feeds under water, rising to the surface at intervals to chew the food and replenish the air supply. One captive individual observed in a tank at Badger Creek Sanctuary, Healsville, Victoria, Australia, spent most of each 24-hour day in the non-breeding season seeking food at the bottom of its tank. At that time a single night's food consisted of 400 large earthworms, 338 beetle grubs, and 38 small crayfish. The total weight of the food was 790 grams (1.75 pounds), and approached that of the adult.

The platypus lives in a burrow in the bank of a stream. Typically these burrows are approximately 10 m. (30 feet) in length and have two entrances, one of which is below the water level. The small diameter of the burrows squeezes the water from the fur as the platypus enters the den. A nest is usually constructed at the inner end of the burrow. This is constructed about 12 days after mating (in October) and is made of leaves and grasses, soaked in water, and carried to the nesting chamber by the female. The nesting material is wadded into tight packets and transported beneath the tail to the nest. The nesting chamber thus has a high relative humidity necessary for the development of the eggs. The nest is completed during a relatively short period of time in which all efforts are devoted to nest building, and practically none to feeding. A captive female built a nest in an 18-hour period. The first egg is laid one or two days after the nest is completed, thus the egg has undergone a developmental period of 14 to 15 days in the body of the female. A total of one to three eggs are laid, with two being the usual number. Each egg is approximately 20 mm. (0.8 inch) in length and only slightly less in diameter. The eggs have strong, white, flexible shells that stick together by means of a sticky substance with which they are coated. Incubation requires some nine to ten days; during this time the female rarely leaves the burrow and eats little or nothing. Probably during this period most of her time is spent curled around the eggs, keeping them warm to insure proper incubation.

After the eggs hatch, the female again spends much of her day feeding. Lactation apparently does not begin until some days after the young have hatched. No nipples are on the mammary glands. The milk oozes out on hairs.

When hatched, the young are approximately 25 mm. (1 inch) in length, blind, naked, and helpless. Reportedly the female holds them to her abdomen with her tail so they can obtain milk, thus forming a "false marsupium." They remain helpless for some time and are unable to crawl until they are almost as large as the parent. The young are unable to control body temperature until they are more than 2 months old. At this time the body length is only 228 mm. (9 inches), the eyes are still unopen, the beak is short, and the hair is barely developed. At 3 months the eyes are open and the body is well furred, but the animal can still hardly crawl. At 4 months it crawls actively and for the first time leaves the burrow. One individual has been kept alive in captivity for 4 years (Holmes, 1939).

In the earlier years of Australia's history, the platypus was trapped for its fur. At present trapping is strictly prohibited by law.

ONE RECENT GENUS

Ornithorhynchus Blumenbach. Duckbilled platypus, Au.

8

Order Marsupialia

Marsupials

The marsupials are a diverse group of mammals that are well known because of three of their members, the opossum, the kangaroo, and the koala (teddy bear). The ordinal name is derived from the fact that the females usually have a well-developed marsupium, or pouch, in which the young are carried and nourished.

CHARACTERISTICS

The limbs are varied, showing the results of considerable radial adaptation. The skull has a relatively small braincase; the jugal bone in the zygomatic arch forms a part of the glenoid fossa; the palate is often incompletely ossified, resulting in large palatine vacuities; the angle of the ramus of mandible is inflected; and the auditory bullae are absent. The teeth are usually numerous, heterodont, tuberculosectorial, and of only one set (P4 may have a predecessor, but it is rudimentary or abortive). As compared to the placental mammals the molar and premolar formula is reversed (P $\frac{3}{3}$, M $\frac{4}{4}$ instead of P $\frac{4}{4}$, M $\frac{3}{3}$) and there are usually fewer incisors in the lower jaw than in the upper jaw. Postcranial features include epipubic (marsupial) bones on the pelvic girdle and the coracoids are reduced to an apophysis on the scapula. The soft anatomy features include a shallow cloaca present in the females, which also have a double vagina and two uteri. The marsupium, containing mammary glands, is usually present on the abdomen of the females. The males have a penis that is bifurcate and testes located in front of the penis. The brain is smaller than in the placental mammals. Reproduction is viviparous, but the uterine development is brief and a placenta is rarely present. After birth the young move to the marsupium where development continues.

RANGE

Marsupials occur in Australia, Tasmania, New Zealand (introduced), Celebes, New Guinea and many adjacent islands, South

America, and North America. Geologically, marsupials are known
from the Upper Cretaceous to Recent.

Family DIDELPHIDAE

Opossums

The opossums, restricted to North, Central, and South America
(Fig. 8–1), are the most primitive living marsupials. In fact, according to some vertebrate paleontologists, little morphological difference

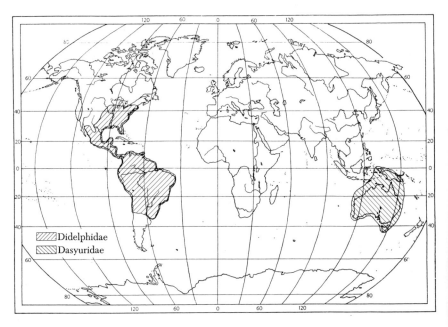

Fig. 8–1. The distribution of families Didelphidae and Dasyuridae.

is evident between the living Virginia opossum (*Didelphis marsupialis*) of the eastern United States and the ancestral opossums of
the Late Mesozoic Period. The family name is derived from *di*
(= two) and *delphi* (= brothers).

STRUCTURE

The dentition is characterized by small, conical upper incisors
and the fact that the teeth are all rooted. The dental formula is

I ⁵⁄₄, C ¹⁄₁, P ³⁄₃, M ⁴⁄₄ = 50. In the limbs, the fore and the hind feet each have five digits, the first digit of the hind foot (hallux) is large, nailless, and opposable. Diagnostic external features include a tail that is generally long, naked, and prehensile. The marsupial pouch is absent or incomplete in most genera.

NATURAL HISTORY

Opossums show considerable variation in their habits and ecological requirements. The Virginia opossum, *Didelphis marsupialis,* is a well-known mammal of the eastern United States (Fig. 8–2). It is about the size of a house cat, has a grizzled gray pelage of long hair, a white head, black legs, naked ears, and a piglike snout. Weight varies with the season of the year (decreasing throughout the winter and early spring, then increasing, see Fitch and Sandidge, 1953), but sexually mature males usually weigh between 1360 and 2700 grams (3 and 6 pounds). Hamilton (1958) recorded one male that weighed 5037 grams (11 pounds, 2 ounces).

The Virginia opossum rarely prepares a den of its own but utilizes some natural cavity in the ground or a burrow prepared by some other animal. In this retreat it prepares a nest of dried leaves and grasses. According to Hamilton (1958), this material is collected in a unique way. "The opossum gathers a mouthful of nest material, passes it under the body with its forefeet, then the curved tail grabs it and transports it to the den site."

The diet of the opossum varies with the season. In general, diet is determined by availability of food. In the warmer months insects and fruits make up a large percentage of the food. Mammals (perhaps, occasionally, as carrion), earthworms, amphibians, birds, mollusks, green vegetation, reptiles, and grains are important food items.

The reproduction of the opossum has been studied in detail by many workers (Hartman, 1923, 1952; Hamilton, 1958, and others). The breeding season varies slightly with geographic range, but, in general, begins in January and lasts through October. The female comes into heat at 28-day intervals and bears at least two litters per year. At the time of ovulation a large number of ova are shed (twenty two was the average number shed in one series of counts). After fertilization, these zygotes undergo a short developmental period in the uterus of the female. Unlike the embryos of the higher mammals, these do not develop a placenta nor do they imbed in the uterine wall. Rather, the embryonic chorion, with its many blood vessels, lies in close contact with the maternal tissues in one of the many folds in the wrinkled, fluffy walls of the uterus. Food for the

Fig. 8–2. An American opossum (*Didelphis marsupialia*). (Ernest P. Walker.)

developing embryo is provided and the elimination of embryonic wastes is accomplished by diffusion and osmosis between the blood vessels in the chorion and those in the uterine walls.

After a gestation period that averages 12.5 days in length, the young are born. At this time the poorly developed young (some-

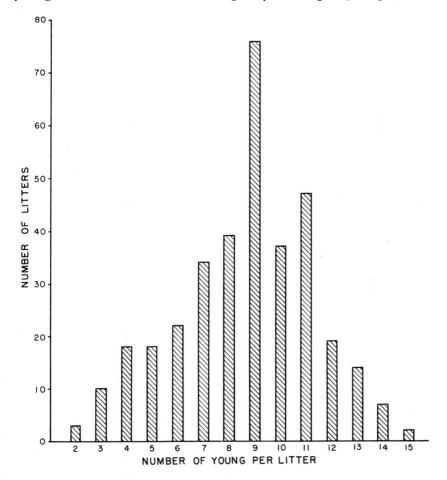

Fig. 8–3. The number of young per litter in 346 opossums from New York (after Hamilton, 1958, prepared by Jane Eppinga).

times described as a living abortion), is approximately 14 mm. in crown-rump length and weighs about 0.16 grams. They are so small that about twenty individuals can easily fit into a teaspoon. In most morphological features they are still embryonic in appearance. The hind limbs, for example, are mere limb buds. The forelimbs, on the other hand, are relatively well developed, muscular, and have well-developed claws. Shortly before parturition the female cleans out the marsupial pouch and assumes a sitting position with the hind legs extended. Upon birth, the female cleans the amnionic fluid from the young by tongue-lapping and the young make the 50 mm. (2 inches) trip from the vaginal opening to the marsupium by a swimming motion with the forelegs and head. Once the young has reached the pouch, it grasps a teat and remains attached for several weeks. Although it is not uncommon for twenty-five or more young to be born, the average number found in the pouch is approximately nine. In general, the others were not successful in making the trip from the vaginal opening to the pouch. Further, since each young remains attached to a nipple, the maximum number of pouch young is determined by the number of nipples present. The usual number of teats present is thirteen, but varies from nine to as many as seventeen. Thus, if more young than there are teats succeed in making the trip, they are still lost, for they cannot secure food.

Hamilton (1958) counted the number of young in the pouches of 346 female opossums in New York State. His findings are presented in Fig. 8–3. The development rate of the young is slow. At the end of 60 days the young are only about the size of a house mouse. At the end of 100 days they first begin to leave the pouch for short periods.

The woolly opossum (*Caluromys*) is nocturnal and covered with a thick, woolly pelage that is bright reddish on the upper parts and cream-colored ventrally. The long prehensile tail is furred on the basal half. This opossum is only slightly smaller than *Didelphis marsupialis;* average measurements are: total length, 635 mm.; tail, 375 mm.; hind foot, 35 mm. Woolly opossums are almost completely arboreal and apparently feed on fruit, insects, and bird's eggs.

RECENT GENERA

Total, 12.

Caluromys J. A. Allen. Woolly opossum, C.A., S.A.
Caluromysiops Sanborn. Opossum, S.A.
Monodelphis Burnett. Short-tailed opossum, C.A., S.A.
Glironia Thomas. Opossum, C.A.
Dromciops Thomas. Montios del monte, S.A.
Lestodelphys Tate. Opossum, S.A.
Marmosa Gray. Murine opossum, C.A., S.A.
Philander Brisson. Four-eyed opossum, C.A., S.A.
Metachirus Burmeister. Brown-masked opossum, C.A., S.A.
Lutreolina Thomas. Little water opossum, S.A.
Didelphis Linnaeus. Common opossum, S.A., C.A., N.A.
Chironectes Illiger. Water opossum, C.A., S.A.

Family DASYURIDAE

Australian Meat- and Insect-eating Marsupials

The dasyurids are carnivorous and insectivorous marsupials restricted in distribution to the Australian region (Fig. 8–1). They vary in size from small forms the size of a mouse to the Tasmanian devil and the marsupial "tigers," which are the size of large dogs. The family is conveniently divided into four subfamilies, the marsupial mice and rats, the native cats and tigers, the Tasmanian wolf, and the marsupial anteater.

STRUCTURE

The dentition is varied, but in all, the incisors are small, $\frac{4}{3}$ in number, the canines are large and trenchant, and the cheek teeth are tritubercular. The dental formulas are varied, ranging from I $\frac{4}{3}$, C $\frac{1}{1}$, P $\frac{2}{2}$, M $\frac{4}{4} = 42$ to I $\frac{4}{3}$, C $\frac{1}{1}$, P $\frac{3}{3}$, M $\frac{5}{6} = 52$. In the limbs, the forelegs are smaller than the hind legs, the forefeet have five digits, while the hind feet may have either four or five digits. The hallux, when present, is small and clawless, and the other toes are always independent. External features include the presence of a long, hairy, non-prehensile tail. The marsupium is varied, ranging from rudimentary to well-developed structure that opens downward and backward.

NATURAL HISTORY

Each of the four subfamilies has somewhat different habits, so they are discussed separately.

The marsupial mice and rats, or phascogales (Subfamily Phascogalinae) include some thirty species that are grouped in thirteen genera. They range in size from that of a house mouse to that of the Norway rat (*Rattus*). The marsupium is varied in its development and even in one genus it may be well developed or so reduced that it is represented only by shallow folds of skin. The number of teats ranges from eight to twelve.

The phascogales are mostly nocturnal, spending the day in hollow logs or holes in the ground or under rocks. They are primarily carnivorous, feeding mainly on insects and small animals, although they probably take some vegetable matter. One species, the yellow-footed marsupial mouse, *Phascogale flavipes*, inhabits caves and crevices in sandstone ledges, where it constructs a compact nest of dry leaves. It has ridged pads on the feet, as well as long claws, which enable it to climb trees and vines and even to run "swiftly upside down over the roofs of caves" (Troughton, 1947).

The little marsupial mouse, *Phascogale subtilissma*, is the smallest living marsupial. It is usually less than 95 mm. (less than 3.75 inches) in total length. The tail is slightly longer than the head and body. It lives chiefly in heavy grasses where it feeds on insects. Members of one genus, *Antechinomys*, are modified for saltatorial locomotion. The ears are large, the hind feet and legs are elongated, the forelegs are reduced, and the tail is long and tufted at the top. These jerboa marsupials are extremely rare and almost nothing is known of their habits.

The Subfamily Dasyurinae includes five species of native and tiger cats (*Dasyurus*) and the Tasmanian devil (*Sarcophilus*). They both are characterized by dentition that is modified for a flesh diet and there are similarities in the structure of the ear, muzzle, and pads on the feet. Members of the genus *Dasyurus* are weasel-like in shape and size and are more or less arboreal in habit. They are nocturnal spending the day in holes in the ground, in rock crevices, and in hollow logs. They are ferocious carnivores feeding on mammals, birds, and bird's eggs. The marsupium is present only during the reproductive season and contains only six to eight teats, although as many as twenty-four young may be born at a time. The young are born in early May and are carried in the pouch until late August.

The Tasmanian devil (*Sarcophilus harrisii*), the largest member of the family, reaches a length of approximately 1010 mm. (40 inches), of which the tail comprises 300 mm. (12 inches). It is blackish in color, with a few white spots on the sides, rump, and venter. Although it may have occurred on the mainland of Australia in Recent times, it is now restricted to Tasmania. Strictly terrestrial, it feeds on mammals, birds, reptiles, and carrion. Reportedly it makes raids on chickens and sheep. The females have a well-developed pouch that opens posteriorly and contains four nipples. The breeding season is in April; after a gestation period of 31 days the two to four young are carried in a pouch.

The Subfamily Thylacininae contains a single species, *Thylacinus cynocephalus*, the Tasmanian "wolf" or "tiger." It is about the size of a collie dog, approximately 1650 mm. (65 inches) in total length, of which the thick-based tapering tail comprises approximately 508 mm. (20 inches). It is covered with short hair, brownish in color, and has a series of sixteen to eighteen dark chocolate stripes across the posterior part of the back. The thylacine is an excellent example of convergent evolution in that it has many of features characteristic of dogs. In running, it stands more on its toes than does any other marsupial, giving it a doglike stance. The dentition is similar to that of the dog in that it consists of long canines for grasping and killing, carnassial or flesh-shearing premolars, and powerful molars for crushing bones. Originally widespread in Australia in Late Pleistocene times, the thylacine (or Tasmanian wolf) is now known only from Tasmania. Even there it is rapidly becoming extinct, primarily through human effort, because the thylacine reportedly preferred the introduced sheep as food to a diet of native wallabies and other Tasmanian mammals, birds, and lizards. It is nocturnal, spending the days concealed in dens in rocks and in shallow caves. The marsupium, which opens posteriorly, contains four nipples. Two to four young are carried in the pouch for 3 months.

The Subfamily Myrmecobiinae contains a single species, of the genus *Myrmecobius*. These marsupial anteaters are modified for a diet of ants. They have elongated snouts, a long, extensile tongue, and degenerate teeth. Occasionally these animals are considered to be a separate family. The marsupial anteaters, once fairly common in wooded areas of Australia, where they are dependent upon fallen logs for food and shelter, are rapidly becoming extinct. The clearing of land, brush fires, and introduced mammals have all contributed to their disappearance. Being both nocturnal and diurnal and not having either rapid locomotion or the ability to climb trees, they are easily killed by the introduced dogs and cats and are one of the first marsupials to disappear as a result of competition with man. They are about the size of a large rat and have a characteristic pattern of bands transversely across the back. They feed on ants and termites found in and around fallen logs of the white gum and jam trees. No marsupium is present in the female; the young cling to the teats (four in number) and are protected only by the coarse pelage of the mother.

RECENT GENERA

Total, 20.

Subfamily Phascogalinae. Pouched "mice" and relatives.
   Phascogale Temminck. Marsupial rats, Au., Tasmania, New Guinea.
   Antechinus MacLeay. Broad-footed marsupial mice, Au.
   Planigale Troughton. Flat-skulled marsupial mice, Au.
   Murexia Tate and Archbold. Long-tailed marsupial mice, New Guinea.
   Nesophascogale Stein. Marsupial rat, New Guinea.
   Parantechinus Tate. Marsupial rat, New Guinea.
   Phascolosorex Matschie. Chestnut-bellied marsupial rat, New Guinea.
   Pseudantechinus Tate. False broad-footed marsupial mice, Au.
   Myoictis Gray. Marsupial mouse, New Guinea.
   Dasyuroides Spencer. Crested-tailed marsupial rats, Au.
   Dasycercus Peters. Crested-tailed marsupial mice, Au.

Sminthopsis Thomas. Narrow-footed marsupial mice, Au.
Antechinomys Krefft. Jerboa marsupials, Au.
Subfamily Dasyurinae. Flesh-eating marsupials.
    Dasyurus E. Geoffroy. Eastern native cats, Au., Tasmania.
    Dasyurinus Matschie. Western native cats, Au.
    Satanellus Pocock. Little northern native cats, Au.
    Dasyurops Matschie. Tiger cats, Au.
    Sarcophilus F. Cuvier. Tasmanian devils, Tasmania.
Subfamily Thylacininae. Tasmanian wolves.
    Thylacinus Temminck. Tasmanian wolves, thylacines, Tasmania.
Subfamily Myrmecobiinae. Banded anteaters.
    Myrmecobius Waterhouse. Banded anteaters, Au.

Family NOTORYCTIDAE

Marsupial Moles

Marsupial moles are another example of convergent evolution, illustrating the independent development of fossorial adaptations found in some of the insectivores and rodents. This family is restricted to Australia (Fig. 8–4).

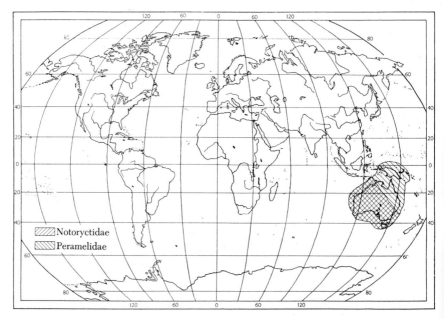

Fig. 8–4. The distribution of families Notoryctidae and Peramelidae.

STRUCTURE

The dentition consists of the following teeth: I $\frac{4}{4}$ or $\frac{3}{3}$, C $\frac{1}{1}$, P $\frac{2}{2}$, M $\frac{4}{4}$. The upper molars are tritubercular. The limbs are short and stout, an adaptation for fossorial life. There are five digits on each foot, and the claws on the third and fourth digit of the forefoot are greatly enlarged. The cervical vertebrae are fused. The external features are those characteristic of fossorial animals. The eyes are vestigial, and the ears have no external pinna. The snout is covered by a horny shield. A well-developed marsupium, opening posteriorly, is present. The tail is reduced to a short stub.

NATURAL HISTORY

The marsupial mole is covered with a fine, silky pelage that varies from almost white to a golden-red color and has an iridescent sheen. It is generally solitary and, like most fossorial mammals, is both nocturnal and diurnal, spending most of its time below the surface of the ground. It is known from a very few specimens taken in the desert and semidesert regions of Australia. Unlike the true mole, it does not leave a permanent tunnel as it burrows through the soil. After burrowing through the ground for distances as great as several yards, it emerges and travels over the surface, leaving a characteristic track. In captivity, it is restless and shrewlike. Food, in captivity, consists of adult insects, insect larvae, and earthworms. During the reproductive season, the female constructs a permanent burrow in which the young (usually one, occasionally two) are raised.

ONE GENUS

Notoryctes Stirling. Marsupial "mole," Au., Tasmania.

Family PERAMELIDAE

Bandicoots

The Family Peramelidae includes a group of marsupials that have the many incisors characteristic of the Dasyuridae and the specialized hind foot modifications characteristic of more specialized Australian marsupials (Fig. 8–4).

STRUCTURE

The dentition is made up of sharp, cutting, insectivorous-type teeth. The canines are slender and pointed, the premolars are narrow and simple-rooted, and the molars are either triangular or quadrate. The hind limbs are larger than the forelimbs. The forefeet have two or three of the middle digits with claws, while the others are rudimentary or absent. The hindfoot has the hallux rudimentary or absent, the second and third digits reduced in diameter and united so that they appear to be a single digit with two claws, and the fourth digit elongated and bearing a large claw. External features include, in addition to the characteristic foot mentioned above, a long, hairy, non-prehensile tail and a long, pointed snout. A marsupium, opening posteriorly, is present. Some species are subfossorial.

NATURAL HISTORY

The bandicoots are more or less solitary forms that are either nocturnal or crepuscular. They are varied in food habits and, on this basis, the five genera appear to be divisible into three groups: an omnivorous group, a carnivorous group, and a herbivorous group.

The short-nosed bandicoots (*Thylacis*), the long-nosed bandicoots (*Perameles*), and the New Guinea bandicoots (*Echymipera*) are omnivorous. The short-nosed bandicoots, some species of which reach lengths up to 458 mm. (18 inches), are noted for digging holes in the ground to locate insect grubs on which they feed. They will occasionally feed on underground bulbs of plants. They build a nest of dried sticks, coarse grass, and leaves. In dry situations, the nest is in a hole in the ground, with the top of the nest at ground level; in damp situations, it is usually constructed above ground level. The long-nosed bandicoots appear to have similar habits. Both of these genera are not doing well in competition with man and his introduced animals, and have disappeared from many areas where they were formerly common.

The bilkies or rabbit bandicoots (*Macrotis*) are more carnivorous than the other bandicoots. Bilkies are about the size of a full-grown rabbit; they have long, silky, blue-gray fur; long, rabbit-like ears; and a long, well-furred tail ending in a small naked spur. The tail is black basally and white on the terminal portion. The bilkies are the only bandicoots that actually construct a burrow in the ground for use as a daytime retreat; reportedly they are excellent burrowers, being able to burrow faster than a man can dig with a shovel. Their tunnels descend in a steep and widening spiral for 5 or more feet. Food of the bilkies consists primarily of insects, larvae, and small mice taken only at night. Insect larvae are often secured by digging shallow holes around the bases and roots of plants. Formerly abundant and widespread, the bilkies are now disappearing from much of their range. The combined effects of trapping for fur (prior to

1923 large numbers of pelts were sold each year), killing for "sport," the attempts at extermination of the introduced rabbits (traps and poisons), and the effects of the introduced fox have resulted in the complete extermination of the bilkies in many areas, and the few surviving populations are in submarginal habitats where they, too, are likely to be exterminated.

The rare or recently extinct pig-footed bandicoot (*Chaeropus*), once widely distributed in the more arid portions of central Australia, was apparently primarily herbivorous. It has been kept in captivity for as long as six weeks on a diet of lettuce, grass, bread, and bulbous roots and did not kill or eat mice and grasshoppers placed in the cage with them. The pig-footed bandicoot is about the size of a young rabbit. It builds a nest in a hollow in the ground with the top level with the surface.

RECENT GENERA

Total, 8.

Perameles E. Geoffroy. Common and long-nosed bandicoots, Au., New Guinea.
Echymipera Lesson. New Guinea bandicoots, New Guinea.
Macrotis Reid. Rabbit bandicoots, Au.
Chaeropus Ogilby. Pig-footed bandicoots, Au.
Thylacis Illiger. Short-nosed bandicoots, Au.
Rhynchomeles Thomas. Long-nosed bandicoot, Ceram Island.
Peroryctes Thomas. Bandicoot, New Guinea.
Microperoryctes Stein. Mouse bandicoot, New Guinea.

Family CAENOLESTIDAE

Mouse Opossums

The mouse opossums are a rare group of small marsupials known only from South America (Fig. 8–5). Almost nothing has been written about this group.

STRUCTURE

The dentition is adapted for an insectivorous diet. The middle lower incisors are enlarged; the lower canines and the lower premolars are small and unicuspid; the upper canines are normal; the upper premolars are triconodont; and the molars are subtriangular or quadrate in shape. The dental formula is I $\frac{4}{3}$, C $\frac{1}{1}$, P $\frac{3}{3}$, M $\frac{4}{4}$. The hind limbs are slightly larger than the forelimbs. Digits $\frac{5}{5}$; on the forefoot digits I and V have blunt nails; on the hind foot the hallux is weak and bears a nail; the other digits bear well-developed, sharp claws. External features include a long tail, quadrilateral in cross-section, thickly covered with short, stiff hairs. They are shrew-like in general appearance. No marsupium is present in adult females.

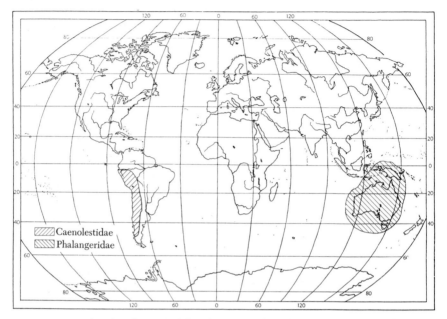

Fig. 8–5. The distribution of families Caenolestidae and Phalangeridae.

NATURAL HISTORY

Mouse opossums are known only from a few localities in Bolivia, Ecuador, Peru, and Chile. They are solitary, terrestrial, and insectivorous mammals that are crepuscular or nocturnal in habit. *Caenolestes fuliginosus* is known from the Andes Mountains in Venezuela, Columbia, Ecuador, and Peru at elevations from 6000 to 12,000 feet, where it lives near timberline and in grassy openings in mountain valleys. It has also been taken in dense growth, beneath a canopy of trees, and in thick grasses in swampy areas (Gregory, 1922). *Caenolestes caniventer* has been taken in subtropical forests in Ecuador, where it is abundant in brushy ravines near water (Tate, 1931). The total length of this species is 241 mm. (about 9.5 inches).

The Chilean rat opossum, *Rhyncholestes*, is known only from three specimens from two localities in southern Chile. One of the localities is in a heavy, temperate forest at the southern end of Chiloe Island; the other, on the mainland, is under deep growth in a cool and moist situation, at an elevation of 3000 feet. It is a small marsupial (Total length: male, 215 mm.; female, 175 mm. Tail: male, 87 mm.;

female, 65 mm. Hind foot: 19–24 mm.) with a loose, uniformly dark-brown pelage above and below. The rostrum of the skull is much elongated. The female has no marsupium and has five teats. Nothing has been recorded concerning the natural history of this rare animal (Osgood, 1943).

RECENT GENERA

Total, 3.

Caenolestes Thomas. Rat opossum, S.A.
Lestoros Ochser. Rat opossum, S.A.
Rhyncholestes Osgood. Chilean rat opossum, S.A.

Family PHALANGERIDAE

Possums and Phalangers

The Australian possums and phalangers are a group morphologically intermediate in many ways between the dasyurids and the kangaroos. They are widely distributed in the Australian region (Fig. 8–5).

STRUCTURE

The dentition is characterized, as are all of the following families of marsupials, by a reduction in the number of incisors. Posterior to the six upper and two lower incisors (which are large and strong), the teeth are extremely varied within the family. The teeth between I1 and P4 are often extremely minute and rudimentary and are not constant in number in a given species nor, for that matter, on the two sides of the jaw in the same individual. Generally P4 is sharp-edged; the molars may have sharp cutting cusps or may be bluntly tuberculate, bordering on bunodont. The dental formulae vary from a maximum of I $\frac{3}{1}$, C $\frac{1}{1}$, P $\frac{2}{1}$, M $\frac{4}{4}$ to I $\frac{3}{1}$, C $\frac{1}{1}$, P $\frac{1}{1}$, M $\frac{0}{0}$. The limbs have five digits on each foot; the hind foot is syndactylous, with the second and third toes united; and both the fore and hind feet are prehensile. External features include a long and generally prehensile tail (rudimentary in some forms) and a well-developed marsupium (containing two to four teats) opening anteriorly.

NATURAL HISTORY

In general, members of this family are nocturnal, arboreal, and phytophagous. Although not generally gregarious, they are frequently found in pairs or family groups. Gliding membranes are independently developed in three genera, *Acrobates, Petaurus,* and *Schoinbates.* The family is conveniently divided into three sub-families: (1) the primitive insectivorous or omnivorous Phalange-rinae, (2) the highly specialized nectarivorous Tarsipedinae, and (3) the herbivorous Phascolarctinae.

Members of the Subfamily Phalangerinae, which includes twelve genera, are a varied group. The smaller mouselike member, *Acrobates* (the pygmy glider), and *Cercaërtus* (pygmy possums) are probably the primitive living members of the family, and are highly insectivorous, a characteristic reflected in the structure of the teeth. In addition to insects, pollen and nectar are taken to some extent. The pygmy glider is modified for volant locomotion by having a gliding membrane extending from the fore to the hind limb and a long feather-like tail that serves as a rudder.

The striped possums (*Dactylopsila*) have characteristic conspicu-ous black and white markings on the body. Like the aye-aye (Pri-mate) of Malagasy, they are modified for a diet of insect grubs which they secure from crevices and holes in trees and fallen logs. The fourth finger is greatly elongated and is provided with a curved claw for extracting insects from crevices, and the incisors are enlarged for gnawing into wood to get at insects and the honey of wild bees.

Leadbeater's possum, *Gymnobelideus,* known only from five specimens, is about 305 mm. (12 inches) in length, with the tail slightly longer than the head and body. It is quite similar in appear-ance to the lesser gliders but does not have gliding membranes. The dentition indicates that the diet is probably insectivorous, perhaps supplemented by nectar and honey.

The lesser gliders (*Petaurus*) have semi-insectivorous dentition and well-developed gliding membranes. They feed on insects and the buds, blossoms, and fruits of various native trees and shrubs, which they secure on nocturnal "flights" from tree to tree. The day-time is spent in holes in hollow trees.

The nocturnal brush-tailed possums (*Trichosurus*) are primarily herbivores, although they do take some carrion. They are widely dis-tributed in Australia, even taking up residence in the attics of houses. Their fur is in demand on the fur market and in 1931–32 more than one million skins were sold.

The honey possum (*Tarsipes spenserare*) is the only member of the Subfamily Tarsipedinae. It is small, about the size of a mouse, has three well-marked dark brown stripes on the back, and is highly specialized for a diet of nectar and soft-bodied insects. The snout is much elongated, the tongue is elongated and extensile, and the lips have flanges which overlap to form a channel for sucking nectar and pollen. The teeth are degenerate, much as in the anteaters; the limbs are highly modified for their arboreal habitat; and the long tail is prehensile. Honey possums are nocturnal, somewhat colonial, and migrate with the season to various species of plants currently in blossom. They apparently hibernate during cold spells. As indicated above, they feed primarily on the pollen and nectar of native flowers and on the soft bodies of insects. Attempts at keeping honey possums alive in captivity for long periods of time have not been successful. They occasionally construct a nest in or near the ground but are known to take over abandoned bird nests high in trees.

The Subfamily Phascolorctinae contains five genera, including *Phascolarctos*, the koala (one species); *Schoinobates*, the greater glider-possum (one species); and *Pseudocheirus*, the ring-tailed possums (six species).

The koala, or "teddy bear," shows extreme adaptations for an arboreal habitat. The limbs are extremely prehensile and the tail is greatly reduced. The fingers, two of which are opposable, are strongly clawed. The great toe is enlarged, clawless, and opposable to the well-clawed digits of the hind feet. The fur is thick and woolly. Adult koalas reach a length of about 910 mm. (3 feet). Well-developed cheek-pouches, presumably associated with the bulky diet of tree leaves, are present. The name "koala" is derived from a native word meaning that it does not drink. Apparently the natural diet, restricted to the leaves of about twelve species of eucalyptus trees, furnishes enough moisture so that free water is not required. The female produces one young per litter and usually breeds only every other year. The young is born after a gestation period of 35 days. At this time it is only 20 mm. in length and weighs about 5.5 grams. It remains in the pouch for 8 months and is carried by the mother until it is almost a year old. Adult size is not reached until it is 4 years old. The demand for fur of the koala led to an open season in Queensland, Australia, in 1927. At that time some 10,000 trapping licenses were issued and some 600,000 skins were taken. Apparently the population has not recovered from this severe overtrapping and a concurrent clearing of the forests, for now koalas are verging on extinction.

The ring-tailed possums, *Pseudocheirus*, all have long, tapered tails with naked prehensile tips, that are normally carried curled into a ring. They live in trees where they construct a large dome-shaped nest on a limb or in a hollow in the tree trunk. Like the koala, the diet of the ringtails is completely herbivorous, consisting of the leaves and blossoms of a large series of trees and shrubs. They are almost completely nocturnal in habit.

The greater glider possum, *Schoinobates*, is also restricted to a diet of leaves. It is large, attaining a total length of approximately 810 mm. (32 inches), of which 510 mm. (20 inches) consists of a long tail covered with soft, fluffy fur. It has a gliding membrane extending from the knee of the foreleg to the foot of the hind leg. Troughton (1943) reported that "one animal, in six successive glides, was once observed to cover a distance of 590 yards . . . (it left the top of a eucalyptus tree 100 feet high and glided to the foot of another 70 yards away); then it immediately climbed and from the summit glided to the next at 80 yards, and lost no time in ascending three more trees at distances of 110, 120, and 90 yards, finally gliding to another 120 yards away, in which it remained." Although extremely adept at climbing and gliding, the glider possum is very clumsy and slow on the ground.

RECENT GENERA

Total, 18.

Subfamily Phalangerinae. Phalangers, Australian possums.
    Phalanger Storr. Cuscus, Au., New Guinea.
    Trichosurus Lesson. Common phalangers, Au.
    Acrobates Desmarest. Pygmy flying "possums," Au.
    Distoechurus Peters. Pen-tailed phalangers, New Guinea.
    Cercaërtus Burmeister. Dormouse possums, New Guinea, Au.
    Eudromicia Mjöberg. Pygmy possums, Au., New Guinea, Tasmania.
    Gymnobelideus McCoy. Leadbeater's possums, Au.
    Petaurus Shaw. Gliding possums, Au., New Guinea.
    Dactylopsila Gray. Striped possums, Au.
    Dactylonax Thomas. Striped possum, New Guinea.
    Wyulda Alexander. Scaly-tailed possum, Au.
    Spilocuscus Gray. Cuscus, Au.
Subfamily Tarsipedinae. Honey possum.
    Tarsipes Gervais and Verreaux. Honey possum, Au.
Subfamily Phascolarctinae.
    Phascolarctos Blainville. Koala, Au.
    Pseudocheirus Ogilby. Ring-tailed possums, Au., New Guinea.
    Hemibelideus Collett. Brush-tipped, ring-tailed possum, Au.
    Petropseudes Thomas. Rock-haunting, ring-tailed possum, Au.
    Schoinobates Lesson. Flying phalangers, Au.

Family PHASCOLOMIDAE

Wombats

Wombats are stout, clumsy marsupials adapted for a subfossorial habitat and a herbivorous diet. They live in Tasmania and Australia south of the tropics (Fig. 8–6).

STRUCTURE

The dentition consists of teeth that are rootless and have persistent pulp. The incisors are large and strong, and the premolars are small. The dental formula is I ⅟₁, C ⁰⁄₀, P ⅟₁, M ⁴⁄₄. The limbs are short and stout, with digits ⅗. The hallux is short and nailless, but the

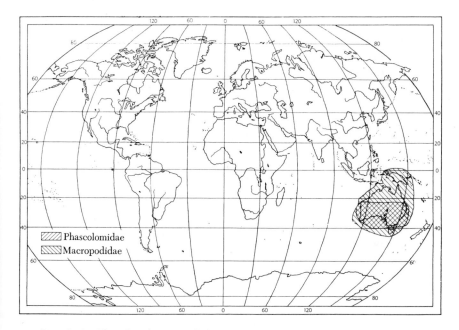

Fig. 8–6. The distribution of families Phascolomidae and Macropodidae.

other digits all have shovel-like nails for digging in the ground. External features include characters indicative of its subfossorial habits. The tail is rudimentary, the body is heavy and thick, and the fur is long, coarse and almost lacking in underfur. The ears are short.

NATURAL HISTORY

The family contains three genera, all of which are relatively uniform in morphology and habits. Wombats (Fig. 8–7) reach a rather large size, up to 1060 mm. (3.5 feet) in length and weights up to 80 pounds; all are nocturnal, subfossorial herbivores. They construct burrows in the ground, often up to 100 feet in length and large enough in diameter to permit a small child to crawl into them. At the end of the burrow is a nest of dry grasses. The diet is entirely herbivorous, consisting primarily of grasses but including some roots, the bark of certain trees, shrubs, and some fungi. The females have one young per litter and one litter per year.

Fig. 8–7. Wombats. *Left*, the fine-haired wombat (*Lasiorhinus latifrons*); *right*, the coarse-haired wombat (*Phascolomis hirsutus*).

RECENT GENERA

Total, 2.

Phascolomis E. Geoffroy. Common wombat, Au.
Lasiorhinus Gray. Hairy-nosed wombat, Au.

Family MACROPODIDAE

Wallabies and Kangaroos

This family, which includes the well-known kangaroo, is restricted to the Australian region (Fig. 8–6).

STRUCTURE

The dentition consists of sharp, cutting incisors, small canines, and broad, ridged molars with low, blunt tubercules. The molars and premolars move forward during the life of the individual by bone absorption anteriorly and deposition posteriorly. The dental formula is I ¾₁, C ⅑₀, P ⅖₂, M ⁴₄ or I ¾₁, C ⁰₀, P ⅖₂, M ⁴₄. The limbs are highly modified for a saltatorial locomotion. The hind limbs are greatly enlarged, the forelegs reduced. The forefeet have five digits, while the hind foot has the hallux reduced or absent. Digits II and III are slender and united (syndactylous), digit IV is elongated and bears a strong claw, and digit V is similar but smaller. External features include a long, hairy tail, somewhat prehensile in some forms, and a large marsupium opening anteriorly. Members of this family vary in size from 460 mm. to 2.5 m. (1.5 to 8 feet) in total length.

NATURAL HISTORY

All members of the family are saltatorial. Some are secondarily arboreal and most are excellent swimmers. They are usually sociable and sometimes gregarious. Most kinds are diurnal, but a few are nocturnal. The larger species are strictly herbivorous, but some of the smaller species are somewhat insectivorous. In all cases where the reproductive pattern is known, females have but one young per litter and one litter per year. The family is divided into two subfamilies, the rat-kangaroos, Subfamily Potorinae and the kangaroos and wallabies, Subfamily Macropodinae.

The Subfamily Potorinae (with five genera) contains the more primitive members of the family. In this group the middle upper incisors are enlarged, the upper canines are well developed, the premolars are grooved, and the molars decrease in size from the first molar to the fourth molar. One genus, *Hypsiprymnodon* (musky rat-kangaroo), appears to be intermediate between the phalangerids and macropodids. They have a well-developed hallux and a more or less naked, scaly tail, while other members of the subfamily have the hallux missing and the tail covered with hair. Based on these and other differences musky rat-kangaroos have often been placed in a separate subfamily. Musky rat-kangaroos are small, with a total length of about 310 mm. (12 inches), of which the tail comprises approximately 155 mm. (6 inches). They live in damp and marshy areas around rivers and lakes where they secure their insectivorous diet by turning over leaves, bark, and other ground debris.

The rat-kangaroos (genera *Bettongia*, *Aepyprymnus*, *Caloprymnus*, and *Potorous*) are mainly nocturnal, spending the daytime in grass nests usually built in depressions in the ground and covered with debris. The grass for these nests is transported by the prehensile tail. Reportedly they feed on grasses, yamlike tubers, and underground fungi. The nails of the forefeet are much enlarged for digging after these foods. According to Guiler (1958) the long-nosed rat-kangaroo (*Potorous tridactylus*) of Tasmania is strictly nocturnal and feeds by digging small holes in the ground to secure insects, grubs, and worms. They are seminomadic in habit, and show no territorial behavior. There are two breeding seasons per year, one in early spring (August to November) and one in the summer (January to February).

The subfamily Macropodinae (with twelve genera) contains the larger and more advanced members of the family. In this group the middle upper incisors are not much larger than the adjacent ones, the upper canines are rudimentary or absent, the premolars are not greatly enlarged, and the transversely ridged molars increase in size from the first molar to the fourth molar. The common names of wallabies, wallaroos, and kangaroos are applied to these animals. Like many common names, there is no great correlation between the common and the scientific names. In general the main difference between the groups is in size. The length of the hind foot is a fairly clear indicator of this size difference. The small wallaroos have a hind foot up to 155 mm. (6 inches) in length; the typical wallabies have a hind foot between 65 and 250 mm. (2.5 and 10 inches) in length; while the kangaroos and wallaroos have a hind foot in excess of 250 mm.

The hare-wallabies (*Lagorchestes*) are small, solitary, and brightly colored. Formerly widespread, they are now facing extinction in most parts of Australia. Like other members of the subfamily, they feed on vegetation.

The great gray kangaroo, *Macropus major*, is the largest of the living marsupials. It may "stand" 7 feet tall and weigh 200 pounds. The longest recorded total length is 9 feet 7 inches. Over a 300-yard course they can maintain a speed of 25 miles per hour and over a shorter course can reach even greater speeds. On being chased, they have been known to jump fences 9 feet high, but such leaps are exceptional. They appear to have no definite breeding season, but most young are born in the winter.

RECENT GENERA

Total, 17.

Subfamily Macropodinae. Kangaroos and wallabies.
    Lagorchestes Gould. Hare-wallabies, Au.
    Lagostrophus Thomas. Hare-wallabies, Au.
    Petrogale Gray. Rock wallabies, Au.
    Peradorcas Thomas. Short-tailed wallabies, Au.
    Onychogalea Gray. Silky wallabies, Au.
    Thylogale Gray. Scrub wallabies, Au., New Guinea.
    Protemnodon Owen. Large wallabies, Au., New Guinea.
    Macropus Shaw. Red and gray kangaroos, Au., New Guinea, Tasmania.
    Setonix Lesson. Short-tailed wallabies, Au.
    Dendrolagus Muller. Tree kangaroos, Au., New Guinea.

Dorcopsis Schlegel and Muller. Tree wallabies, New Guinea.
Dorcopsulus Matschie, Tree wallabies. New Guinea.
Subfamily Potorinae. Rat-kangaroos.
Bettongia Gray. Bettons, "Jerboa" kangaroos, Au.
Aephprymnus Garrod. Large "rat" kangaroo, Au.
Caloprymnus Thomas. Plain "rat" kangaroo, Au.
Potorous Desmarest. Potoroos, Au.
Hypsiprymnodon Ramsay. Musk kangaroo, Au.

9

Order Insectivora

Insectivores

The insectivores are a group of ancient origin and differentiation. Some doubt exists that all of the families indicated below belong to an order of unified origin (see Simpson, 1945) but, because all are primitive in many respects and because all have certain anatomical characteristics in common, they are usually grouped in one order.

CHARACTERISTICS

The limbs are usually pentadactylous (five digits) and usually plantigrade. The first digit is never opposable in either the fore or the hind foot. Claws are present on the digits. The skull has the braincase little elevated above the face line and is usually broad and flat. The brain cavity is small. The orbits usually open posteriorly. The zygomatic arches are often reduced and may be entirely absent. The teeth are often of the typical number for placental mammals (forty-four) and are generally primitive in structure. Two sets of heterodont teeth are present and the molars are tuberculosectorial. The incisors are often enlarged or reduced and the canines differ only slightly from the incisors or premolars. Postcranial skeletal features include separate radius and ulna, with the tibia and fibula often fused distally. The clavicles are almost always present and the lumbar vertebrae often have distinct intercentra. In the soft anatomy, the primitive nature of the insectivores is indicated by the small brain with short cerebral hemispheres. External features include the short, close-set fur with the hairs all of one kind. The eyes are usually minute and occasionally have no external opening. The external ears are usually short. The reproductive system is characterized by the presence of a bicornuate uterus. In some forms there is a well-defined, but shallow, cloaca. In the males the testes are abdominal or inguinal and are never enclosed in a scrotum.

RANGE

Insectivores occur on most of the continents and large islands except Australia and the greater portion of South America.

Family SOLENODONTIDAE

Solenodon, Alamiqui

The solenodons are a primitive group known, as Recent forms, only from the West Indies (Cuba and Haiti). As fossils, members of the family are known from continental North America (Fig. 9–1).

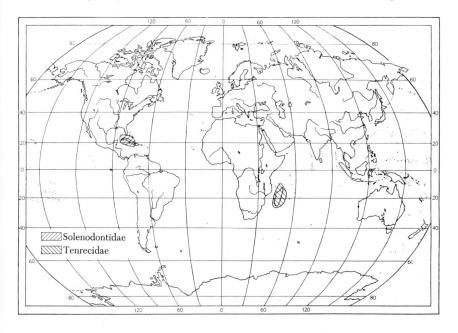

Fig. 9 1. The distribution of the families Solenodontidae and Tenrecidae.

STRUCTURE

The dentition is characterized by a reduction in the number of premolars. The first upper incisors are enlarged and diastema is present between them and the second upper incisors. The upper molars are tritubercular and the cusps arranged in a "V." The dental formula is I ⅗, C ¼, P ⅗, M ⅗ = 40. The skull is markedly constricted between the orbits and has a small braincase. Zygomatic arches and postorbital processes are absent. The lambdoidal crest is well developed and projects posteriorly over the occiput. The limbs have five digits, each with a strong claw. The claws on the forelimbs are larger than those on the rear limbs. The external features include a large, ratlike body form; a long, naked tail; and a long, cylindrical snout with lateral nares. The eyes and external ears are both small, and the vibrissae are numerous and large. Musk glands are present in the axillary and inguinal region; and the mammae are post-inguinal, located on the buttocks.

NATURAL HISTORY

Solenodons (Fig. 9–2) are rat-sized, with measurements of total length 500 mm.; tail 215 mm.; hind foot 65 mm. They are nocturnal animals that move in a zig-zag shambling walk and reportedly are unable to move in a straight line. When hurried, they frequently tumble into a heap (Allen, 1908). Their food consists of insects,

Fig. 9–2. The Cuban solenodon (*Solenodon paradoxus*). (Ernest P. Walker.)

especially ants, small vertebrates, and some fruit. The insects are secured by rooting in the earth with the elongated snout and by opening up rotten logs with their strong claws. Upon occasion they enter native huts in search of cockroaches. Although not proved, natives believe the solenodon has a poisonous saliva. The one to three young are born naked, toothless, and with eyes closed. Solenodons apparently prefer forests and brushy areas.

RECENT GENERA

Total, 1.

Solenodon Brandt. Solenodon, Cuba and Haiti.

Family TENRECIDAE

Tenrecs

The tenrecs, known only from Malagasy, have undergone adaptive radiation to fill various food habits, and resultantly, are highly diversified (Fig. 9–1).

STRUCTURE

The dentition is variously reduced, with all showing a reduction in the number of molars and others also in the number of incisors and premolars. The dental formulas are I $2 \text{ or } 3/2 \text{ or } 3$, C $1/1$, P $3/2 \text{ or } 3$, M $2 \text{ or } 1/2 \text{ or } 3$. The skull is not notably constricted between the orbits, the braincase is small and cylindrical, and zygomatic arches and postorbital processes are absent. The limbs are variously modified for ambulatory, aquatic, fossorial, and arboreal locomotion. The tibia and fibula are united or free. The external features show the results of considerable adaptive radiation. Some are terrestrial, others aquatic, fossorial, or arboreal. Young *Tenrec* have a longitudinal line of strong spines along the back which, in the adult, are replaced by a crest of long, rigid hairs. The females have twelve pair of thoracic and inguinal mammae.

NATURAL HISTORY

The tenrecs (*Tenrec*) occur throughout most of Malagasy from sea level to elevations slightly over 3000 feet but seem to prefer brushlands and drier forests. They are terrestrial and primarily nocturnal. The daylight hours are usually spent in burrows in the ground or in hollow logs. They feed on earthworms, snails, insects, small vertebrates, and fruit. When angered, the tenrec sometimes erects the long crest of spiny bristles on the back of its head, and tosses its head. During the dry season (winter) from May to October, tenrecs hibernate in burrows or in hollow logs. Ovulation usually occurs shortly after the females leave hibernation and embryo counts range from eighteen to twenty-five. Up to twenty-one young have been recorded in a single litter. The young probably keep together and follow the adults until they are at least one-third grown (Rand, 1935).

Hemicentetes is a terrestrial form that inhabits brushlands and the edges of forests. It has a small area of heavy spines in the middle of the back. These spines are strong enough so that they will stick into a person's hands. When walking, its hind feet stand out at right angles to the body. It apparently does not hibernate and spends the day in shallow burrows (Rand, 1935).

Setifer is the Malagasy hedgehog. It, too, is a nocturnal inhabitant of the brushland and forest. Like *Hemicentetes*, the hind feet are at right angles to the body when they walk. They are covered with matted, stiff spines and have a rather offensive odor. Apparently *Setifer* does not hibernate (Rand, 1935). The *Limnogale* is an aquatic genus; *Microgale*, arboreal; and *Oryzorictes*, fossorial. Little is known concerning their habits.

RECENT GENERA

Total, 10.

Tenrec Lacépède. Tenrec, Malagasy.
Setifer Froriep. Hedgehog-tenrec, Malagasy.
Hemicentetes Mivart. Streaked tenrec, Malagasy.
Dasogale Grandidier. Malagasy.
Echinops Martin. Malagasy.
Oryzorictes Grandidier. Rice tenrec, Malagasy.
Microgale Thomas. Long-tailed tenrec, Malagasy.
Cryptogale Grandidier. Malagasy.
Limnogale Major. Aquatic tenrec, Malagasy.
Geogale Milne Edwards and Grandidier. Burrowing tenrec, Malagasy.

Family POTAMOGALIDAE

Otter-shrew

STRUCTURE

The dentition consists of forty teeth, with a formula of I $\frac{3}{3}$, C $\frac{1}{1}$, P $\frac{3}{3}$, M $\frac{3}{3}$. The central upper incisors are enlarged, caniniform, and slightly separated. The upper molars have the cusps arranged in a broad "V." The skull is slightly constricted between the orbits, the braincase is small, and the zygomatic arches and postorbital processes are lacking. The sagittal and lambdoidal crests are prominent. The limbs are plantigrade and have aquatic modifications. The tibia and fibula are united distally. There are five digits on each foot and a web present between digits two and three of the hind foot. The claws are short, strong, and curved. The external features include a long, cylindrical body that continues posteriorly into a thick, laterally compressed tail and a broad, flat muzzle anteriorly. The nostrils project anteriorly and are protected by valves. The mouth is ventral. The body is covered with a short, thick fur, brown above and whitish below.

NATURAL HISTORY

Otter-shrews are aquatic animals about 610 mm. (2 feet) long, of which approximately half is made up of the laterally compressed tail. In swimming the tail furnishes the propulsive power, while the limbs are folded backward along the sides of the body. They live along the banks of streams and along brackish coastal estuaries. According to Sanderson (1937) their food consists of crustacea and no fish, but, according to Weber (1928) they do feed on fish. Cabrera (1925) indicated that otter-shrews have one pair of inguinal mammae while Weber (1928) indicated that five pair of inguinal mammae are present.

The range is restricted to western equatorial Africa (Fig. 9–3).

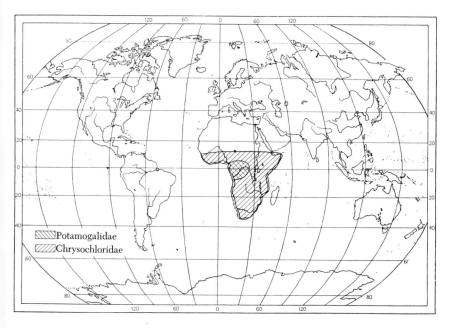

Fig. 9–3. The distribution of the families Potamogalidae and Chrysochloridae.

RECENT GENERA

Total, 3.

Potamogale Du Chaillu. Otter-shrew, Af.
Micropotamogale Heim de Balsac. Otter-shrew, Af.
Mesopotamogale Heim de Balsac. Otter-shrew, Af.

Family CHRYSOCHLORIDAE

Golden Moles

The golden moles are fossorial mammals restricted to the continent of Africa from 5° North Latitude south to the Cape of Good Hope (Fig. 9–3).

STRUCTURE

The dentition is varied. The upper molars are tritubercular and have very tall crowns. The deciduous teeth are not lost until the young are relatively advanced in age. The dental formulas are: I $\frac{3}{3}$, C $\frac{1}{1}$, P $\frac{3}{3}$, M $\frac{3}{3}$ = 40 or I $\frac{3}{3}$, C $\frac{1}{1}$, P $\frac{3}{3}$, M $\frac{2}{2}$ = 36. The skull is conical in shape and is not constricted between the orbits. The zygomatic arches and tympanic bullae are well developed but postorbital processes are absent. The limbs have the tibia and fibula united. The anterior limbs are greatly enlarged for fossorial locomotion. The humerus is greatly thickened and has many tuberosities and crests for muscle attachment. The forearm has a third bone extending from the palm almost to the elbow, which appears to be an ossification of one of the flexor tendons. The forefoot has four digits, the outer two of which are small, while the middle ones are large and have very powerful claws. The external features are characterized by a mole-like appearance and small size (90 to 115 mm. in total length). The eyes are covered by skin; the external ears are short and are concealed in the thick, glossy fur. The upper surfaces have a brilliant metallic luster, varying in color from golden bronze to green and violet. The mammae, both thoracic and inguinal, are in cuplike depressions.

NATURAL HISTORY

The golden mole (*Chrysochloris*) makes a series of tunnels just under the surface of the ground where it searches for the worms, grubs, and other insects, upon which it feeds. Occasionally these tunnels are so near the surface that the earth is raised, much as is done by the North American moles. It has been reported as hibernating in southwestern Africa. One female was found to contain two embryos. The number of litters per year is not known.

The related giant forest mole (*Chrysospalax*) is primarily a nocturnal surface feeder, rooting with its snout for adult insects and grubs in the leaves and leaf mold of the forest floor. Giant forest moles occupy the same permanent burrow in the ground year after year.

RECENT GENERA

Total, 6.

Chrysochloris Lacépède. Cape golden mole, Af.
Eremitalpa Roberts. Golden mole, Af.
Amblysomus Pomel. Golden mole, Af.
Chlorotalpa Roberts. Golden mole, Af.
Chrysospalax Gill. Giant forest mole, Af.
Cryptochloris Shortridge and Carter. Golden mole, Af.

Family ERINACEIDAE

Hedgehogs

STRUCTURE

The dentition is more omnivorous than insectivorous in type. The upper molars have one small median and four principal cusps. The dental formulas are: I ⅗, C ¼, P ¾, M ⅗ = 44 (*Echinosorex* and *Hylomys*) and I ⅗, C ¼, P ⅗, M ⅗ = 36 (*Erinaceus*). The skull has a slender zygomatic arch that is occasionally incomplete. Auditory bullae and postorbital processes are absent. The limbs are

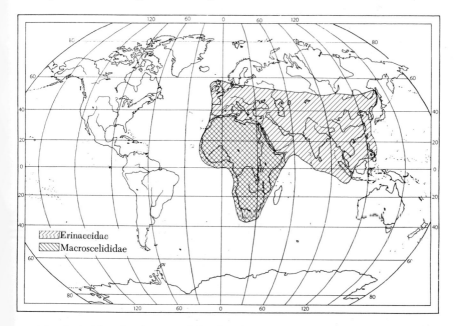

Fig. 9–4. The distribution of the families Erinaceidae and Macroscelididae.

generally plantigrade. The tibia and fibula are united proximally. Each limb has five digits except in *Atelerix*, which has the hallux missing on the forefeet. The external features are varied. These are large insectivores. The smallest member of the family is *Hylomys*, about 6 inches in length; the largest is *Echinosorex albus*, the largest living insectivore, which is about 24 inches long. Members of the Subfamily Erinaceinae with the hairs of the back modified into spines, roll up into a ball when irritated. The range of this family includes most of Europe, Asia, and Africa (Fig. 9–4).

NATURAL HISTORY

The hedgehogs are divided into two subfamilies, the Echinosoricinae or hairy hedgehogs, and the Erinaceinae or spiny hedgehogs.

Fig. 9–5. The Eurasian hedgehog (*Erinaceus europaeus*). (Ernest P. Walker.)

The spiny hedgehogs, Subfamily Erinaceinae, are characterized by having the hairs of the back modified into spines, an extremely reduced tail, and the reduction or absence of I3 and P4. Four genera are recognized in the subfamily. They occur in Europe, Asia, and Africa.

The hedgehogs (*Erinaceus*, Fig. 9 5), widespread throughout Africa, Europe, and most of Asia, are stockily built nocturnal animals with the hair of the back modified into stiff spines. When alarmed they curl up into a ball but make no other effort to defend themselves. In the colder parts of the range, winter is spent in hibernation in a nest in the ground, rock crevice, or similar situation. In temperate Europe the hedgehog has two litters, the first born in May or June and the second in July, August, or September. Two to four young are born in a well-constructed nest of grass or leaves after a gestation period of approximately 30 days. At birth the spines are soft and the eyes are not open. The spines do not harden until the animal is about 3 weeks old. In southwest Africa the young are born in the summer (November). Food consists of insects, worms, slugs, various small vertebrates, eggs, roots, and fruit. Liu (1937) investigated the stomach contents of forty-seven hedgehogs taken near Peiping in northern China. There he found that about 95 per cent of the food was maggots (63.88 per cent *Chrysomya;* 27.94 per cent *Musca,* and 2.96 per cent *Eristalis*), 4 per cent was other animal material (mainly insects) while only 1 per cent was plant material.

The hairy hedgehogs, Subfamily Echinosoricinae, are more normal in external appearances. The pelage is not modified into spines; the tail, sometimes short, is never extremely reduced; and I3 and P4 are present. Four genera are recognized in the subfamily, which is restricted to southern and eastern Asia. The gymnures are spineless, ratlike relatives of the hedgehog that occur in the Malayan region and the Philippines. They are covered with a coat of fur with many overlying long, coarse guard hairs. They feed mainly on termites and cockroaches but do eat other available insects. *Hylomys,* only about 150 mm. (6 inches) long, is the smallest member of the family. The common gymnure or moon rat (*Echinosorex*) reaches length up to 610 mm. (24 inches), of which approximately one-third is the tail. They are said to nest in holes in rocks or hollow logs and to feed on fruit (Harrison and Traub, 1950).

RECENT GENERA

Total, 8.
Subfamily Echinosoricinae. Hairy hedgehogs.
    Echinosorex De Blainville. Moon rat, S.As.
    Hylomys Muller. Lesser gymnures, S.As.
    Podogymnura Mearns. Philippine gymnures, Philippines.
    Neotetracus Trouessart. Chinese gymnure, E.As.
Subfamily Erinaceinae. Spiny hedgehogs.
    Erinaceus Linnaeus. Hedgehog, Eu., As.
    Atelerix Pomel. African hedgehog, Af.
    Hemiechinus Fitzinger. Long-eared hedgehog, N.Af., As.
    Paraechinus Trouessart. Desert hedgehogs, N.Af., S.As.

Family MACROSCELIDIDAE

Elephant Shrews

STRUCTURE

The dentition is varied. The canines resemble premolars in all but *Rhynchocyon.* The molars are broad and have the cusps arranged in a "W." The skull has a comparatively large braincase. The zygomatic arches are strong and tympanic bullae are present. The orbit is surrounded by bone. The limbs are adapted for saltatorial locomotion. The proximal ends of the tibia and fibula are united. The metatarsal elements are much longer than the tarsal elements. The forelimbs are shorter than the hind limbs, and there is a tendency toward a reduction in the number of digits. External features include a characteristic body form similar to that of the kangaroo rat and a much elongated muzzle. The tongue is somewhat extensile. The range of this family is restricted to Africa (Fig. 9–4).

NATURAL HISTORY

The black-eared elephant shrew (*Macroscelides*) lives in the arid parts of South Africa, on sandy or gravelly plains, where it constructs shallow burrows under the low, scattered bushes. They are diurnal, active in the cool hours of the day, and hop from one clump of bush to another, with the tails raised. The females have three pairs of mammae. One or two young are born at a time in a rather advanced stage of development. At birth they are covered with hair, and have the eyes open at birth or soon afterward.

The rock elephant shrews (*Elephantulus*) are widely distributed in Africa, from Algeria, south to the Cape of Good Hope. They are mostly diurnal but become crepuscular during the hot season. In cooler weather, they are often observed basking in the sun. When moving rapidly, they hop on their hind feet, with the tail carried high. Their food consists primarily of insects. The gestation period of *Elephantulus myurus* is 56 days (van der Horst, 1946), with, usually, only two young per litter. These shrews have a glandular pad on the underside of the tail which consists of sebaceous and sudoriferous glands. This glandular pad is at the point where the tail touches the ground when the animal lands after a jump. Lang (1923) suggests that this is a type of secondary sexual gland that, being most active in the breeding season, serves as a scent gland to mark the trail over which the animal has passed.

RECENT GENERA

Total, 5.

Macroscelides Smith. Elephant shrews, Af.
Nasilio Thomas and Schwann. Short-nosed elephant shrews, Af.
Elephantulus Thomas and Schwann. Rock elephant shrew, Af.
Petrodomus Peters. Rock elephant shrew, C.Af.
Rhynchocyon Peters. Checkered-back elephant shrew, E.Af.

Family SORICIDAE

Shrews

The soricids are a diverse group of small insectivores that occur worldwide except for Australia, Greenland, and most of South America (Fig. 9–6).

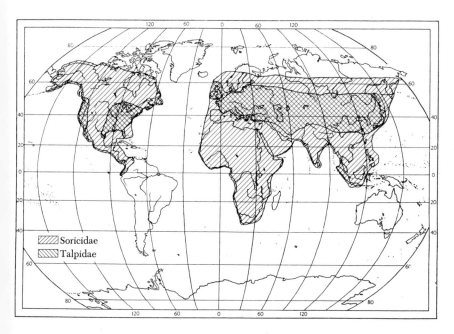

Fig. 9–6. The distribution of the families Soricidae and Talpidae.

STRUCTURE

The dentition is varied and deciduous teeth are shed *in utero.* The middle incisors are elongated and the middle lower incisors are directed forward. According to some interpretations, no lower canines are present. The skull is long and narrow; the zygomatic arches are incomplete; and the auditory bullae are absent. The limbs are usually generalized plantigrade. The tibia and fibula are united. The humerus and femur are short and stout. The feet have five digits. External features include the small to minute size; the mouse-like shape; and the very dense, soft, and velvety fur. The eyes are small and the snout is long and pointed. The genus *Nectogale* has webbed toes and disklike adhesive pads on the ventral surface of the feet.

NATURAL HISTORY

The soricids have a remarkably high metabolic rate. They do not hibernate, and even in the coldest part of their range are active during the whole year. In areas of snow they construct molelike runways in the snow. Their daily activities cannot be classified as nocturnal or diurnal; rather, they are active throughout most of the 24 hour period, with scattered short periods of rest. They normally require two-thirds or more of their own weight in food each 24 hours. Food consists of various insects, worms, and small vertebrates. Some species, at least, have a poisonous saliva which probably stuns or kills their prey. The voice of the soricids is extremely high-pitched, and they probably have the ability to hear sounds above the range of the human ear. Kahmann and Ostermann (1951) have suggested that echolocation may be important. Most soricids are terrestrial but some, such as the Asiatic water shrew (*Chimarrogale*), are amphibious.

The family is divided into three subfamilies: Soricinae, the red-toothed shrews of Eurasia and North America; Crocidurinae, the white-toothed shrews of Eurasia and Africa; and Scutisoricinae, the armored shrew of Africa.

The red-toothed shrews, Soricinae, are characterized by the presence of red pigments in the teeth. The subfamily includes eight genera, one of which (*Sorex*) is Holarctic in distribution, four of which (*Microsorex, Blarina, Cryptotis,* and *Notiosorex*) are North American, and three of which (*Soriculus, Neomys,* and *Blarinella*) are Eurasian in distribution.

The short-tailed shrew (*Blarina brevicauda,* Fig. 9–7) occurs widely in the eastern United States. Its measurements are: total length, 130 mm.; tail, 30 mm.; hind foot, 16 mm. This shrew and the male duckbilled platypus are the only known kinds of mammals that have a venom. In the shrew venom is used to disable and perhaps kill prey, such as mice and various invertebrates. Pearson (1942) described this as follows: "The shrew venom is produced in the submaxillary glands and is led by a pair of ducts to an opening near the base of the lower incisor teeth. The median pair of lower incisors projects far forward, forming a groove along which the venom can flow into a wound. This injection system is less efficient than hollow fangs and is almost ineffective against humans. No human fatalities resulting from shrew bites are known, and only a few local reactions have been reported." Rood (1958) maintained short-tailed shrews (*Blarina*) in captivity for several months. He found that their eyesight was very poor and saw no evidence of their being able to distinguish objects by sight. Further, the sense of smell is not well developed. Hearing, however, is acute, and the sense of touch and vibration are well developed. In captivity they were usually active only a few minutes at a time and then rested for a few minutes. In constructing burrows in soil, they use the front feet alternately to loosen dirt and then kick it to the surface with the hind feet. When enough dirt is at the surface, it is pushed and smoothed out with the pointed nose. In captivity they ate many things but preferred live

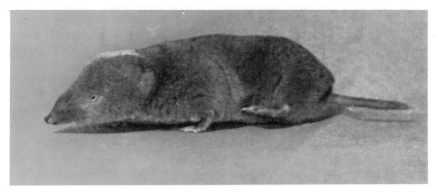

Fig. 9–7. A short-tailed shrew (*Blarina brevicauda*). (Ernest P. Walker.)

food, mainly insects and earthworms. On the average they would eat half of their body weight in food each 24 hours. Rood found no evidence that the short-tailed shrew feeds on mice, for in captivity they could not capture mice in the same cage.

The desert shrew, *Notiosorex*, occurs in the Lower and Upper Sonoran life zones of southwestern United States and northern Mexico. Its average measurements are: total length, 86 mm.; tail, 26 mm.; hind foot, 10 mm. Few specimens are known and little has been learned about its life history. Huey (1936) kept an adult in captivity for 10 days by feeding it various insects, earthworms, and sowbugs.

The white-toothed shrews, Crocidurinae, characterized by the absence of pigment in the teeth, occur widely in Asia and Africa. Of the eleven genera in the subfamily, two (*Crocidura* and *Suncus*) occur in Europe, Asia, and Africa; four occur only in Africa; and six occur only in Asia.

The most widely distributed genus (*Crocidura*, the musk shrews) contains several species that occur in Europe, Asia, Africa, on many of the Malayan islands, and in the Philippines, Formosa, and Japan.

Their food consists primarily of insects, earthworms, slugs, and occasionally small rodents and reptiles. Reportedly they are almost exclusively nocturnal in Southwest Africa, but most authors ascribe more typical soricid habits to this group.

The large musk shrew, or house shrew (*Suncus murinus*), is about 250 mm. (10 inches) in total length, of which the tail comprises 105 mm. (4 inches). It has a powerful, lasting musky scent. It is, in many places in the Orient, a commensal of man, living in his house and on his boats. It feeds primarily on cockroaches and other insects, although it does take some food intended for human consumption. The house shrew has been transplanted by man to many islands in the Pacific. Recently it has appeared in Guam and in Hawaii.

The small musk shrew (*Suncus estruscus*) has been called the smallest living mammal. Its total length is about 80 mm., of which the tail comprises approximately 34 mm. The sand shrews (*Diplomesodon*) of Asia have fringes developed on the feet, large ears, and well-developed vibrissae. They run slowly but can dig in sand quite rapidly.

The Asiatic water shrews (*Chimarrogale*) occur in and near mountainous streams in Japan, Borneo, and Sumatra. They reach lengths of about 205 mm. (8 inches), of which the tail comprises approximately 75 mm. (3 inches). The hind feet are enlarged and have a well-developed fringe of flattened stiff hairs on the lateral margins of each toe. The ears are reduced and have valvular antiragi for closing the ear underwater. Reputedly they walk along the bottoms of streams where they feed on aquatic insects, small fish, and amphibians. The entrances to their burrows are usually under water.

The Tibetan water shrew (*Nectogale*) is even more modified for an aquatic habitat. The snout is elongate, the ears are even more reduced and are valvular, the tail has median and lateral keels of short, stiff hairs for swimming, and the toes are webbed. The feet have disklike pads, which may serve as adhesive disks for climbing on wet stones (Pruitt, 1957).

The armored shrews, Scutisoricinae, are restricted to Africa. Only one genus, *Scutisorex,* is in the subfamily. They are closely related to musk shrews, genus *Crocidura*, in most osteological features except in the vertebral column (Winge, 1941). The lumbar vertebrae, especially, are modified in that they are increased in number (eleven instead of the usual six) and size. Further, the vertebrae have developed a dense network of rodlike projections, mostly in an anterioposterior direction. These modifications of the vertebrae have

greatly increased the strength of the backbone, so much so that reportedly a man can stand on an armored shrew without doing it any
harm. This adaptation is presumed to be associated with a burrowing habit of arching the back and forcing the earth upward to form
tunnels.

RECENT GENERA

Total, 20.

Subfamily Soricinae. Red-toothed shrews.
    Sorex Linnaeus. Common shrews, Eu., As., N.A.
    Microsorex Baird. Pygmy shrew, N.A.
    Soriculus Blyth. Oriental shrews, As.
    Neomys Kaup. Water shrews, Eu., As.
    Blarina Gray. Short-tailed shrews, N.A.
    Blarinella Thomas. Asiatic short-tailed shrews, As.
    Cryptotis Pomel. Little shrew, N.A., northern S.A.
    Notiosorex Baird. Desert shrew, N.A.
Subfamily Crocidurinae. White-toothed shrews.
    Crocidura Walgler. Musk shrew, Eu., As., Af.
    Praesorex Thomas. African forest shrews, W.Af.
    Suncus Ehrenberg. Thick-tailed shrew, Eu., As., Af.
    Feroculus Kelaart. Kelaart's long-clawed shrew, Ceylon.
    Solisorex Thomas. Long-clawed shrew, Ceylon.
    Myosorex Gray. Mouse shrew, S.Af.
    Surdisorex Thomas. African short-tailed shrew, E.Af.
    Diplomesodon Brandt. Sand shrews, As.
    Anourosorex Milne Edwards. Mole shrews, As.
    Chimarrogale Anderson. Asiatic water shrew, As.
    Nectogale Milne Edwards. Tibetan water shrew, As.
Subfamily Scutisoricinae. Armored shrews.
    Scutisorex Thomas. Armored shrews, Af.

Family TALPIDAE

Moles and Shrew-Moles

STRUCTURE

The dentition includes tritubercular upper molars with the outer
tubercles "V"-shaped. The deciduous teeth are shed at a relatively
advanced age. The skull has a complete zygomatic arch. The orbital
and temporal fossae are confluent, and auditory bullae are absent.
The limbs are modified for fossorial locomotion. The humerus is
short and massive, with many tuberosities. The front teeth are much
broadened for digging and are permanently turned outward from
the body. External features include the characteristic mole shape,

the long naked muzzle, minute eyes, and ears without a conch. The fur is thick, soft, and velvety. The range of this family is primarily the temperate parts of Europe, Asia, and North America (Fig. 9–6).

NATURAL HISTORY

The Talpidae constitute a group of molelike insectivores modified for a fossorial life. The head is tapered, the eyes and ears are reduced, and the hands are widened and provided with strong claws. The legs are shortened, and the muscles of the arms and shoulders are enlarged and powerful. The family is divisible into five subfamilies: the primitive shrew-moles of eastern Asia, Uropsilinae; the semiaquatic desmans of Europe and western Asia, Desmaninae; the Old World moles of Europe and Asia, Talpinae; the "American" moles of North America and eastern Asia, Scalopinae; and the semiaquatic star-nosed moles of eastern North America, Condylurinae.

The shrew-moles, Subfamily Uropsilinae, known only from eastern Asia, are characterized by the presence of a relatively unmodified hand, prominent external ears, and relatively strong zygomatic arches. Two genera (*Uropsilus* and *Nasillus*) are recognized in this subfamily. External measurements of *Uropsilus* are: total length, 135 mm.; tail, 65 mm.; and hind foot, 15 mm. Members of the genus *Nasillus* are slightly larger: total length, 145 mm.; tail, 60 mm.; and hind foot, 16 mm. This latter genus, known only from a single species, is a high-alpine species known from mountain meadows at elevations of 11,000 to 14,000 feet (Allen, 1938).

The desmans, Subfamily Desmaninae, are semiaquatic moles known from Europe and western Asia. Two genera are known in the subfamily.

The Old World moles, Subfamily Talpinae, have well-developed fossorial modifications in that the hands are enlarged, the external ears are absent, and the zygomatic arch is very small. They differ from the "American" moles in that the anterior incisors are small and are followed by enlarged canines, and the tail is about the same length as the hind foot. Four genera are recognized in this subfamily. The common Old World moles (*Talpa*) burrow through soft ground by forcing the snout and head forward by the action of the strong arms and shoulders. The feet are used to secure purchase on the sides of the tunnel while the head is being pushed forward. The earth is then shoved aside by raising the head. In harder ground the hands are used as scrapers to remove dirt (Matthews, 1952). They construct extensive burrow systems where they spend most of their time feeding mainly on various small animals including earthworms, adult insects, and insect larvae.

The "American" moles, Subfamily Scalopinae, have well-developed fossorial modifications but differ from the Old World moles in that the anterior incisors are larger than the following teeth and the tail is as long or longer than twice the length of the hind foot. The eastern mole, *Scalopus aquaticus,* reaches lengths up to 200 mm., of which the tail comprises 35 mm. The hind foot is 20 mm. in length. It occurs in the eastern United States. Arlton (1936) made a classical study of the ecology of this mole. In general, it seems to prefer loess or woodland soils, usually avoiding loose, sandy, or rocky soils. It digs by placing the forefeet close to the snout and pushing the earth aside. The snout is used not for loosening or moving dirt but in locating purchases for the forefeet in the next movement of dirt, until, within a few seconds, the body is half buried. When in this position, the mole turns over on its side and pushes the dirt upward, using the forefeet in this action. Deep tunnels are constructed by bringing the waste dirt to the surface. The size of the burrow systems varies but may cover an area as large as 3540 square m. The eastern mole apparently has three periods of activity, 2–6 A.M., 10 A.M.–2 P.M., and 9–11 P.M. In one 8-hour period during the daylight hours 91.4 liters of soil were brought to the surface and 4.6 m. of surface tunnels were constructed. In a similar period, nocturnal activity resulted in 58.4 liters of soil being brought to the surface and the construction of 2.7 m. of surface tunnels. Food of the eastern mole consists mainly of earthworms, adult insects, and insect larvae, although some vegetable materials are eaten.

The western moles, *Scapanus,* are restricted to the Pacific coastal areas of the western United States. They are similar in size and habits to the eastern mole. Grim (1958) maintained California moles (*Scapanus latimanus*) in captivity for several weeks. He found that the moles learned to use the water dispensers almost immediately. In feeding they would scrape dog food into the mouth with the almost prehensile nose. Living food was "cleaned" with the hands before it was put into the mouth. In captivity they would eat, on the average, 70 per cent of the body weight in canned dog food in a 24 hour period. Even more earthworms (averaging 85 per cent of the body weight) were eaten in a similar period, presumably because the intestinal contents of earthworms contain so much· dirt that would not be available as food to the mole. Jerusalem crickets and slugs appeared to be preferred to earthworms or dog food.

The hairy-tailed mole (*Parascalops breweri*) (reaching sizes as large as: total length, 150 mm.; tail, 35 mm.; hind foot, 33 mm.) is restricted to the northeastern United States and extreme southeastern Canada. Fay (1954) reported that in captivity the hairy-tailed mole ate two to three times its body weight in earthworms in a 24 hour period. A female, weighing 41 grams, ate 132.4 grams of worms; and a 45-gram male, 116.8 grams of worms. Hamilton (1939a) found no evidence of rhythmic activity in this species; rather, it appears to be active at any hour of the day or night, and is probably slightly more active during the daylight hours.

The star-nosed mole, Subfamily Condylurinae, constitutes only one genus with one species restricted to the northeastern United States and southeastern Canada. The star-nosed mole (*Condylura,*

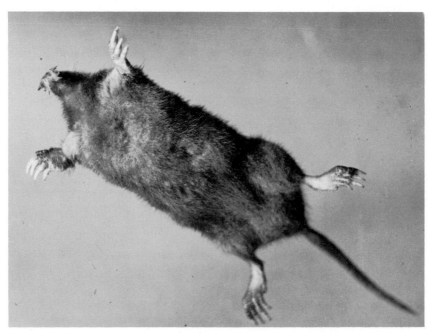

Fig. 9–8. A star-nosed mole (*Condylura cristata*). Note finger-like projections around nose. (Ernest P. Walker.)

Fig. 9–8) has a series of twenty-two soft, finger-like projections from the nose, thus the common name. Measurements of an adult are: total length, 178 mm.; tail, 76 mm.; hind foot, 27 mm.; and weight, 48 grams. It is found in a variety of habitats but is most common in swamps or along streams, where it feeds upon adult and larval insects. It can swim and has been observed to dive to the bottom of streams where it feeds on small crustacea and even small fish. It may share a muskrat house with its owners, building its own nest in the wall of the muskrat house. It has a home range of approximately one acre. Eadie and Hamilton (1956) studied reproduction in the star-nosed mole and found that they have but a single litter per year. The breeding season is in the spring, February to June, and the number of embryos varies from two to seven and averaged 5.4. The young reach adult size by the end of the summer and breed in the spring of the second year.

RECENT GENERA

Total 16.

Subfamily Uropsilinae. Shrew-moles.
    Uropsilus Milne Edwards. Shrew-mole, As.
    Nasillus Thomas. Shrew-mole, E.As.
Subfamily Desmaninae. Desmans.
    Desmana Guldenstadt. Desman, Eu., As.
    Galemys Kaup. Almizilero, Eu.
Subfamily Talpinae. Old World moles.
    Talpa Linnaeus. Common Old World moles, Eu., As.
    Mogera Pomel. Pomel's mole, E.As.
    Parascaptor Gill. White-tailed mole, E.As.
    Scaptochirus Milne Edwards. Musk mole, As.
Subfamily Scalopinae. American moles.
    Scaptonyx Milne Edwards. Spindle-tailed shrew-mole, E.As.
    Neurotrichus Gunther. American shrew-mole, N.A.
    Urotrichus Temminck. Japanese shrew-mole, Japan.
    Scapanulus Thomas. Owen's mole, E.As.
    Parascalops True. Hairy-tailed mole, eastern N.A.
    Scapanus Pomel. Western American mole, western N.A.
    Scalopus E. Geoffroy. Eastern American mole, eastern N.A.
Subfamily Condylurinae. Star-nosed mole.
    Condylura Illiger. Star-nosed mole, N.A.

10

Order Dermoptera

Flying Lemurs

The "flying lemur" is neither a lemur nor does it fly. It was originally considered to be a member of the Order Chiroptera (bats), then an aberrant insectivore and, of late, has been raised to an ordinal rank.

CHARACTERISTICS

The limbs are modified for a volant type of locomotion. The fore and hind limbs are equal in length and have an extensive thin membrane (patagium) that connects the neck to the forelimbs, the forelimbs to the hind limbs, and the hind limbs to the tail. The limbs are so modified that the animal is unable to stand upright on the ground. Only the claws of the digits extend beyond this membrane. The skull has a complete orbital ring of bone and well-developed postorbital process. The dentition is adapted for a diet of leaves. The molars are multicuspid and sharp-pointed. The teeth erupt late so that the milk dentition (except the third premolar) and the molars are in use at the same time. The dental formula is I $\frac{2}{2}$, C $\frac{1}{1}$, P $\frac{3}{3}$, M $\frac{3}{3}$ = 34. Features of the soft anatomy include the primitive brain with the cerebral hemispheres short and but slightly convoluted and the digestive tract adapted for a bulky herbivorous diet. The stomach has a well-developed cecum, and a large cecum exists at the junction of the small and large intestine. The females have a bifid uterus with two distinct openings into the vagina and a pair of pectoral mammae in the axilla of each forearm. In the males the penis is pendant and a well-developed scrotum is present.

RANGE

Living members of this order are restricted to the oriental region (Fig. 10–1). As fossils this order is known only from the Upper Paleocene and Lower Eocene of North America.

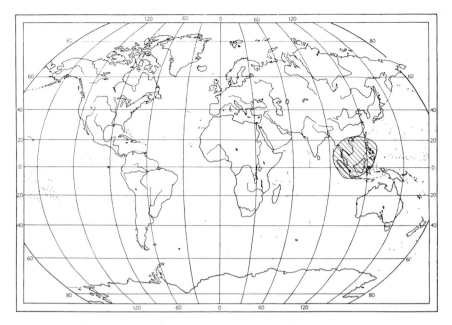

Fig. 10–1. The distribution of the Family Cynocephalidae.

Family CYNOCEPHALIDAE

Flying Lemurs

STRUCTURE

The structure of this, the only living family in the Order Dermoptera, is as outlined above. In external appearance the flying lemur is about 610 mm. (24 inches) in length, and has extreme adaptations for volant life. In addition to the limb adaptations indicated above, the ears are small and almost naked and the eyes are large and prominent. The hair is fine and silky, thicker above than below. The males are a dark chocolate-brown color while the females are usually gray and occasionally reddish tan.

NATURAL HISTORY

Wharton (1950) has recorded several observations on the flying lemur of the Philippines (*Cynocephalus volans*, Fig. 10–2). They are nocturnal, usually spending the day in holes in hollow trees (not hanging to tree trunks as recorded by Cabrera, 1925). They leave the den trees at dusk and apparently follow the same gliding routes night after night. Reportedly they can glide for distances up to 70 yards, although Wharton did not record any distances. They feed on the leaves, buds, and fruits of a series of trees. In feeding, a front foot pulls the leaves within reach of the mouth. While walking in the branches and feeding, the flying lemur always hangs upside down.

Fig. 10–2. A gliding lemur (*Cynocephalus volans*). (John N. Hamlet.)

One young per litter and one litter per year appears to be normal. The gestation period is approximately 60 days. The young cling to the abdomen of the mother as she hangs from a tree or in a den. When the mother feeds, the young is left hanging alone until she returns. Flying lemurs are often snared and used for food by natives in the Philippines and other parts of the Orient.

ONE RECENT GENUS

Cynocephalus Boddaert. Flying lemur, E.As.

11

Order Chiroptera

Bats

Bats are the only mammals with true flight. Both the fore and hind limbs are so modified that locomotion by other means is almost impossible. Not only have many unique structural features resulted from modifications for flight but, within this general plan, much adaptive radiation has occurred, usually associated with diet differences; so that bats represent a complex group of mammals. Only in recent years has much, other than strict morphology, been learned about them.

CHARACTERISTICS

The limbs are modified for flight. The forelimbs are greatly modified, with digits two to five greatly elongated. The radius is longer than the humerus; the ulna is vestigial. The hind limbs are relatively small, posteriorly directed, and are used to support the bat when it is not flying.

The dentition is usually relatively simple, heterodont, and complete; although there is a tendency for a reduction in the number of incisors and premolars. The canines are well developed and the molars are usually tubercular. The dental formula is various; it may be as low as I $\frac{1}{2}$, C $\frac{1}{1}$, P $\frac{1}{2}$, M $\frac{1}{1}$ = 20 but never exceeds I $\frac{2}{3}$, C $\frac{1}{1}$, P $\frac{3}{3}$, M $\frac{3}{3}$ = 38. The adult skull shows no evidence of sutures. It is extremely variable in shape but is often inflated in the auditory region.

The postcranial features includes a strong shoulder girdle, a keeled sternum, and a much reduced pelvic girdle. A calcar (an extension of the calcaneum) is usually present to support the posterior edge of the interfemoral membrane. The long bones are slender and marrowy.

Features of the soft anatomy include a brain with smooth cerebral hemispheres that do not extend back over the cerebellum. The females have a simple uterus that is more or less cornuate. The males have a pendant penis and testes that may be abdominal or inguinal.

The most obvious external feature is well-developed flight membranes. The elongated fingers support a thin wing that, posteriorly, is attached to the hind limb. An interfemoral membrane is often present between the tail and the hind limbs.

RANGE

Bats are worldwide in distribution, occurring on all land masses except those within the Arctic and Antarctic Circles. As a general rule the number of species as well as the number of individuals decrease as one goes toward the poles. Olaf Ryberg (1947) compiled the altitudinal distribution of the 1950 named forms (species and subspecies) of bats. He found that only 230 forms (approximately 10 per cent) had been recorded from elevations of more than 2000 feet; 100 forms from more than 6000 feet; and only 19 from more than 10,000 feet. He concluded that mountains of 6000 feet are barriers to most bats, and even 2000 feet is a barrier to 90 per cent of all bats.

RELATIONSHIPS

Little is known from direct evidence as to the relationships of bats. They are known as fossils from only a few fragmentary remains. The earliest remains are from the Eocene and already show typical bat modifications. Bats are presumed to be an ancient diversification of the insectivores.

SUBORDER MEGACHIROPTERA

Living bats are divided into suborders: Megachiroptera, with only one family, and Microchiroptera, with sixteen families. In Megachiroptera the second digit of the hand has a well-developed claw (absent in the other suborder), the margin of the ear forms a complete ring, and no tragus is present. The bony palate is continuous behind the last molar, and the cheek teeth have smooth crowns that have a longitudinal furrow.

Family PTEROPIDAE

Fruit-eating Bats

This family shows great variation in size and food habits ranging from the large fruit-eating flying "foxes" to tiny nectar-feeding forms.

STRUCTURE

The dentition of this family is varied but in general the crowns of the molars are smooth and have a well-developed median longitudinal groove. The individual cusps are generally indistinct. In one subfamily (Macroglossinae) the incisors and molars are reduced in size. The dental formulae vary from I $\frac{1}{1}$, C $\frac{1}{1}$, P $\frac{3}{3}$, M $\frac{1}{1}$ = 24 or I $\frac{1}{0}$, C $\frac{1}{1}$, P $\frac{3}{3}$, M $\frac{1}{2}$ = 24, to I $\frac{2}{2}$, C $\frac{1}{1}$, P $\frac{3}{3}$, M $\frac{2}{3}$ = 34. The skull is usually generalized, and the rostrum is generally more or less elongated. The bony palate projects posteriorly behind the molars, and a well-developed postorbital process is present. The floor of the braincase is not raised. The limbs are more generalized than are those of the other families of bats. The thumb always has a claw; the second digit of the hand usually has one. The second digit always maintains a large degree of independence from the third digit. The humerus has both the trochiter and the trochin small. The external features include ears that have the conch united to the base to form a complete ring, the absence of a tragus, and a tail that is generally reduced or absent. When present the tail is inferior to and not incorporated in the interfemoral membrane.

NATURAL HISTORY

The range of this family is restricted to the warmer parts of the Old World (Fig. 11–1). It is divided into four subfamilies: Pteropinae, the fruit bats; Macroglossinae, the long-tongued fruit bats; Nyctimeninae, the tube-nosed fruit bats; and Harpyionycterinae, the harpy fruit bats.

The fruit bats (Pteropinae), which include twenty-nine genera, are widely distributed in the warmer parts of the Old World. They are characterized by: a short tail or none at all; a claw always present on the second digit; tongue not greatly extensile nor the lower jaw modified; and teeth normal. One of the best known groups of this subfamily are the flying foxes (*Pteropus*). These are widely distributed in southern Asia, Australia, and the islands of the southern and western Pacific Ocean and are tailless bats with foxlike faces and long, slender muzzles. Most kinds of flying foxes spend the day hanging in trees where they often congregate in such large numbers as to break the branches of the trees in which they roost. One "camp," as these day roosts are called, in northern Australia was estimated to contain 32,000 individuals. Most species are large and one, *Pteropus neohibernicus* of New Guinea, reaches wingspreads of 1830 mm. (about 5.5 feet). Flying foxes feed on fruits of various sorts, often congregating in an orchard where they completely ruin a crop in a single night. At least in some parts of their range the fruit bats undergo seasonal migrations associated with the seasonal production of fruits by various trees. In captivity, fruit bats have been kept for a number of years. A *Pteropus giganteus* was kept for 17 years, 2 months; a *Rousettus leachi* for 19 years, 9 months (Allen, 1939).

The long-tongued fruit bats (Macroglossinae), which include seven genera, occur in the warmer parts of the Old World. They are characterized by: a tongue that is greatly extensile; a lower jaw that

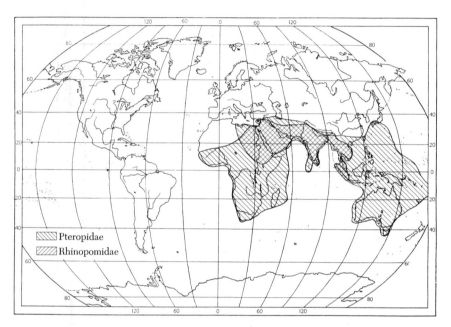

Fig. 11–1. The distribution of the families Pteropidae and Rhinopomidae.

is spoon-shaped in front; lower incisors that lie forward and flat; reduced teeth; and the occasional absence of a claw on the second digit (*Econycteris*). They are pollen- and nectar-feeding forms.

The tube-nosed fruit bats (Nyctimeninae), which include only two genera, are restricted to the area from Timor, through New Guinea, to the Solomons. They are characterized by: the presence of a well-developed tail and the tubelike extension of the nostrils. Members of the genus *Nyctimene* have irregular yellow spots on the forearm, wing, and ear membranes, probably as a protective device to help conceal these bats as they hang in trees during the day. Although some specimens taken contained only insect remains in the stomach, it is generally assumed that the diet consists of ripe, soft fruits and that the tube-nose is of aid in keeping the nasal passages free of food (Troughton, 1943). Tube-nosed bats are solitary.

The harpy fruit bat (Harpyionycterinae), is known only by a single genus from the Philippines. It is characterized by: normal frugivorous teeth, short face, and extremely strong intermaxillary bones. Some doubt exists as to the validity of this subfamily. Winge (1941) comments that it should probably be placed in the Pteropinae as a near relative of *Dobsonia*.

RECENT GENERA

Total, 39.

Subfamily Pteropinae. Fruit bats.
 Cynopterus F. Cuvier. Short-nosed fruit bats, S.As., E. Indies.
 Chironax Andersen. Black-capped fruit bats, E. Indies.
 Thoopterus Matschie. Short-nosed fruit bat, E. Indies.
 Dyacopterus Andersen. E.Indies.
 Penthetor Andersen. Lucas' short-faced fruit bat, E.Indies.
 Sphaerias Miller. Blanford's fruit bat, Burma.
 Ptenochirus Peters. E.Indies.
 Megaerops Peters. Tailless short-nosed fruit bat, E.Indies.
 Balionycteris Matschie. Spotted-winged fruit bat, Borneo.
 Rousettus Gray. Rousette bats, Af., S.As., W.Pacific.
 Pteropus Brisson. Flying foxes, Malagasy, S.As., Au., S. and W. Pac.
 Boneia Jentink. Celebes.
 Neopteryx, Hayman. S.As.
 Acerodon Jourdan. S. As.
 Pteralopex Thomas. S.As.
 Aethalops Thomas. Pygmy fruit bats, As.
 Styloctenium Matschie. Celebes.
 Dobsonia Palmer. Bare-backed fruit bats, SW.Pacific.
 Haplonycteris Lawrence. Celebes.
 Myonycteris Matschie. Little collared fruit bats, Af.
 Epomops Gray. Epaulet bats, Af.
 Epomophorous Bennett. Epauleted fruit bats, Af.
 Micropteropus Matschie. Dwarf epauleted fruit bats, Af.
 Scotonycteris Matschie. Af.
 Nanonycteris Matschie. Af.
 Hypsignathus H. Allen. Hammer-head bats, Af.
 Casinycteris Thomas. Af.
 Plerotes Andersen. Fruit bat, Af.
 Eidolon Rafinesque. Yellow-haired fruit bats, Af., As., Au., Pacific.
Subfamily Macroglossinae. Long-tongued fruit bats.
 Eonycteris Dobson. Dawn bats, S.As., E.Indies.
 Macroglossus Schinz. Long-tongued fruit bats, S.As., Au., W.Pacific.
 Syconycteris Matschie. Blossom bat, Au., W.Pacific.
 Megaloglossus Pagenstecher. African long-tongued fruit bat, W.Af.
 Melonycteris Dobson. W.Pacific.
 Nesonycteris Thomas. Solomon Island long-tongued fruit bat, Solomons.
 Notopteris Gray. Long-tailed fruit bat, W.Pacific.
Subfamily Nyctimeninae. Tube-nosed fruit bats.
 Nyctimene Berkhausen. Tube-nosed bats, E.Indies, Au.
 Paranyctimene Tate. Lesser tube-nosed bats, E.Indies.

Subfamily Haryionycterinae Thomas. Harpy fruit bat.
  Haryionycteris Thomas. Harpy fruit bat, Philippines.

SUBORDER MICROCHIROPTERA

The Microchiroptera contains sixteen families. In contrast to the Megachiroptera: the second digit of the hand does not end in a claw; the margin of the ear does not form a complete ring; a tragus is usually present; the bony palate does not continue behind the last molar; and the cheek teeth usually have sharp cusps separated by transverse grooves.

Family RHINOPOMIDAE

Mouse-tailed Bats

STRUCTURE

The dentition is of the insectivorous type with a formula of I ½, C ¼, P ½, M ⅔ = 28. The skull is broad and stout and has a transverse ridge or globular swelling on each side above the nares. Postorbital processes are absent and the premaxillaries, which are free, have a well-developed nasal branch and a much reduced palatal branch. In the vertebral column the seventh cervical and first thoracic vertebrae are not fused. In the limbs the second and third fingers each have two distinct phalanges; and in the third finger there is no trace of a third phalange. The feet are normal and the fibula is free and threadlike. The humerus has a small trochiter that does not articulate with the scapula. External features include an excessively long and slender tail, extending far beyond a narrow interfemoral membrane. The ears are large, extending beyond the nostrils when laid forward, and are united at the base across the forehead, and the tragus is simple. The muzzle has a distinct ridge-like dermal outgrowth down the center and the nostrils are unusual, appearing as transverse valvular slits.

NATURAL HISTORY

The range of this family is from northeastern Africa, eastward through southern Asia, to Burma and Sumatra (Fig. 11–1). Mouse-tailed bats are gregarious and are frequently found in deserted buildings and in tombs, generally in the desert and semidesert regions. Little is known about these bats. They presumably hibernate in winter.

ONE GENUS

Rhinopoma E. Geoffroy. Mouse-tailed bats, N.Af., S.As.

Family EMBALLONURIDAE
Sheath-tailed Bats

STRUCTURE

The dentition is normal insectivorous type but the formulae vary from I $\frac{1}{3}$, C $\frac{1}{1}$, P $\frac{2}{2}$, M $\frac{3}{3}$ = 30 to I $\frac{2}{3}$, C $\frac{1}{1}$, P $\frac{2}{2}$, M $\frac{3}{3}$ = 34. The skull has well-developed postorbital processes that are either slender and distinct (Emballonurinae) or broad and almost hidden by a wide supraorbital ridge (Diclidurinae); and free premaxillaries that are always incomplete, consisting primarily of well-developed nasal branches. In the vertebral column the seventh cervical and first thoracic vertebrae are unfused. In the limbs the second finger has a fully developed metacarpal but no phalanges; the third finger has two phalanges. The fibula is complete and threadlike. The clavicle is either not expanded (Emballonurinae) or greatly expanded (Diclidurinae). External features include the presence of a simple tragus; a tail that perforates the interfemoral membrane and appears to be loose on the dorsal surface; and a reflexed proximal phalanx of the third finger, resulting in a folded wing. Several species have distinct sacs along the anterior edge of the wing membrane.

NATURAL HISTORY

The range of this family is worldwide in the tropics except Australia (Fig. 11–2). Geologically it is known from the Eocene or Oligocene in Europe. Sheath-tailed bats are small, slender, and insectivorous. The family is divided into two subfamilies: Emballonurinae, or sac-winged bats, which occur throughout the range of the family; and the Diclidurinae, or ghost bats, which occur only in the tropical Americas. In the Emballonurinae, the sharp-nosed bat, *Rhynchonycteris*, ranges from southern Mexico southward to northern Peru and central Brazil. In general these are small, butterfly-like bats with a whitish dorsal stripe. Dalquest (1957) has recorded observations on one species, *Rhynchonycteris naso*, in southern Mexico. It is smaller and more slender than the little brown bat (*Myotis lucifugus*) of the United States or *Pipistrellus pipistrellus* of the Old World. The long interfemoral membrane is supported by greatly elongated calcars, and is furred on the basal portion. It is about 60 mm. in total length. The sharp-nosed bat inhabits the jungle, usually along relatively slow-moving streams. It is highly colonial, and in over 200 daytime resting places observed by Dalquest usually lived in groups of ten to twenty-five individuals. An exceptional roost of about 100 individuals was observed. Every colony, except those of nursing females, was located hanging over water, either under trees, branches, logs, or rock ledges. Here they so resemble patches of lichens that they cannot be observed until closely approached. Food consists of small insects, such as mosquitoes and midges. Food is taken as the bat flies over water in hunting flights that begin shortly after dusk. One night roost was observed under a concrete bridge spanning a dry arroyo. Here the bats, from a distance of 20 feet, appeared to be large tropical cock-

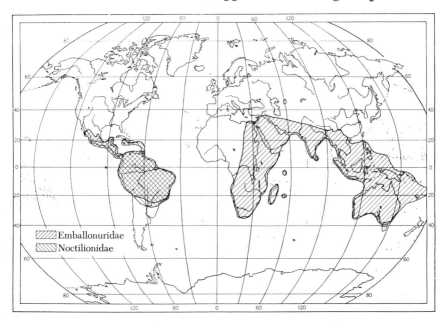

Fig. 11–2. The distribution of the families Emballonuridae and Noctilionidae.

roaches. The sharp-nosed bat has a single young at a time but may have more than one litter per year. Females with young apparently inhabit hollow logs lying on the ground, and not the usual roosts over water.

Various species of the sheath-tailed bats, *Emballonura*, occur in Malagasy, southern Asia and the South Pacific where they are often extremely common. Some species spend the daytime hanging in small groups in low-growing palms but feed on insects around the tops of tall trees (Tate, 1947).

The Diclidurinae, or ghost bats, known from three genera, occur only in the tropical parts of the New World. This subfamily differs in that the postorbital process is extremely broad and the clavicle is greatly expanded. The color of the ghost bats is pale to white.

Ghost bats are solitary cave dwellers, about which little has been written.

RECENT GENERA

Total, 13.

Subfamily Emballonurinae

    Emballonura Temminck. Sheath-tailed bats, Malagasy, S.As., S.Pacific.
    Coleura Peters. African sheath-tailed bats, E.Af.
    Rhynchonycteris Peters. Proboscis bats, tropical A.
    Saccopteryx Illiger. White-lined bats, tropical A.
    Cormura Peters. Wagner's sac-winged bat, tropical A.
    Peropteryx Peters. Peters' sac-winged bats, tropical A.
    Peronymus Peters. White-winged bats, S.A.
    Centronycteris Gray. Shaggy-haired bats, tropical A.
    Balantiopteryx Peters. Least sac-winged bats, tropical A.
    Taphozous I. Geoffroy. Tomb bats, Af., S.As., Au.

Subfamily Diclidurinae.

    Diclidurus Maximilian. Ghost bats, tropical A.
    Depanycteris Thomas. S.A.
    Cyttarops Thomas. S.A.

Family NOCTILIONIDAE

Bulldog Bats

STRUCTURE

The molar dentition is of the normal insectivorous type but the first upper incisors are enlarged, almost rodent-like, and conceal the second upper incisors. The dental formula is I $\frac{2}{1}$, C $\frac{1}{1}$, P $\frac{1}{2}$, M $\frac{3}{3} = 28$. The skull has premaxillaries with well-developed nasal and palatal branches that are fused with the maxillaries so that the palate is closed anteriorly. Postorbital processes are absent. In the vertebral column the seventh cervical and first thoracic vertebrae are unfused. In the limbs the second finger has the metacarpel as long as that of the third finger and has a single rudimentary phalanx. The third finger has two phalanges. The fibula is cartilaginous at the proximal end. The hind legs are elongated and bear large curved claws. External features include a normal muzzle, but the orifice of the mouth is transverse; and the very full lips form distinct cheek pouches and a well-developed tragus. The ears are narrow and sharp-pointed; the tail extends only half the length of the inter-femoral membrane. The interfemoral membrane is supported pos-teriorly by extremely long calcars.

NATURAL HISTORY

The range of this family is restricted to the tropical New World (Fig. 11–2). The bulldog bat (*Noctilio leporinus*) occurs from southern Mexico, southward to central Brazil. It has short close hair, long limbs, and large feet. It frequently spends the daytime in caves and crevices along the shore, but has been taken in hollow trees. The food consists of insects, including many winged ants, scarabaeoid beetles, mole crickets and stink bugs, and fish. Bloedel (1955), by observing and photographing captive individuals, determined for the first time how the bulldog bat captures fish. The fish are gaffed by the sharp claws of the extremely large and specialized hind feet. This is in contrast with most previous theories which held that the interfemoral membrane was used to capture the minnows. He thought that echolocation might be used at short range to locate the fish but concluded that chance contact would be sufficient to furnish enough minnows to adequately feed the bulldog bat.

The related species (*Noctilio labialis* = *Dirias minor* of some authors) is primarily insectivorous and gregarious. Colonies of several hundred individuals have been observed in attics of buildings.

ONE GENUS

Noctilio Linnaeus. Hare-lipped bats, tropical A.

Family NYCTERIDAE

Hispid or Slit-faced Bats

STRUCTURE

The dentition is the normal insectivorous type; the dental formula is I ⅔, C ¼, P ½, M ⅜ = 32. The skull has postorbital processes but these are obscured by broad supraorbital ridges. The premaxillaries consist of palatal branches only which completely fill the space between the mandibles. The vertebral column has the seventh cervical and first thoracic vertebrae fused and the first pair of ribs enlarged and strengthened. In the limbs the second finger has no phalanges, the third finger has two phalanges, and the fibula is present. External features include large ears that have a simple tragus and are connected at the bases by a low band of flesh; cutaneous outgrowths along the margin of the muzzle; and a long tail (about one-half the total length) that is included in the interfemoral membrane all the way to the tip.

NATURAL HISTORY

The range of this family is restricted to Africa and the Malayan area of Asia (Fig. 11–3). Only one genus (*Nycteris*) is known. Slit-faced bats are mainly African in distribution where they are gregarious, often congregating in large numbers in caves and producing much guano. Small groups have been found in buildings, culverts, hollow trees, and similar places. These insectivorous bats have been known to pick spiders, beetles, and other large insects from the walls

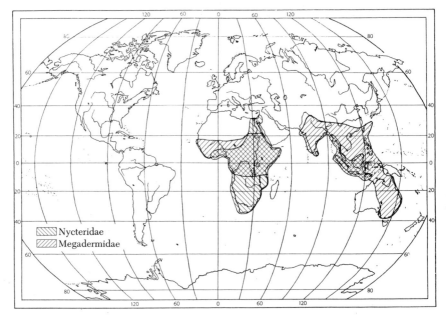

Fig. 11–3. The distribution of the families Nycteridae and Megadermidae.

of a veranda, even when it was well lighted (Shortridge, 1934). There is one young per litter and reportedly two litters in quick succession each year although the latter is highly improbable.

ONE GENUS

Nycteris E. Geoffroy and Cuvier. Slit-faced bats, Af., Malaya.

Family MEGADERMIDAE

Large-winged Bats

STRUCTURE

The dentition is reduced in number, especially the upper incisors. The upper canines are enlarged and project forward. The dental formulae are, I $\frac{0}{2}$, C $\frac{1}{1}$, P $\frac{1}{2}$, M $\frac{3}{3}$ = 26 or I $\frac{0}{2}$, C $\frac{1}{1}$, P $\frac{2}{2}$, M $\frac{3}{3}$ = 28. The skull has postorbital processes which are short or nearly absent and are nearly obscured by wide supraorbital ridges. The premaxillaries are absent. The vertebral column has the seventh cervical and the first thoracic vertebrae fused with the first ribs and the presternum into a solid ring of bone. In the limbs the second finger has one phalanx, and the third finger has two phalanges. The fibula is thread-like and is less than half the length of the tibia. External features include large ears that are joined halfway up the inner edges and contain a bifid tragus; a well-developed leaf on the nose; and a tail so reduced that it is not evident externally.

NATURAL HISTORY

The range is the tropical Old World: Africa, Asia, and Australia (Fig. 11–3). Geologically the family is known from the Eocene or Oligocene to the Miocene in Europe. The large-winged bat (*Megaderma*) occurs from India and the Malay Peninsula to Java and Borneo. It is colonial, roosting in caves, hollow trees, or attics of houses where it is usually the only species present. Food consists of large insects, small bats, frogs, lizards, mice, and even fish. In India it has been reported as entering cages and killing canaries.

The great-eared bat (*Lavia*) of tropical Africa is gray and yellowish in color and has orange wings. It is apparently a solitary bat that hangs in bushes during the day. Its bright color is associated with its habit of resting in trees for other cave-dwelling members of the family are dull colored. The presence of a long-eared bat in a tree is often betrayed by the almost constant motion of its long ears (Shortridge, 1934).

RECENT GENERA

Total, 3.

Megaderma E. Geoffroy. False vampires, Af., S.As.
Macroderma Miller. Giant false vampires, Au.
Lavia Gray. Yellow-winged bats, tropical Af.

Family RHINOLOPHIDAE

Horseshoe-nosed Bats

STRUCTURE

In the dentition the upper incisors are rudimentary; the lower incisors are well developed as are the first and second molars. The third upper molar and the second and third premolars (when present) are reduced in size or are rudimentary. The dental formula is

I ½, C ¼, P ⅔, M ⅗ = 32. The skull is without postorbital processes, and the premaxillaries are reduced extending anteriorly from the palate without additional contact with the maxillaries. The vertebral column has the seventh cervical and first thoracic vertebrae fused with the first ribs, part of the second ribs, and the presternum into a solid ring of bone. In the limbs the second finger is without phalanges; the third has two; and the toes have three phalanges except the hallux, which has only two. External features include large ears that lack tragi and well-developed leaflike cutaneous folds around the nostrils.

NATURAL HISTORY

The range of this family is Old World, including Europe, Asia, Africa, and Australia (Fig. 11–4). The horseshoe bat (*Rhinolophus*) occurs in most of Europe and Asia, the East Indies, Australia, and throughout Africa. It is typically a cave bat, although colonies have been reported from mine tunnels, quarries, and buildings. They often occupy different caves in the winter than in the summer. Some species are solitary in habit. The horseshoe bats are insectivorous. Some species "hawk" for moths, hanging on the end of a branch, taking short flights to capture an insect, and then return to the same vantage point. One young per litter and one litter per year are normal. At least in the northern part of their range, horseshoe bats hibernate. When resting, horseshoe bats completely wrap the wings around the body, even hiding the eyes.

RECENT GENERA

Total, 2.

Rhinolophus Lacépède. Horseshoe bats, Eu., Af., As., Au.
Rhinomegalophus Bourret. Horseshoe bats, Au.

Family HIPPOSIDERIDAE

Old World Leaf-nosed Bats

Some authorities have combined this family with Rhinolophidae, which appears to be logical, as few major differences are evident.

STRUCTURE

The structure of this family is quite similar to that of the last family, Rhinolophidae. It differs as follows: the dental formulae are

I ½, C ¼, P ²⁄₂, M ³⁄₃ = 30 or I ½, C ¼, P ½, M ³⁄₃ = 28; and the
toes have only two phalanges instead of three.

NATURAL HISTORY

The greater leaf-nosed bats (*Hipposideros*) which include some
130 species distributed throughout the Old World tropics, include
some of the largest insectivorous bats. Pratt's round-leaf horseshoe
bat (*Hipposideros pratti*), of southern Asia, reaches a length of 166
mm., with a forearm 90 mm. long. (Fig. 11–4.)

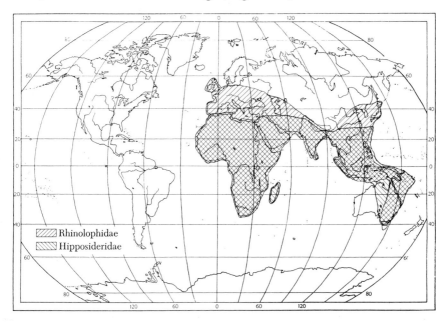

Fig. 11–4. The distribution of the families Rhinolophidae and Hipposideridae.

Sexual dimorphism in this family is extreme with the posterior
noseleaf varying in size and shape with the sex of the individual.
They are cave dwelling and highly colonial. Another species, *Hipposideros commersoni*, in southwestern Africa, has been reported to
hang from the upper branches of trees exposed to bright sunlight,
while others were roosting in the roof of a building. They have the
habit of hanging from a branch of a tree and darting out at passing
insects, and reportedly returning night after night to the same spot.
Occasionally they return to the spot to leisurely devour the insect.
At other times, they have been observed to snap large insects from
the leaves of a tree or from the tops of tall grasses (Shortridge,
1934).

RECENT GENERA

Total, 9.

Hipposideros Gray. Greater horseshoe bats, tropical Old World.
Asellia Gray. Trident bats, NE.Af.
Anthops Thomas. Flower-faced bats, Af.
Cloeotis Thomas. African trident bats, E.Af.
Coelops Blyth. Hairy-faced horseshoe bats, S.Af., S.As.
Paracoelops Dorst, Au
Rhinonicteris Gray. Golden horseshoe bats, Au.
Triaenops Dobson. E.Af., Malagasy, Iran.
Aselliscus Tate. Tate's trident bats, S.As.

Family PHYLLOSTOMATIDAE

American Leaf-nosed Bats

STRUCTURE

The dentition is extremely varied, ranging from the normal insectivorous type of tubercular molars to smooth-crowned molars adapted for fruit eating. The dental formulae are various, ranging from I $\frac{2}{2}$, C $\frac{1}{1}$, P $\frac{2}{2}$, M $\frac{2}{2}$ = 28 to I $\frac{2}{2}$, C $\frac{1}{1}$, P $\frac{2}{3}$, M $\frac{3}{3}$ = 34. In the limbs the second finger has a small distinct phalanx, the third finger has three phalanges, and the slender fibula is incomplete. External features include the presence of a simple leaflike growth on the nose. The tail and interfemoral membrane are various but the tail never extends appreciably beyond the free edge of the interfemoral membrane. A tragus is present but is variable in structure.

NATURAL HISTORY

The range of this family is the New World from southern United States, southward through most of South America (Fig. 11–5). It is so diverse in structure and habits that it is divided into seven subfamilies: Chilonycteriinae, Phyllostomatinae, Glossophaginae, Carollinae, Sturnirinae, Stenoderminae, and Phyllonycterinae.

The mustache bats (Subfamily Chilonycteriinae) differ from the other Phyllostomatidae in that the trochiter does not articulate with the scapula; the hind leg has an unusually long calcarial spur; and the tibia is unusually long and strongly compressed. The dentition is of the normal insectivorous type. The dental formula is I $\frac{2}{2}$, C $\frac{1}{1}$, P $\frac{2}{3}$, M $\frac{3}{3}$ = 34. External features include the absence of a nose-leaf (a wartlike protuberance may occur above the nares), the presence of platelike outgrowths on the lower lips, and a tail that projects through the upper surface of the interfemoral membrane. Members of this subfamily (three genera) are colonial, cave dwelling, and insectivorous. Two color phases, a brown phase and a "reddish" phase, are known in most species. Felten (1956) reported that Parnell's mustached bat, *Chilonycteris parnelli*, spends the daytime in deep caves or tunnels that have high temperatures and high relative humidity; and they are usually associated with other species.

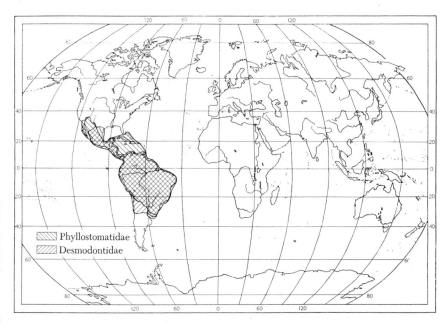

Fig. 11–5. The distribution of the families Phyllostomatidae and Desmodontidae.

In the big-eared, leaf-nosed bats (Subfamily Phyllostomatinae), the nose-leaf is well developed, the ears are large, and the molars are of the normal tubercular type. Twelve genera are known. The food habits of members of this subfamily are varied, ranging from insectivorous to frugivorous. The California leaf-nosed bat (Fig. 11-6) is primarily insectivorous but also feeds on the ripe fruits of various cacti. The little big-eared bat, *Micronycteris megalotis*, is more or less solitary in habit. One or two bats, usually one of each sex, are found hanging by one foot in shallow caves, highway tubes, or occasionally in dense foliage of trees. They emerge after darkness and feed on many kinds of fruit. In San Luis Potosí, Mexico, Dalquest (1953) found them feeding on small guavas. The bats picked the fruit as they hovered in the air, then carried it to another tree where it was eaten. Felten (1956) recorded observations on the spear-nosed bat, *Phyllostomus discolor* in El Salvador, Central America. He found these bats in large colonies in dark caves and hollow trees. Fragments of fruit (figs and other species) were invariably found under these colonies. In captivity they fed on stationary and moving insects (including moths), fruits, and honey water. Meat and blood were not touched.

Fig. 11–6. A California leaf-nosed bat (*Macrotus californicus*). Note the well-developed nose-leaf, or flap of bare skin, above nose. (Bruce J. Hayward.)

In the long-tongued bats (Subfamily Glossophaginae), a small nose-leaf is present, the ears are short and rounded, the tail is short, the muzzle is elongated, the tongue is highly extensile and is covered with bristle-like papillae and the cheek teeth are narrow and elongate (Fig. 11–7). Thirteen genera are known all of which apparently feed on nectar and pollen as well as some insects. They are mostly cave dwellers. The shrew-faced bat, *Glossophaga soricina*, inhabits hot humid caves and mine tunnels, buildings, and hollow trees, usually sharing its quarters with several other species. In captivity Felten (1956) found that it fed on honey water, fruit (especially ripe bananas), and insects. Insects appeared to be the preferred food during the 14 months they were kept in captivity. The honey water was also taken at all times of the year. It was taken while the bats hovered near petri dishes suspended from the roof of a cage. The various genera in the subfamily show a progressive elongation of the rostral region of the skull, presumably associated with a nectivorous diet. The long-nosed bat (*Leptonycteris nivalis*, Fig. 11–8) feeds on the nectar and pollen of agaves and saguaros in southern Arizona.

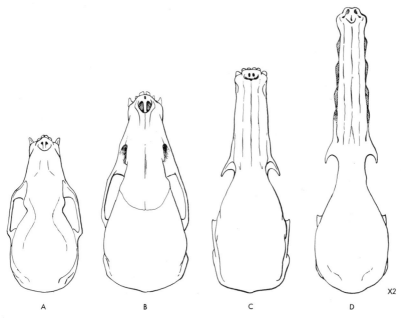

A   B   C   D

Fig. 11–7. The skulls of four genera of bats in the Subfamily Glossophaginae. Note the progressive elongation of the rostral region, an adaptation for feeding on nectar in flowers. (A) *Glossophaga soricina*; (B) *Leptonycteris nivalis*; (C) *Choeronycteris mexicana*; (D) *Musonycteris harrisoni*.

In the common short-tailed bats (Subfamily Carollinae) a small, pointed nose-leaf is present; the ears are rather short; the tail reaches about the middle of the naked, moderately developed interfemoral membrane; the muzzle is short; the tongue is normal; and the teeth are somewhat modified for a fruit diet. This subfamily includes only two genera. Felten (1956) found the short-tailed bat, *Carollia perspicallata*, to be widespread in caves and mine tunnels in El Salvador, where it is colonial but often occurs in clusters of other species. Dalquest (1953) thought that in Mexico this species fed entirely on fruit, primarily wild figs and other wild fruits, but to some extent on bananas.

The yellow-shouldered bats (Subfamily Sturnirinae) have normal nose-leaf, short ears, no external tail, a narrow interfemoral membrane that is densely furred, short rostrums, and teeth modified for a frugivorous diet. Three genera are known in this subfamily and all are frugivorous. Little is known concerning their habits for they have not been taken in day roosts. Dalquest (1953) took specimens of *Sturnira* in mist-nets stretched across arroyos, small clearings in forests, and over a pond. In southern Sonora, Mexico, the author has observed *Sturnira* as they fed on wild figs.

Fig. 11–8. A long-nosed bat *(Leptonycteris nivalis)* hovering over a flower. Note the long, extensile tongue and the elongated rostrum. (Bruce J. Hayward.)

In the short-faced bat (Subfamily Stenoderminae) a nose-leaf is usually present (sometimes rudimentary or absent), the ears are short, the tail is reduced or absent, the interfemoral membrane is narrow, the muzzle is short and wide, the teeth are modified for a frugivorous diet, and one or two white facial stripes are usually present. The subfamily contains nineteen genera. The members of this subfamily are the typical fruit-eating phyllostomatid bats. They inhabit deep and shallow caves, tunnels, hollow trees, and some hang under large leaves such as that of the banana plant.

In the flower bats (Subfamily Phyllonycterinae), the ears are moderately large; and the tail is short and extends on the dorsal surface of the interfemoral membrane. The rostrum and the tongue are elongated. The tongue has many long, bristle-like papillae. The diet consists of pollen and nectar of various flowers. These bats, known from two genera, are restricted to the West Indies.

RECENT GENERA
Total, 52.

Subfamily Chilonycteriinae. Mustache bats.
    Chilonycteris Gray. Mustache bat, tropical A.
    Pteronotus Gray. Naked-backed bat, tropical A.
    Mormoops Leach. Leaf-chinned bat, tropical A.
Subfamily Phyllostomatinae. Big-eared, leaf-nosed bats.
    Micronycteris Gray. Small big-eared bats, tropical A.
    Macrotus Gray. Leaf-nosed bats, southern N.A., W.Indies.
    Lonchorhina Tomes. Sword-nosed bat, W.Indies, Northern S.A.
    Macrophyllum Gray. Long-legged bat, Brazil.
    Tonatia Gray. Round-eared bats, tropical A.
    Mimon Gray. Spear-nosed bats, tropical A.
    Phyllostomus Lacépède. Spear-nosed bats, tropical A.
    Phylloderma Peters. Spear-nosed bats, S.A.
    Trachops Gray. Fringe-lipped bats, tropical A.
    Chrotopterus Peters. Woolly false vampire bats, tropical A.
    Vampyrum Rafinesque. Neotropical false vampire bats, tropical A.
Subfamily Glossophaginae. Long-nosed bats.
    Glossophaga E. Geoffroy. Shrew-faced bats, tropical A.
    Lionycteris Thomas. S.A.
    Lonchophylla Thomas. Long-nosed bats, tropical A.
    Platalina Thomas. S.A. (Peru).
    Monophyllus Leach. Long-tongued bats, W.Indies.
    Anoura Gray. Tailless bats, tropical A.
    Choeronycteris Tschudi. Hog-nosed bats, tropical N.A.
    Choeroniscus Thomas. Godman's long-nosed bats, tropical A.
    Scleronycteris Thomas. S.A.
    Hylonycteris Thomas. Underwood's long-nosed bats, C.A.
    Leptonycteris Thomas. Long-nosed bat, tropical N.A.
    Lichonycteris Thomas. Brown-nosed bat, tropical A.
    Musonycteris Schaldach and McLaughlin. Banana bat, Mexico.
Subfamily Carolliinae. Common short-tailed bats.
    Carollia Gray. Short-tailed bat, tropical A.
    Rhinophylla Peters. South American short-tailed bat, tropical S.A.
Subfamily Sturnirinae. Yellow-shouldered bats.
    Sturnira Gray. Yellow-shouldered bats, tropical A.
    Corvira Thomas. S.A.
    Sturnirops Goodwin. Hairy-footed bat, Costa Rica.
Subfamily Stenoderminae. Short-faced bats.
    Brachyphylla Gray. Fruit-eating bats, W.Indies.
    Uroderma Peters. Tent-making bat, tropical A.
    Platyrrhinus Saussure. Broad-nosed bats, tropical A.

Vampyrodes Thomas. Great stripe-faced bat, S.A.
Vampyressa Thomas. Yellow-eared bats, tropical A.
Vampyriscus Thomas. S.A.
Chiroderma Peters. Big-eyed bat, tropical A.
Ectophylla H. Allen. White bats, C.A., Guiana.
Artibeus Leach. Fruit-eating bats, tropical A.
Enchisthenes Andersen. Little fruit-eating bats, tropical A.
Ardops Miller. Tree bats, Lesser Antilles.
Phyllops Peters. Fig-eating bats, W.Indies.
Ariteus Gray. Jamaican fig-eating bat, Jamaica.
Stenoderma E. Geoffroy. Red fruit bat, Puerto Rico.
Pygoderma Peters. Isamon bats, tropical A.
Centurio Gray. Wrinkle-faced bat, C.A., tropical A.
Sphaeronycteris Peters. S.A.
Ametrida Gray. S.A.
Subfamily Phyllonycterinae. Flower bats.
Erophylla Miller. Brown flower bats, W.Indies.
Phyllonycteris Gundlach. Smooth-toothed flower bats, W.Indies.

Family DESMODONTIDAE

Vampires

STRUCTURE

In the dentition the molars have no trace of a crushing surface and both the premolars and molars are reduced to tiny blades. The incisors are large, recurved, and bladelike. The dental formulae are: I $\frac{2}{2}$, C $\frac{1}{1}$, P $\frac{1}{2}$, M $\frac{2}{2}$ = 26 and I $\frac{1}{2}$, C $\frac{1}{1}$, P $\frac{1}{2}$, M $\frac{1}{1}$ = 20. The skull lacks postorbital processes. In the limbs the third finger has three phalanges. The fibula is large and functional. External features include a nose-leaf, small ears with tragi, no tail, and a narrow strip of interfemoral membrane.

NATURAL HISTORY

The range of this family is restricted to the subtropical and tropical New World (Fig. 11–5). The most widely distributed member of the family, *Desmodus rotundus,* is a medium-sized bat (total length 84 mm., forearm 55 mm.) that has no tail or interfemoral membrane. They spend the daytime in caves and, to some extent, in hollow trees and buildings. Day roosts are characterized by the presence of pools of tarlike digested blood that accumulate below the roosting colony. A single colony may include more than 100 individuals. They feed primarily on the blood of horses and burros but will feed on almost any warm-blooded animal including cows, sheep, goats, chickens, and man.

Vampires can be kept readily in captivity by feeding them on a diet of defibrinated blood. Their feeding habits in captivity have been described by Ditmars and Greenhall (1935). The blood was lapped from the bowl by stretching the tongue out through the split in the lower lip, thus obtaining the food without placing the lips in contact with the blood. After feeding they crawled back to the resting place.

RECENT GENERA

Total 3.

Desmodus Maximilian. Vampire bats, tropical A.
Diaemus Miller. White-winged vampire bats, tropical S.A.
Diphylla Spix. Hairy-legged vampire bats, tropical A.

Family NATALIDAE

Funnel-eared Bats

It is thought that these bats, as well as the following two families, Furipteridae and Thyropteridae, were isolated in South America during Tertiary times and are recent invaders of southern North America (Allen, 1939).

STRUCTURE

The dentition is of small teeth of the normal insectivorous type; the molars have sharp cusps; the dental formula is: I $\frac{2}{3}$, C $\frac{1}{1}$, P $\frac{3}{3}$, M $\frac{3}{3}$ = 38. The skull is delicate and has complete premaxillaries but postorbital processes are absent. The vertebral column has all the lumbar vertebrae (except the two posterior ones) fused into a single inwardly curved compressed bone. In the limbs the second finger has no phalanges; the third has two; and the fibula is threadlike. The hind legs are unusually long. External features include small size, distinctly funnel-shaped ears with tragus, and elongated legs. The tail is normal and extends to the end of the well-developed interfemoral membrane.

NATURAL HISTORY

The range of this family is restricted to the tropical and subtropical New World (Fig. 11–9). The funnel-eared bat, *Natalus*, occurs in colonies in deep caves, usually in association with other

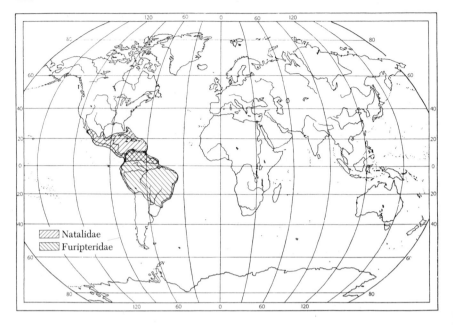

Fig. 11–9. The distribution of families Natalidae and Furipteridae.

species of bats. Little is known of their habits but they appear to be insectivorous, probably do not hibernate, and they have but one young per year.

ONE GENUS

Natalus Gray. Funnel-eared bats, C.A., W. Indies, S.A.

Family FURIPTERIDAE

Smoky Bats

The smoky bats may have been much more common in past times but are unsuccessful in competition with the more progressive recent invaders of South America (Allen, 1939).

STRUCTURE

The dentition consists of tubercular premolars and molars; the canines are reduced to a premolar shape. The dental formula is I ⅔, C ¼, P ⅔, M ⅜ = 36. The skull is like that of Natalidae except the premaxillaries only have rudimentary palatal branches. The vertebral column is as in the Natalidae. In the limbs the first finger is reduced and is included in the wing membrane; the third finger has two phalanges and the fibula. External features include funnel-shaped ears with tragi, a tail ending slightly beyond the middle of the interfemoral membrane, and a rudimentary thumb included in the wing membrane.

NATURAL HISTORY

The range of this family is restricted to South America (Fig. 11–9). The genus *Furipterus* is known from only a single species that occurs in Columbia, the Guianas, and Brazil (de Cunha Vierira, 1955). It is rare in collections and little is known of its habits. Presumably it is insectivorous. The second genus in this family, *Amorphochilus*, also with only one known species, is equally rare and unknown. It has been recorded from Peru and Chile. Osgood (1914) reports capturing two individuals, one male and one female, as they were flying around in a room late at night.

RECENT GENERA

Total, 2.

Furipterus Bonaparte. Smoky bats, tropical S.A.
Amorphochilus Peters. Smoky bats, tropical S.A.

Family THYROPTERIDAE

Disk-winged Bats

STRUCTURE

The dentition is tubercular, with weak canines. The dental formula is I $\frac{2}{3}$, C $\frac{1}{1}$, P $\frac{3}{3}$, M $\frac{3}{3}$ = 38. The skull is essentially the same as in Natalidae. The vertebral column does not have the lumbar vertebrae fused. In the limbs the thumb has a distinct claw, the second finger has the metacarpal reduced to half the size of the metacarpal of the third finger. The toes have only two phalanges; and the third and fourth toes, together with their claws, are fused together from their bases to their tips. The fibula is reduced, thread-like, and only half the length of the tibia. External features include funnel-shaped ears with tragi, and suction pads on the thumb and on the soles of the feet.

NATURAL HISTORY

The disk-winged bats, known only from a single genus, occur from British Honduras, southward into northern South America

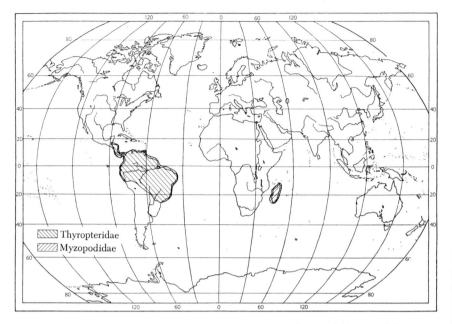

Fig. 11–10. The distribution of families Thyropteridae and Myzopodidae.

(Fig. 11–10). They are small in size (total length, 66 mm.; tail, 26 mm.; forearm, 31 mm.) and appear to be rather fragile. Their habits are little known. They are insectivorous and usually roost individually, often being found clinging to the inside of rolled-up banana fronds (Allen, 1939).

ONE GENUS

Thyroptera Spix. Disk-winged bats, C.A. and tropical S.A.

Family MYZOPODIDAE

Golden Bat

STRUCTURE

The dentition and skull are essentially as in Natalidae and Furipteridae. The dental formula is I ⅔, C ¼, P ⅗, M ⅗ = 38. In the vertebral column the lumbar vertebrae are unfused. In the limbs the metacarpal of the second finger is well developed; the third finger has three bony phalanges; the toes have only two phalanges; the third and fourth toes together with their claws are fused throughout their whole length; and the fibula is threadlike. External features include the relatively large ears that have the meatus partially closed by large mushroom-like structures arising from their bases and the presence of suction cups on the thumbs and on the bottoms of the feet.

NATURAL HISTORY

Nothing is known of the habits of this small, rare, insectivorous bat that occurs only in Malagasy (Fig. 11–10).

ONE GENUS

Myzopoda Milne Edwards and Grandidier. Sucker-footed bats, Malagasy.

Family VESPERTILIONIDAE

Vespertilionid Bats

STRUCTURE

The dentition consists of molars that are tubercular in the typical insectivorous manner and varied dental formulae ranging from I ½, C $\frac{1}{1}$, P ½, M $\frac{3}{3}$ = 28 to I $\frac{2}{3}$, C $\frac{1}{1}$, P $\frac{3}{3}$, M $\frac{3}{3}$ = 38. The skull does not have postorbital processes and the premaxillae are without palatal branches, resultantly the palate is widely emarginate anteriorly. The vertebral column is unfused except in one *Tomopeas* which has the seventh cervical and first thoracic vertebrae fused. In the limbs the third finger has three phalanges, the most distal of which is cartilaginous, except at its base. External features include ears which are usually separate and with a normal tragus; a simple muzzle and lips; and a complete interfemoral membrane in which the tail extends little, if any, beyond its free edge.

NATURAL HISTORY

The vespertilionid bats are a widespread (Fig. 11–11) and relatively uniform group that is divided into six subfamilies: the Vespertilioninae, or common bats; the Miniopterinae, or bent-winged bats; the Murininae, or tube-nosed insectivorous bats; the Kerivoulinae, or trumpet-eared bats; the Nyctophilinae, or big-eared bats; and the Tomopeatinae, or Peruvian bat.

The common bats (Vespertilioninae) are a somewhat diverse group (thirty genera) that is characterized by a combination of characters including unkeeled ears with well-developed basal lobes; the seventh cervical and first dorsal vertebrae unfused; sternum long and slender; and the second upper premolar reduced or absent.

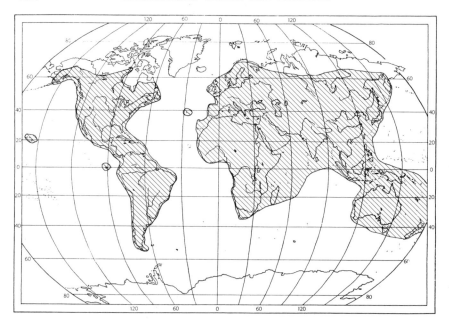

Fig. 11–11. The distribution of Family Vespertilionidae.

Members of 'this subfamily are widely distributed, especially in the temperate zones of both the Old World and the New World. The Mexican big-eared bat (Fig. 11–12) shows the well-developed ears and tragus clearly.

Most of the studies of the life history, embryology and physiology of bats have been made on members of this subfamily. Most are relatively small insectivorous forms that may be solitary, in small groups, or in large colonies. In temperate regions most species hibernate in the winter, usually in a cave, mine tunnel, or similar place. In the spring many move from the hibernal to summer roosts. Spermatogenesis occurs in late summer and mating occurs in September or October or during hibernation. Spermatozoa remain in the female reproductive tract until ovulation and fertilization occurs in the spring (April–May). The gestation varies, even within a given species, and is apparently influenced by the environmental temperatures. Only one young per litter and one litter per year appears to be the rule, although some species routinely have two young per litter (e.g., the hoary bat, Fig. 11–13) and at least one may have as many as four young per litter. In nature some individuals have been known to live as long as 20 years.

The bent-winged bats (Miniopterinae), known from only a single genus, are widely distributed in northern Africa and southern

Europe and Asia. The subfamily is characterized by the reduction in size of the second upper premolar and the presence of an extremely elongated second phalanx in the third finger. This phalanx is three times the length of the first phalanx and at rest, is flexed against the upper part of the wing. The tail is exceptionally long, being equal to or greater than the length of the head and body. In the skull, the rostrum is short and rounded and the cranium proper

Fig. 11–12. A Mexican big-eared bat (*Plecotus phyllotis*). Note the extremely large ears and well-developed tragus. (Bruce J. Hayward.)

Fig. 11–13. A hoary bat (*Lasiurus cinereus*). This bat normally spends its days roosting in trees. Note how the interfemoral membrane is covered with fur. (Bruce J. Hayward.)

is exceptionally elevated. Because of the great length of the wings the bent-winged bats have a flight pattern that is rapid, sustained, and swallow-like. They are cave-dwelling and insectivorous, flying at great heights soon after sundown (Tate, 1947).

The tube-nosed insectivorous bats (Murininae), known from two genera from southern Asia, are characterized by normal-sized second upper premolar and nostrils that are elongated into tubes. The dorsal surface of the interfemoral membrane is covered by dense fur. Most species are brownish gray in color but some are reddish and one is a golden yellow.

The trumpet-eared bats (Kerivoulinae) are known from only two genera from Africa and southern Asia to the Solomon Islands. They are characterized by a funnel-shaped ear that has a long, pointed tragus. These tiny, butterfly-like bats are covered with dense woolly fur. They are thought to be tree dwellers.

The long-eared bats (Nyctophilinae), with three genera, occur in western North America and southern Asia. They are characterized by a low nose-leaf or horseshoe-shaped ridge bearing the nostrils and by big ears.

The Peruvian bat (Tomopeatinae), known from only a single genus with but one species from Peru, is characterized by the presence of a rudimentary keel on the ear, but no anterior basal lobes, and in having the seventh cervical and first dorsal vertebrae fused. Morphologically, it appears to be a primitive form, somewhat intermediate between the vespertilionids and the molossids, and may represent the last remnants of an early form (Allen, 1939). It has the delicate form and tail structure of the vespertilionids and the ear structure and vertebral characteristics of the molossids.

RECENT GENERA

Total, 38.

Subfamily Vespertilioninae. Common bats.

Myotis Kaup. Little brown bats, almost worldwide.
Pizonyx Miller. Fishing bats, N.A.
Lasionycteris Peters. Silver-haired bats, N.A.
Pipistrellus Kaup. Pipistrelles, N.A., Eu., As., Au., Af.
Glischropus Dobson. Thick-thumbed bats, S.As.
Nyctalus Bowdich. Noctule bats, Af., Eu.
Eudiscopus Conisbee. Disk-footed bats, Philippines.
Eptesicus Rafinesque. Big brown bats, almost worldwide.
Rhinopterus Miller. Horny-skinned bats, Af.
Hesperoptenus Peters. Tickell's bats, southern As.
Tylonycteris Peters. Club-footed bats, southern As.
Mimetillus Thomas. Moloney's flat-headed bat, Af.
Philetor Thomas. Af.
Histiotus Gervais. Big-eared brown bats, S.A.
Laephotis Thomas. DeWhinton's long-eared bat, Af.
Vespertilio Linnaeus. Frosted bats, Eu., As.
Otonycteris Peters. Long-eared bats, N.Af., As.
Nycticeius Rafinesque. Evening bats, N.A. As., Au., Af.
Scotomanes Dobson. Harlequin bats, southern Asia.
Rhogeëssa H. Allen. Little yellow bats, tropical A.
Baeodon Miller. Baeodon, tropical N.A.

Scotophilus Leach. Yellow bats, Af., As.
Chalinolobus Peters. Groove-lipped bats, Af., Au., New Zealand.
Glauconycteris Dobson. Butterfly bats, Af.
Cistugo Thomas. Wing-gland bats, Af.
Lasiurus Gray. Hoary and red bats, N.A., S.A.
Barbastella Gray. Barbastelles, N.Af., Eu., W.As.
Plecotus I. Geoffroy. Long-eared bats, Eu., As., N.Af., N.A.
Euderma H. Allen. Spotted bat, N.A.
Subfamily Miniopterinae. Bent-winged bats.
Miniopterus Bonaparte. Long-winged bats, N.Af., S.Eu., S.As.
Subfamily Murininae. Tube-nosed insectivorous bats.
Murina Gray. Tube-nosed insectivorous bats, S.As., Malaya, Japan.
Harpiocephalus Gray. Hairy-winged bats, S.As.
Subfamily Kerivoulinae. Trumpet-eared bats.
Kerivoula Gray. Painted bats, Af., S.As.
Anamygdon Troughton. Solomons.
Subfamily Nyctophilinae. Long-eared bats.
Antrozous H. Allen. Pallid bats, N.A.
Nytophilus Leach. Big-eared bats, E.Indies, Au.
Pharotis Thomas. E.Indies.
Subfamily Tomopeatinae.
Tomopeas Miller. S.A. (Peru).

Family MYSTACINIDAE

New Zealand Short-tailed Bats

STRUCTURE

The dentition is tubercular, with sharp cusps on the molars. The dental formula is I $\frac{1}{1}$, C $\frac{1}{1}$, P $\frac{2}{2}$, M $\frac{3}{3}$ = 28. The skull lacks postorbital processes and the premaxillae have well-developed palatal branches. In the limbs the second finger has one phalanx; the third finger has three bony phalanges; the fifth finger is longer than the third metacarpal; the fibula is complete and functional; and the foot is short and broad. External features include a short tail about half the length of the narrow interfemoral membrane, broad wings, and supplementary talons on the claws of the toes and thumb.

NATURAL HISTORY

These rare and little-known bats of the forested areas of New Zealand (Fig. 11–14) are known from a single species. They live in hollow trees and, unlike other species of bats, do little flying. They apparently secure their food by chasing the insects in the branches of trees. Harper (1945) indicates that this bat is on the verge of extinction and may, in fact, be extinct, perhaps as a result of clearing

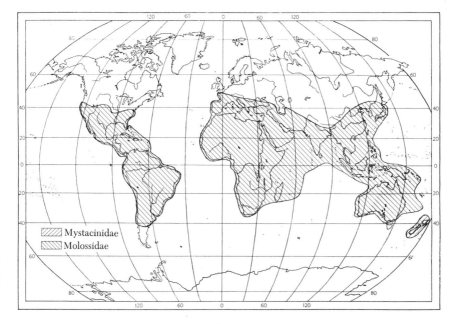

Fig. 11–14. The distribution of families Mystacinidae and Molossidae.

of the forests. The bat was apparently never very common and nothing is known of its life history.

ONE GENUS

Mystacina Gray. New Zealand short-tailed bats, New Zealand.

Family MOLOSSIDAE

Free-tailed Bats

STRUCTURE

The dentition is of the tubercular type and the dental formulae vary from I ⅟₁, C ⅟₁, P ½, M ⅜ = 26 to I ⅓, C ⅟₁, P ⅖, M ⅜ = 32. In the skull postorbital processes are absent and nasal branches of the premaxillae may be present or absent. The vertebral column has the seventh cervical and first thoracic vertebrae fused and the first pair of ribs thickened. In the limbs the second finger has a rudimentary phalanx; the third, three; the fifth finger is greatly shortened, being scarcely longer than the second metacarpal; and the short, strong legs have well-developed fibulas. External features include ears with small tragi and well-developed antitragi; no cutaneous outgrowths around the nose; and a short but complete interfemoral membrane with the tail extending conspicuously beyond its free edge. The two outer toes have characteristic spoon-shaped hairs.

NATURAL HISTORY

The molossid bats are primarily colonial species that often congregate in large colonies in suitable habitats throughout the warmer parts of the world (Fig. 11–14). All are insectivorous.

Fig. 11–15. Brazilian free-tailed bats (*Tadarida brasiliensis*) hanging on a cave wall. (Photo by Bruce J. Hayward.)

The Mexican free-tailed bat (*Tadarida brasiliensis mexicana*, Fig. 11–15), of the southwestern United States and Mexico, has been the subject of a number of studies in recent years. Mating occurs in the spring at about the time of ovulation. Shortly after this the females congregate in maternity colonies, often consisting of several million individuals. Here they each give birth to a single young. During this time the males are widely scattered, roosting singly or in small groups in caves, tunnels, buildings, rock crevices, or under the bark of trees. In the late summer, the maternity colonies break up and most individuals migrate southward, where they congregate in extremely large colonies in caves in central Mexico.

RECENT GENERA

Total, 10.

Eomops Thomas. Af.

Molossops Peters. Dog-faced bats, tropical A.

Cheiromeles Horsfield. Naked bats, S.As., E.Indies.

Xiphonycteris Dollman. Free-tailed bat, Af.

Tadarida Rafinesque. Free-tailed bats, worldwide in warmer regions.

Platymops Thomas. Flat-headed, free-tailed bats, Af.

Otomops Thomas. Big-eared, free-tailed bats, Af., S.As.

Molossus E. Geoffroy. Velvety free-tailed bats, tropical A.

Promops Gervais. Dome-palate mastiff bats, tropical A.

Eumops Miller. Mastiff bats, tropical A.

12

Order Primates

Primates

The primates as an order are mostly arboreal animals that are vegetarians or omnivores although a few are terrestrial and a few, insectivorous. Unlike other kinds of mammals, mating behavior in most primates is not limited in either sex to short, definitely determinable periods of the year.

CHARACTERISTICS

The limbs are plantigrade and usually have five digits. The digits usually have nails but some have claws. The thumbs and great toes are usually opposable. The clavicles are well developed; and the radius and ulna are never united. The skull has the orbits, usually surrounded by bone, directed forward. The dentition is of at least three kinds of teeth during at least one time of life; the molars are more complex than the premolars. The dental formulae are various ranging from I $\frac{1}{1}$, C $\frac{0}{0}$, P $\frac{1}{0}$, M $\frac{3}{3}$ = 18 to I $\frac{2}{2}$, C $\frac{1}{1}$, P $\frac{3}{3}$, M $\frac{3}{3}$ = 36. Features of the soft anatomy include a stomach that is generally simple, usually one pair of thoracic mammae and a brain that always has a posterior lobe and a calcarine fissure. External features show progressive adaptations for an arboreal habitat.

RANGE

The distribution of the order is essentially tropical and subtropical Old and New World, with the exception of man, who is cosmopolitan.

SUBORDER PROSIMII

Primates are usually divided into two major groups: Suborder Prosimii and Suborder Anthropoidea. In the more primitive group, Prosimii, the face is more or less elongate, the orbit is widely confluent with the temporal fossa, the cerebral hemispheres of the brain are only slightly convoluted, and the first upper pair of incisors are separated in the midline.

Family TUPAIIDAE

Tree Shrews

The relationships of the tree shrews are uncertain, to say the least. They are either very primitive primates or else very aberrant members of the Order Insectivora and have been placed with equal justification in each order.

STRUCTURE

The dentition includes broad upper molars with the cusps arranged in a "W," upper incisors that are large, caniniform, and separated in the midline and canines that are reduced in size. The dental formula is I $\frac{2}{3}$, C $\frac{1}{1}$, P $\frac{3}{3}$, M $\frac{3}{3}$ = 38. The skull has a comparatively large braincase (when compared with insectivores—but small compared with the higher primates), well-developed zygomatic arches, and a rostrum that is prolonged anteriorly. The limbs are of the general arboreal type, with the radius and ulna and the tibia and fibula separate. External features include a squirrel-like shape, feet naked beneath, pointed head, and rounded ears. The long tail is prehensile in at least some forms, and the fur is thick and soft. Females have one, two, or three pair of mammae which are axillary and/or inguinal.

NATURAL HISTORY

The range of this family is the Philippines and southern China to India, southward through Java, Sumatra, and the adjacent islands (Fig. 12–1). Two subfamilies are recognized: the tree shrews (Tupaiinae) and the pen-tailed shrews (Ptilocercinae). The pen-tailed shrews (known only from a single genus) are characterized by the presence of a large terminal tuft of hair on the tail and large, membranous ears (instead of small, cartilaginous ears).

The tree shrews, Tupaiinae, are squirrel-like in shape and size. They reach lengths as great as 14 inches of which the tail comprises 6.5 inches. They are extremely active and excitable animals and are antisocial. In captivity they fight each other or jointly attack and destroy the weakest one. In nature they form territories that are actively defended against other individuals of the same species. Food consists of insects and fruits.

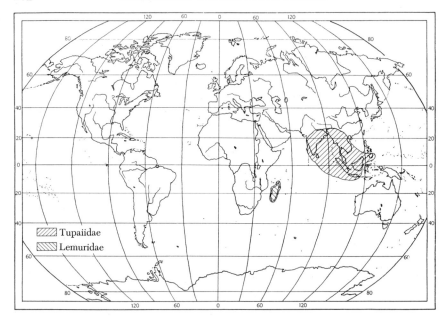

Fig. 12–1. The distribution of families Tupaiidae and Lemuridae.

RECENT GENERA

Total, 5.

Subfamily Tupaiinae. Tree shrews.

   Tupaia Raffles. Tree shrews, India, China, E.Indies, Philippines.

   Anathana Lyon. Indian tree shrew, India.

   Dendrogale Gray. Small tree shrews, SE.A., Borneo.

   Urogale Mearns. Philippine tree shrews, Philippines.

Subfamily Ptilocercinae. Pen-tailed shrews.

   Ptilocercus Gray. Pen-tailed shrews, E.Borneo, E.Indies, Malaya.

Family LEMURIDAE

Lemurs

STRUCTURE

In the dentition C1 is large, conical, and compressed; p1 is caniniform; the first upper incisors are separated from each other by a wide diastema; and the lower incisors and canines are procumbent. The dental formula is I $\frac{2}{2}$, C $\frac{1}{1}$, P $\frac{3}{3}$, M $\frac{3}{3}$ = 36. In the skull the orbit and temporal fossa are widely confluent beneath the orbital bar. The limbs are not disproportionately long, the tarsus is only slightly elongate (except in two species), and the calcaneum is always less than one-fourth the length of the tibia. The fibula is well developed and distinct from the tibia. All of the digits (except the second of the hind foot) have flat nails. The external features are extremely varied, associated with the radial adaptations that have occurred in the family. They range in size from 300 mm. (12 inches) in total length to as much as 1425 mm. (56 inches). The limbs and body are slender; the eyes are large and closely set; a long, furred tail is present. Some forms are arboreal, some terrestrial, and some are bipedal.

NATURAL HISTORY

The lemurs, confined to Malagasy and adjacent islands (Fig. 12–1), are divided into two subfamilies: Lemurinae and Cheirogaleinae. The Cheirogaleinae, or mouse lemurs and dwarf lemurs, are small in size (total length 300 to 600 mm.) and are generally arboreal forms that have a tail longer than the head and body. The Lemurinae or true lemurs are larger (up to 1425 mm. in total length) and are usually terrestrial forms with the tail about equal to or less than the length of the head and body.

Harper (1945) has summarized most of the available information on the status and habits of the known forms. The broad-nosed lemurs (*Hapalemur*), with two species, reach lengths as great as 610 mm. (24 inches). They are herbivorous, feeding on grasses and bamboo leaves, and are most common in bamboo forests. They are gregarious, usually traveling in groups of two or three, and are usually nocturnal. The lemurs (*Lemur*), with five species, include the largest members of the family. Most are diurnal or crepuscular, and inhabit open rocky country. They are herbivorous, feeding on various wild fruits, figs, and bananas and, in the winter season, prickly pear. Being quite gregarious they are often seen in parties of up to fifteen in number. They may have young, one to three in number, at any time of the year.

The weasel lemurs (*Lepilemur*), with two species, are nocturnal herbivores that feed on fruits and the buds and leaves of certain trees. The mouse lemurs (*Cheirogaleus*), with three species, reach lengths as great as 580 mm., of which the tail comprises 275 mm. They are nocturnal, arboreal, and apparently feed on fruits and perhaps honey. They hibernate during the cold season, subsisting on fat that is stored around the base of the tail. In general the mouse lemurs are now rare.

The dwarf lemur (*Microcebus*), with two species, includes the smallest living primates. One of the species, as an adult, is 300 mm.

in total length, of which the tail comprises 150 mm. Dwarf lemurs are nocturnal and arboreal. They feed on honey, fruit, and insects. They have two or three young in a litter that are born at the beginning of the rainy season after a gestation period of approximately 4.5 months. The fork-marked lemur (*Phaner*), with a single species, reaches a length of 600 mm. of which the tail comprises 350 mm. It is nocturnal, arboreal, and feeds on fruits and honey.

RECENT GENERA

Total, 6.

Subfamily Lemurinae. Lemurs.
   Hapalemur I. Geoffroy. Broad-nosed lemurs, Malagasy.
   Lemur Linnaeus. Lemurs, Malagasy.
   Lepilemur I. Geoffroy. Weasel lemurs, Malagasy.
Subfamily Cheirogaleinae. Mouse and dwarf lemurs.
   Cheirogaleus I. Geoffroy. Mouse lemurs, Malagasy.
   Microcebus I. Geoffroy. Dwarf lemurs, Malagasy.
   Phaner Gray. Fork-marked lemurs, Malagasy.

Family INDRIDAE

Woolly Lemurs

STRUCTURE

The dentition consists of enlarged first upper incisors that are separated by a wide diastema; elongated procumbent lower incisors; upper canines enlarged and sharp; lower canines elongate and procumbent; and first lower premolar caniniform. The dental formula is I $\frac{2}{1\,or\,2}$, C $\frac{1}{0\,or\,1}$, P $\frac{2}{2}$, M $\frac{3}{3} = 30$. The skull has the braincase enlarged and globular and a shortened rostrum. The limbs have a large, opposable hallux and a small, slightly opposable pollex. The digits of the foot are united by a web of skin that extends to the first phalanx. The hind limbs are greatly developed, although the foot is normal in size. External features include a tail that is either short (*Indri*) or long. The face is short and monkey-like; and the second digit of the foot has an elongated claw. The pelage varies from white to brownish black in color.

NATURAL HISTORY

Three genera, restricted to Malagasy and adjacent islands (Fig. 12–2), are known in this family: the woolly lemurs (*Avahi*) and the indri (*Indri*), with but a single species each; and the skifakas (*Pro-*

pithecus), with three species. The indri, with its short tail, reaches a length of 720 mm. (28.5 inches), of which the tail comprises 70 mm. The woolly lemur reaches a length of 690 mm., of which the tail comprises 390 mm.; the skifakas are smaller.

Members of this family are diurnal, arboreal, and vegetarian. They feed on leaves, fruits, buds, and flowers. One species, *Indri*, reportedly also takes small birds. They mate in the rainy season and,

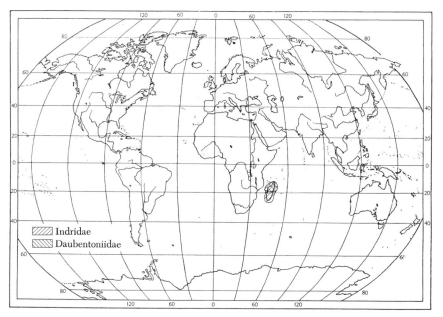

Fig. 12–2. The distribution of families Indridae and Daubentoniidae.

at least in *Indri*, a single young is born after a gestation period of 60 days. The female carries her young on her back for a number of months. The indrisoid lemurs spring upright from branch to branch of trees and can jump as far as 30 feet, thus giving rise to a belief that they can fly. They usually travel in bands of eight to twelve individuals. Early reports (in the 1780's) indicated that the natives tamed the indri and used them like dogs in hunting.

RECENT GENERA

Total, 3.

Avahi Jourdan. Woolly lemurs, Malagasy.
Propithecus Bennett. Skifakas, Malagasy.
Indri E. Geoffroy. Endrinas or indris, Malagasy.

Family DAUBENTONIIDAE

Aye-aye

STRUCTURE

The dentition consists of very large, compressed and curved incisors with persistent pulps; incisors with enamel on the anterior surface only; no canines; and flat-crowned molars with indistinct tubercules. The dental formula is I $\frac{1}{1}$, C $\frac{0}{0}$, P $\frac{1}{0}$, M $\frac{3}{3}$ = 18. The skull is relatively large and rounded. The orbit is surrounded by a ring of bone posteriorly but ventrally is confluent with the temporal fossa. The limbs are long and slender. The digits are pointed and have compressed claws, except the thumb, which has a nail. The middle digit of the hand has an unusually elongated claw. The thumb and great toe are opposable. External features include the short face, large naked ears, and a long bushy tail.

NATURAL HISTORY

The family, known only from northern Malagasy (Fig. 12–2), is represented by a single living species, the aye-aye (*Daubentonia madagascariensis*). It is cat-sized (total length 875 mm., tail 475 mm.) and is dark brown to nearly black in color. It lives in the bamboo forests of the interior of Malagasy and does not appear to be common anywhere. The aye-aye is solitary in habit, although on rare occasions two are seen together. It is nocturnal and arboreal and is adept at moving through tree branches. It feeds on the pith of bamboo and sugar cane and on larval and adult wood-boring beetles. Food is secured by rodent-like incisors and an elongated claw on the middle finger. The female builds a large nest and gives birth to a single young in February or March.

ONE GENUS

Daubentonia E. Geoffroy. Aye-aye, Malagasy.

Family LORISIDAE

Lorises and Pottos

STRUCTURE

The dentition consists of a dental formula of I $\frac{2}{2}$, C $\frac{1}{1}$, P $\frac{3}{3}$, M $\frac{3}{3}$ = 36. The second upper incisors are greatly reduced or absent in *Nycticebus*. The lower incisors are procumbent, with i2 enlarged and caniniform. The canines are long and sharp; the premolars, bicuspid; and the lower molars, quadritubercular. The skull has a large orbit. The limbs are generalized for arboreal locomotion. The forelimbs and the hind limbs are nearly equal in length. The index finger is very short and nailless or absent. The thumb and great toe are opposable and diverge from the other digits. External features include a round head; very large eyes; short, rounded ears; and short woolly pelage. The tail is long, short, or rudimentary. Members of this family are completely arboreal and the limbs are not adapted for running or jumping.

NATURAL HISTORY

The range of this family is Equatorial Africa, India, Ceylon, East Indies, and the Philippines (Fig. 12–3). Four genera are known: the slender loris (*Loris*) of India and Ceylon; the slow loris (*Nycticebus*)

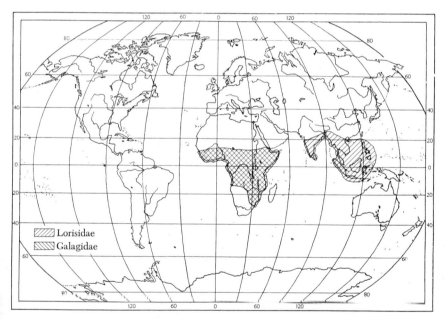

Fig. 12–3. The distribution of families Lorisidae and Galagidae.

of southern Asia; and the pottos (*Arctocebus* and *Perodicticus*) of Africa. All are arboreal, often moving by slow hand-over-hand progression (brachiation), through the trees. They are nocturnal and feed on a variety of insects, fruits, and berries. In gathering food with their hands, they often hang suspended by the hind limbs. Daylight hours are spent in heavy foliage or in hollow trees. They breed twice a year in any season and have one or two young after a gestation period of from 90 days (*Nycticebus*) to 108 days (*Loris*). Although the young are precocial (at birth their eyes are open and they are covered with fur) the adult female carries them until they are almost adult sized (Fig. 12–4). In captivity the slender loris will live as long as 10 years. They usually are solitary in behavior, and

Fig. 12–4. A slow loris (*Nycticebus coucang*). Note young hanging beneath mother. (Ernest P. Walker.)

have well-developed senses of sight, hearing, and smell. The slow loris reaches a length of 455 mm. (18 inches) (and has no tail) and weighs up to 1 pound. Measurements of the pottos are: total length, 420 mm.; tail, 60 mm.; hind foot, 78 mm. The stomach contents of specimens included: white grubs, caterpillars, and snails (Hollister, 1924).

RECENT GENERA

Total, 4.

Loris E. Geoffroy. Slender lorises, India, Ceylon.
Nycticebus I. Geoffroy. Slow lorises, S.As., E.Indies to Philippines.
Arctocebus Gray. Angwantibos or calabor pottos, Af.
Perodicticus Bennett. Pottos, Equatorial Af.

Family GALAGIDAE

Galagos

STRUCTURE

The dentition consists of a dental formula of I $\frac{2}{2}$, C $\frac{1}{1}$, P $\frac{3}{3}$, M $\frac{3}{3} = 36$. The upper incisors are subequal in size; the lower incisors are procumbent, with the second enlarged and caniniform. The second upper and third lower premolars are caniniform; the molars are tritubercular. The skull has an enlarged rostrum and large orbits. The limbs are adapted for leaping and jumping and decidedly unequal. The femur, tibia, and fibula are elongated. External features include large ears, long bushy tail, long limbs, and short woolly pelage.

NATURAL HISTORY

Two genera are known in this family: *Galago,* known by a variety of common names including galago, bush baby, and night-ape; and *Euoticus,* known as the needle-clawed galagos, bushy-tailed lemur, and night-ape. Both are restricted to Equatorial Africa (Fig. 12–3). They are arboreal, progressing by leaps through the branches of trees. On the ground they hop and often spring up and move obliquely for distances up to 10 feet. They are nocturnal and spend the day in heavy foliage or in hollow trees. The diet is varied, ranging from insectivorous to omnivorous. Fruits, berries, small birds, eggs, and lizards are taken in addition to insects. They are often found in small groups. One or two young are born between April and October after a gestation period of 120 days. The young may either be left in a nest of leaves in the trees or carried, hanging on to the ventral surface of the mother. The young nurse 3.5 months and are mature at 20 months. *Galago* has lived 13 years in captivity and *Euoticus* has lived 9 years, 9.5 months (Shortridge, 1934). The measurements of an adult male *Galago lasiotis* are: total length, 630 mm.; tail, 360 mm.; hind foot, 88 mm. (Hollister, 1924). This is one of the larger species in the genus.

GENERA

Total, 2.

Galago E. Geoffroy. Galagos, Bush babies, Af.
Euoticus Gray. Needle-clawed galagos, Equatorial Af.

Family TARSIIDAE

Tarsiers

STRUCTURE

The dentition consists of the following teeth: I $\frac{2}{1}$, C $\frac{1}{1}$, P $\frac{3}{3}$, M $\frac{3}{3} = 34$. The first upper incisors are enlarged and closely appressed; the lower incisors are not procumbent. The canines are relatively small. The molars are tuberculate. The skull has a broad, globular braincase. The orbits are large and are almost completely separated from the temporal fossa by a bony septum. The limbs are adapted for leaping on the ground or in trees. The forelimbs are much shorter than the hind limbs. The fibula is slender and is fused for the distal half to the tibia. Digits $\frac{5}{5}$, with nails, except the second and third of the hind foot which have claws. External features include: a globular head with a short muzzle and large naked ears; a short body with long slender legs; and a long tail. The digits have enlarged pads on their tips. The pelage is long and silky.

NATURAL HISTORY

One genus is known in this family and its range is restricted to scattered islands of the East Indies from Sumatra to the Philippines (Fig. 12–5). Tarsiers are arboreal and terrestrial. They reach lengths up to 330 mm. (13 inches) and weigh about 6 ounces. They move through trees with froglike leaps and on the ground, walk or leap. They are crepuscular or nocturnal, spending the daylight hours clinging to vertical branches. Tarsiers are basically insectivorous, feeding on a variety of insects including grasshoppers and beetles, but will also take lizards, frogs, and other small animals. The prey is captured by springing through the air and grabbing it with

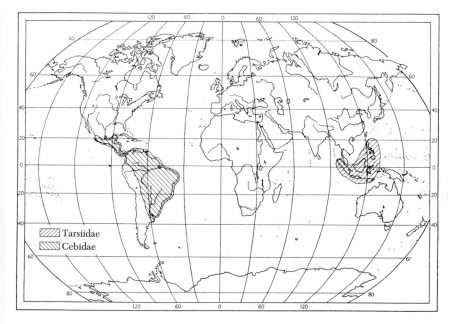

Fig. 12–5. The distribution of families Tarsiidae and Cebidae.

both hands. The tarsier is polyestrous and breeds at any time of the year. At birth the single young is well furred, has the eyes open, and is capable of climbing. It is carried, clinging to the abdomen of its mother, for several months. In captivity they live up to 3 years.

ONE GENUS

Tarsius Storr. Tarsiers, E.Indies to Philippines.

SUBORDER ANTHROPOIDEA

Primates of this suborder have the snout and face shortened into more or less a caricature of the human face. Digits in this group have nails instead of claws (except the marmosets); there is no space between the upper incisors; and the orbit is completely separated from the temporal fossa by a bony plate. The cerebral hemispheres are richly convoluted. The suborder is divided into three super-families; the South American monkeys, Ceboidea; the Old World monkeys, Cercopithecoidea; and the higher primates, Hominoidea.

SUPERFAMILY CEBOIDEA, NEW WORLD MONKEYS AND MARMOSETS

The New World monkeys have probably evolved separately from the other Anthropoids since Eocene times. Externally they differ in that the nasal septum is broad and the nostrils open laterally; the thumb is only partially or not at all opposable (may be reduced or absent); and cheek pouches and ischial callosities are absent. Cranially they differ in that there is no bony external auditory meatus, although a tympanic bulla is present; and the cheekbone is broadly in contact with the parietal. Two families are recognized in this superfamily.

Family CEBIDAE

New World Monkeys

STRUCTURE

The dentition consists of unspecialized incisors; canines that vary from short to strong; premolars that are bicuspid; and quadricuspid molars. The dental formula is I $\frac{2}{2}$, C $\frac{1}{1}$, P $\frac{3}{3}$, M $\frac{3}{3}$ = 36. The skull is usually rounded and has a short rostrum and large braincase. A broad intermarial cartilage is usually present. The limbs have nails on all of the digits. The thumb is present and usually opposable. The great toe is often absent; when present it diverges widely from the other digits. External features include a slender build with long, slender limbs and a long tail that is often prehensile. The nose is flat, and the ears are short and rounded. The pelage is varied, long and silky, short and coarse, or even woolly.

NATURAL HISTORY

The range of this family is from southern Mexico, southward through Central America, to tropical South America (Fig. 12–5). New World monkeys are quite diverse, morphologically, and living members are usually divided into six subfamilies although some writers have considered each to be a distinct family.

The night monkeys, Aotinae, are characterized by extremely enlarged eyes and a brain that is the least enlarged in this family. The sakis, Pitheciinae, are entirely frugivorous and are restricted to the Amazon Basin. The howler monkeys, Alouattinae, have the throat modified for a howling call. A laryngeal pouch is much enlarged and the hyoid bone is enlarged into a large capsule. The tail is long and prehensile. The squirrel monkeys, Cebinae, have short thumbs and enlarged brains. The tail is long but not naked at the tip. The spider monkeys (Fig. 12–6), Atelinae, have the thumb absent or reduced and closely appressed to the second digit. The tail is prehensile, naked on the venter, and the limbs are unusually long.

Fig. 12–6. A spider monkey (*Ateles geoffroyi*). (Ernest P. Walker.)

Goeldi's marmoset, Callimiconinae, is restricted to the Amazon Basin.

All members of this family are completely arboreal, perhaps more so than any other primate group. They are extremely agile, climbing and swinging rapidly through tree tops by means of their hands, feet, and prehensile tail. They are typically diurnal (the Aotinae are nocturnal) and gregarious, traveling around in family groups or troops up to fifty in number. The diet consists of insects, birds, eggs, fruits, and berries. Reportedly the Pitheciinae are almost entirely frugivorous.

RECENT GENERA

Total, 12.

Subfamily Aotinae. Night monkeys.
  Aotus Itumbaldt. Night monkeys, tropical S.A.
  Callicebus Thomas. Titi monkeys, tropical S.A.
Subfamily Pitheciinae. Sakis.
  Cacajao Lesson. Ukaris, Amazon Basin, S.A.
  Pithecia Desmarest. Sakis, Guianas and Amazon Basin, S.A.
  Chiropotes Lesson. Red-backed sakis, Guianas and Amazon Basin, S.A.
Subfamily Alouattinae. Howler monkeys.
  Alouatta Lacepede. Howler monkeys, tropical A., n. to Mexico.
Subfamily Cebinae. Squirrel monkeys.
  Cebus Erxleben. Capuchins, tropical A., Nicaragua to Brazil.
  Saimiri Voigt. Squirrel monkeys, tropical C. and S.A.
Subfamily Atelinae. Spider monkeys.
  Ateles E. Geoffroy. Spider monkeys, tropical A., Mexico to the Amazon.
  Brachyteles Spix. Woolly spider monkeys, Brazil.
  Lagothrix I. Geoffroy. Woolly monkeys, tropical S.A.
Subfamily Callimiconiae.
  Callimico Ribeiro. Goeldi's marmoset, Amazon.

Family CALLITHRICIDAE

Marmosets

STRUCTURE

The dentition is characterized by a reduction in the number of molars as compared to the cebids. The dental formula is I $\frac{2}{2}$, C $\frac{1}{1}$, P $\frac{3}{3}$, M $\frac{2}{2}$ = 32. The skull is rounded and the braincase is relatively small. The limbs are elongated, with especially elongated hands and feet. The digits have pointed claws except the thumb, which has a flat nail. The thumb is enlarged and opposable; the great toe is reduced in size and not opposable. External features include an elongated body and appendages, including a long, non-prehensile tail; forelimbs that are shorter than the hind limbs, and large, tufted ears. The face is naked. The pelage, long and soft, varies from black through gray and reddish-brown to golden in color.

NATURAL HISTORY

The marmosets, restricted to tropical Central and South America (Fig. 12–7), are known by four living genera. They are small, squirrel-sized, and have long silky hair. They are arboreal and usually travel in small bands, running and climbing through tree branches

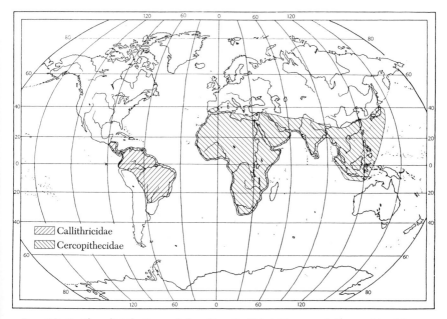

Fig. 12–7. The distribution of families Callithricidae and Cercopithecidae.

and occasionally jumping from branch to branch. After a gestation period of 140 to 150 days the young, usually three in number, are born. The male is quite active in helping with the care of the young. Some, such as the crested marmoset (Fig. 12–8), have a conspicuous median crest of long white hairs on the forehead.

RECENT GENERA

Total, 4.

Callithrix Erxleben. Marmosets, tropical S.A.
Cebuella Gray. Pygmy marmosets, tropical S.A.
Saguinus Hoffmannsegg. Bare-faced marmosets, C.A., tropical S.A.
Leontideus Cabrera. Lion-headed marmosets, tropical S.A.

Fig. 12–8. Crested marmosets (*Saguinus oedipus*). (Ernest P. Walker.)

SUPERFAMILY CERCOPITHECOIDEA, OLD WORLD MONKEYS

The Old World monkeys have a narrow nasal septum; resultantly the nostrils are close together and face forward or downward. In contrast to the New World monkeys, the thumb is usually opposable and tail is never prehensile. Cranial characteristics separating these cercopithecoids from the ceboids include tympanic bulla, absent cheekbone not in contact with the parietal. Cheek pouches and ischial callosities are often present.

Family CERCOPITHECIDAE

Old World Monkeys

STRUCTURE

The dentition is characterized by a reduction in the number of premolars. The dental formula is I $\frac{2}{2}$, C $\frac{1}{1}$, P $\frac{2}{2}$, M $\frac{3}{3}$ = 32. The upper canines are large and tusklike; the lower canines recurved; and the molars elongated anteroposteriorly. The skull has a highly concave palate that extends posterior to the molars; small flattened bullae with a long, bony external auditory meatus; and a narrow internarial septum. The limbs are equal in length; and locomotion on the ground is quadripedal and plantigrade. The thumb and great toe, if present, are opposable. External features include medium to large size with rounded muzzles, tail varying from short to long and never prehensile, and highly colored ischial callosities (hairless callused areas on the skin in the region of the ischial bone).

NATURAL HISTORY

The Old World monkeys, which occur in southeastern Europe, Africa, southern Asia, and the East Indies (Fig. 12–7), are divided into two subfamilies, or, by some workers, into two families. The Colubinae (languars and proboscis monkeys) are characterized by a diet of leaves, with a correspondingly large sacculate stomach. The tail is very long and straight. The face and the nose are short in all but one genus. The cheek pouches are reduced in size. Six genera are known.

The Cercopithecinae (macaques; mangabeys, Fig. 12–9; apes; baboons; and drills) are omnivorous and do not have enlarged sacculate stomachs. The face and nose are usually elongate, the tail is often reduced or absent, and large cheek pouches are present. Ten genera are known.

The macaques (*Macaca*) include the well-known rhesus monkey and range from northern Africa, through southern Asia, the East Indies, and northward into the Philippines and Japan. An adult female rhesus monkey measured 580 mm. (23 inches) in total length; tail, 150 mm.; hind foot, 145 mm. Monkeys of this genus are often tamed as pets and, in some areas, are used as food. In the wild they travel in large troops, breed at any season of the year, and bear one or two young after a gestation period of 146 days. In zoos they have lived as long as 28 years (Allen, 1938).

Fig. 12–9. A mangabey (*Cercocebus fuliginosus*). (Ernest P. Walker.)

The baboons (*Chaeropithecus, Comopithecus,* and *Theropithecus*) are restricted in distribution to Africa. They reach lengths of 1330 mm. (52 inches) of which the tail comprises 550 mm. (22 inches). The hind foot is 235 mm. (Hollister, 1924). Although a large old male weighed 90 pounds, the average weight is 40 to 50 pounds for males and 32 to 42 pounds for females (Shortridge, 1934).

The drills (*Mandrillus*) are larger and more ferocious than baboons. When disturbed they will stand their ground instead of fleeing like most other monkeys. Their gestation period is 270 days and one individual lived in a zoo for 46 years (Shortridge, 1934).

RECENT GENERA

Total, 16.

Subfamily Cercopithecinae.

Macaca Lacépède. Macaques, incl. rhesus monkeys, N.Af., S.As., E.Indies, Philippines, Japan.

Cynopithecus I. Geoffroy. Black apes, Celebes.

Cercocebus E. Geoffroy. Mangabeys, Equatorial Af.

Allenopithecus Lang. Allen's swamp monkeys, Af.

Chaeropithecus Gervais. Baboons, Af.

Comopithecus J. A. Allen. Hamadryas baboons, E.Af., SW.As.

Mandrillus Ritgen. Mandrills and drills, tropical Af.

Theropithecus I. Geoffroy. Gelada baboons, Ethiopia.

Cercopithecus Linnaeus. Guenons, Af.

Erythrocebus Trouessart. Red monkeys, Equatorial Af.

Subfamily Colobinae.

Presbytis Eschscholtz. Languars, S.As., E.Indies.

Pygathrix E. Geoffroy. Douc languars, S.As.

Rhinopithecus Milne Edwards. Snub-nosed languars, China. Tibet.

Simias Miller. Pagi Island languars, Sumatra.

Nasalis E. Geoffroy. Proboscis monkeys, Borneo.

Colobus Illiger. Guerezas, Equatorial Af.

SUPERFAMILY HOMINOIDEA

Members of this superfamily are characterized by the presence of a large braincase and a raised cranium, giving a definite forehead. Ischial callosities are extremely reduced or absent.

Family PONGIDAE

Gibbon, Orangutan, Chimpanzee, Gorilla

STRUCTURE

The dentition is similar to the anthropoid primates in number and general arrangement of the teeth. The skull has the upper jaw prognathus and has prominent saggital crests. In the limbs the pectoral appendages are much longer than the pelvic. The fingers and thumb are long, and the thumb is opposable. The great toe is short and somewhat opposable. In quadripedal locomotion the knuckles are in contact with the ground and the middle carpels of the fingers have horny plates that are already indicated in the embryo. External features include a large, man-like appearance; protruding jaws; a height that reaches 72 inches; often use bipedal locomotion; round, naked ears; and naked faces. The pelage is short, shaggy, and coarse. The tail is absent.

NATURAL HISTORY

The living members of this family, restricted to the dense tropical forests of southeastern Asia, Sumatra, Borneo, and Equatorial Africa (Fig. 12–10), are divided into two subfamilies: Hylobatinae, the gibbons; and Ponginae, the orangutans, chimpanzees, and gorillas. Some recent authors consider these two groups as representing separate families.

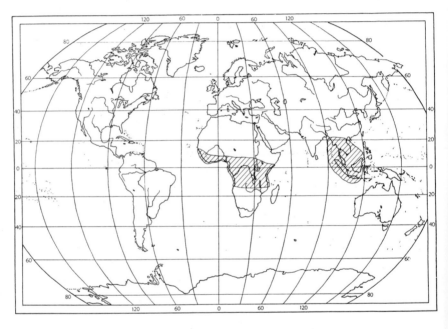

Fig. 12–10. The distribution of Family Pongidae.

The gibbons, *Hylobates*, with three species, occur in southeastern Asia and the East Indies. They are of slender build, often moving through trees by brachiation, although on occasion they do use bipedal locomotion. Unlike most mammals the gibbons, gorillas, and chimpanzees do not appear to be able to swim (Bourliere, 1954). Gibbons move in family groups consisting of two parents and a number of young. The family group lives in an actively defended territory. The female gives birth to a single young after a gestation period of 200 to 212 days. The female carries the young by holding them low over the pelvis and upper part of the leg. The young reaches sexual maturity in 8 to 10 years.

The siamang gibbons, *Symphalangus*, of Sumatra and the Malay Peninsula have the second and third toes united in a common integument. They reach a height of approximately 3 feet and have an arm span of 5 feet.

The orangutan, *Pongo*, known from one living species, occurs in Borneo and Sumatra. It has, relatively, the longest arms and the shortest legs of any member of the family. The body is bulky, rarely over 4 feet high, yet weighs 160 pounds. The arm spread is 7.5 feet. Orangutans are perfectly arboreal and have a high degree of intelligence and acute hearing. In nature they build a crude platform of sticks on which they sleep at night and rest during the day. Orangutans normally travel in small family parties of from two to four individuals. Their numbers are being greatly reduced in most of the range.

The chimpanzee, *Pan*, known from two living species, are restricted to equatorial Africa. An adult male stands about 5 feet, the female, 4 feet. The males weigh between 125 and 175 pounds; the females, 100 to 150 pounds. Chimpanzees are only partially bipedal. After a gestation period of 8 to 9 months the females give birth to a single young that weighs about 2.25 pounds. The parents care for the young for up to 6 years. They often travel in troops of up to twenty individuals.

The gorillas, *Gorilla*, are known from a single living species in Equatorial Africa. Adult male gorillas reach heights of 72 inches and weights up to 600 pounds. Gorillas are only partially bipedal, and when walking, the hands are flexed, with the dorsal surface of the knuckles in contact with the ground. Temporary shelters of branches are often constructed and serve as night shelters for this diurnal animal. Gorillas usually travel in groups consisting of a dominant male, three or four adult females and eight to ten dependent and immature individuals of both sexes. In captivity they live as long as 30 years.

RECENT GENERA

Total, 5.

Subfamily Hylobatinae.

Hylobates Illiger. Gibbons, SE.As.

Symphalangus Gloger. Siamang gibbons, Sumatra, Malay Peninsula.

Subfamily Ponginae.

Pongo Lacépède. Orangutan, Borneo, Sumatra.

Pan Oken. Chimpanzees, Equatorial Af.

Gorilla I. Geoffroy. Gorillas, Equatorial Af.

Family HOMINIDAE

Man

STRUCTURE

The dentition is similar to the other anthropoids, differing in relatively minor characteristics. The canines are much reduced in size and the tooth row is short and rounded. The dental formula is I 2/2, C 1/1, P 2/2, M 3/3 = 32. In the skull prognathism and the supra-orbital prominences are reduced and the chin is well developed. In the limbs the digits have flattened nails. The thumb is highly opposable, and the great toe has lost its power of opposition.

ONE RECENT GENUS

Homo Linnaeus. Man, worldwide.

13

Order Edentata

American Anteaters, Sloths, and Armadillos

CHARACTERISTICS

The limbs are varied, being adapted for terrestrial, fossorial, or arboreal locomotion. The radius and ulna are separate; the tibia and fibula may be separate, fused distally, or fused at both ends. The skull varies considerably among the three families and reflects differences in food habits. The premaxillaries are weakly developed, rarely involved in the lateral boundaries of the nares openings. The zygomatic may be complete, incomplete, or rudimentary. The teeth are modified for a diet of small objects. Incisors and canines are absent. The cheek-teeth are absent or else simple, without enamel, and growing from persistent pulps. When present the molars vary from four to ten or sometimes more in number. Postcranial features include the presence of a clavicle (rudimentary in Myrmecophagidae); a variable number of dorsal and caudal vertebrae; fusion of the sacral vertebrae with the sacrum; and, occasionally, six cervical vertebrae (instead of the seven that is usual in most mammals). Soft anatomy. There is a common urinary and genital duct in the females; in the males the testes lie in an abdominal cavity between the rectum and the bladder. External features are varied. Edentates range in size from quite small to extremely large animals. Some kinds are terrestrial, some show fossorial adaptations, while still others are arboreal.

RANGE

Edentates are found in South and Central America, north into southeastern United States.

Family MYRMECOPHAGIDAE

Anteaters

STRUCTURE

The dentition is completely absent, not even milk dentition is evident. The skull is long and low; rostrum tubular, rounded above and flattened below. The zygomatic arch is incomplete. The limbs are varied. Digit III of the forefoot is much enlarged and has a long, strong claw; the others are shorter and have shorter claws or are reduced. The hind foot has four or five subequal short-claw digits. External features include a thick covering of hair; the presence of a single pair of pectoral mammae; a well-developed, heavily furred tail (prehensile and naked at the tip in *Tamandua*). The mouth cavity is tubular, and in feeding a long slender tongue extends from the mouth. The tongue is covered by a sticky material that is produced by the greatly enlarged submaxillary glands. A further modification, associated with the absence of teeth and the insectivorous diet, is the presence of a gizzard-like stomach that has a thin-walled cardiac portion and a muscular pyloric portion.

NATURAL HISTORY

The range of this family is restricted to the Neotropical realm, north to southern Mexico (Fig. 13–1). It contains three living genera, two arboreal and one terrestrial. The giant anteater, *Myrmecophaga,* is terrestrial and walks with the toes of the forefoot so strongly flexed that the weight is borne by the end of the fifth and the dorsal surface of the third and fourth digits. They reach lengths in excess of 6 feet, of which the tail comprises some 2 feet and stand 2 feet high at the shoulder. Food is obtained by tearing open termite nests with the long clawed forefeet and then rapidly extending the sticky tongue into their midst. The giant anteaters are found in low, swampy savannas; along river banks; and in deep, humid forests from Guatemala, southward into tropical South America.

The four-toed anteater, *Tamandua,* and the two-toed anteater, *Cyclopedes,* are both arboreal inhabitants of dense primeval forests from southern Mexico, southward into tropical South America. The four-toed anteater will run readily on the ground and occasionally hides in holes in the ground, although hollow trees appear to be used more often. The strong claws on the forefeet of these arboreal forms are used to destroy the bark and expose insects. Both have prehensile tails that are naked, at least on the terminal portion. The tamandua, slightly larger than a house cat, has a slender body and reaches a length of approximately 1220 mm. (4 feet), of which the tail comprises approximately half. The two-toed anteater is rat-sized, about 410 mm. (16 inches) long including a 230 mm. (9 inch) tail. The pelage is long and semiwoolly.

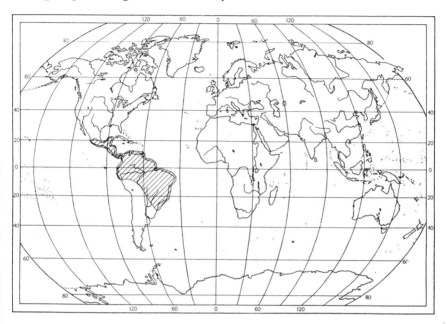

Fig. 13–1. The distribution of Family Myrmecophagidae.

RECENT GENERA

Total, 3.

Myrmecophaga Linnaeus. Giant anteaters, C. and S.A.
Tamandua Gray. Tamanduas or collared anteaters, C. and S.A.
Cyclopedes Gray. Two-toed anteater, C. and S.A.

Family BRADYPODIDAE

Tree Sloths

STRUCTURE

The dentition consists of cheek-teeth that have cupped grinding surfaces. The dental formula is I %, C %, P and M $\frac{5}{4} = 18$. The skull has an incomplete zygomatic arch and small premaxillaries. The lower jaw has a well-developed corocoid process. In the limbs the forelimbs are longer than the hind limbs. The feet are long and curved, and have only two or three digits which form a hook adapted to suspending the animal from a bough of a tree. The digits are encased for nearly their full length in a common integument. External features include a thick covering of hair that is often greenish in color due to the presence of algae on the hair. The tail is rudimentary, and the head is short and rounded. The external ears are inconspicuous.

NATURAL HISTORY

The range of this family is restricted to the tropical forest of South and Central America (Fig. 13–2). It includes only two living genera, the three-toed sloths (*Bradypus*) and the two-toed sloths

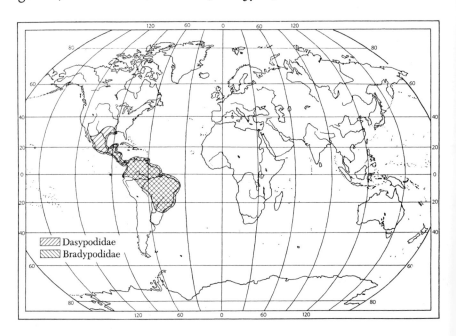

Fig. 13–2. The distribution of families Bradypodidae and Dasypodidae.

(*Choloepus*). Both are strictly arboreal herbivores that are nocturnal and usually solitary. Sloths are relatively inactive and are usually slow of movement, although, when pressed, they can move rather rapidly among branches of trees. They hang suspended below the branches by the recurved feet and claws and move by a "hand-over-hand" locomotion involving all four feet and legs. They can crawl along a level surface only with great difficulty, since their greatly modified limbs are inefficient on the ground. The two-toed sloth (Fig. 13–3) has no tail, and reaches lengths as great as 660 mm. (26 inches). The three-toed sloth has a short tail, 65 to 75 mm. (2.5 to 3 inches) long, and reaches lengths as great as 685 mm. (27

Fig. 13–3. Two-toed sloths (*Choloepus didactylus*). (Ernest P. Walker.)

inches). These sloths appear to be heterothermic for the rectal temperatures of a captive individual ranged from 81.8 to 98.3°F. (Kredal, 1928).

RECENT GENERA

Total, 2.

Bradypus Linnaeus. Three-toed sloth, C.A., S.A.
Choloepus Illiger. Two-toed sloth, C.A., S.A.

Family DASYPODIDAE

Armadillos

STRUCTURE

The dentition consists of numerous simple teeth in the posterior part of the jaws. These teeth are rootless and continue to grow throughout life. The usual dental formula is I %, C %, and P and M $^{7\ to}$ %$_{7\ to\ 9}$ = 28 to 36. The giant armadillos, *Priodontes,* may have as many as forty teeth in each jaw and one specimen had ninety teeth. The skull has a complete zygomatic arch, small premaxillaries, and a tympanic that is prolonged into a tubular auditory meatus curving upward around the base of the zygoma. The limbs have the tibia and fibula fused at the distal ends. External features include the presence of ossified skin over most of the body. The resultant armor consists of a cephalic shield (over the shoulder region); and a variable number of movable rings between the scapular shield (over the shoulders) and the pelvic shield (over the hips). The tail is encased in bony rings, and the limbs are covered by bony scutes.

NATURAL HISTORY

The range of this family is tropical and temperate South America, northward into southeastern United States (Fig. 13–2). It has had a long geologic history, and most known forms are extinct. The living members are divisible into two subfamilies: the pichiciegos (Chlamyphorinae) and the armadillos (Dasypodinae). The pichiciegos have no movable bands in the body of armor, rather they are covered by a series of uniform plates and have, posteriorly, vertically placed shields that are rigidly ankylosed with the posterior part of the pelvis. The tail protrudes from a notch in the lower border of this shield. The skull is short and pointed. Two genera, both South American in distribution, are known in this subfamily. The pichiciegos have greatly enlarged claws for digging and reportedly use the posterior shield to close their burrow.

The armadillos, Subfamily Dasypodinae, occur from southeastern United States, southward through Central America, and most of South America. They have an armor with three to thirteen movable rings between the scapular and the pelvic shields. The skull is elongated and tapering. Currently, seven living genera are recognized.

The nine-banded armadillo, *Dasypus novemcinctus,* reaches a length as great as 813 mm. (32 inches) of which the tail comprises up to 370 mm. (14.5 inches). Adults weigh as much as 17 pounds. They are terrestrial and burrowing in habits. Food consists primarily of insects although some vegetable material and some carrion is taken. Fitch, Goodrum, and Newman (1932) analyzed the contents of 104 stomachs taken throughout the year in western Louisiana. They found the food indicated in Table 13–1.

TABLE 13–1

Food of the Armadillo *(Dasypus novemcinctus)* Based on Analysis of the Stomach Contents of 104 Individuals

Food Item	Per Cent of Total Volume
Animal foods (total 90.2 per cent)	
Vertebrates	
Amphibians and reptiles	4.5
Invertebrates	
Arthropoda (total, 79.3 per cent)	
Insecta (total, 65.5 per cent)	
Beetles and larvae	44.6
Orthoptera	8.5
Lepidoptera	4.7
Diptera	4.2
Hymenoptera	3.9
Hemiptera	1.6
Myriapoda	8.5
Arachnida	2.1
Isopoda	1.2
Snails, slugs, and earthworms	6.4
Plant foods	
Fruits, berries, seeds, and mushrooms.....................	9.8

SOURCE: Based on Fitch, Goodrum, and Newman (1932).

The armadillo is unusual in its reproduction in that implantation is delayed (up to 14 weeks), and the single ovum almost invariably gives rise to identical quadruplets. The young are born in nests at the end of a simple burrow in the ground and remain with the mother for several months.

The Central American armadillo (*Cabassous centralis*) occurs from Guatemala, southward into South America. They reach lengths up to 450 mm. Ingles (1953) observed the feeding habits of one individual on Barro Colorado Island. It would search for ground-dwelling termites and ants by digging holes, up to a foot in depth, to some dead root or stump that contained the insects. Its large sickle-like claws cut roots up to 6 mm. (0.25 inch) in diameter as it dug after prey. Once located, insects were extracted from their tunnels by the armadillo's long extensile tongue.

The South American three-banded armadillo, *Tolypeutes,* when disturbed, reportedly curls up into a ball and, protected by its armor, rolls away from its enemies. The giant armadillo (Fig. 13–4) of South America reaches weights up to 104 pounds.

Fig. 13–4. A giant armadillo (*Priodontes gigantea*). This large South American armadillo reaches lengths of 46 inches and weights of 104 pounds. (Ernest P. Walker.)

RECENT GENERA

Total, 9.

Subfamily Dasypodinae. Armadillos.
    Chaetophractus Fitzinger. Quirquinchos, S.A.
    Euphractus Wagler. Six-banded armadillos, S.A.
    Zaedyus Ameghino. Piches, S.A.
    Priodontes Cuvier. Giant armadillos, S.A.
    Cabassous McMurtrie. Eleven-banded armadillos, S.A.
    Tolypeutes Illiger. Three-banded armadillos, S.A.
    Dasypus Linnaeus. Nine-banded armadillos, southern N.A., S.A.
Subfamily Chlamyphorinae. Pichiciegos.
    Chlamyphorus Harlan. Lesser pichiciegos, S.A.
    Burmeisteria Gray. Greater pichiciegos, S.A.

14

Order Pholidota

Pangolins or Scaly Anteaters

The limbs have digits ⅘. The forefeet have long digging claws at the end of short legs; the hind legs are longer and stouter and have short nails on the digits. The skull is somewhat tapered anteriorly and has incomplete zygomatic arches. The jugals are reduced or absent and the pterygoids are well developed. The mandibles are reduced to simple, bladelike bones, with no angular of corocoid processes. Teeth are completely absent in all adult forms. Postcranial features include the absence of a clavicle in the shoulder girdle and the absence of articular processes on the lumbar vertebrae. Soft anatomical features include a long vermiform tongue that is highly extensile. The details of the anatomy of the reproductive tract resemble that of the ungulates and not at all those of the typical American edentates. External features include the presence of large, overlapping horny scales that form an armor over the dorsal surface of the neck and body and completely over the tail. The head is small and pointed; the tail is long and broad. The eyes and ears are in elongated grooves in the side of the head.

RANGE

Southern Asia and western Africa (Fig. 14–1).

Family MANIDAE

Pangolins

The single family in this order has but one genus, and has the characteristics outlined in the ordinal discussion.

NATURAL HISTORY

The general appearance of the pangolins is reptile-like, since they are covered by broad, overlapping horny scales. These scales are formed of modified hairs and are brown in color. Basically a timid animal, the pangolin rolls itself into a ball when alarmed, presenting only the hard scales to the enemy. Captive animals sleep curled up in a ball. In walking, the animal usually is bipedal and balances on the tail. When the forelegs are used the toes are bent under, with the long claws touching the ground. They are strictly nocturnal in habit.

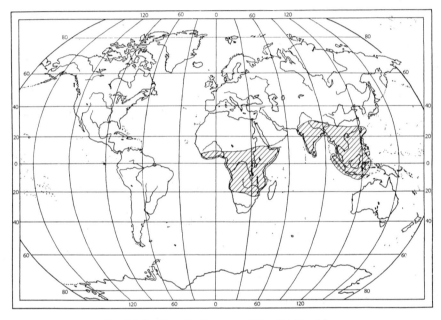

Fig. 14–1. The distribution of Family Manidae.

The Chinese pangolin, *Manis pentadactyla,* reaches a total length of up to 1170 mm. (46 inches), of which the tail comprises approximately 405 mm. (16 inches), and weighs up to 17 pounds. They feed on a diet of termites and other insects which they secure by burrowing into terrestrial termite nests or by climbing trees and tearing open the nests of arboreal termites. The young (usually one, sometimes two) are born in nests at the end of burrows, often 8 to 10 feet underground.

ONE GENUS

Manis Linnaeus. Pangolin, Af., As.

15

Order Lagomorpha

Pikas, Rabbits, and Hares

CHARACTERISTICS

The limbs have the tibia and fibula fused and the fibula articulating with the calcaneum. In general the hind limbs are longer than the forelimbs. The elbow and knee joints are non-rotating. The digits ($\frac{5}{5}$) have claws. The skull has the sides of the maxilla fenestrated; a short palate, not extending to the end of the tooth row; and elongate incisive foramina that terminate between the cheek teeth. The orbitosphenoid is large and the supraorbital processes are well developed. The glenoid process is not anteroposteriorly elongated. The teeth are reduced in number and are modified for a herbivorous diet. The dental formula is I $\frac{2}{1}$, C $\frac{0}{0}$, P $\frac{3}{2}$, M $\frac{2 \text{ or } 3}{3}$ = 26 or 28. The incisors are evergrowing, with enamel extending around to the posterior surface. The second upper incisors, reduced in size, are without cutting edges, and are located directly posterior to the first upper incisors. The cheek teeth have cusps of uncertain homologies and are not known definitely to be of tritubercular origin. Features of the soft anatomy include a spiral valve in the well-developed cecum; a prepenial scrotum and the absence of an os penis. External features include the extreme reduction or absence of a tail.

RANGE

The lagomorphs are present on most of the continents and many of the larger islands. They have been introduced in Australia and New Zealand.

Family OCHOTONIDAE

Pikas

STRUCTURE

The dentition consists of the following teeth: I $\frac{2}{1}$, C $\frac{0}{0}$, P $\frac{3}{2}$, M $\frac{2}{3}$ = 26. The second upper premolar is unlike the third in size and shape. The cutting edge of the first upper incisor is V-shaped. The last lower molar is simplified. The skull lacks a postorbital process on the frontal bone. The rostrum is slender and the nasal bones are widest anteriorly. The jugal is long and projects far posterior to the zygomatic arm of the squamosal. The auditory bullae are somewhat inflated with spongy materials. The limbs are characteristic in that the hind limbs are but little larger than the forelimbs. External features include small size (220 mm. in total length); tail apparently absent; and short, rounded ears.

NATURAL HISTORY

The range of this family is western North America and northern Asia, generally restricted to rocky areas and, especially in the southern part of the range, high mountainous areas (Fig. 15–1). The

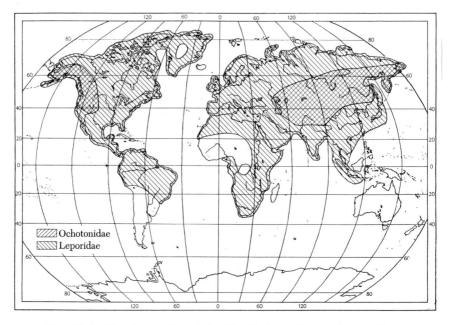

Fig. 15–1. The distribution of families Ochotonidae and Leporidae.

single living genus is divided into approximately fourteen species, all of which appear to be similar in habits. Pikas are diurnal and colonial, living in rocky and rock talus slide situations. They often lie on a rock, basking in the sun, but are usually difficult to see since their coat color blends with the color of the rocks. They rarely venture far from the protection of the rocks. External measurements of

Ochotona princeps are: total length, 162–216 mm.; hind foot, 25–35 mm.; and weight, 108 to 129 grams.

Pikas feed on green grasses in the summer months. They also harvest grasses which they stack on rocks in the sunlight to cure as hay. In threatening weather the whole colony works to store drying hay under rocks, out of the rain. This hay furnishes food for the winter season. The female probably has two litters of young per year, between May and September. The young, two to five, usually three, are born in a grass-lined nest under rocks, or in a burrow in the ground.

ONE RECENT GENUS

Ochotona Link. Pikas, As., N.A.

Family LEPORIDAE

Rabbits and Hares

STRUCTURE

The dentition is characterized by the presence of a small m3 (except in *Pentalagus*) and a dental formula of I $\frac{2}{1}$, C $\frac{0}{0}$, P $\frac{3}{2}$, M $\frac{2 \text{ or } 3}{3} = 26$ or 28. P2 is like P3 in form and m3 is divided by a transverse enamel plate. The cutting edge of I1 is straight. The skull has a wide rostrum, with the nasals widest posteriorly. Post-orbital processes of the frontal are present and well developed. The jugal projects less than halfway from the zygomatic root of the squamosal to the external auditory meatus. The auditory bullae are small and not inflated with spongy material. The hind limbs are much longer than the forelimbs. External features include ears that are longer than wide, often long, and the presence of a short but evident tail.

NATURAL HISTORY

The living rabbits and hares, which occur throughout the world (Fig. 15–1), are divided into nine genera. The Ryukyu rabbit, *Pentalagus*, is known from a single living species and is restricted to the Ryukyu Islands. It is unique in that the molars are reduced to $\frac{2}{3}$. The rock hares, *Pronolagus*, are known from some four or five species in Africa. According to Shortridge (1934) these rabbits are nocturnal, coming out of hiding places in rock crevices or under boulders shortly after sunset. They never stray far from their rock cover in feeding. During the breeding season the rock hares pluck hair from their bodies to line the nest where one or two young are born. The volcano rabbit, *Romerolagus*, is known from a single species from a restricted area in the high mountains of central Mexico. These rabbits have a rudimentary tail, reach a total length of 311 mm., and have a hind foot that is 52 mm. Volcano rabbits live in well-defined runways in dense grass, and are mainly nocturnal.

The hares (*Lepus*), with approximately twenty-five species, occur in Europe, Asia, Africa, and North America. They vary in size, one of the largest being the antelope jackrabbit of southwestern United States and northwestern Mexico. This species (*Lepus alleni*) reaches a total length of 670 mm. including a tail length of 70 mm. Its hind foot is 145 mm. long and the ears are 175 mm. in height from the notch. The average weight of sixty-one adult males from Arizona was 8.2 pounds. These hares are crepuscular and often inhabit open country where the combination of large ears, for detecting an enemy at a great distance, and their greatly enlarged hind limbs, for running at speeds up to 45 miles per hour, enables them to avoid their enemies. Two to eight young are born after a gestation period of up to 40 days. More than one litter is produced each year by certain species. The young are precocial and actively follow the adult female shortly after birth.

The cottontail rabbits (*Sylvilagus*), with approximately seventeen species, are widely distributed in North and South America. The cottontails are, in general, smaller than the lepids. The swamp rabbit (*Sylvilagus aquaticus*) of southeastern United States is one of the largest in the genus, with a total length of 540 mm., including a tail length of 71 mm. Lowe (1958) has recorded several observations on its habits. It usually inhabits the flood plains of rivers and creeks where it may escape detection by remaining motionless, often until a person is within a foot of it. The swamp rabbit is an accomplished swimmer. The females build a nest in a depression in the earth and this depression is lined with fur. The altricial young, one to four in number, are born either in April or in September. The average home range of an adult is 19 acres.

The Old World rabbits (*Oryctolagus*), with but one species, occurs in Europe and northern Africa. It was introduced and has become established in Australia, New Zealand, and North America. Mykytowycz (1958) has made an enlightening study of the social behavior of these rabbits. A small colony of marked individuals was established in a pen 1.75 acres in area. Observations were made on behavior at all hours of the day and night. It was discovered that a rigid order of rank was maintained in the colony—bucks over bucks, does over does—and that the highest-ranking buck controlled the group. Fights were rare; order was maintained by chase and retreat. An individual newly introduced into the population was treated hostilely by all and was attacked by the dominant individuals. The removal of the dominant buck caused disturbance among all of the males, but the second-ranking male always won. If, after a few days, the original leader was returned a long and vicious fight resulted, and the loser was always degraded to the lowest rank.

RECENT GENERA

Total, 9.

Pentalagus Lyon. Ryukyu rabbit, As.
Pronolagus Lyon. Rack hares, Af.
Romerolagus Merriam. Volcano rabbits, N.A.
Caprolagus Blyth. Bristly rabbits, As.
Lepus Linnaeus. Hares, Eu., As., Af., N.A.
Poëlagus St. Leger. Scrub hares, As.
Sylvilagus Gray. Cottontail rabbits, N.A., S.A.
Oryctolagus Lilljeborg. Old World rabbits, Eu., N.Af.
Nesolagus Major. Sumatran short-eared rabbits, Sumatra.

16
Order Rodentia
Rodents

The Order Rodentia is large, both in terms of numbers of individuals and in numbers of different kinds. It contains approximately one-third of the named species of mammals in the world. They are old, being known from Early Eocene deposits and are well circumscribed, being obviously rodents even in the earliest known fossils.

CHARACTERISTICS

The limbs are usually plantigrade (occasionally semi-plantigrade); the tibia and fibula are separate or fused; the radius and ulna are unfused; and the elbow joint permits free rotary motion of the forearm. The skull has an anteroposteriorly elongated glenoid fossa, thus the articular condyle of the mandible is capable of anteroposterior motion; the orbit is broadly united with the temporal fossa; the premaxilla has a process reaching to the frontal; and auditory bullae are present which involve at least the tympanic. The teeth are characteristic of the order. There is one upper and one lower large, chisel-shaped incisor on each side and a wide diastema between these and the cheek teeth. The incisors grow from persistent pulp and have the enamel restricted to the anterior face of the tooth. Canines are absent. The cheek teeth (premolars and molars or molars only) are usually similar in size and shape and form an unbroken series. The dental formula is somewhat varied, but is not known to exceed I $\frac{1}{1}$, C $\frac{0}{0}$, P $\frac{2}{1}$, M $\frac{3}{3}$ = 22. Postcranial features include a narrow scapula and, usually, a well-developed clavicle. Features of the soft anatomy include a simple stomach, a cecum without a spiral valve, and a relatively large brain with the cerebral hemispheres smooth and not covering the cerebellum.

SUBORDER SCIUROMORPHA, SQUIRREL-LIKE RODENTS

The rodents are divided into three suborders: Sciuromorpha, or squirrel-shaped rodents; Myomorpha, or mouse-shaped rodents; and Hystricomorpha, or porcupine-shaped rodents. The following features characterize the Suborder Sciuromorpha. The skull has a slender zygomatic arch that is formed chiefly by the jugal. The infraorbital canal is small, seldom wider than the width of the first molar and never slitlike. There are always more than three cheek teeth in each half of the jaw. The lateral processes of the supra-occipital are well developed. Postcranial features include the presence of separate tibia and fibula. In the soft anatomy there is, characteristically, no part of the masseter muscle passing through the infraorbital canal.

Family APLODONTIDAE

Mountain Beaver

STRUCTURE

The dentition includes evergrowing cheek teeth that are simplified in pattern. The dental formula is I $\frac{1}{1}$, C $\frac{0}{0}$, P $\frac{2}{1}$, M $\frac{3}{3}$ = 22. P3 is a simple peg. The skull is usually flat and wide. The zygomatic arch is not especially enlarged. The posterior horns of the hyoid are attached to the thyroid cartilage and the anterior horns have two well-developed segments. The limbs have the tibia and fibula unfused. The feet are somewhat modified for a fossorial life in that they are large and have strong claws. External features include the short legs, ears, and tail and a stout body. The mountain beaver is about the size of a large muskrat. The fur is short and dense.

NATURAL HISTORY

The range of this family is restricted to the Pacific Coast and coastal ranges of North America, from extreme southern British Columbia southward to San Francisco Bay. They occur from sea level to 9700 feet in elevation (Fig. 16–1). Mountain beavers (*Aplodontia*) are rather gregarious, fossorial animals that are mainly nocturnal and are very shy. They dig burrows in the deep soil in riparian situations. The burrows vary from 4 to 10 inches in diameter and may extend for distances up to 300 yards. External measurements are: total length, 365 mm.; tail, 35 mm.; hind foot, 58 mm.; weight, 450 grams.

Their diet consists entirely of green vegetation and they appear to require rather high humidity and an abundant supply of food. Ingles (1959) made an intensive study of the activity of the mountain beaver in Northern California. Field observations, as well as observations on captive animals, revealed that they may be active outside their burrows at any time of the day or night but are 50 to

60 per cent more active at night. During the summer they have six to seven periods of activity each 24 hours, with activity peaks at 3 A.M., 11 A.M., 3 P.M., and 10 P.M. The activity periods vary in length, up to 2 hours and 45 minutes, and average longer at night than during the day.

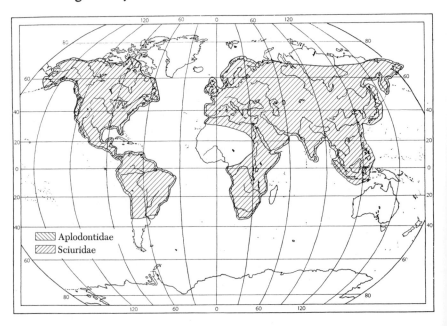

Fig. 16–1. The distribution of families Aplodontidae and Sciuridae.

Only one litter (usually numbering two to three young) is born each year in the month of April after a gestation period of 30 days. The young are blind and scantily haired at birth.

ONE RECENT GENUS

Aplodontia Richardson. Mountain beaver, western N.A.

Family SCIURIDAE

Squirrels

STRUCTURE

The dentition consists of cuspate, rooted, and not especially simplified cheek teeth. The dental formula is I $\frac{1}{1}$, C $\frac{0}{0}$, P $\frac{2 \text{ or } 1}{1}$, M $\frac{3}{3} = 20$ or 22. The skull has a postorbital process present on the frontal bone, a feature unique to this family. The zygomatic plate is broad, and the zygomatic arch is moderately developed. The auditory bullae are prominent but usually not greatly modified. The limbs have four toes on the front feet and five toes on the hind feet. The tibia and fibula are never fully fused. External features are quite varied. The eyes are usually large, while the pinna of the ear varies from small to large and is often tufted. The tail, varying from long to short, is usually well haired. Internal cheek pouches are usually present.

NATURAL HISTORY

The range of this family is worldwide except in the Australian region, Malagasy, and southern South America (Fig. 16–1). The sciurids are generally diurnal (the flying squirrels are nocturnal) and primarily herbivorous, feeding on seeds, nuts, fruits, and vegetation. They show considerable adaptive radiation, some being volant, others arboreal or terrestrial, and a few showing fossorial trends. Although generally solitary, some species live in large colonies. The family includes forty-seven genera and approximately 1350 named forms.

They are divided into two subfamilies, the typical ground and tree-living forms, Sciurinae; and the flying squirrels, Petauristinae. The Sciurinae are divided into six tribes.

The European and American tree squirrels, Tribe Sciurini, contains six genera. The pygmy squirrels, *Microsciurus*, of Central and South America are the smallest in this tribe. External measurements are: total length, 232 to 260 mm.; tail, 100 to 120 mm.; hind foot, 33 to 40 mm. The European and American tree squirrels usually have long bushy tails and pointed ears that often have tufts. They usually build nests in trees; do not hibernate; and feed on a variety of fruits, nuts, and tree buds. These squirrels are extensively hunted for food and sport.

The chickaree, Tribe Tamiasciurini, of North America, contains but a single genus. External measurements are: total length, 270 to 385 mm.; tail, 92 to 158 mm.; hind foot, 35 to 57 mm. The chickaree is an animal of the forests and lives in both conifers and hardwoods. It is usually solitary but pairs are formed during the mating season, late winter and early spring. After a gestation period of 36 to 40 days, three to seven (usually five or six) young are born in an altricial condition.

The Asiatic and African tree squirrels, Tribe Funambulini, with nine genera, includes the largest tree squirrel. The long-tailed giant squirrel *Ratufa macrura*, measures as much as: total length, 1030 mm.; tail, 519 mm.; hind foot, 93 mm. Members of this tribe are both nocturnal and diurnal. They feed on a variety of berries, fruits, nuts, and other vegetable materials.

The oriental tree squirrels, Tribe Callosciurini, include nine genera. They are moderate in size, have untufted ears, and highly complex male reproductive organs. They are extremely varied in color, with many forms having stripes.

The African ground squirrels, Tribe Xerini, with four genera, are terrestrial and usually occupy open areas. They are all diurnal and feed on vegetable materials. *Geosciurus* live in colonies in hard-packed soil areas, much as do the North American prairie dogs.

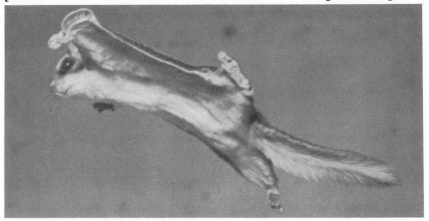

Fig. 16–2. A flying squirrel (*Glaucomys volans*). Note the modifications of the limbs and tail. (Ernest P. Walker.)

The northern ground squirrels, Tribe Marmotini, with five genera, are well known to most inhabitants of the temperate part of the Northern Hemisphere. This group includes the marmots, prairie dogs, ground squirrels, and chipmunks. All appear to be diurnal and primarily terrestrial. Members of this tribe are known to aestivate and hibernate.

The flying squirrels (Fig. 16–2), Subfamily Petauristinae, with thirteen genera, are all modified for a volant type of locomotion. They are arboreal and feed on a variety of vegetable items. One of the largest species, *Petaurista petaurista* of southeastern Asia, reaches a total length of 910 mm. of which the tail is 482 mm.

RECENT GENERA

Total, 47.

Subfamily Sciurinae. Ground and tree squirrels.

    Tribe Sciurini. European and American tree squirrel.

        Sciurus Linnaeus. Tree squirrels, Eu., As., N.A., S.A.

Syntheosciurus Bangs. Neotropical ground-tooth squirrels, C.A.

Microsciurus J. A. Allen. Dwarf tree squirrel, C.A., S.A.

Sciurillus Thomas. South American pygmy squirrel, S.A.

Prosciurillus Ellerman. Celebes pygmy squirrel, S.A.

Rheithrosciurus Gray. Groove-toothed squirrel, Borneo.

Tribe Tamiasciurini. Chickaree, N.A.

Tamiasciurus Trouessart. Chickaree, N.A.

Tribe Funambulini. African tree squirrels, Af., As.

Funambulus Lesson. Palm squirrel, As.

Ratufa Gray. Oriental giant squirrel, As.

Protoxerus Major. Oil palm squirrel, As.

Epixerus Thomas. African palm squirrel, Af.

Funisciurus Trouessart. African striped squirrel, Af.

Paraxerus Major. African bush squirrel, Af.

Heliosciurus Trouessart. Sun squirrel, Af.

Myosciurus Thomas. African pygmy squirrel, Af.

Hyosciurus Tate and Archbold. Long-snouted squirrel, As.

Tribe Callosciurini. Oriental tree squirrels, As.

Callosciurus Gray. Tricolored squirrels, As.

Tamiops J. A. Allen. Asiatic striped squirrel, As.

Menetes Thomas. Berdmore's squirrels, As.

Rhinosciurus Gray. Long-nosed squirrels, As.

Lariscus Thomas and Wroughton. Black-striped squirrel, As.

Dremomys Heude. Long-nosed squirrel, As.

Sciurotamias Miller. Rock squirrels, As.

Glyphotes Thomas. Bornean squirrels, Borneo.

Nannosciurus Trouessart. Oriental pygmy squirrels, As.

Tribe Xerini. African ground squirrels, Af., As.

Atlantoxerus Major. Barbary ground squirrels, Af.

Xerus Hemprich and Ehrenberg. African ground squirrel, Af.

Geosciurus A. Smith. African ground squirrel, Af.

Spermophilopsis Blasius. Long-clawed ground squirrel, As.

Tribe Marmotini. Northern ground squirrels, Eu., As., N.A.

Marmota Frisch. Marmots, Eu., As., N.A.

Cynomys Rafinesque. Prairie dogs, As., N.A.

Citellus Oken. Ground squirrels, Eu., As., N.A.

Tamias Illiger. Eastern chipmunk, N.A.

Eutamias Trouessart. Western chipmunk, As., N.A.

Subfamily Petauristinae. Flying squirrels.

Petaurista Link. Giant flying squirrels, As.

Aeromys Robinson and Kloss. Black flying squirrels, As.

Eupetaurus Thomas. Woolly flying squirrels, As.

Pteromys Cuvier. Old World flying squirrels, Eu., As.

Glaucomys Thomas. American flying squirrels, N.A.

Hylopetes Thomas. Indo-Malayan flying squirrels, S.As.

Petinomys Thomas. Dwarf flying squirrel, As.

Aeretes G. Allen. Grooved-tooth flying squirrel, China.

Trogopteris Heude. Complex-toothed flying squirrel, As.

Belomys Thomas. Hairy-footed squirrel, As.

Pteromyscus Thomas. Small-eared flying squirrel, As.

Petaurillus Thomas. Pygmy flying squirrel, SE.As.

Iomys Thomas. Javanese flying squirrel, SE.As.

Family GEOMYIDAE

Pocket Gophers

STRUCTURE

The dentition consists of the following teeth: I $\frac{1}{1}$, C $\frac{0}{0}$, P $\frac{1}{1}$, M $\frac{3}{3} = 20$. The cheek teeth are evergrowing and the molars have the enamel reduced to plates either on the anterior or posterior surface of the tooth. The skull is massive and angular, and the auditory region is not greatly inflated. The infraorbital canal is long, narrow, and opens on the lateral side of the rostrum, anterior to the zygomatic plate. The squamosals usually have strong ridges which tend to unite (especially in old males) to form a sagittal crest. The zygomatic arches are strong. The limbs are modified for a fossorial life. The forelegs have long powerful claws, while the hind feet are more generalized. External features include the short, almost naked tail and the presence of large external fur-lined cheek pouches. The eyes and ears are small.

NATURAL HISTORY

The pocket gophers, with eight living genera, are restricted to North America (Fig. 16–3). They are fossorial, constructing exten-

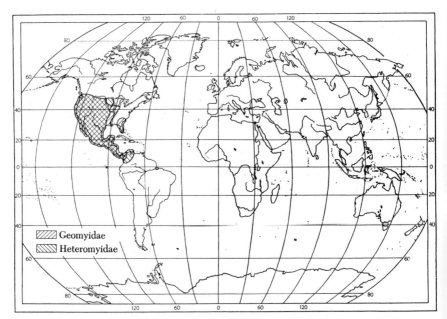

Fig. 16–3. The distribution of families Geomyidae and Heteromyidae.

sive burrows in the ground. The size and length of the burrows vary with the soil type in which the pocket gopher lives. In a flood-irrigated alfalfa field in California, Miller (1957) found that the burrows of the valley pocket gopher, *Thomomys bottae*, varied from 31 to 275 feet in length, had an average diameter of 2.6 inches, and an average volume of 3.87 cubic feet. The typical burrow system consisted of two parts; a larger network of shallow tunnels (6 to 8 inches below the surface) and a smaller network at a deeper level (20 to 22 inches) that contained three or four nests and an occasional food cache.

Pocket gophers feed on the roots and tubers of various plants. They are occasionally detrimental to agriculture, causing damage to irrigation ditches and to certain root crops. Dingle (1956) found that in a reforestation program in eastern Washington up to 30 per cent of the young ponderosa pines were killed by pocket gophers in a 3-year period. Pocket gophers have two to eleven young per litter and as many as two litters per year.

RECENT GENERA

Total, 8.

Geomys Rafinesque. Eastern pocket gophers, N.A.
Thomomys Maximilian. Western pocket gophers, N.A.
Pappogeomys Merriam. Tuzas, Mexico.
Cratogeomys Merriam. Yellow pocket gophers, N.A.
Orthogeomys Merriam. Tuzas, Mexico, C.A.
Heterogeomys Merriam. Hispid pocket gopher, Mexico.
Macrogeomys Merriam. Taltuzas, C.A.
Zygogeomys Merriam. Tuzas, Mexico.

Family HETEROMYIDAE

Kangaroo Rats and Allies

STRUCTURE

The dentition consists of I $\frac{1}{1}$, C $\frac{0}{0}$, P $\frac{1}{1}$, M $\frac{3}{3}$ = 20. The cheek teeth are rooted except in *Dipodomys* and are of simple structure. The incisors are thin and compressed. The skull is never modified for a fossorial life but is thin and papery. The tympanic and mastoid regions are inflated or highly inflated. The infraorbital canal is as in the geomyids. The limbs are often modified for saltatorial locomotion. The hind foot is long and narrow, the forefoot is short but has well-developed claws. External features include a tail that is as long as or longer than the body and the presence of external fur-lined cheek pouches.

NATURAL HISTORY

The heteromyid rodents are, primitively, animals of warm sub-tropical and tropical forests that have successfully invaded the arid Great American Desert (Fig. 16–3). Living members are divided into three subfamilies: the spiny pocket mice, Heteromyinae; the pocket and kangaroo mice, Perognathinae; and the kangaroo rats, Dipodomyinae. All are apparently nocturnal, spending the daytime in burrows in the ground. The heteromyids are polyestrous and have a litter of one to eight altricial young that are born in a nest in a burrow.

The Heteromyinae, with two genera, morphologically and by habitat preference, appear to be the most primitive group. In this group the bullae are not greatly inflated and saltatorial modifications are not evident. The habitat requirements range from semiarid sub-tropical situations to heavy tropical rain forests. *Heteromys gold-mani* appears to be one of the larger species. Its measurements are: total length, 300 to 350 mm.; tail, 170 to 201 mm.; hind foot, 35 to 41 mm.

The Perognathinae, with two genera, *Perognathus* and *Micro-dipodops*, are slightly more modified for saltatorial locomotion. The bullae vary from well inflated to extremely inflated. Their habitat ranges from semiarid grasslands to extreme desert conditions. *Pe-rognathus californicus,* one of the largest species in the group, measures: total length, 190 to 235 mm.; tail, 103 to 143 mm.; hind foot, 24 to 29 mm. Pocket mice feed on a variety of seeds, green plant material, and some insects, and most kinds actively store hoards of seeds in their burrows. Probably most species can survive for long periods without free water and some, at least, thrive in cap-tivity for weeks at a time on a diet of dry seeds. Physiological modi-fications including resorption of water from kidney wastes and the production of metabolic water plus the habits of spending the day-time and even hot, dry nights in their burrows, make possible life without free water.

The Dipodomyinae, with the single living genus *Dipodomys*, are extremely modified for saltatorial locomotion and have the bullae ex-tremely inflated. The habitat ranges from grasslands to extremely arid desert situations. *Dipodomys deserti* appears to be the largest species, having the following measurements: total length, 305 to 377 mm.; tail, 180 to 215 mm.; hind foot, 50 to 58 mm.; weight, 83 to 138 grams. The kangaroo rats are bipedal and use the tail as a balancing organ in locomotion.

RECENT GENERA

Total, 5.

Subfamily Perognathinae.
  Perognathus Maximilian. Pocket mice, N.A.
  Microdipodops Merriam. Kangaroo mice, N.A.
Subfamily Dipodomyinae.
  Dipodomys Gray. Kangaroo rats, N.A.
Subfamily Heteromyinae.
  Liomys Merriam. Spiny pocket mice, N.A.
  Heteromys Desmarest. Forest spiny pocket mice, C.A., northern S.A.

Family CASTORIDAE

Beaver

STRUCTURE

The dentition includes strongly developed incisors and the presence of rooted but extremely hysodont teeth. The dental formula is I $\frac{1}{1}$, C $\frac{0}{0}$, P $\frac{1}{1}$, M $\frac{3}{3}$ = 20. The skull is massive and has a strong zygomatic arch; a broad, deep rostrum; and a narrow braincase. The limbs are modified for aquatic locomotion. The hind feet have a web of skin between the digits. The feet are plantigrade and the digits $\frac{5}{5}$. The claws of the second and third digits of the foot are divided and are used in grooming. External features include its large size (being the second largest rodent known) and a dorsoventrally flattened tail that is covered with scales. The fur is thick and consists of well-developed guard hairs and dense underfur. The short ears and nares are valvular.

NATURAL HISTORY

The range of this family includes Europe, Asia, and North America (Fig. 16–4). The general habits of beavers are well known. They are aquatic, living in ponds and streams where woody vegetation such as willow is nearby. They often build dams of sticks, mud, and rocks and live in dome-shaped structures made of the same materials. These lodges usually have two or more underwater entrances. In many areas, especially in larger ponds and streams, they do not build dams and lodges, rather they dig a den in the bank. A beaver can swim up to 750 m. underwater and can remain submerged for slightly more than 5 minutes. Beavers feed on the bark and leaves of trees and, in areas with severe winters, store food.

The gestation period of the beaver has been variously reported as from 42 to 128 days; they have one to six young per litter with three being the usual number. They do not reach sexual maturity until the second year after their birth.

ONE RECENT GENUS

Castor Linnaeus. Beaver, N.A., Eu., As.

SUBORDER MYOMORPHA, RATLIKE RODENTS

The skull has a zygomatic arch in which the jugal element seldom extends far forward and is supported by the zygomatic process of the maxilla. The infraorbital canal is enlarged and usually slitlike. There

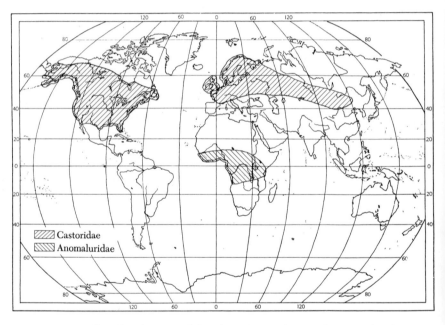

Fig. 16–4. The distribution of families Castoridae and Anomaluridae.

are usually only three cheek teeth in each half of the lower jaw. In the upper jaw there are usually three cheek teeth on each side but there may be four or only two. Postcranial features include the presence of tibia and fibula united at each end. In the soft anatomy the supraficial division of the masseter muscle passes forward in front of the orbit and attaches to the side of the rostrum, while the deep division of this muscle enters the orbit and passes through the infraorbital foramen and then attaches to the side of the rostrum.

Family ANOMALURIDAE

Scaly-tailed Squirrels

STRUCTURE

The dentition consists of rooted, flat-crowned, and relatively brachydont cheek teeth and incisors. The dental formula is I $\frac{1}{1}$, C $\frac{0}{0}$, P $\frac{1}{1}$, M $\frac{3}{3} = 20$. The cheek teeth have a crown pattern of narrow cross ridges separated by wide recurring spaces. The skull has the infraorbital foramen much enlarged for the transmission of part of the masseter muscle. The bullae are large but not excessively inflated. The limbs are modified for arboreal locomotion. The thumb is reduced or absent, and a gliding membrane extends from the fore-limb to the hind limb in all except *Zenkerella*. The flying membrane is extended by means of a cartilage rod attached to the olecranon. External features include usually the presence of a gliding membrane and a series of scales on the ventral surface of the tail. The eyes and ears are large, and the tail is tufted distally.

NATURAL HISTORY

The scaly-tailed squirrels are restricted to the heavy tropical and subtropical forests of western and central Africa (Fig. 16–4). Two subfamilies, each with two genera, are recognized: Anomalurinae and Zenkerellinae. The scaly-tailed squirrels are adapted for climbing trees. They are nocturnal and spend the daylight hours in hollow trees often 120 feet above the ground. Three of the four genera have gliding membranes and at dusk climb to the top of the den tree and glide toward small openings in the forest.

The food consists of fruits, seeds, nuts, and leaves. One young per litter and two litters per year have been reported.

RECENT GENERA

Total, 4.
Subfamily Anomalurinae.
Anomalurus Waterhouse. Scaly-tailed squirrels, Af.
Anomalurops Matschie. Narrow-tailed squirrel, Af.
Subfamily Zenkerellinae.
Idiurus Matschie. African small flying squirrel, Af.
Zenkerella Matschie. Flightless scaly-tail, Af.

Family PEDETIDAE

Spring Haas

STRUCTURE

The dentition consists of incisors and evergrowing cheek teeth. The dental formula is I $\frac{1}{1}$, C $\frac{0}{0}$, P $\frac{1}{1}$, M $\frac{3}{3}$ = 20. The premolars are not reduced in size, and the cheek teeth have a simplified crown pattern. The skull is massive and has extremely inflated mastoids.

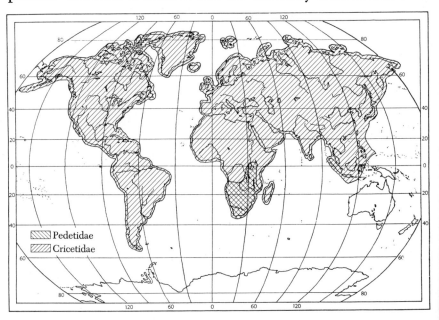

Fig. 16–5. The distribution of families Pedetidae and Cricetidae.

The zygomatic arch is thickened, and the infraorbital foramen is greatly enlarged. The rostrum is broad and deep. The limbs are modified for saltatorial locomotion. The tibia and fibula are fused, the forefeet have five digits, the hind feet have four. The hind feet are much enlarged, with claws that are hooflike. External features include a tail that is as long as or longer than the head and body, and long ears. The tail has a characteristic thick black terminal brush of hair. The eyes are extremely large (26 mm. in diameter) and reflect the light brilliantly at night.

NATURAL HISTORY

The range of this family is central and southern Africa (Fig. 16–5).

The spring haas is a large nocturnal rodent that is modified for bipedal, saltatorial locomotion and has inflated bullae. They can jump as much as 2 m. in a single leap. External measurements are: total length, 837 mm.; tail, 430 mm.; hind foot, 151 mm. They are local in distribution and occur in deep sandy soils in arid and semiarid regions. They live in colonies of several dozens of individuals, each pair in its own burrow. Each burrow is surrounded by a large heap of sand. The secondary openings to the burrow are not surrounded by sand. They feed on grass bulbs and other roots which are dug out of the ground. They come out only after dark, often traveling long distances to feeding grounds, sometimes as far as 6 miles. According to Shortridge (1934) "In severe drought they have been known to travel twenty miles in one night to parts where rain has fallen." In places they are destructive to crops, digging out and devouring the root systems of oats, wheat, and barley. The spring haas has one young per litter. In captivity a spring haas lived 7.5 years.

ONE RECENT GENUS

Pedetes Illiger. Spring haas, Af.

Family CRICETIDAE

Cricetid Rats and Mice

STRUCTURE

The dentition is varied. The dental formula is I ⅓, C %, P %, M ⅔ = 16. The cheek teeth are cuspate (with cusps arranged in two rows), laminate, or prismatic. When cuspate the laminae bearing the cusps are separated by wide re-entrant folds. The skull is variously shaped. The infraorbital canal is generalized with a rounded upper portion transmitting part of the masseter muscle and a narrow lower portion transmitting the nerve. Postorbital processes are always absent. The limbs are usually generalized but are modified for aquatic life in some genera (for example, *Ondatra*), fossorial life in others (Myospalacinae), and tending toward saltatorial in still others (Gerbillinae). External features are quite varied. The size ranges from a total length of 100 mm. (*Baiomys*) up to 915 mm. (*Ondatra*).

NATURAL HISTORY

The range is worldwide except for Australia (Fig. 16–5). The cricetid rodents are so diverse and widely distributed that little can be stated in general terms concerning their habits. The family is usually divided into five subfamilies and the larger subfamilies are divided into tribes. The following outline indicates these subdivisions.

Subfamily Cricetinae, with 60 genera divided into three tribes, is a highly diverse group of mice. The Tribe Hesperomyini (with fifty-three genera) is restricted to the New World, from Alaska to Patagonia. These are more or less generalized rodents with generally long tails. The pack rat (Fig. 16–6) is one of the larger members of this tribe. The Tribe Cricetini (with six genera) is restricted to Europe, Asia, and northern Africa. These are generally mouse-like

Fig. 16–6. A pack rat (*Neotoma albigula*). (Bruce J. Hayward.)

animals with short tails, heavy-set bodies and well-developed cheek pouches. The Tribe Myospalacini (with one genus) is restricted to Asia. These are geomyid-like cricetid rodents that are extremely adapted for a fossorial life. The body is thick and chunky, the limbs are short and powerful and have long claws, the tail is short, and the eyes and ears are reduced. These mole mice bear four to five young at the end of April. They make burrows up to 125 feet in length and feed on roots and grain. Measurements are: total length, 291 mm.; tail, 38 mm.; hind foot, 50.6 mm.

Subfamily Nesomyinae (with seven genera) is restricted to Malagasy. Little has been recorded concerning their habits.

Subfamily Lophiomyinae, or crested hamsters (with one genus), is restricted to Africa, and little is known about them. The dorsal and lateral surfaces of the cranium have a very granular surface. External measurements of an adult male are: total length, 507 mm.; tail, 215 mm.; hind foot, 51 mm. These crested hamsters are often reported as being arboreal but, according to Hollister (1919) this is probably a myth based on a secondhand account of native collectors. The few specimens reported by Hollister had been trapped in rock crevices and one placed in the fork of a tree soon fell out and gave no indication of climbing ability.

The voles and lemmings, Subfamily Microtini, are thick-set animals with bluntly rounded muzzles. The greater part of the length of each limb is within the general body contour, thus resulting in a short-legged appearance. The tail is generally short, never as long as the head and body, and often slightly longer than the hind foot. The subfamily is divided into three tribes.

The Tribe Lemmini (with four genera) occurs in Europe, Asia, and North America. They are characterized by having the lower incisors entirely on the lingual side of the molars, with the posterior end extending no farther than the alveolus of the third lower molar.

The Tribe Microtini (with fifteen genera) also occurs in Europe, Asia, and North America. They are characterized by having the lower incisors passing from the lingual to the labial side of the molars between the bases of the roots of the second and third lower molars and with the posterior end of the incisor terminating in or near the condylar process of the mandible.

The Tribe Ellobiini (with a single genus) occurs in Europe and Asia and is a microtine rodent that is modified for a life underground. The external ears are rudimentary as is the tail. The hair is soft and plushlike. The feet and claws, however, are not especially enlarged, for this mouse reportedly does its digging with its teeth.

The Subfamily Gerbillinae (with thirteen genera) occurs in Europe, Asia, and Africa. These are xerophytic mammals, most of which are bipedal and saltatorial. The typical large African gerbils (*Tatera*) have the following measurements: total length, 348 mm.; tail, 188 mm.; hind foot, 38 mm.; ear, 21 mm. (Hollister, 1919). They occur in large colonies in sandy soil where they dig burrows in the ground, often to a depth of three or more feet, and leaving a large pile of sand at the entrance of the burrow. The burrows have extensive interconnections underground and are occupied by one or more family groups. Gerbils feed on bulbs, roots, seeds, and insects. They breed at all seasons of the year and bear from two to eight young in a litter and may have as many as four litters per year. The young are sexually mature at the age of 3 months (Shortridge, 1934).

RECENT GENERA

Total, 99.

Subfamily Cricetinae.

Tribe Hesperomyini. New World mice.

Oryzomys Baird. Rice rats, N.A., S.A., Galapagos.

Melamomys Thomas. Swamp rice rats, S.A.

Neacomys Thomas. Spiny rice rats, C.A., S.A.

Scolomys Anthony. Spiny mice, S.A.

Nectomys Peters. Neotropical water rats, C.A., S.A.

Rhipidomys Tschudi. Climbing mice, C.A. S.A.

Thomasomys Coues. Thomas' Paramo mice, S.A.

Phaenomys Thomas. Rio de Janeiro rice rats, S.A.

Chilomys Thomas. Columbian forest mice, S.A.

Tylomys Peters. Climbing rats, S.A.

Ototylomys Merriam. Tree rats, C.A.

Nyctomys De Saussure. Vesper rats, C.A.

Otonyctomys Anthony. Yucatàn vesper rats, Mexico.

Rhagomys Thomas. Brazilian arboreal mice, S.A.

Reithrodontomys Giglioli. American harvest mice, N.A.

Peromyscus Gloger. White-footed mice, N.A.

Ochrotomys Osgood. Golden mice, S.A.

Baiomys True. Pygmy mice, N.A.

Onychomys Baird. Grasshopper mice, N.A.

Akodon Meyen. South American field mice, S.A.

Zygodontomys J. A. Allen. Cane mice, C.A., S.A.

Microxus Thomas. Field mice, S.A.

Podoxymys Anthony. Mt. Roraima mice, S.A.

Lenoxus Thomas. Peruvian rats, S.A.

Oxymycterus Waterhouse. Burrowing mice, S.A.

Blarinomys Thomas. Brazilian shrew-mice, S.A.

Notiomys Thomas. Long-clawed South American mice, S.A.

Scapteromys Waterhouse. Water rats, S.A.

Scotinomys Thomas. Brown mice, C.A.

Calomys Waterhouse. Vesper mice, S.A.

Eligmodontia Cuvier. Highland desert mice, S.A.

Wiedomys Hershkovitz. Weid's red-nosed mice, S.A.

Pseudoryzomys Hershkovitz. Red-nosed mice, S.A.

Phyllotis Waterhouse. Pericores, S.A.

Irenomys Thomas. Chilean rats, S.A.

Chinchillula Thomas. Chinchilla mice, S.A.

Punomys Osgood. Puna mice, S.A.

Neotomys Thomas. Andean swamp rats, S.A.

Reithrodon Waterhouse. Rabbit rats, S.A.

Euneomys Coues. Patagonian chinchilla mice, S.A.

Holochilus Brandt. Web-footed rats, S.A.

Sigmodon Say and Ord. Cotton rats, N.A., S.A.

Andinomys Thomas. Andean mice, S.A.

Neotomodon Merriam. Volcano mice, Mexico.
Neotoma Say and Ord. Wood rats, N.A.
Nelsonia Merriam. Nelson's wood rat, Mexico.
Xenomys Merriam. Colima wood rat, Mexico.
Ichthyomys Thomas. Fish-eating rats, S.A.
Anotomys Thomas. Fish-eating rats, S.A.
Daptomys Anthony. Aquatic rats, S.A.
Rheomys Thomas. Central American water mice, S.A.
Neusticomys Anthony. Fish-eating rats, S.A.
Tribe Cricetini. Hamsters.
Calomyscus Thomas. Mouselike hamsters, As.
Phodopus Miller. Dwarf hamsters, As.
Cricetulus Milne Edwards. Ratlike hamsters, Eu., As.
Cricetus Leske. Hamsters, Eu., W.As.
Mesocricetus Nehring. Golden hamsters, E.Eu., W.As.
Mystromys Wagner. White-tailed rats, Af.
Tribe Myospalacini. "Mole" mice.
Myospalax Laxmann. "Mole" mice or zohors, As.
Subfamily Nesomyinae. Malagasy rats.
Macrotarsomys Milne Edwards and Grandidier. Malagasy.
Nesomys Peters. Malagasy.
Brachytarsomys Gunther. Malagasy.
Eliurus Milne Edwards. Malagasy.
Gymnuromys Major. Malagasy.
Hypogeomys Grandidier. Malagasy.
Brachyuromys Major. Malagasy.
Subfamily Lophiomyinae. Crested hamster.
Lophiomys Milne Edwards. Crested hamster, Af.
Subfamily Microtinae
Tribe Lemmini. Lemmings
Dicronstonyx Gloger. Collared lemmings, Eu., As., N.A.
Synaptomys Baird. Lemming mice, N.A.
Myopus Miller. Wood lemmings, Eu., As.
Lemmus Link. Brown lemmings, Eu., As., N.A.
Tribe Microtini. Voles.
Clethricnomys Tilesius. Red-backed mice, Eu., As., N.A.
Eothenomys Miller. Père David's vole, As.
Alticola Blanford. High-mountain voles, As.
Hyperacrius Miller. Kashmir vole, As. (India).
Dolomys Nehring. Snow voles, Eu.
Arvicola Lacépède. Bank or water vole, Eu., As.
Ondatra Link. Muskrat, N.A., introduced in Eu.
Neofiber True. Round-tailed muskrat, N.A.
Phenacomys Merriam. Heather vole, N.A.
Pitymys McMurtrie. Pine mice, Eu., As., N.A.
Blanfordimys Argyropulo. Afghan vole, C.As.
Microtus Schrank. Meadow mice or voles, Eu., As., N.Af., N.A.
Lagurus Gloger. Sagebrush vole, As., N.A.
Prometheomys Satunin. Long-clawed mole voles, Caucasus.
Tribe Ellobiini. "Mole" lemming.
Ellobius Fischer. "Mole" lemming, E.Eu., As.
Subfamily Gerbillinae. Gerbils, sand rats, antelope rats.
Monodia Heim de Balsac. Gerbil, Af.

Gerbillus Desmarest. Gerbils or sand rats, Af., As.
Tatera Lataste. Large gerbils, Af.
Taterillus Thomas. Small, naked-soled gerbils, Af.
Desmodillus Thomas and Schwann. Short-eared rats, Af.
Desmodilliscus Wettstein. Small, short-eared rats, Af.
Pachyuromys Lataste. Fat-tailed mice, Af.
Ammodillus Thomas. Gerbil, Af.
Meriones Illiger. Jirds, E.Eu., As., N.Af.
Sekeetamys Ellerman. Ellerman's gerbil, Af.
Brachiones Thomas. Przewalski's gerbils, As.
Psammomys Cretschmar. Diurnal sand rats, N.Af., W.As.
Rhombomys Wager. Great gerbils, E.Eu., As.

Family SPALACIDAE

Mole Rats

STRUCTURE

The dentition consists of rooted cheek teeth and a dental formula of I $\frac{1}{1}$, C $\frac{0}{0}$, P $\frac{0}{0}$, M $\frac{3}{3}$ = 16. The inner and outer re-entrant folds become isolated on the crown surface in the adult animal. The incisors are greatly enlarged, being used for digging in the ground. The skull has the supraorbital region sloping forward and the zygomatic plate narrowed and turned downward. The limbs are not especially modified for fossorial life. The claws are very short and blunt. External features include modifications for a fossorial habit. The eyes are without external orifices and are functionless. The tail is absent, and the pinna is reduced to a low ridge. The nose is broad, padded, and horny and is used in pushing and packing loose soil. The fur is short and reversible, like that of the mole.

NATURAL HISTORY

The range of this family is restricted to the eastern Mediterranean region (Fig. 16–7). The mole-rat (*Spalax*) is a fossorial rodent that digs burrows up to 40 yards in length and 4 feet in depth in dry and often rocky soils. It apparently emerges to the surface only at night. It is completely blind and dissection reveals only a tiny eye, about the size of a pinhead, that is situated beneath the epidermis and has no traces of either ocular muscles or an optic nerve associated with it. In Iraq, Reed (1958) found *Spalax leucodon* to occur from elevations as low as 750 feet, where the total annual rainfall is 17 inches or less, upwards at least to the tree line (5500 feet), where the rainfall is probably somewhere between 40 and 50 inches

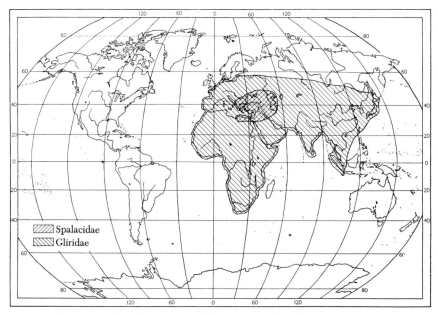

Fig. 16–7. The distribution of families Spalacidae and Gliridae.

each year. Their presence in a region is evident from the mounds of earth thrown up at the mouth of the burrows. Mating occurs in the spring and two young per litter is normal. The adults hibernate during the winter.

ONE RECENT GENUS

Spalax Guldenstadt. Mole-rat, Eastern Mediterranean region.

Family RHIZOMYIDAE

Bamboo Rats

STRUCTURE

The dentition consists of thick, stout incisors and semihypsodont or hypsodont cheek teeth. The dental formula is I $\frac{1}{1}$, C $\frac{0}{0}$, P $\frac{0}{0}$, M $\frac{3}{3}$ = 16. The skull has the neural portion of the infraorbital foramen reduced or completely obliterated by the fusion of the zygomatic plate to the side of the rostrum. The cranium is large, triangular, and flattened dorsoventrally. The limbs are more or less adapted for fossorial locomotion. The limbs and claws are short. External features include a scantily haired tail that is slightly longer than the hind foot; ears hidden in the hair; and the pelage soft and dense.

NATURAL HISTORY

The range is the Indo-Malayan region and East Africa. The African mole-rat (*Tachyoryctes*) is common in mountainous areas of East Africa, often occurring at elevations up to 11,000 feet, where they inhabit open grassy plots in the bamboo belt and openings in the forests. Here they construct burrows in the ground, and build a bulky nest of dried grasses in a side pocket of the tunnel system. Their burrows have been compared to those of the pocket gophers of North America. When on the surface, they crawl slowly and soon begin to dig a burrow. Measurements of an adult male are: total length, 298 mm.; tail, 63 mm.; hind foot, 30 mm. In the single case recorded, only one embryo was found in a female (Hollister, 1919).

The bamboo rats, *Rhizomys* and *Cannomys*, of eastern Asia, feed in the evening on roots and shoots of bamboo, unhusked rice, yams, and pumpkins. They construct underground burrows, using their teeth to dig dirt from the tunnel. Three to four young per litter have been reported in *Rhizomys*.

RECENT GENERA

Total, 3.

Tachyoryctes Ruppel. African mole-rat, Af.
Rhizomys Gray. Bamboo rats, As.
Cannomys Thomas. Lesser bamboo rats, As.

Family MURIDAE

Old World Rats and Mice

STRUCTURE

The dentition is varied. The dental formula is I $\frac{1}{1}$, C $\frac{0}{0}$, P $\frac{0}{0}$, M $\frac{2 \text{ or } 3}{2 \text{ or } 3}$. The cheek teeth are cuspate (with the cusps arranged in three rows) or laminate. When the crown pattern is laminate the folds are pressed closely together. The skull has the infraorbital foramen enlarged, as compared to Cricetidae, and the zygomatic plate usually broadened and tilted upward. The limbs are somewhat varied but in all the great toe of the hind foot is rudimentary and has the claw reduced. External features typically include a mouse or ratlike shape and a long, naked, and scaly tail. The size is generally small. The range is the Old World, but it is now introduced worldwide.

NATURAL HISTORY

The members of this family are so numerous and diverse that little can be said of their habits. Currently the living genera are divided into six subfamilies.

The Subfamily Murinae, with seventy-one genera, is widely distributed in the temperate and tropical Old World. They include species ranging from 110 to over 600 mm. in total length. It includes the well-known commensals of man, the house mouse, *Mus musculus;* the Norway rat, *Rattus norvegicus;* and the roof rat, *Rattus*

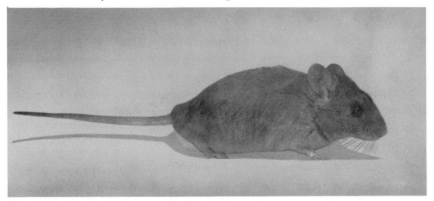

Fig. 16–8. A multimammate rat (*Rattus coucha*). (Ernest P. Walker.)

rattus. In Australia, members of this group have undergone adaptive radiation and some have developed prehensile tails, and others saltatorial locomotion. Fig. 16–8 shows one of the African members of this subfamily.

The Subfamily Dendromurinae, or tree mice, is restricted to Africa, south of the Sahara. Six genera are included in the subfamily. External measurements of a large male *Dendromus* are: total length, 217 mm.; tail, 117 mm. Although not exclusively arboreal, members of this subfamily are apparently never found far from forests. All appear to be nocturnal and feed on insects, berries, and seeds. Some species live in short burrows in the ground, others live in nests in low bushes. In southwest Africa the fat mouse, *Steatomys,* reportedly sleeps throughout the winter in a grass nest at the end of a burrow (Shortridge, 1934).

The Subfamily Otomyinae, with three genera, is restricted to Africa. These are microtine-like in general appearance, especially in the presence of large hypsodont molars. The third molar is the largest of the three. External measurements of *Otomys* are: total length, 307 mm.; tail, 102 mm.; hind foot, 33 mm. (Hollister, 1919). Members of this subfamily are nocturnal or diurnal and usually construct a series of interconnected runways in swamps or along the edges of rivers (*Otomys*) or brushy areas (*Parotomys*), and have been taken as high as 13,700 feet elevations in the mountains of East Africa (Hollister, 1919). They usually construct a large nest of sticks, thorns, or grasses in and around the bases of bushes (much the same as the pack rats, *Neotoma*, of North America) or reeds, but occasionally utilize underground dens. Food consists of stems of reeds and various wild plants. The young range from two to four per litter, and several litters may be produced each year (Shortridge, 1934).

The Subfamily Phloeomyinae, with seven genera, occurs in southeastern Asia and the East Indies, northward to the Philippines. They are large rats with reduced bullae.

The Subfamily Rhynchomyinae, or shrew rat, is known from but a single genus and species from Mount Data, northern Luzon, Philippines. Other than the fact that it feeds on insects and soft-bodied worms, little is known of its habits (Carter *et al.*, 1946).

The Subfamily Hydromyinae, or water rats, with thirteen genera, occurs from Australia through the East Indies. They are characterized by a reduction in the dentition to two upper and two lower molars in some forms. The genus *Hydromys* is highly specialized for an aquatic habitat. Its members have long, flattened heads, small ears, partially webbed broad feet, and molars modified for crushing food. The fur is short and thick. They are nocturnal and feed on mussels, snails, and crayfish, and occasionally kill even adult water birds. Their nest is usually found at the end of a burrow in the bank of a stream. Measurements of a *Hydromys chrysogaster* are: total length, 656 mm.; tail, 320 mm.; hind foot, 66 mm.; ear, 19 mm. (LeSouef and Burrell, 1926).

RECENT GENERA

Total, 101.

Subfamily Murinae.

Hapalomys Blyth. Asiatic climbing rats, S.As.
Vernaya Anthony. Vernay's climbing mice, As.
Vandeleuria Gray. Long-tailed climbing mice, As.
Tokudaia Kuroda. Ryukyu spiny rats, Ryukyu Islands.
Micromys Dehne. Old World harvest mice, Eu., As.

Apodemus Kaup. Wood mice, Eu., As., N.Af.
Thamnomys Thomas. Doringboomrotte, Af.
Grammomys Thomas. African thicket rats, Af.
Carpomys Thomas. Fruit rats, Philippines.
Mindanaomys Sanborn. Mindanao rats, Philippines.
Batomys Thomas. Luzon forest rats, Philippines.
Pithecheir Cuvier. Malayan tree rats, E.Indies.
Hyomys Thomas. New Guinea giant rats, New Guinea.
Conilurus Ogilby. House-building "jerboa" rat, Au.
Zyzomys Thomas. Thick-tailed rats, Au.
Mesembriomys Palmer. Rabbit-eared rats, Au.
Oenomys Thomas. Rufous-nosed rats, Af.
Mylomys Thomas. African groove-toothed rats, Af.
Dasymys Peters. Shaggy-haired rats, Af.
Arvicanthis Lesson. Striped or grass mice, Af.
Hadromys Thomas. Manipur brush rats, SE.As.
Golunda Gray. Indian brush rats, As.
Pelomys Peters. Groove-toothed swamp rats, Af.
Lemniscomys Trouessart. Striped grass mice, Af.
Rhabdomys Thomas. Striped field mice, Af.
Hybomys Thomas. Three-striped mice, Af.
Hylenomys Thomas. Congo mice, Af.
Millardia Thomas. Soft-furred rats, As.
Dacnomys Thomas. Large-toothed giant rats, S.As.
Eropeplus Miller and Hollister. Celebes soft-furred rats, E.Indies.
Stenocephalemys Frick. Ethiopian narrow-headed rats, Ethiopia.
Thallomys Thomas. Acacia rats, Af.
Rattus Fischer. Typical rats, native Old World, introduced worldwide.
Nilopegamys Osgood. African water rats, Af.
Tryphomys Miller. Mearn's Luzon rats, Philippines.
Gyomys Thomas. Australian field mice, Au.
Leporillus Thomas. Australian stick-nest rats, Au.
Pseudomys Gray. Australian false mice, Au.
Pogonomelomys Rummler. Mosaic-tailed rats, Au.
Melomys Thomas. Banana rats, E.Indies, Au.
Solomys Thomas. Naked-tailed rats, E.Indies.
Xenuromys Tate and Arnold. Giant rats, New Guinea.
Uromys Peters. Giant naked-tailed rats, E.Indies, Au.
Malacomys Milne Edwards. Big-eared swamp rats, Af.
Haeromys Thomas. Pygmy tree mice, E.Indies.
Chiromyscus Thomas. Asiatic tree mice, SE.As.
Zeletomys Osgood. Broad-headed mice, Af.
Diomys Thomas. Manipur mice, S.As.
Muriculus Thomas. Striped-back mice, Af.
Mus Linnaeus. House mice, native Old World, introduced worldwide.
Leggadina Thomas. Australian native mice, Au.
Colomys Thomas and Wroughton. African tree rats, Af.
Nesoromys Thomas. Ceram Island rats, E. Indies.
Crunomys Thomas. Philippine swamp rats, Philippines.
Macruromys Stein. New Guinea jumping rats, E.Indies.

Lorentzimys Jentink. New Guinea jumping mice, E.Indies.
Lophuromys Peters. Harsh-furred mice, Af.
Leimacomys Matschie. Groove-toothed forest mice, Af.
Notomys Lesson. Australian kangaroo mice, Au.
Mastacomys Thomas. Broad-toothed rats, Au.
Echiothrix Gray. Shrew-rats, Celebes, E.Indies.
Melasmothrix Miller and Hollister. Celebes long-clawed mice, Celebes.
Acomys I. Geoffroy. Spiny mice, Af., W.As.
Uranomys Dollman. African big-toothed mice, Af.
Bandicota Gray. "Bandicoot" rats, As.
Nesokia Gray. Pest rat, As.
Beamys Thomas. Long-tailed pouched rats, Af.
Saccostomus Peters. African pouched rats, Af.
Cricetomys Waterhouse. Giant pouched rats, Af.
Anisomys Thomas. Powerful-toothed rats, New Guinea.
Neanthomys Toschi. Af.
Subfamily Dendromurinae. African tree mice.
    Dendromus A. Smith. African climbing mice, Af.
    Malacothrix Wagner. Long-eared mice, Af.
    Prionomys Dollman. Tree mice, Af.
    Petromyscus Thomas. Rock mice, Af.
    Steatomys Peters. Fat mice, Af.
    Deomys Thomas. Congo forest mice, Af.
Subfamily Otomyinae.
    Otomys Cuvier. Swamp rat, Af.
    Myotomys Thomas. Bush otomys rats, Af.
    Parotomys Thomas. Karo-rotte, Af.
Subfamily Phloeomyinae.
    Lenomys Thomas. Celebes rats, E.Indies.
    Pogonomys Milne Edwards. Prehensile-tailed rats, New Guinea.
    Chiropodomys Peters. Pencil-tailed tree mice, As.
    Mallomys Thomas. Giant tree rats, New Guinea.
    Papagomys Sody. Flores Island giant tree rats, Flores Island, Indonesia.
    Phloeomys Waterhouse. Slender-tailed cloud rats, Philippines.
    Crateromys Thomas. Bushy-tailed cloud rats, Philippines.
Subfamily Rhynchomyinae. "Shrew" rat.
    Rhynchomys Thomas. "Shrew" rat.
Subfamily Hydromyinae. Water rats.
    Chrotomys Thomas. Luzon striped rats, Philippines.
    Celaenomys Thomas. Shrewlike rats, Philippines.
    Crossomys Thomas. Water rats, Philippines, New Guinea.
    Xeromys Thomas. False water rats, Au.
    Hydromys E. Geoffroy. Australian water rats, Au.
    Parahydromys Poche. Mountain water rats, Au.
    Neohydromys Laurie. New Guinea water rat, New Guinea.
    Leptomys Thomas. Water rat, New Guinea.
    Microhydromys Tate and Arnold. Small water rat, New Guinea.
    Paraleptomys Tate and Arnold. Water rat, New Guinea.
    Baiyankamys Hinton. Baiyanka water rat, New Guinea.
    Pseudohydromys Rummler. New Guinea water rats, New Guinea.
    Mayermys Laurie and Hill. Shaw-Mayer's mice, New Guinea.

Family GLIRIDAE

Dormice

STRUCTURE

The dentition consists of incisors and brachyodont cheek teeth. The dental formula is $\frac{1}{1}$, $\frac{0}{0}$, $\frac{1}{1}$, $\frac{3}{3} = 20$. The cheek teeth have a series of ridges extending across the crowns. The skull has the infraorbital foramen little specialized, although it does transmit some muscles. The bullae are usually enlarged, and postorbital processes are absent. The limbs have the tibia and fibula strongly fused. External features include a squirrel-like appearance and slight modifications for arboreal life. The tail is long and bushy. The eyes and ears are large.

NATURAL HISTORY

The range is the Old World (Fig. 16–7). Dormice are divided into two subfamilies: Graphiurinae and Glirinae. Graphiurinae, with but a single genus restricted to Africa south of the Sahara, differs from the other subfamily in that the cheek teeth are more basin-shaped, the skull is constricted between the frontals and the nasals project anteriorly beyond the incisors. It has been considered to be a separate family by some writers. African dormice, *Graphiurus*, are nocturnal, and live in hollow trees and rock crevices. External measurements of an adult *G. murinus* are: total length, 185 mm.; tail, 85 mm.; hind foot, 18 mm. (Hollister, 1919). They feed on insects, fruits, nuts, seeds, and other vegetable matter; become extremely fat in the fall of the year; and spend the winter months in hibernation. They have two to five young in a litter (Shortridge, 1934).

The Glirinae, with six genera, occur in Europe, Asia, and North Africa. They are scansorial and nocturnal and feed on a variety of animal and vegetable matter. These dormice become extremely fat and hibernate. They breed in May or June and, after a gestation period of 22 days, give birth to two to six young in a nest in a hollow tree or on a tree limb. In captivity they live as long as 5½ years.

RECENT GENERA

Total, 7.

Subfamily Glirinae.
    Glis Brisson. Common dormice, Eu.
    Muscardinus Kaup. Hazel mice, Eu., W.As.
    Eliomys Wagner. Golden dormice, N.Af., Eu., W As.
    Dryomys Thomas. Tree dormice, E.Eu., As.

Glirulus Thomas. Japanese dormice, Japan.
Myomimus Ognev. Asiatic dormice, As.
Subfamily Graphiurinae.
Graphiurus Smuts. African dormice, Af.

Family PLATACANTHOMYIDAE
Spiny Dormice

STRUCTURE

The dentition consists of the following teeth: I $\frac{1}{1}$, C $\frac{0}{0}$, P $\frac{0}{0}$, M $\frac{3}{3}$ = 16. The cheek teeth have a series of oblique parallel ridges extending across the crowns and are subhypsodont. The skull has a series (or a single large pair) of foramina in the palate between the tooth rows. The bullae are small and the infraorbital foramen is normal in shape and size. The zygomatic plate is narrow. The limbs are modified for an arboreal habitat. The thumb is replaced by a pad, and the hind feet are slender and elongate. The claws are slender and compressed. External features include its size, about that of a large house mouse; nearly naked ears; and a long tail that is bushy, at least terminally.

NATURAL HISTORY

The range of this family is the southern parts of India and China (Fig. 16–9). Little is known of the habits of the two species of this family. Spiny dormice, *Platacanthomys lasiurus,* are known only from southern India. It has a long bushy tail with the distal hairs arranged like the web of a feather. The pelage is a mixture of soft hairs and broad, flat spines. The ears are long and pointed. Measurements are: total length 209 mm.; tail, 96 mm.; hind foot, 25 mm. The hairs on the tail extend 30 mm. beyond the tip of the tail. In southern India the spiny dormice have been found in hollow trees in rocky ravines. They construct a nest of shredded plant materials and feed on various plant materials including roots, fruit, and hot peppers. A captive female gave birth to four young.

The Chinese pygmy dormouse, *Typhlomys cinereus,* known only from southern China, measures: total length, 198 mm.; tail, 109 mm.; hind foot, 20 mm.; ear, 16 mm. It inhabits forests up to 4000 feet in elevation.

RECENT GENERA

Total 2.

Platacanthomys Blyth. Spiny dormice, As. (India).
Typhlomys Milne Edwards. Chinese pygmy dormice, S E. As.

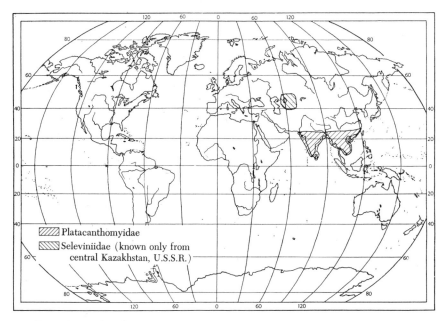

Fig. 16–9. The distribution of families Platacanthomyidae and Seleviniidae.

Family SELEVINIIDAE

Selvin's Mice

STRUCTURE

The dentition consists of cheek teeth that are simple and very small; each of the cheek teeth has only a single root; and the upper incisors are grooved. The dental formula is I $\frac{1}{1}$, C $\frac{0}{0}$, P $\frac{0}{0}$, M $\frac{3}{3}$ = 16. The skull has the auditory bullae greatly inflated, a comparatively small infraorbital foramen, and long palatal foramina. The limbs show saltatorial modifications. External features include the chunky body with a long, well-furred tail, and external ears that extend beyond the fur. The pelage, up to 10 mm. long in winter-taken specimens, is grayish above and whitish below.

NATURAL HISTORY

The seleviniids, known from a single genus and a single species in central Kazakhstan, U.S.S.R. (Fig. 16–9), are saltatorial, insectivorous inhabitants of arid and semiarid habitats. According to Ognev (1928–1950), they require up to three-quarters of the body weight in food each day. They are crepuscular and nocturnal, spending the day sleeping in a burrow and hibernate when the ambient temperature falls to 3° C.

ONE GENUS

Selevinia Belosludov and Bashanov. Selvin's mice, As.

Family ZAPODIDAE

Jumping Mice

STRUCTURE

The dentition consists of incisors that are sometimes grooved and cheek teeth that are brachyodont or semihypsodont. The dental formula is I $\frac{1}{1}$, C $\frac{0}{0}$, P $\frac{0\,or\,1}{0}$, M $\frac{3}{3} = 16$ or 18. The skull has the infraorbital foramen large, and uninflated bullae. The zygoma are simple, and the mandible is weakly developed. The limbs show saltatorial modifications in some forms. External features are generalized in the rare genus *Sicista*. In *Zapus* and *Napaeozapus* saltatorial modifications are evident including elongated tail and hind limbs.

NATURAL HISTORY

The range of this family is restricted to Eurasia and North America (Fig. 16–10). The zapodids are divided into two subfamilies: Sicistinae and Zapodinae. The Sicistinae, known from a single genus, occur in higher mountains of northern Europe and Asia. In these the cheek teeth are brachyodont, the upper incisors are ungrooved, and the appendages are not modified for saltatorial locomotion. They are called birch mice since they are common in birch thickets up to 10,000 feet in elevation. Measurements are: total length, 177 mm.; tail, 113 mm.; hind foot, 18 mm.; weight, 8 gm.

The Zapodinae, with three genera, occur in North America and in part of China. The following are typical measurements. *Zapus*: total length, 188–216 mm.; tail, 112–134 mm.; hind foot, 28–31 mm. *Napaeozapus*: total length, 220–225 mm.; tail, 131–160 mm.; hind foot, 29–33 mm. They are nocturnal, solitary, and saltatorial. They have two to eight young in late June or early July and occasionally have a second litter. The gestation period is approximately 18 days. In late summer, jumping mice become extremely fat, then hibernate in burrows lined with grass and hair. They emerge from hibernation only after the spring season is well advanced. Food consists of fruit, seeds, buds, and insects.

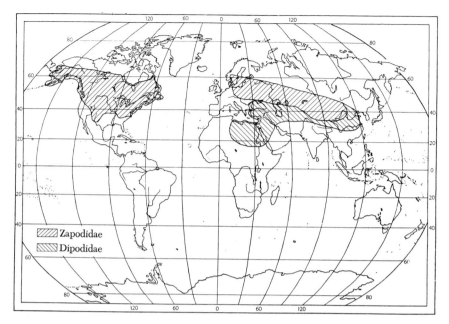

Fig. 16–10. The distribution of families Zapodidae and Dipodidae.

RECENT GENERA

Total, 4.

Subfamily Sicistinae.
  Sicista Gray. Birch mice, Eu., As.
Subfamily Zapodinae.
  Zapus Coues. Meadow jumping mice, N.A.
  Eozapus Preble. Szechwan jumping mice, As. (China).
  Napaeozapus Preble. Woodland jumping mice, N.A.

Family DIPODIDAE

Jerboas

STRUCTURE

The dentition consists of somewhat hypsodont cheek teeth with P4 reduced or absent. The dental formula is I $\frac{1}{1}$, C $\frac{0}{0}$, P $\frac{0 \text{ or } 1}{0}$, M $\frac{3}{3} = 22$ or 24. The crown pattern is the normal cricetid type. The skull has the mastoid and tympanic bullae expanded and the infraorbital foramen greatly enlarged. The zygomatic plate is narrow and below the infraorbital foramen. The limbs are modified for saltatorial locomotion. The hind limbs have digits I and V reduced or absent and digits II, III, and IV fused. The fibula is reduced to a threadlike structure. External features include the obvious adaptations for saltatorial locomotion: elongated hind feet and legs, and elongated tail. The tail has a large terminal tuft of hairs, and the eyes are large.

NATURAL HISTORY

The range of this family is primarily the deserts of the Old World from Central Asia through the African deserts (Fig. 16–10). The jerboas are divided into three subfamilies: the true jerboas, Dipodinae; the dwarf jerboas, Cardiocraniinae; and the long-eared jerboas, Euchoreutinae.

The Dipodinae, with seven genera, are widely distributed in the arid portions of Europe, Asia, and Africa; have large ears; cheek teeth with low or moderate cusps and well-marked re-entrant folds; jugals in two portions unconnected by a curvature; rostrums not enlarged; cervical vertebrae often fused; and the three median metatarsals fused into a common bone.

The jerboas are saltatorial and generally bipedal. They are nocturnal and crepuscular, and construct burrows where they store food and hibernate during the winter. They feed on leafy vegetation and seeds of grasses and herbs. They breed shortly after leaving hibernation and, after a gestation period of 42 days, give birth to one to five young.

The Cardiocraniinae, with two genera restricted to central Asia, have small ears; cheek teeth as in the Dipodinae; jugals in two portions connected by a curvature; bullae excessively inflated (probably the maximum in the order, occupying one-third of the upper surface of the skull); and metatarsals that are not fused.

The Euchoreutinae, with a single genus restricted to Asia, have abnormally large ears; cheek teeth that are high-cusped and have shallow re-entrant angles, jugals that slope gradually upward toward the lacrymal; well-inflated bullae; elongated rostra; and the three median metatarsals fused to form a common bone.

RECENT GENERA

Total, 10.

Subfamily Dipodinae. Jerboas.

    Dipus Zimmerman. Feather-footed jerboas, E.Eu., As.
    Paradipus Vinogradov. Comb-toed jerboas, As.
    Jaculus Erxleben. Desert jerboas, Af.
    Stylodipus G. Allen. Thick-tailed jerboas, Af.
    Allactaga Cuvier. Five-toed jerboas, Eu., As.
    Alactagulus Nehring. Jerboas, As.
    Pygeretmus Gloger. Flat-tailed jerboas, As.

Subfamily Cardiocraniinae. Dwarf jerboas.
  Cardiocranius Satunin. Five-toed dwarf jerboas, As.
  Salpingotus Vinogradov. Three-toed dwarf jerboas, As.
Subfamily Euchoreutinae. Long-eared jerboas.
  Euchoreutes Sclater. Long-eared jerboas, As.

SUBORDER HYSTRICOMORPHA, PORCUPINE-LIKE RODENTS

The skull has a massive zygomatic arch in which the jugal element is not supported by the zygomatic process of the maxilla. The infraorbital foramen is extremely large, usually larger than the diameter of the foramen magnum. The angle of the lower jaw arises from the outer wall of the incisive socket, rather than from the lower border of the dentary. The dental formula in all forms is I ¼, C %, P ¼, M ⅔ = 20. The cheek teeth are usually hypsodont, often grow from persistent pulp, and are usually flat-crowned in adult individuals. Postcranial features include the presence of separate tibia and fibula bones.

Family HYSTRICIDAE

Old World Porcupines

STRUCTURE

The dentition consists of incompletely rooted cheek teeth that have narrow re-entrant folds that are not regular. They vary from moderately to strongly hypsodont. The dental formula is I ¼, C %, P ¼, M ⅔ = 20. The skull has the facial portion inflated by pneumatic cavities, an enlarged infraorbital canal, and little or no interorbital constriction. The bullae are relatively small. The limbs are short, plantigrade, and pentadactyl. External features include a heavy body that is covered with well-developed spines and a short tail that is covered with short spines. The soles of the feet are naked; the thumbs, rudimentary.

NATURAL HISTORY

The Old World porcupines (Fig. 10 11) are divided into two subfamilies: Hystricinae, the true porcupines, with two genera; and Antherurinae, the brush-tailed porcupines, with two genera. They are all vegetarians, feeding on fruits, berries, roots, tubers, bark of trees, and cultivated crops such as melons, pumpkins, and corn. *Hystrix* is the only genus whose habits are well known. They are nocturnal and either occupy some burrow dug by another animal or dig their own burrow system. They frequently move as much as 10 miles nightly from the den to the feeding ground, often over fairly well-defined trails. In captivity they have two litters per year, each after a gestation period of 6 to 8 weeks. Normally there are two young per litter. They have been known to live 20 years in captivity.

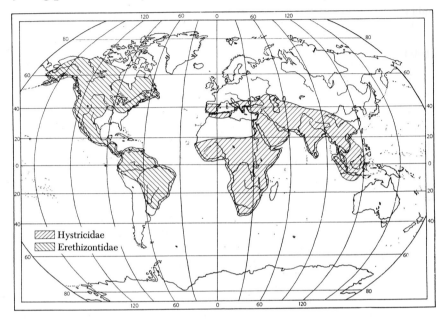

Fig. 16–11. The distribution of families Hystricidae and Erethizontidae.

RECENT GENERA

Total, 4.

Subfamily Hystricinae. Old World porcupines.
   Thecurus Lyon. Indonesian porcupines, As., E.Indies.
   Hystrix Linnaeus. Old World porcupines, As., Af., Eu.
Subfamily Antherurinae. Brush-tailed porcupines.
   Atherurus Cuvier. Brush-tailed porcupines, As.
   Trichys Gunther. Long-tailed porcupines, As.

Family ERETHIZONTIDAE

New World Porcupines

STRUCTURE

The dentition consists of the following teeth: I ⅟₁, C %, P ⅟₁, M ⅗ = 20. The cheek teeth are rooted and subhypsodont, with flat crowns. The skull has prominent bullae and the upper base of the zygoma is above the anterior part of the tooth row. The inferior border of the angular process of the mandible is strongly enrolled. The limbs are comparatively short, with feet that are modified for climbing. The claws are long and curved. The function of the thumb is taken over in some forms by a broad, movable pad. External features include a thick-set short body covered dorsally with sharp spines mixed with long hairs.

NATURAL HISTORY

The New World porcupines (Fig. 16–11) are divided into two subfamilies: Erethizontinae and Chaetomyinae.

The Erethizontinae, with three genera, have wide re-entrant folds in the cheek teeth and no special modifications of the orbit region. It includes the widely distributed North American porcupine, *Erethizon dorsatum.* They have the quills situated primarily on the back, tail, and hindquarters. Measurements are: total length 648–860 mm.; tail, 148–300 mm.; hind foot, 86–124 mm. A weight of approximately 15 pounds is average but some fat old males weigh as much as 35 pounds. They feed on the cambium layer of many woody plants and, to some extent on buds, twigs, and young pine needles. After a gestation period of about 7 months a single young is born.

The prehensile-tailed porcupines, *Coëndou,* have prehensile tails that are modified for contact on the dorsal surface of the distal end. Quills are widely distributed over their bodies. Prehensile-tailed porcupines are nocturnal and arboreal. Relatively little is known of their habits. Goldman (1920) reported that they are occasionally found concealed in matted vines in the tops of trees when timber is felled, and that the stomach of one specimen was filled with such vegetable matter as leaves and probably fruit.

The Chaetomyinae, or thin-spined porcupine, with a single known species, are restricted to South America. The re-entrant folds of their cheek teeth are so narrow that the upper cheek teeth appear to be laminate. The orbit is almost ringed by bone.

RECENT GENERA

Total, 4.
Subfamily Erethizontinae. New World porcupines.
    Erethizon Cuvier. North American porcupines, N.A.
    Coëndou Lacépède. Prehensile-tailed porcupines, C.A., S A.
    Echinoprocta Gray. Upper Amazon porcupines, S.A.
Subfamily Chaetomyinae. Thin-spined porcupines.
    Chaetomys Gray. Thin-spined porcupine, S.A.

Family CAVIIDAE

Guinea Pigs and Allies

STRUCTURE

The dentition is modified for a herbivorous diet. The cheek teeth are evergrowing and are comparatively simple. The skull has the angular process of the mandible drawn backward and not distorted outward, as in the Erethizontidae. The palate and the paraoccipital

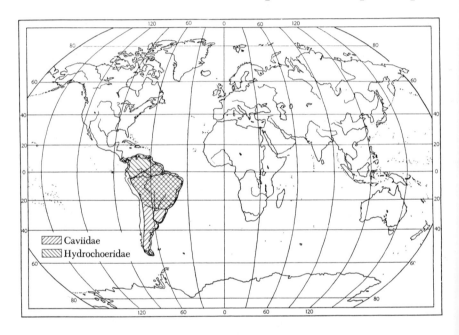

Fig. 16–12. The distribution of families Caviidae and Hydrochoeridae.

processes are short. The lacrimal is moderately large. The limbs have the tibia and fibula partially fused and the digits reduced to ⅘. External features are varied but the tail is vestigial in all forms.

NATURAL HISTORY

The range is restricted to South America, primarily from Venezuela, southward to southern Argentina (Fig. 16–12). The Caviidae are exclusively vegetarian, diurnal, and often colonial. Their inroads on agricultural crops make them unwanted pests in some areas. None are known to hibernate. Two subfamilies are recognized: Caviinae and Dolichotinae. The Caviinae, or guinea pigs, have robust bodies with short limbs and ears, large heads and small size. Two genera are known. Measurements of three male *Cavia musteloides* from southern Peru are: body length, 210–235 mm.; hind foot, 36–38 mm.; ear, 21–23 mm. (Pearson, 1951). Pearson reported that this species was one of the most common mammals in

Fig. 16–13. Guinea pigs (*Cavia porcellus*). (Ernest P. Walker.)

the region. They are diurnal and make burrows in ditches and stone walls along roads and frequently live in tunnels dug by other mammals. After a gestation period of 60 days, they produce two to four young. The young reach sexual maturity in 2 months.

Cavia porcellus, the guinea pig (Fig. 16–13), was in domestication by the Indians when the white man arrived and was used by the Indians as food.

The Dolichotinae, or Patagonian "hares" (Fig. 16–14), have rabbit-like bodies, with long thin limbs, large eyes, and relatively large ears. The subfamily is represented by one genus with two known species. These hystricomorph rodents run and leap like rabbits. They are social, often living in groups of up to thirty in number.

RECENT GENERA

Total, 3.
Subfamily Caviinae. Guinea pigs.
　Cavia Pallas. Guinea pigs, cavies, S.A.
　Kerodon Cuvier. Mocos, S.A.
Subfamily Dolichotinae. Patagonian "hares."
　Dolichotis Desmarest. Patagonian "hares," S.A.

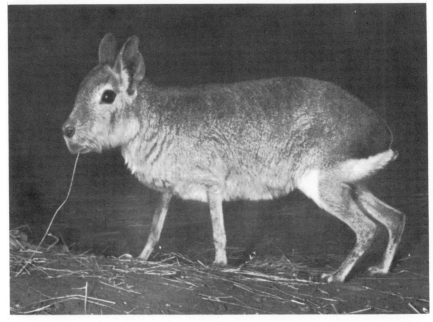

Fig. 16–14. A Patagonian cavy *(Dolichotis patagonica)*. (Ernest P. Walker.)

Family HYDROCHOERIDAE

Capybara

STRUCTURE

The dentition consists of the following teeth: I ¼, C %, P ¼, M ⅜ = 20. The cheek teeth are evergrowing and complex. M3 is elongate, longer than the combined lengths of the other cheek teeth; m3 is also elongated. Both teeth have occlusal surface patterns made up of broadly joined transverse lamellae. The skull has the zygomatic structure similar to that in the Caviidae. The palate is somewhat elongated and the tooth rows strongly convergent anteriorly. The paraoccipital processes are greatly enlarged. The limbs have the digits reduced to ⅘. The digits are semiwebbed. External features include a massive robust body, with a large head and short limbs. The ears are short and rounded; the eyes are small. The tail is vestigial.

NATURAL HISTORY

The range of this family includes tropical America from Panama southward (Fig. 16–12). The Hydrochoeridae, or capybaras, are the largest living rodents. A single genus, with two species, is known. Measurements of a male are: total length, 1250 mm.; hind foot, 200 mm. Weights as great as 50 kg. (more than 110 pounds) have been recorded. Capybaras are primarily diurnal and are entirely herbivorous. They feed in bands of ten to twenty, sometimes grazing with cattle. They also feed on grains, melons, and squashes. They are generally quiet animals that run little and do not dig burrows in the ground. They do wallow in muddy pools and may make shallow beds in the ground. When alarmed they will enter water and hide in floating vegetation with only their nostrils exposed. There is but a single breeding season each year and after a gestation period of 104 to 126 days, three to eight young are born. The young are precocious and shortly after birth are able to follow the mother into water and swim.

ONE RECENT GENUS

Hydrochoerus Brisson. Capybaras, C.A., S.A.

Family DINOMYIDAE

False Paca

STRUCTURE

The dentition includes cheek teeth that are extremely hypsodont and are probably evergrowing. The occlusal surface consists of a series of lamellae. The dental formula is I $\frac{1}{1}$, C $\frac{0}{0}$, P $\frac{1}{1}$, M $\frac{3}{3}$ = 20. The skull has the palate constricted anteriorly and the angular process of the mandible distorted outward and heavily ridged. The bullae are moderate in size. The limbs have digits $\frac{4}{4}$. The feet are broad, and the claws are long and powerful. External features include a robust body with an elongate head, short ears, and short limbs. The tail is well-haired and slightly longer than the hind foot. The pelage is short, dense, and rather harsh.

NATURAL HISTORY

The false paca, or pacarana, is known from a single species. It is restricted in distribution to the relatively uninhabited valleys and lower slopes of the Andes (Fig. 16–15) where the climate is mild and the rainfall abundant.

Relatively little is known of the habits of false pacas. They are rare and may be on the verge of extinction. They are terrestrial, diurnal, and herbivorous. In captivity they are slow-moving, sit on

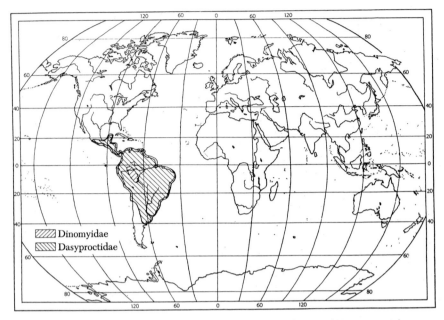

Fig. 16–15. The distribution of families Dinomyidae and Dasyproctidae.

their haunches and hold food in their forepaws while eating, and never use the powerful claws for digging. They reach weights of 22 to 33 pounds.

ONE GENUS

Dinomys Peters. False pacas, S.A.

Family DASYPROCTIDAE

Pacas

STRUCTURE

The dentition includes incisors that are relatively thin and cheek teeth that are hypsodont and semirooted. The dental formula is I ⅕, C 0⁄0, P ⅕, M ⅗ = 20. The skull is diverse, but all have relatively large lacrimals. The limbs are modified for cursorial locomotion. They are elongated and have the toes reduced. The forefeet are functionally artiodactylous, having four toes terminating in strong, thick, and blunt claws that are almost hooflike. The hind feet are functionally perissodactylous, with three main digits. External features vary with the subfamily but include a relatively large slender body with an elongate head, moderate to small ears, elongate limbs, and a tail that is reduced or absent.

NATURAL HISTORY

The range of this family is North, Central, and South America from southern Mexico, south to northern Argentina, and some of the West Indies (Fig. 16–15). They are terrestrial, herbivorous, and cursorial. Two subfamilies with relatively great morphological differences are recognized: Cuniculinae and Dasyproctinae. The Cuniculinae, or pacas, with one known genus, have large cheek teeth, with deep re-entrant angles, and a uniquely enlarged and inflated zygomatic arch that covers a broad inner cheek pouch. The body is relatively heavy, and the digits are subungulate. The pelage is short, has a characteristic pattern of four lines or rows of whitish spots on each side, and a general brownish color. Pacas live in burrows and are usually nocturnal. They feed on plants, herbs, fruits, tubers, and roots. When alarmed, they take to water readily. Two litters per year with two to four young per litter appears to be common. The pacas are widely hunted for food throughout their range.

The Dasyproctinae, or agoutis, with two genera, have relatively small cheek teeth; a normal, unmodified zygomatic arch; and a less bulky body. The pelage is short; coarse; and usually uniformly blackish, brownish, or reddish dorsally. They dig burrows in the ground and bury food. There appears to be no special breeding season. After a gestation period of 104 days, two to four precocial young are born. Agoutis are generally solitary in habit and, in undisturbed situations, are diurnal, but, where hunted by man, they become crepuscular.

RECENT GENERA

Total, 3.
Subfamily Cuniculinae. Pacas.
  Cuniculus Brisson. C.A., S.A.
Subfamily Dasyproctinae. Agoutis.
  Dasyprocta Illiger. Agoutis, C.A., S.A.
  Myoprocta Thomas. Tailed Agoutis, S.A.

Family CHINCHILLIDAE
Chinchillas

STRUCTURE

The dentition includes relatively narrow incisors and evergrowing cheek-teeth that have a pattern of tightly compressed transverse laminae. The dental formula is I $\frac{1}{1}$, C $\frac{0}{0}$, P $\frac{1}{1}$, M $\frac{3}{3} = 20$. The skull has large lacrimals that are usually in contact with the jugals; long, narrow palatine foramina; anteriorly constricted palate; and an elongated angular process that is but slightly deflected laterally. The limbs have the fibula reduced but not fused with the tibia. The hind feet are relatively long. The forefeet have five digits (thumb reduced), and the hind feet have three or four digits. External features include a relatively large head, with large eyes and rounded ears that vary from short to long. The hind limbs are long and muscular, the forefeet short. The tail is long and well-haired.

NATURAL HISTORY

The range of this family is South America, where it is restricted to the highlands of Peru, Chile, Bolivia, Argentina, and parts of the pampas of Argentina (Fig. 16–16). They are terrestrial, herbivorous,

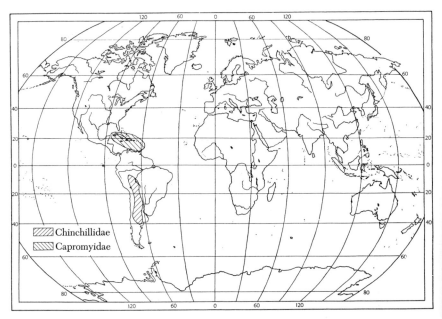

Fig. 16–16. The distribution of families Chinchillidae and Capromyidae.

diurnal or nocturnal, seek shelter in burrows or rock crevices, and are not known to hibernate.

The true chinchilla, *Chinchilla*, is known from a single species. They formerly existed from sea level in Chile upward in the mountains to elevations as high as 11,000 feet. Because of excessive hunting and trapping pressures, the native chinchillas of Bolivia, Peru,. and Chile are greatly restricted in number and distribution (Osgood,

1943). External measurements of two females taken in Chile are: total length, 425 and 376 mm.; tail, 151 and 136 mm.; hind foot, 59 and 57 mm.; ear 63 and 62 mm. (Osgood, *op. cit.*). The chinchillas were acclimated to captivity and were raised extensively in captivity, especially in the United States, where they were sold primarily for breeding purposes. In captivity the chinchilla bears one to six young twice yearly.

The mountain viscachas, *Lagidium*, are distributed widely at higher elevations in the Andes of southern Chile and central and northern Peru. Measurements of 288 adults from Caccachara, Peru are: total length, 144 males—range 561 to 655 mm.; 144 females—average 613 mm. (range 549 to 685 mm.); tail, 269 mm. (239 to 320 mm.), 269 mm. (231 to 304 mm.); hind foot, 92 mm. (85 to 102 mm.), 93 mm. (84 to 99 mm.); ear, 64 mm. (57 to 72 mm.), 64 mm. (56 to 74 mm.) (Pearson, 1951). Mountain viscachas are diurnal, herbivorous, and gregarious. They live only near rocks and venture up to 75 yards from the rocks for food. They live in burrows under the rocks, with family groups of two to five occupying the same burrow and colonies of up to seventy-five individuals living in the immediate area. The females bear one or two young after a gestation period of 3 months. The young are precocial, being fully haired, having the eyes open, and able to eat plant food immediately (Pearson, 1948).

The plains viscachas, *Lagostomus*, occur in open, exposed situations in the pampas of Argentina, where they dig extensive burrows in the ground. One entrance may serve more than one burrow and a series of interconnected burrows, with four to thirty entrances covering 10 to 20 sq.m., may be occupied simultaneously by a number of individuals. The entrances to the burrows are large enough, in some cases, for a man to fall in up to his waist.

RECENT GENERA

Total, 3.

Lagostomus Brookes. Plains viscachas, S.A.
Lagidium Meyen. Mountain viscachas, S.A.
Chinchilla Bennett. Chinchillas, S.A.

Family CAPROMYIDAE

Hutias

STRUCTURE

The dentition includes evergrowing cheek-teeth that have the crowns and a pattern of folds filled with cement. The upper cheek-teeth are slightly hypsodont. The dental formula is I $\frac{1}{1}$, C $\frac{0}{0}$, P $\frac{1}{1}$, M $\frac{3}{3}$ = 20. The skull is long and flattened. The paraoccipital processes usually stand apart from the bullae. The limbs are short; the digits are $\frac{5}{5}$. External features include a stout body, and a tail that is long and prehensile or greatly reduced.

NATURAL HISTORY

Members of this family are restricted to the West Indies (Fig. 16–16). The hutias are herbivorous, terrestrial or arboreal, and diurnal. They feed on bark, buds, leaves, and fruit; some reportedly take lizards. Up to four precocial young are born in a litter. They are widely hunted for food and sport. Hutias are divisible into two subfamilies: Capromyinae and Plagiodontinae.

The Plagiodontinae have unique cheek-teeth: the upper molars have a single fold on each side and these are long, parallel to each other, obliquely arranged on the tooth and filled with cement. The lower cheek-teeth have two long inner and one shallow outer fold. The jugal is more simplified than in the Capromyinae, and the tail is naked (Ellerman, 1940). Measurements are: total length, 475–551 mm.; tail, 127–153 mm.; hind foot, 67 mm.; ear, 18 mm. (Hall and Kelson, 1959). Two of the four known species are living. These are from Haiti and the Dominican Republic in the West Indies.

The Capromyinae have the enamel pattern of the upper and lower cheek-teeth with five or six folds. The jugal is enlarged and complex; and the tail is long and prehensile (*Capromys*) or strongly reduced (*Geocapromys*). External measurements of six adult *Capromys pilorides* from Cuba are: total length, 710–810 mm.; tail, 170–255 mm.; hind foot, 95–100 mm.; ear, 27–28 mm. (Hall and Kelson, 1959). The average weight of males is 3.0 kg.; of females, 2.5 kg. Large males may weigh as much as 5.0 kg. (Angulo, 1945).

RECENT GENERA

Total, 3.
Subfamily Capromyinae.
    Capromys Desmarest. Cuban hutias, W.Indies.
    Geocapromys Chapman. Bahaman and Jamaican hutias, W.Indies.
Subfamily Plagiodontinae.
    Plagiodontia Cuvier. Hispanolian hutias, W.Indies.

The genus *Procapromys* Chapman, based on a single specimen from Venezuela, is of doubtful significance. The immature specimen may be a young *Capromys pilorides,* probably transported by man to Venezuela (Anthony, 1926).

Family MYOCASTORIDAE

Nutria

STRUCTURE

The dentition consists of cheek teeth that are semirooted, highly hypsodont, and have deep, outer and inner folds that tend to isolate the occlusal surface into islands. The cheek teeth decrease in size and converge anteriorly. The incisors are broad and strong. The dental formula is I $\frac{1}{1}$, C $\frac{0}{0}$, P $\frac{1}{1}$, M $\frac{3}{3}$ = 20. The skull is heavily ridged, somewhat triangular in outline, and has short postorbital and elongated paraoccipital processes. The mandible has the corocoid reduced and the angular process enlarged, elongated, and laterally deflected. The limbs are modified for aquatic locomotion. The thumb is vestigial; the hind feet are larger than the forefeet; and the toes are webbed; with the great toe free. The claws are large and sharp. External features include a stout body of large size, small eyes and ears, and short limbs.

NATURAL HISTORY

The range is southern South America, from southern Brazil south to the Straits of Magellan. It has been introduced in North America

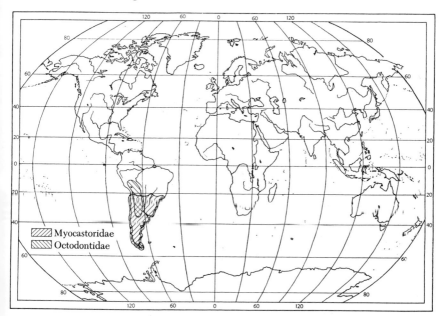

Fig. 16–17. The distribution of families Myocastoridae and Octodontidae.

and Eurasia (Fig. 16–17). Nutrias are represented by one living genus with a single known species. Measurements are: total length, 800–900 mm.; tail, 350–400 mm.; hind foot, 130–140 mm. (Osgood, 1943). The pelage consists of soft dense underfur and harsh overlying guard hairs. Its pelt is widely used in the fur trade. Nutrias live in and around streams and ponds, dig burrows in the banks, and feed on various types of aquatic vegetation. They have a home range approximately 200 yards in radius. Runways are constructed through the aquatic vegetation. The females are polyestrous, undergo postpartal heat 48 hours after the birth of the young, have a gestation period of about 120 days, and bear a litter of two to ten. Two litters per year are usually produced.

In the United States, nutria have been widely raised in captivity (on "fur farms," which apparently exist primarily to sell breeding stock to others) and deliberately introduced in the wild as potential fur-bearers. In many places these introductions have been economically detrimental, rather than beneficial.

ONE GENUS

Myocastor Kerr. Nutrias, S.A. (introduced into N.A. and Eurasia).

Family OCTODONTIDAE

Octodonts or Hedge Rats

STRUCTURE

The dentition includes cheek teeth that are simplified and, in the upper row, have an occluded pattern that is usually "8"-shaped. The dental formula is I $\frac{1}{1}$, C $\frac{0}{0}$, P $\frac{1}{1}$, M $\frac{3}{3}$ = 20. The skull has the bullae moderately to greatly inflated, and no part of the lacrimal canal opening on the side of the rostrum. The bony palate terminates between the tooth rows, and the incisive foramina are never enlarged. The limbs have digits $\frac{5}{5}$. The thumb is reduced in size and bears a nail instead of a claw. The claws are moderate in size, recurved, and sharp. External features include a robust body, a relatively large head with rounded ears of moderate size, and a pointed nose. The tail is short or long, with the hairs at the base short and becoming progressively longer distally, resulting in a trumpet-shaped tufted tail. The toes of the hind feet have a row of stiff, bristly hairs and extend beyond the claws.

NATURAL HISTORY

The range of this family is South America where it is restricted from low to moderate elevations in the Andes from southern Peru south to Bolivia, northwestern Argentina, and Chile (Fig. 16–17). The octodonts, with five genera, are ratlike in general form and size. They are vegetarian, feeding on a variety of tubers, roots, bark, and cacti. They are fossorial, and usually store food in underground chambers associated with their burrows.

The degu, *Octodon*, with three species, occurs in Chile, mainly in the coastal region and inland up to 4000 feet elevation. External measurements of *Octodon degus* are: total length, average: 295 (range 284–310) mm.; tail, 117 (106–130) mm.; hind foot, 36 (35–38) mm. Degus are diurnal, have short ears and a black-tipped tail. They are locally abundant, but are not widespread; little is known of their habits (Osgood, 1943).

The rock rats (*Aconaemys*), with two known species, occur in the high slopes of the Andes and in the coastal ranges of south central Chile. External measurements are: total length, average 232 (range 217–247) mm.; tail, 62 (57–73) mm.; hind foot, 30.8 (30–32) mm. It is a burrowing rodent that is apparently restricted in distribution to forests of araucarias (a "pine" that, like the rock rat, appears to be a primitive form becoming extinct). Rock rats are primarily nocturnal, live in burrows that are often interconnected by shallow runways, and are apparently active all year. Specimens taken in early November included several small young and an adult female that contained two very large fetuses (Osgood, 1943).

The coruro (*Spalacopus*), with two known species, is small, thick-set, and short-tailed. The incisors are procumbent and probably are used in digging the extensive burrow systems characteristic of this rodent.

RECENT GENERA

Total, 5.

Octodon Bennett. Degu, S.A.
Octodontomys Palmer. Boris, S.A.
Spalacopus Wagler. Cururos, S.A.
Aconaemys Ameghino. Rock rats, S.A.
Octomys Thomas. Viscacha rats, S.A.

Family CTENOMYIDAE

Tucu-tucus

STRUCTURE

The dentition consists of incisors that are much thickened and cheek teeth that are much simplified. In the upper cheek teeth the small inner fold is obsolete, resulting in a kidney-shaped pattern. The third molars are greatly reduced in size. The dental formula is I ⅟₁, C ⁰⁄₀, P ⅟₁, M ⅔ = 20. The skull is similar to that of the Octodontidae. The rostrum is broad, a postorbital process is present, and the parietals are well-ridged. The limbs are short and muscular. The toes are strong and have strong claws that are longer on the forefeet than on the hind feet. The soles of the feet are large and are fringed by stiff bristles. External features include a heavy body, large head, thick neck, small eyes, and reduced ears. The tail is short and sparsely covered with short hairs. All of these are obvious modifications for the fossorial habits of this family.

NATURAL HISTORY

The range of this family is restricted to southern South America (Fig. 16–18). Tucu-tucus are very similar to North American pocket gophers, Geomyidae, in habits and general adaptations.

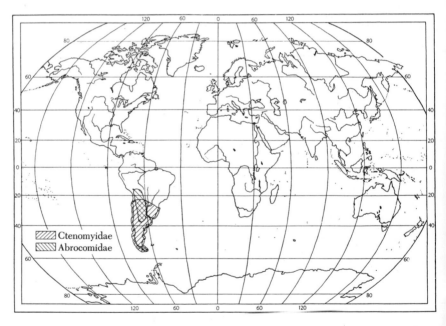

Fig. 16–18. The distribution of families Ctenomyidae and Abrocomidae.

Measurements vary with the species: *Ctenomys magellanicus* measurements are: total length, 276 to 304 mm.; tail, 79 to 82 mm.; hind foot, 37 to 41 mm. (Osgood, 1943). Measurements of *Ctenomys opimus* are: total length: average 271 (range 252–293) mm.; tail,

85 (80–95) mm.; hind foot, 37 (35–39) mm.; ear, 7 (7–8) mm. (Pearson, 1951). Tucu-tucus construct extensive burrows, up to 30 feet in length, and feed on vegetation around the burrow. Large food stocks are stored in the underground burrows. Pearson (1951) reported that *Ctenomys opimus* reveals itself by completely stripping the natural vegetation, a spiny grass, from areas up to 100 feet across. In favorable areas tucu-tucus completely denude between one-fourth and one-half of the vegetation.

ONE RECENT GENUS

Ctenomys Blainville. Tucu-tucus, S.A.

Family ABROCOMIDAE

Chinchilla Rats

STRUCTURE

The dentition includes evergrowing cheek-teeth and narrow incisors. The upper cheek-teeth have one inner and one outer fold, and M3 has an accessory posterior loop. The dental formula is I $\frac{1}{1}$, C $\frac{0}{0}$, P $\frac{1}{1}$, M $\frac{3}{3}$ = 20. The skull has a long, narrow rostrum; rounded braincase; enlarged bullae; and constricted frontals. The short, straight palate has long, narrow incisive foramina. The mandible has the angular process long and slender and the coronoid process low. The limbs are short, the digits are $\frac{4}{5}$, and the nails are weak and hollow ventrally. The hind toes have a fringe of stiff, recurved hairs extending beyond the claw tip. External features include a ratlike shape, a large head, pointed nose, large eyes, and large rounded ears. The tail, always less than half the length of the head and body, is terete and covered by fine, short hairs. The long, soft, and fine pelage is grayish in color.

NATURAL HISTORY

The range is South America where the family is restricted to higher elevations in the mountains of southern Peru, Bolivia, northwestern Argentina, and Chile. Elevational distribution ranges from 4000 to 18,000 feet (Fig. 16–8). Chinchilla rats, with one living genus and two living species, are colonial and vegetarian. They live in rocky crevices or in rocky areas under which they burrow; occasionally they climb trees. Measurements of *Abrocoma bennetti* are: total length, 350–398 mm.; tail, 145–166 mm.; hind foot, 36–39 mm. (Osgood, 1943). External measurements of a large adult female

Abrocoma cinerea are: total length, 256 mm.; tail, 74 mm.; hind foot, 28.5 mm.; ear, 25 mm.

Pearson (1951) suggests that the comb of stiff bristles on the hind toes, in this and other hystricomorph rodents, is used to remove parasites from the fur and to help keep the fine fur untangled. Pearson found chinchilla rats to be rare, restricted in distribution, and not susceptible to baited traps. He found evidence that two is the usual number of young in a litter.

ONE RECENT GENUS

Abrocoma Waterhouse. Chinchilla rats, S.A.

Family ECHIMYIDAE

Spiny Rats

STRUCTURE

The dentition includes flat-crowned, rooted cheek teeth and normal incisors. The dental formula is I $\frac{1}{1}$, C $\frac{0}{0}$, P $\frac{1}{1}$, M $\frac{3}{3}$ = 20. The skull has prominent bullae and broad frontals. The angle of the jaw is slender. The limbs vary with the subfamily. External features include the ratlike size and shape, ears that are of moderate size and broadly rounded or sharply pointed, and pelage that often is spiny.

NATURAL HISTORY

The range of this family is restricted to the tropical New World, from Nicaragua southward to southern Brazil (Fig. 16–19). Spiny rats are a diverse group (fifteen genera) of herbivorous hystricomorph rodents that are adapted for a life in the humid tropics. They normally consume a great deal of free water and quickly die when exposed to high temperatures or aridity. Two subfamilies are recognized: Echimyinae and Dactylomyinae.

The Echimyinae, with eleven genera, do not have the cheek teeth especially broadened. The pelage is harsh and has a tendency to become spiny. The feet are unmodified. Most members of this subfamily are terrestrial or arboreal but one, *Euryzygomatomys*, is fossorial.

The Dactylomyinae, with four genera, have the cheek teeth excessively broad and heavy, and relatively prismatic in pattern. The pelage is soft and does not develop spines, and the digits of the forefeet and hind feet are greatly elongated and somewhat syndactylous.

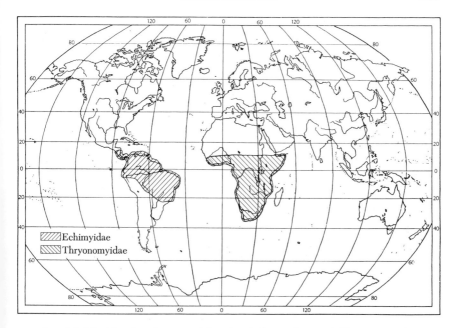

Fig. 16–19. The distribution of families Echimyidae and Thryonomyidae.

In climbing, digits I and II of the hind feet and digits II and III of the forefeet are placed on one side of a limb, while the other digits are placed on the opposite side.

RECENT GENERA

Total, 15.

Subfamily Echimyinae.

Proëchimys J. A. Allen. Spiny rats, C.A., S.A.
Hoplomys J. A. Allen. Harsh-furred spiny rats, C.A., S.A.
Euryzygomatomys Goeldi. Suira, S.A.
Clyomys Thomas. Spiny rat, S.A.
Carterodon Waterhouse. Spiny rat, S.A.
Cercomys Cuvier. Punare, S.A.
Mesomys Wagner. Hedgehog rat, S.A.
Lonchothrix Thomas. Rato d'ouphino, S.A.
Isothrix Wagner. Arboreal rats, S.A.
Diplomys Thomas. Arboreal spiny rats, C.A., S.A.
Echimys Cuvier. Arboreal spiny rats, C.A., S.A.

Subfamily Dactylomyinae.

Dactylomys I. Geoffroy. Arboreal rat, S.A.
Lachnomys Thomas. Tree rat, S.A.
Kannabateomys Jentink. Tree rat, S.A.
Thrinacodus Gunther. Arboreal rat, S.A.

Family THRYONOMYIDAE

Cane Rats

STRUCTURE

The dentition includes semihypsodont, rooted cheek-teeth and powerful incisors. The upper incisors have three deep grooves. The dental formula is: I $\frac{1}{1}$, C $\frac{0}{0}$, P $\frac{1}{1}$, M $\frac{3}{3} = 20$. The skull is massive and heavily ridged. The occipital region of the skull is enlarged and heavy; the bullae are small. The limbs are short and have the digits arranged in a perissodactylous manner. The thumb is absent, and the fifth digit is often reduced. On the hind foot the great toe is greatly reduced or absent. The claws are thick and heavy. External features include a robust body with short limbs, short tail, and short rounded ears that barely extend above the spiny pelage.

NATURAL HISTORY

The range of this family is restricted to Africa south of the Sahara (Fig. 16–19). Cane rats are more or less fossorial, and hide in matted vegetation and holes in the ground during the daytime. They feed on vegetation, especially the softer parts of coarse grasses and shrubs, and the bark of trees. Two to four young are born in a litter.

The typical cane rats (*Thryonomys*) occur in Africa from about 10 degrees N., south throughout most of the continent. They occur in marshes and in the reeds and papyrus stands which border streams and lakes. They can swim well and when pursued, often remain submerged in the water with only the nose above water. They are about the size of muskrats and are used as a source of meat by several native tribes, who conduct organized hunts almost daily in the dry season. In such a drive, the dry reeds are burned, driving the cane rats out into the open where they are killed with a spear or run down by dogs (Shortridge, 1934).

ONE RECENT GENUS

Thryonomys Fitzinger. Cane rats, Af.

Family PETROMYIDAE

Rock Rats

STRUCTURE

The dentition consists of rooted, hypsodont cheek-teeth with a simplified pattern and relatively weak, ungrooved incisors. The dental formula is I ⅓, C %, P ⅓, M ⅔ = 20. The skull is flattened and has greatly inflated bullae. The angular process of the mandible is bent outward. The limbs have narrow feet with short claws. The hind toes have a comb of stiff spines as in the octodontids. The thumb is vestigial and the great toe is reduced. External features include small size; a generalized ratlike external form; a long tail covered with scattered, long soft hairs, and short rounded ears.

NATURAL HISTORY

The range is restricted to rocky areas in southeastern Africa (Fig. 16–20). The rock rats, or dassie-rats, (*Petromys*) live in the

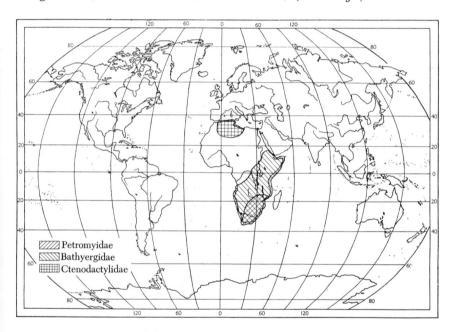

Fig. 16–20. The distribution of families Petromyidae, Bathyergidae, and Ctenodaitylidae.

rocky areas of the arid and semiarid parts of southern Africa. They are diurnal and usually travel singly or in pairs. They feed on vegetation and, to some extent, berries and seeds. They have one or two young per litter and appear to have only one breeding season per year. The fur is extremely soft and silky. The hairs on the tail stand out at right angles and the tail is apparently quite easily lost, for many trapped specimens are missing all or part of it. They are reported to be extremely difficult mammals to skin. The skin has been described as "the consistency of wet blotting paper" and can best be removed by leaving the outer layer of flesh attached to the skin. They have two to four young per litter. The young are born in nests built in the middle of the reed beds. The young are usually hidden under a thin layer of reeds (Shortridge, 1934).

ONE GENUS

Petromys Smith. Rock rat, Af.

Family BATHYERGIDAE

Mole Rats

STRUCTURE

The dentition consists of a variable number of cheek teeth that are strongly hypsodont and rooted, and large incisors. The pattern of the cheek teeth is often reduced to a simplified ring of enamel. The dental formula is I $\frac{1}{1}$, C $\frac{0}{0}$, P $^{0, 2,}\frac{3}{0, 2, 3}$, M $^{0,}\frac{3}{0, 3} = 4$–28. The skull is highly modified for a fossorial habitat. The infraorbital foramen is so reduced that it can transmit little muscle. The frontal is constricted between the orbits. The mandible has a wide angular process that is distorted outward. The limbs are short and have the tibia and fibula fused both proximally and distally. The claws on the large feet are moderate to long, and strong. External features include extreme modifications for a fossorial life. The eyes are small; the external ear is reduced to a ridge of skin around the opening; the limbs are short; and the tail is extremely reduced, but is covered with hair. The pelage is thick and short, or absent. The range is restricted to Africa (Fig. 16–20).

NATURAL HISTORY

The mole rats are almost completely fossorial and apparently travel above ground only rarely. They construct extensive burrows a few inches under the surface in soft soils. They feed on various bulbs and roots, which are gathered and stored in chambers in the runway systems. Some species feed on worms readily. Hibernation or seasonal inactivity occurs during the winter season (Shortridge, 1934). One to five young are produced in a single litter.

Eloff (1951a and b, 1958) has shown that mole rats are blind. They are extremely sensitive to air currents and can detect differences of as little as 2° C. They are well oriented and when the tunnels are destroyed, bore a parallel tunnel, without trial and error, directly to their goal.

RECENT GENERA

Total, 5.

Georychus Illiger. Cape Blesmols, Af.
Cryptomys Gray. African mole rats, Af.
Heliophobius Peters. Mole rats, Af.
Bathyergus Illiger. Sand mole rats, S.Af.
Heterocephalus Ruppell. Naked sand rats, Af.

Family CTENODACTYLIDAE

Gundis

STRUCTURE

The dentition consists of the following: I $\frac{1}{1}$, C $\frac{0}{1}$, P $\frac{1}{1}$ or $\frac{2}{2}$, M $\frac{3}{3}$ = 20 or 24. The cheek teeth are evergrowing and have a practically or completely simplified pattern. The skull is flattened and has a large infraorbital canal and a large lacrimal. The mandible has the coronoid process absent and the angular process elongated. The limbs have the digits reduced to four on each foot, and the claws are not enlarged. The two inner digits of the hind foot have comblike fringes of stiff bristles. External features include a shape similar to that of the guinea pig; small, rounded ears, a short tail, and very soft fur.

NATURAL HISTORY

The range of this family is restricted to rocky and semiarid regions of northern Africa (Fig. 16–20). The gundis are primarily diurnal rodents that live in natural cavities in rocks or ruins and spend long periods basking in the sun. They are chiefly herbivorous but take some seeds. They have one or two precocial young in a litter. The young are furred and are able to run at birth. Measurements are: total length, 210 mm.; tail, 20 mm.

GENERA

Total, 4.

Ctenodactylus Gray. Gundis, Af.
Pectinator Blyth. Specke's pectinator, Af.
Massoutiera Lataste. Gundis, Af.
Felovia Lataste. Gundis, Af.

17

Order Cetacea

Whales

The cetaceans are a group of large-sized, exclusively aquatic mammals that occur in all of the oceans of the world and in the lower courses of many of the larger rivers. This order includes the largest living mammal, the blue whale.

CHARACTERISTICS

The limbs are modified for aquatic life, in that the posterior limbs are absent and the forelimb is not externally divisible into limb elements. The radius, ulna, and digital bones are greatly flattened, and nails are absent on the webbed digits. The skull is greatly modified, with the rostrum and facial portions elongated. The parietals are on the side of the skull, often concealed by the overlapping supraoccipitals. The nasals are reduced. The teeth are simplified or are absent (see subordinal diagnoses). Postcranial features include flattened and more or less fused cervical vertebrae, a reduction in the articular connections of the body vertebrae, and a greatly reduced sternum. The pelvic girdle is reduced and is not in contact with the vertebral column. Features of the soft anatomy include the absence or great reduction of the sebaceous and suderiferous skin glands and the presence of a complex stomach. External features show the great adaptation to an aquatic life. The body is fusiform in shape, with no constriction of the body contour at the neck. The tail is greatly flattened and modified with flukes. The ears lack any trace of a pinna, and the auditory meatus is reduced to a tiny aperture. The skin is thick, smooth, and hairless; under it is a layer of blubber. The external narial opening is usually near the vertex of the head.

RANGE

Whales and relatives are exclusively aquatic and occur in all of the oceans and the lower courses of many larger rivers· of the world.

SUBORDER ODONTOCETI, TOOTHED WHALES

The dentition is varied; teeth are always present and usually numerous, although they may be reduced to a single pair. The skull is asymmetrical on the dorsal surface, especially in the region of the blowholes. The maxillae are expanded and cover most of the orbital process of the frontal bones. The nasal bones form no part of the roof of the nasal passage. Postcranial features include the two-headed anterior ribs and a sternum formed of two or more pieces. External features include a single blowhole.

Family PLATANISTIDAE

Ganges River Dolphin

STRUCTURE

The dentition consists of about twenty-nine pairs of small conical teeth in each jaw. Several teeth at the front of the jaw have pointed crowns and compressed, enlarged roots. The skull has the lacrimal and jugals fused; the palatines not part of the hard palate; the petro-tympanic fused with the cranium; and the narial opening anterior, with a longitudinal oblong opening. Postcranial features include separate cervical vertebrae that are enlarged. The vertebral formula is C-7, D-10, L-9, CD-26 = 52. The sternum consists of three transverse segments. External features include a length of about 8 feet, small eye and ear openings, wedge-shaped head, and a well-developed beak, 180 to 200 mm. long, that is well defined from the forehead. The eyes are so degenerate that they lack a lens.

NATURAL HISTORY

The range of this family is restricted to the Ganges, Indus, and Brahmaputra rivers of India (Fig. 17–1). The Ganges River dolphin or susu, is known from a single species that is restricted in distribution to a few rivers in India. They are almost blind, and probe for food in the river bottom with the long snout. They remain submerged for up to 2 minutes at a time. They feed on various bottom-dwelling fishes and fresh-water crustaceans. Unlike most dolphins, the Ganges River dolphins never leave fresh waters.

ONE RECENT GENUS

Platanista Wagler. Ganges River dolphins, S.As.

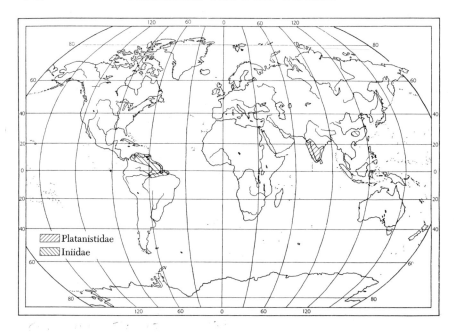

Fig. 17–1. The distribution of families Platanistidae and Iniidae.

Family INIIDAE

Amazon and White Flag Dolphins

STRUCTURE

The dentition consists of numerous teeth in both jaws, but the upper teeth are found only in the maxillaries. The crowns of the teeth are anteroposteriorly compressed and are covered with enamel that has a reticulate or nodular pattern. The skull has an elongate rostrum, and has the narrow facial depression bordered by the upper edges of the maxillaries. The lacrimal and jugal are fused. The palatines form a part of the interior wall of the narial passage and are separated in the midline by the vomers; the nasals are flattened against the frontals on the anterior wall of the braincase. The petro-tympanic is united to the skull by ligaments. Postcranial features include separate cervical vertebrae. External features include a length of 7.5 to 9 feet, a beak that is either decurved (*Inia*) or recurved (*Lipotes*), a low forehead, small eyes, large ear openings, and a small dorsal fin.

NATURAL HISTORY

The range is restricted to fresh-water rivers and lakes of northern South America (Amazon and Orinoco rivers and tributaries) and Tungting Lake in Hunan Province, China (Fig. 17–1). Two genera, each with a single species, are known. The Amazon dolphins (*Inia geoffroyensis*) reach lengths in excess of 9 feet and weights in excess of 300 pounds. The color, which varies with age and with local environments, ranges from blackish to bluish-gray, or even flesh-colored dorsally and generally white ventrally. The blowhole is concentric and symmetrically located on the summit of the head. They swim, usually at a 2-miles-per-hour pace, singly or in small groups. They have acute hearing, use the eyes above water, and probably use echolocation in locating their food. They feed on various fishes, usually less than a foot in length, including kinds that are characteristically bottom-dwellers. These dolphins probably have territorial behavior (Layne, 1958).

The white flag dolphin (*Lipotes vexillifer*) has a dorsal fin that is supposed to look like a flag when seen above water. It is restricted in distribution to the Tungting Lake some 600 miles up the Yangtze River. Adult males reach lengths of 7.5 feet and weigh approximately 300 pounds. The blowhole is asymmetrically situated on the left side behind the forehead. In past years the Chinese fishermen have been reluctant to capture the dolphins, since local legends contend that they are descendant from a princess who flung herself into the water (Kellogg, 1933).

RECENT GENERA

Total, 2.

Inia D'orbigny. Amazon dolphin, S.A.
Lipotes Miller. White flag dolphins, China.

Family PHYSETERIDAE

Sperm Whale

STRUCTURE

The dentition is unique in that there are numerous teeth in the lower jaw (twenty to twenty-five in each half) and no teeth in the upper jaw, although there are numerous small teeth embedded in the gums of the upper jaw. The skull is massive, in comparison with the postcranial skeleton. It has the vomer, entirely exposed in front of the palatines, distinct in the middle of the hard palate; the right nasal is absent. The lower jaw is quite small. The zygoma is complete. Postcranial features include the completely fused cervical vertebrae. The pectoral appendages are small and the phalanges are I (1–2), II (5–8), III (4–8), IV (4–5), V (2–7). A spermaceti organ is present. External features include a head that is almost one-third the total length, and the narial opening (blowhole) to the left of the median line. The snout is high and blunt. The dorsal fin is absent.

NATURAL HISTORY

The range of this family is all oceans, south to the South Shetland Islands and north to Iceland and the Bering Sea. A single living species is known, *Physeter catodon*. Sperm whales are the largest of the toothed whales, with adult males reaching lengths of 65 feet and females, 30 feet. A 59 foot male weighed 52 tons. They travel in gams consisting of one old male and up to twenty females and young. They swim at a speed of approximately 4 knots but, when pressed, reportedly can attain a speed of 12 knots. They have been known to dive to depths of 3240 feet and, on occasion, to remain submerged for 20 to 30 minutes. They feed on squids and octopuses and require up to a ton of food each day. Breeding occurs between August and December and, after a gestation period of about 16 months, one or two young are born. At birth the young are 13 to 14 feet in length, nurse for about 6 months, and reach sexual maturity at 15 months (females) to 2 years (males). The females and their calves are mainly restricted to tropical and subtropical waters but the males move into Arctic and Antarctic waters, especially during the summer season (Kellogg, 1933; Hall and Kelson, 1959).

ONE RECENT GENUS

Physeter Linnaeus. Sperm whales, all oceans.

Family ZIPHIIDAE

Beaked Whales

STRUCTURE

The dentition is reduced. There are no more than two pairs of functional teeth, and these are in the lower jaw. They are generally below the gum in females. The skull has a slender rostrum or beak and is markedly asymmetrical, in that there is a prominence on its vertex behind the nares. The lacrimal and jugal are distinct. Postcranial features include cervical vertebrae that tend to fuse with one another and high neural spines on the lumbar and caudal vertebrae. External features include a well-developed beak, a dorsal fin located posterior to the middle of the body, and the absence of a notch at the junction of the tail and the flukes. There are two to six longitudinal grooves in the throat region. These whales are of medium size, ranging between 15 and 42 feet in length. The flippers are small and rounded. The narial opening is median, semilunar shaped, and is directed forward.

NATURAL HISTORY

The range of this family is all oceans but members are more common in oceans of the Southern Hemisphere. The habits of beaked whales are little known. The bottle-nosed whales (*Hyperoodon*) are known to migrate in schools of four to eleven. They spend the summer months in northern waters and winter as far south as the Mediterranean Sea and Rhode Island. Large adults reach lengths of 30 feet and a 21 foot female weighed 3800 pounds. Squids make up the principal food but occasionally herring and other fish are taken. They usually remain submerged only 10 to 20 minutes but, when harpooned, have been known to remain submerged up to 2 hours.

The goose-beaked whale (*Ziphius cavirostris*) has rarely been seen alive by naturalists, although it is widely distributed in all of the seas. It reaches lengths of 28 feet and reportedly travels in gams of thirty to forty individuals.

RECENT GENERA

Total, 5.

Mesoplodon Gervais. Beaked whales, Atlantic, Pacific, Indian oceans.
Ziphius Cuvier. Goose-beaked whales, all oceans.
Tasmacetus Oliver. Tasmanian beaked whales, S.Pacific.
Berardius Duvernoy. Pacific beaked whales, Pacific.
Hyperoodon Lacépède. Bottle-nosed whales, N.Atlantic, S.Pacific, Antarctica.

Family KOGIIDAE

Pygmy Sperm Whale

STRUCTURE

The dentition consists of nine to fifteen needle-like teeth in each half of the lower jaw and, rarely, a pair of teeth in each upper jaw. The skull has a small, narrow mandible that does not reach the anterior end of the rostrum; and a short symphysis. The lacrimal is massive and fused with the jugal. The zygoma is incomplete; the palatine bones are small. Postcranial features include fused cervical vertebrae and the presence of a spermaceti organ. External features include a length of 9 to 13 feet, of which the head occupies approximately one-sixth; the lower jaw is underslung; the rostrum is short; the narial opening is to the left of the median line of the head; and the pectoral appendages are small and tapering.

NATURAL HISTORY

There is but a single living species of this little-known whale. Its range is the Atlantic, Pacific, and Indian oceans. Nothing is known of their habits nor of their reproductive behavior except that two females washed up on shore (one in Holland and one in India both in the month of December) each had a single embryo that was 8 to 9 inches in length. Reportedly they feed on cuttlefish and shore crabs.

ONE RECENT GENUS

Kogia Gray. Pygmy sperm whale, Atlantic, Pacific, Indian oceans.

Family MONODONTIDAE

White Whale and Narwhal

STRUCTURE

The dentition is varied, with only two upper teeth on each side in *Monodon* and thirty-two to forty teeth in the other forms. In *Monodon* the left upper tooth (and occasionally both) enlarges into a coiled tusk that may reach a length of 8 or more feet in males. In females this is undeveloped or short. The skull has an enlarged braincase and reduced temporal fossa. Postcranial features include cervical vertebrae that are unfused. The phalanges are I (1–2), II (6–7), III (4–5), IV (3–4), V (3–4). External features include the absence of a dorsal fin, the presence of broad flippers and asymmetrical tails. The external nares are posterior to the eyes. These whales are of small size, ranging between 15 and 20 feet in length.

NATURAL HISTORY

The range of this family is north polar waters, south to the St. Lawrence River. Two monotypic genera are known. Narwhals (*Monodon monoceros*) live in arctic waters. They reach lengths of approximately 12 feet. Male narwhals are unique in that the upper left canine is greatly enlarged into a twisted tusk that may reach lengths of 9 feet. They live in gams of five to seven of the same sex and congregate in large schools during the migration seasons, moving southward in the fall and northward in the spring. In the spring they are often found in openings in the thawing ice of the Arctic Sea, apparently avoiding being attacked by killer whales. Food consists of a variety of fishes, cuttlefish, and shrimp. The food is crushed between the jaws and swallowed without being chewed. The young are approximately 5 feet in length at birth and remain with their mothers for extended periods of time.

The white whales (*Delphinapterus leucas*), which reach lengths of 12 to 14 feet, are unique in that the adults are entirely white. They travel in gams of up to twelve in number; do not migrate; and feed on fish, cuttlefish, and crustaceans. They are fast swimmers, often reaching speeds of up to 6 knots.

RECENT GENERA

Total, 2.

Delphinapterus Lacépède. White whales, northern oceans.
Monodon Linnaeus. Narwhals, Arctic, N.Atlantic.

Family DELPHINIDAE

Dolphins and Porpoises

STRUCTURE

The dentition is varied. Teeth are in both jaws and are usually numerous with up to 260 teeth present, but *Grampus* has only four to fourteen teeth confined to the anterior part of the lower jaw. The skull has the lacrimal and molar bones indistinct and articulating posteriorly with the squamosal. The rostrum is as long as, or longer than, the cranial portion. Postcranial features include the two most anterior cervical vertebrae fused. The phalanges are varied, and there are fewer than eight double-headed ribs. External features include the presence of a dorsal fin and the presence of a tail at the junction of the flukes. The tail is notched posteromedially and the anterior limbs are sickle shaped. Size varies from small to medium (4 to 30 feet in length).

NATURAL HISTORY

The range of this family includes all of the oceans and lower parts of the large rivers of the world, being more common in warmer waters. The dolphins and porpoises are the most numerous and diversified group in the order. They are generally gregarious, often traveling in gams of up to 1500 individuals, although groups of ten to 100 are more common. Most are playful, often racing ships and leaping from the water. Food consists primarily of various fishes, cuttlefish, and crustaceans, although the white dolphin (*Sotalia tenzii*) is believed to be completely vegetarian and the killer whales (*Orcinus orca* and *O. rectipinna*) are more predaceous. Killer whales hunt in packs, feeding on fishes, penguins, walruses, seals, and large whales.

Extensive migrations are known in the grampus (*Grampus griseus*) and probably occur in other species. The Pacific white-sided dolphins (*Lagenorhynchus obliquidens*) have well-developed seasonal movements. They spend the winter and spring in the near-shore waters feeding primarily on anchovy. In the summer and fall the anchovy move into even shallower waters. During this time the dolphins move into offshore waters where they feed mainly on saury (Brown and Norris, 1956).

RECENT GENERA

Total, 19.
Subfamily Delphininae. Dolphins.
  Steno Gray. Rough-toothed dolphins, oceans except polar.
  Sotalia Gray. White dolphins, Indian Ocean, W.Af., eastern S.A.
  Stenella Gray. Spotted dolphins, Atlantic.
  Delphinus Linnaeus. Common dolphins, all oceans.
  Grampus Gray. Grampus, all oceans except polar.
  Tursiops Gervais. Bottle-nosed dolphins, all oceans except polar.
  Lagenorhynchus Gray. Striped dolphins, all oceans except polar.
  Feresa Gray. Slender blackfish, Pacific Ocean.
  Cephalorhynchus Gray. Commerson's dolphins, southern seas.
  Orcinus Fitzinger. Killer whales, orcas, all seas.
  Pseudorca Reinhardt. False killer, all seas.
  Orcaella Gray. Irrawaddy River dolphins, S.As.
  Globecephala Lesson. Blackfish, pilot whales, all seas except polar.
  Lissodelphis Gloger. Right whale dolphins, all seas.
  Lagenodelphis Fraser. Bornean dolphins, Pacific Ocean.
  Stenodelphis Gervais. La Plata River dolphins, S.A.
Subfamily Phocoeninae. Porpoises.
  Phocoena Cuvier. Harbor porpoises, all seas except polar.
  Phocoenoides Andrews. Dall porpoises, Pacific Ocean.
  Neomeris Gray. Asiatic porpoises, Indian Ocean, W.Pacific.

SUBORDER MYSTICETI, WHALEBONE WHALES

The dentition is rudimentary in the embryo and absent in adults. The upper jaw has baleen which is a cornified epithelial structure developed from the papillae of the mucous membrane along the maxillary dental arch. The skull is nearly symmetrical and more or less arched to accommodate the baleen. The nasal bones are equal, or nearly so. The lacrimal and jugal bones are not ossified. Post-cranial features include single-headed ribs and a broad, short sternum made up of a single bone. External features include a blowhole made up of two longitudinal slits and the presence of gular grooves in most forms.

Family ESCHRICHTIIDAE

Gray Whale

STRUCTURE

The dentition is absent. The baleen plates are short and few in number and fit into the closed mouth without bending. The baleen is yellowish in color; the largest blades are 18 inches in length. The skull has a narrow rostrum and arched premaxillae. The snout is high and ridged. The supraorbital process of the frontal has a broad base. Postcranial features include the presence of only four digits in the flippers. The cervical vertebrae are not fused and the pelvis is relatively large. External features include the absence of a dorsal fin and a head that is less than one-fourth the total length. Two to four well-developed longitudinal grooves, approximately 6 feet in length, are present on the throat. The size of these whales varies from 30 to 50 feet in length, and the females are larger than the males.

NATURAL HISTORY

The range of the family is the northern Pacific Ocean, south to Jalisco and eastern Korea. Gray whales, represented by a single living species, were hunted almost to extinction in the eastern part of their range, but in recent years, under vigorous protection, have been increasing in numbers. Gray whales generally stay close to the shore and often play and roll in the surf. They feed on sardines in the southern part of their range and on several different species of amphipod crustaceans, called "krill," in the northern part of the range. Apparently two populations exist, both of which spend the summer in the Arctic. One population migrates southward in the eastern Pacific, along the west coast of North America, to as far south as Jalisco, Mexico. The other population migrates southward along the coast of Asia, as far south as Japan and Korea. When migrating these whales move in schools of several individuals and swim at speeds up to 7 or 8 knots.

Breeding takes place in lagoons in the southern part of their range during December and January (just after parturition). The single young is 16 to 18 feet in length at birth and nurses for 6 to 8 months, at which time it is approximately 25 feet in length.

ONE RECENT GENUS

Eschrichtius Gray. Gray whale, N.Pacific.

Family BALAENOPTERIDAE
Fin-backed Whales

STRUCTURE

The dentition is absent. The baleen plates are relatively shorter and broader than in the gray whale. The blades are blue-black or black in color and may be as much as 41 inches in length in the large blue whale. The skull has a flat, broad rostrum. The parietal bones extend anteriorly beyond the posterolateral margins of the nasal bones. Postcranial features include narrow flippers with only four digits. The cervical vertebrae are unfused. External features include the presence of a dorsal fin, and a head that is less than one-fourth the total length. Their size ranges from 25 to 110 feet in length. One blue whale 89 feet in length weighed 119 tons. The skin of the throat has numerous conspicuous longitudinal grooves.

NATURAL HISTORY

Members of this family occur in all oceans. The fin-backed whales, known from three living genera, including six species, vary in length from 33 to 110 feet. They are generally bluish in color dorsally and whitish ventrally. They feed on a variety of small fishes, "krill," and plankton. They travel in schools of up to 200 individuals and are the fastest of the whales. They travel at speeds of 10 to 12 knots and when pressed attain speeds of 14 knots. The gestation period varies from 10 months in some of the smaller species to 12 months in the larger species. Fin-backed whales migrate to warm waters for the breeding seasons.

Rayner (1940) reported on the results from marking whales with serially numbered stainless steel tubes that were shot into the blubber of the animal and later recovered by whaling boats. In all, some 668 blue whales, 3915 fin-backed whales, and 548 hump-backed whales were marked. Percentages of recoveries were 4.9, 3.0, and 6.6, respectively. Most recoveries were from the general region of the place of marking, but several foreign returns were recorded. Among the blue whales, for example, one individual traveled more than 300 miles in 32 days, another more than 500 miles in 88 days.

The hump-backed whales apparently frequent antarctic waters during the summer months; during the winter they move northward to tropical latitudes northwest of Australia and Malagasy where they breed, returning to the same general region the following summer. Marking results reported by Rayner support these conclusions.

RECENT GENERA

Total, 3.

Balaenoptera Lacépède. Rorquals or fin-backed whales, all oceans.
Megaptera Gray. Hump-backed whales, all oceans.
Sibbaldus Gray. Blue or sulphur-bottom whales, all oceans.

Family BALAENIDAE
Right Whales

STRUCTURE

The dentition is absent. The baleen plates are long and flexible, folding on the floor of the closed mouth. The skull has a narrow rostrum that is bowed-down toward the tip and is disproportionately large for the animal's size. Postcranial features include fused cervical vertebrae and a reduced sternum. External features include the presence of a dorsal fin and a head that makes up between one-fourth and one-third of the total length. No grooves are present in the throat region. Size varies from 16 to 70 feet in length and the weight up to 100 tons.

NATURAL HISTORY

Members of this family occur in all oceans. Three living genera, including five species, are known in the right whales. Because these whales were formerly abundant, were slow swimmers, had a buoyant carcass, and produced a great yield of oil, they were given the name "right" whales by the early hunters. These whales have been hunted by man for more than 100 years. The baleen or "whalebone" was formerly in great demand in the manufacture of corsets. Right whales feed on small crustacea and plankton, which they filter from the water through the baleen plates. They do not migrate, and have been practically exterminated in many areas.

RECENT GENERA

Total, 3.

Balaena Linnaeus. Bow-head or Greenland right whale, Arctic.
Eubalaena Gray. Black right whale, all oceans except Arctic.
Caperea Gray. Pygmy right whale, S.Pacific.

18

Order Carnivora

Carnivores

The carnivores are medium- to large-size terrestrial mammals that are modified for feeding on flesh.

CHARACTERISTICS

The limbs are plantigrade or digitigrade and have the tibia and fibula and the radius and ulna complete and separate. There are usually five toes (at least four, all of which have claws). The skull has strong jaws, with the lower jaw having a transversely placed condyle that articulates with a deep glenoid fossa. The zygomatic arches are stout. The teeth are usually generalized for a meat diet. Primitively the dental formula is I $\frac{3}{3}$, C $\frac{1}{1}$, P $\frac{4}{4}$, M $\frac{3}{3}$ = 44. In modern genera there is a tendency toward a reduction of the number of incisors, premolars, and molars. The incisors are small, weak, and pointed. The canines are strong, pointed, and usually recurved. A pair of teeth on each side (often P4, and m1), modified for shearing, are called the carnassials. Soft anatomical features include a single stomach and a well-developed brain, with deep convolutions. External features show considerable adaptive radiation. Size varies from small to large.

RANGE

Except for certain oceanic islands, carnivores occur throughout the world.

Family CANIDAE

Wolves, Dogs, and Allies

STRUCTURE

The dentition is primitive, the dental formula is I $\frac{3}{3}$, C $\frac{1}{1}$, P $\frac{4}{4}$, M $\frac{2 \text{ or } 3}{2 \text{ or } 3}$ = 40 to 44. The cheek teeth are tuberculosectorial and the carnassials, P4 and m1, are well developed. The incisors are unspecialized, and the canines are elongate and pointed. The skull has a long rostrum and the auditory bullae are smooth, inflated, and partially divided internally by an incomplete septum. The bony palate does not extend posterior to the last molar. The limbs are digitigrade, with five digits on each foot. The claws are non-retractile. External features include a long bushy tail, a long, pointed muzzle, large erect ears, and long slender legs.

NATURAL HISTORY

Members of this family are worldwide in distribution. The canids are, in general, moderately sized, digitigrade, cursorial predators, with moderate to long tails. They are all relatively primitive, and are thought to be close to the ancestral stock. The canids are divided into three subfamilies: Caninae, Simocyoninae, and Otocyoninae.

The Caninae, with ten genera, are practically worldwide in distribution. The subfamily includes, in addition to the well-known domestic dog, the wolves, coyotes, jackals, foxes, fennecs, and several exotic South American dogs. Most are monoestrous and, after a gestation period of about 63 days, three to twelve blind and helpless, but haired, young are born. Sexual maturity is reached in 1 to 2 years. Timber wolves (*Canis lupus*) in Wisconsin have home ranges that cover up to 150 square miles. Their winter food consists of white-tailed deer, grass, balsam fir, hemlock, and snowshoe hares, with deer remains being found in 97 per cent of the scats (Thompson, 1952).

The Simocyoninae, with three genera, are restricted to Africa, southern Asia, and South America. The bush dogs (*Speothos*), with two species, have the molars reduced to two above and two below. The legs and tail are short. The African hunting dogs (*Lycaon*) were formerly widely distributed in Africa where they hunted in packs of up to 100 individuals. Their distribution is now greatly reduced. They are crepuscular and, on cool days, diurnal. Two to six young are born in a litter, usually in a grass-lined burrow in the ground. On occasion two or more females may use the same burrow. Measurements are: total length, 1473 mm.; tail, 355 mm.; weight, 60 to 80 pounds (Shortridge, 1934).

The Otocyoninae, with a single genus, are restricted to Africa. These big-eared foxes are nocturnal, usually solitary, and feed on a variety of insects and small rodents. The daylight hours are spent in thick brush. Adults weigh 6 to 8 pounds. The gestation period of the big-eared foxes is apparently somewhat longer than that of most canids, being reported as 70 days. Three to four young are born in a litter (Shortridge, 1934).

RECENT GENERA

Total, 14.

Subfamily Caninae.

Canis Linnaeus. Dogs, wolves, coyotes, jackals, N.A., Eu., As., Af., introduced worldwide.

Alopex Kaup. Arctic foxes, arctic.

Vulpes Brisson. Red and kit foxes, N.A., Eu., As., N.Af.

Fennecus Desmarest. Fennecs, N.Af.

Urocyon Baird. Gray foxes, N.A., northern S.A.

Nyctereutes Temminck. Raccoon dogs, E.As.

Dusicyon Smith. South American foxes, S.A.

Atelocynus Cabrera. Small-eared dogs, S.A.

Cerdocyon Smith. Crab-eating foxes, S.A.

Chrysocyon Smith. Maned wolves, S.A.

Subfamily Simocyoninae.

Speothos Lund. Bush dogs, S.A.

Cuon Hodgson. Indian dholes or red rogs, As.

Lycaon Brookes. African hunting dogs, Af.

Subfamily Otocyoninae.

Otocyon Muller. Big-eared foxes, Af.

Family URSIDAE

Bears

STRUCTURE

The dentition is modified for an omnivorous diet. The dental formula is I $\frac{3}{3}$, C $\frac{1}{1}$, P $\frac{4}{4}$, M $\frac{2}{3}$ = 42. In adults the anterior premolars tend to be lost and the second and third premolars are generally absent or minute. The molars are bunodont, a modification for crushing; the carnassials are not developed. The skull is large and heavy, with a moderately long rostrum and depressed auditory bullae, and with no traces of an internal dividing septum in the bullae. The bony palate extends posterior to the last upper molar. The limbs are plantigrade, with five digits. The toes have non-retractile claws. External features include a short tail, broad feet, and a heavy build.

NATURAL HISTORY

The range of this family is worldwide except Australia, Malagasy, the West Indies and the Ethiopian region of Africa. Approximately eleven living species, of six genera, are known. They are primarily omnivores, feeding on a variety of grasses, roots, fruits, berries, insects, and flesh. The polar bear (*Thalarctos*) is probably strictly carnivorous. In tropical and subtropical regions bears are crepuscular or nocturnal. In the arctic the polar bears are diurnal. Most bears are expert diggers and can climb trees. They have home ranges that are up to 45 miles in diameter. In northern regions bears "hibernate" in winter. This hibernation is a period of inactivity that is not accompanied by a marked lowering of the body temperature and metabolic processes characteristic of true hibernation. Bears "hibernate" in shallow caves and in hollow trees.

Hirasaka (1954) reported that the Japanese bear (*Ursus thibetanus*) builds a "basking couch" of branches and twigs on which to lie in the sun for a few days in order to dry its fur, prior to retiring to the wintering den.

Bears are monoestrous and have delayed implantation. Mating occurs in spring or early summer and, after a gestation period of 6 to 8 months, one or two young are born. Sexual maturity is reached in the sixth year; in captivity bears have been known to live as long as 47 years.

RECENT GENERA

Total, 7.

Tremarctos Gervais. Spectacled bears, S.A.
Selenarctos Heude. Asiatic black bears, As.
Ursus Linnaeus. Brown and grizzly bears, Eu., As., N.A.
Euarctos Gray. American black bear, N.A.
Thalarctos Gray. Polar bear, arctic.
Helarctos Horsfield. Sun bears, As.
Melursus Meyer. Sloth bears, As.

Family PROCYONIDAE

Raccoons and Allies

STRUCTURE

The dentition is somewhat like that of the canids but with a reduction in the premolars and molars. The dental formula is I $\frac{3}{3}$, C $\frac{1}{1}$, P $\frac{3 \text{ or } 4}{3 \text{ or } 4}$, M $\frac{2}{2 \text{ or } 3}$ = 36, 38, or 40. The carnassials are not well developed and the cheek teeth tend to be bunodont. The skull is usually short and broad and has inflated audital bullae. The bulla has no dividing septum. The bony palate extends posteriorly to the last upper molars. The limbs are plantigrade, with five toes on each foot, and the claws are not retractile. External features include a tail that is usually long, often prehensile, and often ringed. Procyonids are frequently arboreal in habits.

NATURAL HISTORY

The range of this family is primarily Neotropical and southern North America with a few forms occurring in the mountains of southeastern Asia (Fig. 18–1). Two subfamilies are recognized: the New World Procyoninae, with seven genera, and the Asiatic Ailurinae, with two genera. The Procyoninae include the well-known

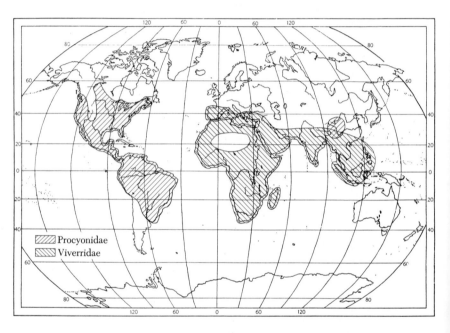

Fig. 18–1. The distribution of families Procyonidae and Viverridae.

raccoons (*Procyon*). Adult male raccoons reach measurements of: total length, 634–950 mm.; tail, 200–405 mm.; hind foot, 96–138 mm.; weight, 1.8 to 22.2 kg. (Hall and Kelson, 1959). They are nocturnal omnivores that are noted for the curious habit of washing their food before they eat it. In northeastern Colorado, in the fall of the year, their food consisted of the following (by volume): animal foods, 27 per cent (grasshoppers, 12.4 per cent; crayfish, 9.8 per cent); plant foods, 64 per cent (corn, 57 per cent; plums, 7 per cent); and detritus, 9 per cent (Tester, 1953). Sharp and Sharp (1956) studied raccoon behavior at a winter feeding station. They found that 78 per cent of those visiting the station fed in pairs or packs; that family units (adult female with young) dominated groups of mixed ages; that any group dominated an individual; and that young of the year are tolerated more than older individuals. Raccoons may have two

Fig. 18–2. A kinkajou (*Potos flavus*). (Ernest P. Walker.)

litters per year and a gestation period of 65 days. The kinkajou (Fig. 18–2) is a tropical member of the family. The coati mundi (*Nasua narica*) tends to travel in bands, occasionally up to 200 individuals, and is often diurnal in its activities.

The Subfamily Ailurinae, or pandas, is restricted to Asia. Two genera are known. The panda, *Ailurus fulgens,* is somewhat like the raccoon in size and form. The giant panda, *Ailuropoda melanoleucus,* has been variously classified as a bear, a procyonid, and as a separate family. In shape it is somewhat like a small bear. Giant pandas have short tails and reach lengths up to 1500 mm. and weights up to 170 pounds. They are confined, in distribution, to bamboo forests high in the mountains of western China. Few specimens have been obtained, and almost nothing is known of their habits. Unlike most procyonids they appear to be completely herbivorous, feeding on bamboo shoots.

RECENT GENERA

Total, 9.

Subfamily Procyoninae. Raccoons and relatives.
   Bassariscus Coues. Cacomistles, N.A.
   Jentinkia Trouessart. Mexican and Central American cacomistles, C.A.
   Procyon Storr. Raccoons, N.A., S.A.
   Nasua Storr. Coati mundis, C.A., S.A.
   Nasuella Hollister. Little coati mundis, S.A.
   Potos E. Geoffroy and Cuvier. Kinkajous, C.A., S.A.
   Bassaricyon Allen. Olingos, C.A.
Subfamily Ailurinae. Pandas.
   Ailurus Cuvier. Lesser pandas, As.
   Ailuropoda Milne Edwards. Giant pandas, As.

Family MUSTELIDAE

Weasels, Skunks, and Allies

STRUCTURE

The dentition shows considerable reduction in numbers of teeth, especially in the posterior molars. The dental formula varies I $\frac{3}{2 \text{ or } 3}$, C $\frac{1}{1}$, P $\frac{2, 3 \text{ or } 4}{2, 3 \text{ or } 4}$, M $\frac{1}{1 \text{ or } 2}$ = 28, 30, 32, 34, or 36. The cheek teeth are typically sectorial, and carnassials are well developed. The skull generally has a short rostrum and the auditory bullae are only slightly inflated. The bony palate usually projects behind the last molar. The limbs are semiplantigrade or digitigrade. There are five toes on each foot, each with a non-retractile claw. External features include a tail that is variable in length, ranging from short to long. Well-developed anal musk glands are usually present. Size varies from 195 mm. (7.75 inches) (*Mustela rixosa*) to 1785 mm. (70 inches) (*Enhydra*) and weight, from 1.33 to 70 pounds. The males are usually larger than the females.

NATURAL HISTORY

The range of this family is worldwide except Australia and Malagasy. The mustelids are a diverse group of twenty-six genera that are divided into five subfamilies: the Mustelinae, or weasels and relatives; the Mellivorinae, or honey badger; the Melinae, or badgers; the Mephitinae, or skunks; and the Lutrinae, or otters.

The Mustelinae (weasels and relatives), with ten genera, are almost worldwide in distribution, being absent only in Australia and Malagasy. They feed primarily on flesh. In Missouri, Korschgen (1958) found the diet of the mink (*Mustela vison*), during December, consisted of the following: frogs, 24.9 per cent; mice and rats, 23.9 per cent; fish, 19.9 per cent; rabbits, 10.2 per cent; crayfish, 9.3 per cent; birds, 5.6 per cent; fox squirrels, 2.2 per cent; muskrats, 1.3 per cent; and other, 2.7 per cent.

The Mellivorinae (honey badgers) includes but a single genus that is restricted to Africa. According to Shortridge (1934), honey badgers are nocturnal and spend the daytime in burrows, caves, or rock crevices. Generally solitary, they possess well-developed anal scent glands. Although honey and the grubs of wild bees appear to be favorite foods, they are, in effect, omnivores, feeding on rats, mice, eggs, reptiles, insects, fruits, and berries.

The Melinae (badgers) with six genera occur in Europe, Asia, and North America. They are semifossorial, with broad bodies, short tails, and broad paws equipped with long strong claws. In general, the males are larger than the females, often reaching a length of 870 mm., of which the tail comprises 150 mm., and weights up to 10 kg. Badgers primarily feed on burrowing mammals but also feed on carrion, lizards, snakes, and birds. The American badger (*Taxidea taxus*) exhibits delayed implantation with fertilization occurring in August or September, implantation in mid-February, and birth some 6 weeks later. The usual litter size is two but may range from one to five.

The Mephitinae (skunks), with three genera, are restricted to North America. The Mephitinae are known for their well-developed anal scent glands. The color of all species is black with various stripes or spots of white, depending upon the species and the individual. As in most mustelids, the males are larger than the females. An adult male *Mephitis mephitis* measured: total length, 710 mm.; tail, 400 mm.; and hind foot, 72 mm. Skunks are omnivores, feeding on a variety of plant and animal foods, including insects and small mammals. The spotted skunk (Fig. 18–3) is the smallest member of the subfamily.

The Lutrinae (otters) with six genera, are almost worldwide in distribution. Members of this subfamily are modified for an aquatic life, with the extreme of this modification being seen in the sea

Fig. 18–3. A spotted skunk (*Spilogale putorius*). (Ernest P. Walker.)

otter (*Enhydra lutris*) of the northern Pacific Ocean area. All have thick, glossy pelts that are much sought after for fur. Otters have small ears; long muscular tails; and enlarged, more or less webbed hind feet.

RECENT GENERA

Total, 26.

Subfamily Mustelinae.

    Mustela Linnaeus. Weasels, ferrets, stoats, minks, N.A., S.A., Eu., As., N.Af.

Vormela Blasius. Marbled polecats, E.Eu., As.
Martes Pinel. Martens, sables, Eu., As., N.A.
Tayra Oken. Tayras, C.A., S.A.
Grison Oken. Grisons, C.A., S.A.
Lyncodon Gervais. Patagonian weasels, S.A.
Ictonyx Kaup. Zorilles, African polecats, Af., W.As.
Poecilictes Thomas and Hinton. North African striped weasels, N.Af.
Poecilogale Thomas. African weasels, Af.
Gulo Pallas. Wolverines, gluttons, Eu., As., N.A.
Subfamily Mellivorinae. Honey badgers.
Mellivora Storr. Honey badgers, Af.
Subfamily Melinae. Badgers.
Meles Brisson. World badgers, Eu., As.
Arctonyx Cuvier. Hog badgers, As.
Mydaus Cuvier. Malayan stink badgers, E.Indies.
Suillotaxus Lawrence. Malayan stink skunk, SE.As.
Taxidea Waterhouse. American badger, N.A.
Melogale I. Geoffroy. Ferret badgers, As.
Subfamily Mephitinae. Skunks.
Mephitis Cuvier. Striped skunks, N.A.
Spilogale Gray. Spotted skunks, N.A.
Conepatus Gray. Hog-nosed skunks, N.A., S.A.
Subfamily Lutrinae. Otters.
Lutra Brisson. River otters, Af., Eu., As., N.A., S.A.
Pteronura Gray. Giant otters, S.A.
Amblonyx Rafinesque. Oriental small-clawed otters, S.As.
Aonyx Lesson. Clawless otters, Af.
Paraonyx Hinton. African small-clawed otters, Af.
Enhydra Fleming. Sea otters, N.Pacific.

Family VIVERRIDAE

Civets and Allies

STRUCTURE

The dentition is generally sectorial with some forms tending toward bunodont modifications. The dental formula is I $\frac{3}{3}$, C $\frac{1}{1}$, P $\frac{3 \text{ or } 4}{3 \text{ or } 4}$, M $\frac{1 \text{ or } 2}{1 \text{ or } 2}$ — 32, 36, or 40. The carnassials are well developed. The skull is generally long and flattened. The auditory bulla is composite and divided by a full septum. The limbs are subdigitigrade. There are usually five digits on each foot, but some species have five in front and four behind while others have four in front and four behind. The claws are semiretractile. External features include a long neck, arched back, long tail, and short limbs. Musk glands are present.

NATURAL HISTORY

The range of this family is restricted to the Old World, including Europe, Asia, Africa, and Malagasy (Fig. 18–1). The Viverridae are a diverse group that is divided into six subfamilies: Viverrinae (civets), Paradoxurinae (palm civets), Hemigalinae (banded palm civets), Galidiinae (Malagasy mongooses), Herpestinae (mongooses), and Cryptoproctinae (fossas).

The Viverrinae, with seven genera, are widely distributed in southern Europe, Asia, and Africa. The African civet (*Civettictis*) is widely distributed in tropical Africa, occurring at both low and high elevations. In color they are a whitish silvery with black spots. They are nocturnal animals, essentially terrestrial, and primarily carnivorous. They feed on smaller terrestrial vertebrates, arthropods, carrion, and, to some extent, wild fruits and berries. The young, usually two or three, are born in a hole in the ground. The genets (*Genetta*), occurring in southern Europe, Asia, and Africa, are somewhat more arboreal and usually live near swamps and rivers.

The Paradoxurinae, or palm civets, with six genera, are mainly Asian in distribution. Members of this subfamily are arboreal and have the terminal pads of the third and fourth digits united. The tail is prehensile, and the anal scent glands are extensive. Palm civets reach lengths of up to 1220 mm. (4 feet), about half of which is the tail. They are nocturnal, expert climbers, and feed on fruit, mice, frogs, lizards, and insects.

The Hemigalinae, or banded palm civets, with six genera, are confined to Asia and Malagasy. They are arboreal, do not have the third and fourth digit united, and have the anal scent glands less developed than in the palm civets. The common name is derived from the color pattern, which is some shade of gray, with a series of dark transverse bands across the back and alternating rings of dark and light on the tail. Total lengths approach 1 m. (3 feet). One genus, *Cynogale*, is adapted for an aquatic habitat, with short ears; reduced tails; and elongate, flattened heads.

The Galidiinae, or Malagasy mongooses, with four genera, are restricted to Malagasy. Like the other mammals of this area almost nothing has been published concerning their habits.

The Herpestinae, or mongooses, with thirteen genera, are mainly African in distribution although one genus also occurs in Asia. Smaller species of mongooses are often social, diurnal animals that hunt in groups of six to twelve or more. They can climb trees but are usually terrestrial, feeding on a wide assortment of small animal life, and living in burrows in the ground.

The Cryptoproctinae, or fossas, with a single genus, are restricted to Malagasy. It is the largest carnivore of Malagasy, reaching lengths approaching 1525 mm. (5 feet), including a tail approximately 610 mm. (2 feet) in length. The fossa is carnivorous, weasel-like in habits, and attacks animals as large as the wild boar and the ox.

RECENT GENERA

Total, 37.
Subfamily Viverrinae. Civets.
  Poiana Gray. African linsangs, Af.
  Genetta Oken. Genets, N.Af., S.Eu., W.As.
  Viverricula Hodgson. Small Indian civets, As.
  Osbornictis J. A. Allen. Congo water civets, Af.
  Viverra Linnaeus. Oriental civets, As.
  Civettictis Pocock. African civets, Af.
  Prionodon Horsfield. Banded linsangs, As.
Subfamily Paradoxurinae. Palm civets.
  Nandinia Gray. African palm civets, Af.
  Arctogalidia Merriam. Small-toothed civets, SE.As., E.Indies.
  Paradoxurus Cuvier. Small-toothed civets, As.
  Paguma Gray. Masked civets, As.
  Macrogalidia Schwarz. Celebes civets, As.
  Arctictis Temminck. Binturongs, As.
Subfamily Hemigalinae. Banded palm civets.
  Fossa Gray. Malagasy civets, Malagasy.
  Hemigalus Jourdan. Banded palm civets, As.
  Chrotogale Thomas. Owston's palm civet, As.
  Diplogale Thomas. Bornean mongooses, As.
  Cynogale Gray. Otter civets, As.
  Eupleres Doyere. Falanoucs, Malagasy.
Subfamily Galidiinae. Malagasy mongooses.
  Galidia I. Geoffroy. Ring-tailed mongooses, Malagasy.
  Galadictis I. Geoffroy. Broad-striped mongooses, Malagasy.
  Mungotictis Pocock. Narrow-striped mongooses, Malagasy.
  Salancia Gray. Brown-tailed mongooses, Malagasy.
Subfamily Herpestinae. Mongooses.
  Suricata Desmarest. Suricates, Af.
  Hespestes Illiger. Mongooses, Af., As.
  Helogale Gray. Dwarf mongooses, Af.
  Dologale Thomas. Af.
  Atilax Cuvier. Marsh mongooses, Af.
  Mungos E. Geoffroy and Cuvier. Striped mongooses, Af.
  Crossarchus Cuvier. Cusimansos, Af.
  Liberiictis Hayman. Af.
  Ichneumia I. Geoffroy. White-tailed mongooses, Af.
  Badiogale Peters. Bushy-tailed mongooses, Af.
  Rhynchogale Thomas. Meller's mongooses, Af.
  Cynictis Ogilby. Yellow mongooses, Af.
  Paracynictis Pocock. Selous' mongooses, Af.
Subfamily Cryptoproctinae. Fossas.
  Cryptoprocta Bennett. Fossas, Malagasy.

Family HYAENIDAE

Hyaenas

STRUCTURE

The dentition is heavy and well adapted for crushing. The dental formula of living forms is I $\frac{3}{3}$, C $\frac{1}{1}$, P $\frac{4}{4}$, M $\frac{1}{1}$ = 34. The carnassials are well developed. The skull is heavy and rugose, with a prominent saggital crest. The inflated auditory bulla is formed primarily by the ectotympanic bone, resultantly the dividing septum is posterior and not too prominent. The limbs are digitigrade with four digits on each foot. The claws are not retractile. External features include forelegs longer than the hind limbs, a coarse spotted or striped fur and a mane. Anal scent glands are present.

NATURAL HISTORY

The range of this family is tropical and subtropical parts of Africa and southern Asia (Fig. 18–4). The Hyaenidae are a group of carnivores that are specialized scavengers possessing massive crushing teeth. This family is divided into two subfamilies: Protelinae, or aardwolves; and Hyaeninae, or hyaenas.

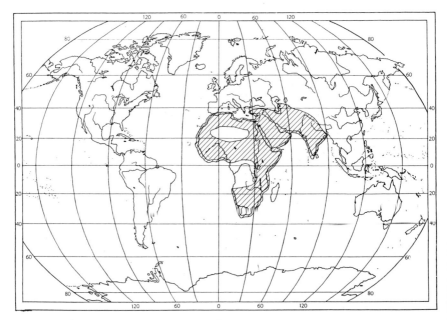

Fig. 18–4. The distribution of Family Hyaenidae.

The aardwolves (Protelinae), with but a single genus and species, are restricted to southern and eastern Africa. They are hyaena-like in general appearance but are smaller and more delicately built. The teeth are reduced in size and are often lost. They are a buffy color with a series of transverse bars of black on the sides and legs. They are about 3 feet in over-all length, and have a short tail approximately 6 inches in length. Food of the aardwolf consists entirely of insects, mainly ants and termites.

The Hyaeninae include two genera, the spotted hyaenas of Africa and the striped hyaenas of southwestern Asia and Africa. They are highly developed as carrion eaters. They weigh up to 110 pounds and have two to four young in a litter.

RECENT GENERA

Total, 3.
Subfamily Protelinae. Aardwolves.
  Proteles I. Geoffroy. Aardwolves, Af.
Subfamily Hyaeninae. Hyaenas.
  Crocuta Kaup. Spotted hyaenas, Af.
  Hyaena Brisson. Striped hyaenas, As., Af.

Family FELIDAE

Cats

STRUCTURE

The dentition is an extreme example of the sectorial modification. The dental formula is I $\frac{3}{3}$, C $\frac{1}{1}$, P $^{2 \text{ or }}\frac{3}{2}$, M $\frac{1}{1} = 28$ or 30. The canines are large and recurved. The skull has the facial region extremely shortened as is reflected by the number of cheek teeth. The auditory bullae are inflated, compound, and divided by prominent septa. The limbs are digitigrade, with five digits on the forefeet and four digits on the hind feet. The claws are retractile. External features include a long tail (except in *Lynx*), and compressed recurved claws, that are retractile. The head is short and rounded, and the muzzle is short. Their eyes have the well-known vertical slit pupil.

NATURAL HISTORY

The range of this family is worldwide except Australia. The Family Felidae includes six genera. The carnivorous habits of the family are well known. Most wild felids are crepuscular or nocturnal. They have large home ranges, and feed on a wide variety of animal foods, usually stalking their prey. The bobcat (*Lynx rufus*), in one study of its food habits in Vermont (Latham, 1950), was found to feed on deer (mainly carrion), mice, rabbits, porcupines, squirrels, birds, fish, insects, and grasses. Most of the larger species of cats are being exterminated or greatly reduced in number as a result of man's activities. Even the well-known African lion is being eliminated from large portions of its former range.

RECENT GENERA

Total, 6.

Lynx Kerr. Lynx, bobcat, Eu., As., Af., N.A.
Felis Linnaeus. Cats, N.A., S.A., Eu., As., Af., worldwide by introduction.
Panthera Oken. Leopards, panthers, tigers, As., Af., S.A.
Neofelis Gray. Clouded leopards, As.
Uncia Gray. Snow leopards, As.
Acinonyx Brookes. Cheetahs, Af., As.

19

Order Pinnipedia

Seals and Walruses

The pinnipeds are specialized aquatic mammals and are usually considered to be most closely related to the Carnivora. In fact several taxonomists consider the pinnipeds to be only subordinally distinct from the groups herein considered to comprise the Order Carnivora. Within the pinnipeds various degrees of aquatic modifications occur. Some, such as the northern fur seal, which still spends much time on the land, retain the ability to use their legs on land; while others such as the harbor seal, which may spend 6 to 8 months at a time at sea, are unable to use their legs as more than props as they wiggle across the beach. Two suborders, based upon the degree of aquatic adaptation, are recognized.

CHARACTERISTICS

The limbs are modified for aquatic locomotion. The elbow and knee are within the body contour. The feet are webbed and paddle-shaped. The skull is generally compressed interorbitally, with a short facial portion and with the broad braincase abruptly expanded. The orbits are large. The teeth, as compared with the Carnivora, are less differentiated. The incisors are always less than ⅗. The molars are never broad and tuberculated, and carnassials are absent. The deciduous teeth are feeble and are shed early. Postcranial features include a reduction in the iliac portion of the pelvic girdle and the absence of clavicles. Soft anatomical features include a relatively large brain with numerous convolutions. External features are those characteristics of aquatic mammals: fusiform body shape, neck reduced, limbs modified into paddles for swimming, and tail very short. Size is medium to large. The body is usually covered with hair.

RANGE

Pinnipeds occur along coastal regions of most of the world.

379

Family OTARIIDAE

Eared Seals

STRUCTURE

The dentition is the least modified in the order. The dental formula is I $\frac{3}{2}$, C $\frac{1}{1}$, P $\frac{4}{4}$, M $^{1 \text{ or } 2}/_1 = 34$ or 36. The outer incisors are caniniform. The canines are large, conical, and recurved. The skull has well-developed orbital processes and slightly inflated auditory bullae. The limbs are all useful in terrestrial locomotion. The hind feet can be turned forward on land. The forelimbs furnish most of the propulsion in the water. External features include the presence of small external ears. The nostrils are at the anterior end of the snout. These are medium- to large-sized seals 4 to 6 feet in length and weighing up to 500 pounds. The males are three to five times as heavy as the females. The family can be divided into the hair seals (*Otaria, Eumetopias,* and *Zalophus*), which have coarse, stiff hair and no underfur; and the fur seals (*Callorhinus* and *Arctocephalus*), which have abundant silky underfur.

NATURAL HISTORY

The range includes the Pacific Ocean and all Southern Hemisphere seas. The Family Otariidae, with six genera, is less completely adapted for the aquatic habitat than are other members of this order. It is roughly divisible into two groups: the sea lions, with coarse stiff hair and no underfur; and the fur seals, with abundant silky underfur. In general, the fur seals are smaller than sea lions. An adult male fur seal (*Callorhinus*) may reach a length of 6 feet and weigh up to 500 pounds, while an adult male sea lion may reach a length of 13 feet and weigh up to 2000 pounds. In all species in the family, males are larger than the females and often weigh five times more than the latter.

All species are gregarious and breed on coasts and islands where they congregate in large numbers during the breeding season. The males set up breeding harems, which they defend actively from other males. During this time, often for 6 weeks or more, these males go without food, living on stored fat. Food of the eared seals consists of fish, molluscs, crustacea, and occasionally birds.

RECENT GENERA

Total, 6.

Otaria Peron. South American sea lions, coastal southern S.A.
Eumetopias Gill. Steller sea lions, N.Pacific.

Zalophus Gill. California and Japan sea lions, Central Pacific.
Neophoca Gray. Australian and New Zealand sea lions, Central Pacific.
Arctocephalus E. Geoffroy and Cuvier. Southern fur seal, anarctic regions.
Callorhinus Gray. Northern fur seal, N.Pacific.

Family ODOBENIDAE

Walruses

STRUCTURE

The dentition has the upper canines greatly enlarged (often 24 inches long) and the lower canines molariform. The number of cheek teeth is extremely variable and these teeth are not readily divisible into premolars and molars. The dental formula is generally given as I ⅒, C ¼, P and M ⅗. The skull does not have a post-orbital process, and the mastoid process is strong. The anterior portion is greatly enlarged to support the enlarged upper canines. The limbs are modified for aquatic locomotion but are of some use on land. The hind limbs can rotate forward as in the sea lions. Each foot has five toes and each toe has an evident nail. External features include the small eyes, the absence of external ears, and the presence of a short-necked thick body. Adult males reach lengths up to 15 feet and weights up to 3000 pounds. Young animals have a covering of stiff hairs, but old animals are almost hairless.

NATURAL HISTORY

The range is the arctic coasts of North America and Europe. The Odobenidae, known from a single living genus, is noted for the extremely large tusks in the males. The walrus is more or less gregarious at all times, non-migratory, and is thought to be monogamous. The single young, weighing 100 to 150 pounds at birth, stays with the mother for approximately 2 years and reaches sexual maturity at the end of 4 to 6 years. The gestation period is 11 to 12 months in length. The breeding season is in April and May in the North Atlantic; June and July in the North Pacific.

Food consists almost entirely of clams that are dug up from the bottom of the sea. Walruses are often found on ice floes and the bare, rough and warty soles of the feet aid in traction on the ice.

ONE RECENT GENUS

Odobenus Brisson. Walrus, arctic regions.

Family PHOCIDAE

Seals

STRUCTURE

The dentition is varied. The dental formula is I $^{2\,or\,3}\!/_{1\,or\,2}$, C $\frac{1}{1}$, P $\frac{4}{4}$, M $\frac{1}{1}$ = 24, 26, or 28. The incisors are conical. The grinding teeth, except the first, are two-rooted and multilobed. The skull has the postorbital process absent and greatly inflated auditory bullae. The limbs are extremely adapted for aquatic locomotion. The hind limbs are of no use in terrestrial locomotion and are functionally a part of the tail. The principal propulsive mechanisms in the water are the hind limbs and the tail. External features include streamlining of the body shape for aquatic locomotion, the absence of external ears, and a covering of stiff fur. They range in size from 3 to 16 feet in length and weigh from 75 to 5000 pounds.

NATURAL HISTORY

The range of the phocids is all of the oceans of the world. They are a diverse group divisible into four subfamilies: Phocinae, Monachinae, Lobodontinae, and Cystophorinae.

The Phocinae, with three genera, are characterized by incisors $\frac{3}{2}$, the posterior four cheek teeth double-rooted, and digits with five well-developed nails. The ribbon, ringed, and harp seals, formerly recognized as separate genera, are now included as subgenera of *Phoca*.

The well-known harbor seal, *Phoca vitulina*, reaches lengths of up to 6 feet and weights up to 300 pounds, in the males; females are smaller. They frequent coastal waters, often being found in harbors and bays, where they appear to form loosely organized colonies but not well-developed harems. Mating takes place in the water, usually in September, and after a gestation period of about 9½ months, a single pup is born. Food is primarily fish. Wilke (1954) found the stomach contents to consist of 83 per cent pollack and 10 per cent herring. The bearded seal, *Erignathus barbatus*, is a bottom-feeding form in which Wilke (1954) found stomach contents to consist of 83 per cent octopus and 13 per cent crabs.

The Subfamily Monachinae is characterized by incisors $\frac{2}{2}$, nails rudimentary or absent, and the first and fifth digits of the hind foot elongated. It includes but a single genus, *Monachus*, the monk seal of tropical and subtropical waters. Adult males reach lengths of 7½ feet. They bask in the sunlight in groups and feed on fishes and molluscs. Monk seals are decreasing in number as a result of man's activities.

The Subfamily Lobodontinae, with four genera, is restricted to the Antarctic. Relatively little is known of their habits.

The Subfamily Cystophorinae is characterized by incisors $\frac{2}{1}$, cheek teeth single-rooted, and toes subequal or with first and fifth elongated. It includes two genera, the hooded and the elephant seals. The male hooded seal, *Cystophora cristata*, reaches a length of 10 feet and a weight of 850 pounds; females are considerably smaller. Males are usually described as having paired inflatable pouches of skin on the nose which become inflated at times of anger. Berland (1958) studied this structure in detail and found that it is a single, bilobed bladder that functions as follows: "By closing one nostril, and by blowing air out through the nose, the mucous nasal septum is made to bulge into the opposite half of the nasal cavity and is extruded through the opposite nostril as a red bladder." Hooded seals are gregarious and migrate southward in the fall of the year. Food consists mainly of fish.

RECENT GENERA

Total, 10.

Subfamily Phocinae.

Phoca Linnaeus. Hair or harbor seals, arctic, N.Atlantic, N.Pacific.

Halichoerus Nilsson. Gray seals, N.Atlantic.

Erignathus Gill. Bearded seals, northern polar seas.

Subfamily Monachinae.

Monachus Fleming. Monk seals, tropical and subtropical seas.

Subfamily Lobodontinae.

Lobodon Gray. Crab-eating seals, antarctic.

Ommatophoca Gray. Ross seal, antarctic.

Hydrunga Gistel. Leopard seal, antarctic.

Leptonychotes Gill. Weddell seal, antarctic.

Subfamily Cystophorinae.

Cystophora Nilsson. Hooded seals, arctic, N.Atlantic, W.Indies.

Mirounga Gray. Elephant seals, S.Pacific, Indian Ocean, Pacific N.A.

20

Order Tubulidentata

Aardvark

This order, with a single living genus, shows the results of an extreme adaptation for burrowing and feeding on small food items (mainly termites).

CHARACTERISTICS

The limbs are plantigrade and show burrowing adaptations. The forefoot does not have a thumb. The other digits are well developed and have strong nails (intermediate between claws and hooves), suited for digging. The hind feet have five toes. The skull has slender, but complete, zygomatic arches and small premaxillaries. The teeth are numerous and apparently heterodont and diphyodont. In adults only four or five simple peglike teeth remain. These lack enamel but are covered by cement. Instead of a pulp cavity, these teeth are transversed by a number of tubules. Soft anatomy features include a long, extensile, but not vermiform, tongue. External features include the heavy build, long ears and snout, and a thin coat of coarse hair. The mouth has a small gape.

RANGE

The aardvarks are restricted to Africa south of the Sahara (Fig. 20–1).

Family ORYCTEROPODIDAE

Aardvark

STRUCTURE

The structure of this, the only living family of Tubulidentata, has been summarized above in the discussion of the ordinal characteristics.

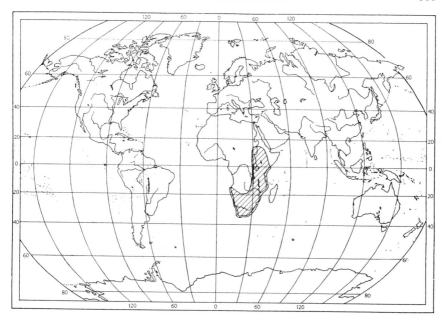

Fig. 20–1. The distribution of Family Orycteropodidae.

NATURAL HISTORY

The aardvark (Fig. 20–2), or ant-bear as it is called in South Africa, reaches a length of 1290 mm., of which the tail comprises 450 mm.; large adults weigh up to 140 pounds. They are common in

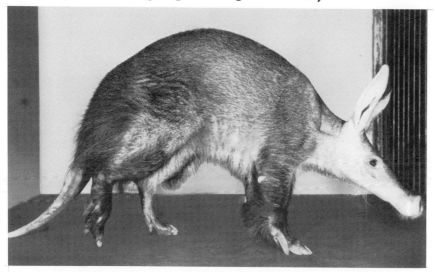

Fig. 20–2. An aardvark (*Orycteropus afer*). (Ernest P. Walker.)

more or less open grass plains, but some are residents of the forest. They construct extensive burrows in the ground, where they spend the day. All are nocturnal, solitary, and utilize a large number of alternate burrows scattered over distances up to several miles. They are extremely wary and hard to capture; they do not live well in captivity. A single young is born usually in midwinter. Food consists exclusively of termites and ants.

ONE RECENT GENUS

Orycteropus E. Geoffroy. Aardvark, Af.

21
Order Proboscidea
Elephants

Formerly, the proboscideans were much more numerous and more widely distributed. The living members, restricted to the tropics of the Old World, show adaptations for large size in the structure of the limbs and in the development of a proboscis (necessary for reaching food on the ground).

CHARACTERISTICS

The limbs are immense pillar-like structures modified to support the great body weight. There are five digits on each foot. The skull is shortened and increased in height to provide leverage for wielding the heavy proboscis. The teeth are modified for a herbivorous diet. The dental formula is I $\frac{1}{0}$, C $\frac{0}{0}$, P $\frac{3}{3}$, M $\frac{3}{3}$ = 26. The single upper incisor is evergrowing and enlarged into a tusk. A single molar is functional at a given time and is replaced from the rear, as it wears away, by the next posterior tooth. The premolars are lost early and have no functional importance. External features include the proboscis, which is the nose extended into a long, muscular, flexible, and prehensile structure, with the nostrils at the terminal end.

RANGE

Elephants are restricted to Africa and southern Asia (Fig. 21–1).

Family ELEPHANTIDAE
Elephants

NATURAL HISTORY

Two living species of elephants are known: the Indian elephant, *Elephas indicas,* and the African elephant, *Loxodonta africana* (Fig. 21–2). The Indian elephant occurs in India, Burma, Cochin China,

387

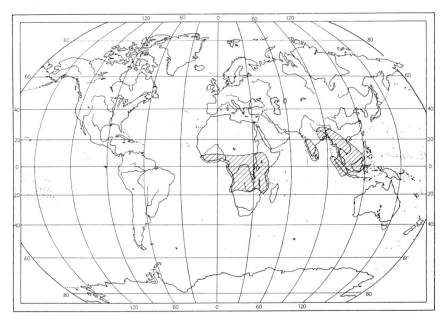

Fig. 21–1. The distribution of Family Elephantidae.

Fig. 21–2. An African elephant (*Loxodonta africana*). (Ernest P. Walker.)

388

Malay Peninsula, Ceylon, and Sumatra. Its trunk has a single pointed tip; the head has two rounded bosses which give it the "wise" look; the back is arched, being higher than at the shoulders; there are five nails on the forefeet and four on the hind feet; and, finally, the molars are more complex than those of the African elephant. Indian elephants have been domesticated for centuries. Today, wild elephants live in herds of fifteen to thirty animals, led by a single large old bull. The herd may contain a number of young bulls as well as many females and calves. Their diet is entirely herbivorous, consisting of large quantities of leaves and small branches, fruits, tubers, and melons. In captivity an adult elephant can eat 500 pounds of hay each day.

An adult elephant stands 9 feet high at the shoulders and weighs 3.5 to 6.0 tons. A single young is born after a gestation period of 18 to 21 months. The newborn calf weighs about 200 pounds and is 3 feet high at the shoulders. It is covered with a dense coat of woolly hair; and its trunk is short, inflexible, and of no use in suckling. Sexual maturity is reached after 12 to 15 years and life expectancy is approximately 50 years. A few, reportedly, have lived for 80 years, but 69 years is the most accurate longevity record known.

The African elephant has a trunk with two pointed tips; lacks the rounded bosses on the head; is highest at the shoulders; has four nails on the forefeet and three on the hind feet; and has less complex molars than the Indian elephant. They are rapidly becoming extinct in large parts of their former range. Being gregarious, they were formerly found in large herds numbering one to four hundred individuals, mainly young bulls, females, and calves.

RECENT GENERA

Total, 2.

Elephas Linnaeus. Indian elephants, As.
Loxodonta Cuvier. African elephants, Af.

22

Order Hyracoidea

Conies

Members of this order are an ancient and unprogressive offshoot of the ungulate stem at a time when modern ungulates were not well differentiated. In past times this order was much more numerous and more diverse than the present remnants. Living hyracoids are characterized by small size, but some extinct kinds reached the size of a horse.

CHARACTERISTICS

The limbs show a reduction in the number of digits; the forefoot has four digits, the hind limbs, three. The digits end in small hooves and the soles of the feet are covered with firm pads to aid in clinging to rocks. The skull is stout and rather flattened. The teeth are reduced. The dental formula is I ½, C %, P ¼, M ⅜ = 34. The cheek teeth are ungulate-like in shape, being selenodont and brachydont and forming a continuous series. The upper incisors are like the rodents' in that they grow from persistent pulp. Postcranial features include the absence of a clavicle. Soft anatomy features include a two-chambered stomach, long intestine, and large caecum, plus an additional pair of large caeca. External features include the small size and the rodent-like appearance resulting from the short ears, the reduced tail, and the squatting attitude.

RANGE

Conies are restricted to Africa and southwestern Asia (Fig. 22–1).

Family PROCAVIIDAE

Conies

NATURAL HISTORY

This is the only living family in the Order Hyracoidea. It contains only three living genera. The cony (*Procavia* and *Heterohyrax*) or rock dassie, as it is called in South Africa, is widely distributed in Africa and Asia Minor. The earliest record of this animal is in the Bible (Psalm civ: 18) where rocks are described as "the refuge of the conies." *Procavia* usually inhabits rocky areas in arid or semiarid regions. They are gregarious, often occurring in colonies of fifty or more individuals, and usually diurnal. They have been recorded from elevations as great as 15,000 feet. The cony is exclusively vegetarian, feeding on grass, leaves, and the bark of shrubs and trees. They have two to three young per litter and probably one litter per year.

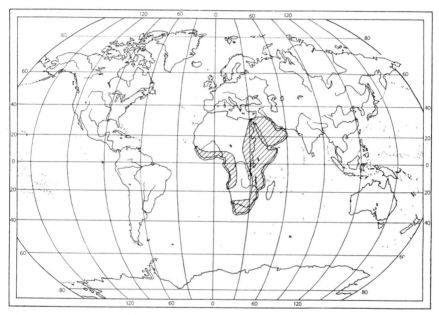

Fig. 22–1. The distribution of Family Procaviidae.

The tree dassie, or tree cony (*Dendrohyrax*), occurs in the forested parts of tropical and subtropical Africa. Unlike the coney it is solitary and nocturnal in habit. They have a characteristic call that is given at frequent intervals throughout the night. This call has been described as "a rattling sound, rather deliberate at the start but growing in rapidity and intensity and then terminating in a series of wailing shrieks." They are almost completely arboreal, only occasionally descending to the ground in their search for food.

RECENT GENERA

Total, 3.

Dendrohyrax Gray. Tree hyraxes, Af.
Heterohyrax Gray. Rock hyraxes, Af.
Procavia Storr. Conies, Af., W.As.

23

Order Sirenia

Manatees and Sea Cows

The Sirenia are a group of subungulates that, secondarily, have become modified for an aquatic life.

CHARACTERISTICS

The hind limbs are absent; the forelimbs are paddle-shaped. The skull is characterized by its large size and the posterior portion of the anterior narial opening. The nasals are absent or rudimentary. The premaxillaries form a long narrow rostrum, and the lower jaw is heavy. The teeth are generally of two kinds, incisors and molars separated by a wide diastema. Milk dentition appears to be absent. Postcranial features include a vestigial pelvis and massive skeletal elements. The vertebrae are not united to form a sacrum. Soft anatomy features include large layers of blubber under the skin; a complex stomach with several chambers; and a small brain with few convolutions. External features include a tail, enlarged horizontally; no external ears; a few scattered hairs.

RANGE

The Sirenia are restricted to coastal waters, bays, estuaries, and large rivers of tropical waters.

Family DUGONGIDAE

Sea Cows

STRUCTURE

The dentition is I $\frac{5}{5}$, C $\frac{0}{0}$, P $\frac{0}{0}$, M $\frac{5 \text{ or } 6}{5 \text{ or } 6}$ = 40 or 42 in the dugong. The extinct Steller's sea cow had no teeth except for a pair of tusklike upper incisors in the males. The molars are not all in place at one time but are replaced by rotation from back to front. The skull has a much enlarged rostrum formed by a union of the premaxillae in front of the narial opening. The forelimbs are modified for aquatic locomotion, broad and finlike. The digits lack nails. The hind limbs are absent. External features include a tail with a central notch and lateral tips pointed.

NATURAL HISTORY

The range of this family is restricted to bays and rivers of the oriental and Australian regions. It formerly occurred in the Bering Straits region (Fig. 23–1). The dugongs are widely distributed throughout the tropical portions of the Indian and Pacific oceans. In over-all length adult males reach 10 feet in length; adult females

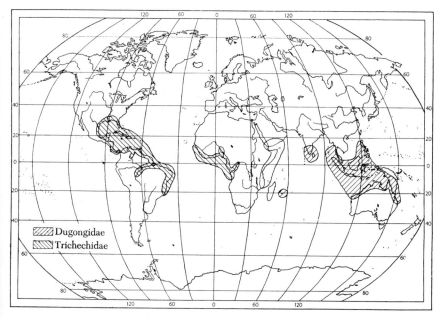

Fig. 23–1. The distribution of families Dugongidae and Trichechidae.

are smaller. They are herbivorous, feeding on various green sea-weeds which they pull into the mouth with prehensile lips. Their sense of hearing is acute; sight, however, is poorly developed. A single young is born in the winter months after a gestation period of approximately 1 year.

A second genus, *Hydrodamalis*, or Steller's sea cow, formerly inhabited the islands of the Bering Sea but was exterminated by Russian hunters and traders about 1768.

ONE RECENT GENUS

Dugong Lacépède. Dugongs, sea cows, Red Sea, Indian Ocean, W.Pacific.

Family TRICHECHIDAE

Manatees

STRUCTURE

The dentition is I $\frac{2}{2}$, C $\frac{0}{0}$, P $\frac{0}{0}$, M $\frac{11}{11} = 52$. Incisors are rudimentary, not tusklike, and disappear before maturity. There are never more than six molars present at one time. The skull has a small rostrum formed by the fusion of the premaxillae in front of the anterior narial opening. External features include a shovel-shaped tail and an upper lip that is split and prehensile.

NATURAL HISTORY

Members of this family occur in rivers and bays of the Atlantic coast of South America, southern North America, and Africa (Fig. 23–1). Manatees are exclusively marine, herbivorous, and extremely slow and inactive. They reach a length of slightly more than 10 feet. The Florida manatee has been known to remain submerged for up to 16 minutes (Bourliere, 1954). After a gestation period of approximately 11 months a single young is born. The female carries the newborn on her back, completely out of the water, for 45 minutes; and during the following 2 hours she gradually submerges it in the water. The young nurses with its head under water while the female browses on aquatic plants.

ONE RECENT GENUS

Trichechus Linnaeus. Manatees, Atlantic, N.A., S.A., Af.

24

Order Perissodactyla

Odd-toed Ungulates

The Order Perissodactyla includes all of the odd-toed, hooved mammals. Living members of the order are generally large, have elongated legs, and have the functional axis of the leg passing through the third toe.

CHARACTERISTICS

The limbs are unguligrade with weight borne on an axis running through the middle digit. The carpals and tarsals are not fused. Well-developed hooves are present on the digits. The skull is elongated in the facial portion and no antlers or horn cores are found in recent forms. The teeth are modified for an herbivorous diet. The premolars and molars form a continuous series and are massive and quadrate. The crown pattern is lophodont (tapir) or bunodont. Postcranial features usually include twenty-three (never fewer than twenty-two) dorsolumbar vertebrae. Features of the soft anatomy include a simple stomach, a large and sacculated caecum, and the absence of a gall bladder. External features may include: a horn or horns. If present they are on, but not attached to, the nasal bone and are always on the midline of the skull. These horns are composed entirely of dermal materials. The skin is often sparsely haired and of great thickness.

RANGE

Perissodactyls occur in parts of South America, Central America, Africa, and southern Asia.

Family EQUIDAE

Horses

STRUCTURE

The dentition consists of the following teeth: I $\frac{3}{3}$, C $\frac{1}{1}$, P $\frac{3 \text{ or } 4}{3}$, M $\frac{3}{3} = 40$ or 42. The upper incisors have wide crowns; P4 is extremely reduced or absent; and the remaining cheek teeth are high-crowned, rootless, and have complex enamel folding. The skull, with the characteristic elongated facial portion, has the orbit completely surrounded by bone, and is modified for space for the ever-growing cheek teeth and heavy jaw muscles. The limbs show extreme adaptation for cursorial locomotion. The digits are reduced to a single functional toe on each foot. Two lateral splints are the only evidence of the other digits. The ulna and fibula are incomplete and are fused distally with the radius and tibia. The external features include the absence of horns and proboscis and the presence of a long tail.

NATURAL HISTORY

The range of feral equids is restricted to parts of Africa and Asia (Fig. 24–1). The Family Equidae contains but a single living genus, *Equus*, and includes the well-known domestic horse. Feral

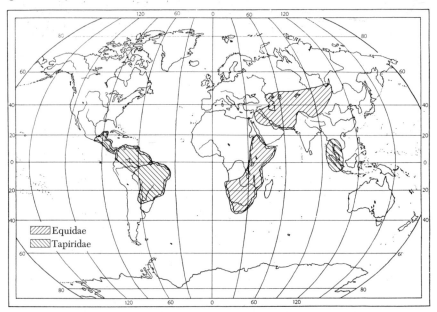

Fig. 24–1. The distribution of families Equidae and Tapiridae.

equids are all large, gregarious, and diurnal herbivores, that are adapted for rapid locomotion in open, grassy areas and hilly country. Most species, including some domestic forms, have a characteristic color pattern of vertical stripes (Fig. 24–2). A single young (or, rarely, two) is born in the spring after a gestation period of 11 to 12 months. Table 24–1 indicates the recent species of equids.

Fig. 24–2. A Mongolian wild horse (*Equus przewalskii*). (Ernest P. Walker.)

TABLE 24–1

Recent Species of the Genus *Equus*

Equus przewalskii	Przewalsky's horse	Western Mongolia
Equus caballus	Domestic horse	
Equus heminus	Wild ass	Mongolia
Equus kiang	Wild ass	Tibet
Equus onager	Wild ass	India to Arabia
Equus asinus	Parent of domestic stock	Africa
Equus quagga	Zebra (recently extinct)	South Africa
Equus burchelli	Zebra	Africa
Equus grevyi	Zebra	Somaliland
Equus zebra	Zebra	Cape Colony, Africa

ONE RECENT GENUS

Equus Linnaeus. Horses, asses, and zebras, As., Af.

Family TAPIRIDAE

Tapirs

STRUCTURE

The dentition consists of the following teeth: I ⅔, C ¼, P 4/4, M ⅓ = 42. The teeth are simpler and more generalized than in other living Perissodactyla. The skull is elevated and compressed and has the orbital and temporal fossa confluent. The limbs are not so modified as in the living horses, being short and pillar-like. The forefeet have four toes, with the third being the longest; the second and fourth, nearly equal; and the fifth, the shortest, not reaching the ground. The hind feet have three toes, with the third being the longest, and the second and fourth being equal in length. External features include the absence of horns; a very heavy body; short legs; reduced tail; and the nose and upper lip elongated into a short proboscis, with the nostrils near the end. The skin is exceedingly thick.

NATURAL HISTORY

The range of living tapirs is restricted to the Malay Peninsula Java, Sumatra, and, in the New World, Central and tropical South America (Fig. 24–1). Only a single living genus, *Tapirus*, with five species, is in this family. External measurements of an adult male from Mexico are: total length, 2020 mm.; tail, 70 mm.; hind foot, 375 mm.; and ear, 140 mm. Tapirs are herbivorous, feeding by browsing on leaves, shoots, and fruits. They are crepuscular or nocturnal inhabitants of wet, shady forests and swamps. They tend to

Fig. 24–3. A South American tapir (*Tapirus terrestris*) with young. (Ernest P. Walker.)

be solitary and are shy and inoffensive. A single young is born after a gestation period of 392 to 405 days (Fig. 24–3.)

Ingles (1953) observed the habits of two 3-year-old Baird's tapirs (*Tapirus bairdi*) on Barro Colorado Island. Their favorite foods, obtained by browsing, were herbs and grasses of a clearing and soft, leafy foliage that hung over a stream. In season they fed on the fallen fruits of the bread fruit and star apple trees. They were observed to defecate while submerged in a lake with only the snout, eyes, and ears above water.

ONE RECENT GENUS

Tapirus Brisson. Tapirs, As., C.A., S.A.

Family RHINOCEROTIDAE

Rhinoceri

STRUCTURE

The dentition of living members of this family consists of the following teeth: I $^{0 \text{ or }}\frac{1}{0 \text{ or } 1}$, C $\frac{0}{0 \text{ or } 1}$, P $\frac{4}{4}$, M $\frac{3}{3}$ = 28, 32, or 34. The incisors are diminished or defective, and upper canines are absent in

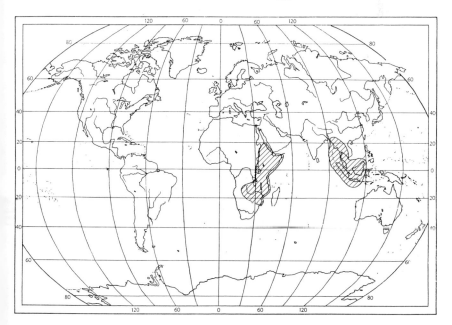

Fig. 24–4. The distribution of Family Rhinocerotidae.

living genera. The premolars are molariform. The skull is large, elongated, and elevated posteriorly by a large transverse crest. The postorbital process is absent, thus the orbital and temporal fossa are confluent. The nasals are large, ossified, and standing out freely above the premaxillae. The limbs are extremely short and pillar-like. Each foot has three well-developed toes that terminate in hooves. The middle toe is the longest. External features include its huge size; a thick, "armor-plated" skin with few hairs; and one or two horns, on the midline of the head. The upper lip is more or less prehensile.

NATURAL HISTORY

The range is restricted to Africa south of the Sahara, southern Asia, Sumatra, Java, and Borneo. (Fig. 24–4). Four genera are recognized in this family. Rhinoceri are herbivorous, feeding on shrubs, leaves, and fruits. Crepuscular or nocturnal in habits, they are usually found in moist, wooded areas, often near water. The greater one-horned rhinoceros, *Rhinoceros unicornis,* stands approximately 5½ feet high at the shoulders and weighs up to 4000 pounds. Its single young, born after a gestation period reported to be approximately 19 months, stands about 2 feet high and weighs about 110 pounds at birth. The sense of sight is dull, but the senses of hearing and scent are well developed.

RECENT GENERA

Total, 4.

Rhinoceros Linnaeus. Indian rhinoceri, As.
Didermocerus Brookes. Sumatran rhinoceri, As.
Diceros Gray. African black rhinoceri, Af.
Ceratotherium Gray. White rhinoceri, Af.

25

Order Artiodactyla

Even-toed Ungulates

The Order Artiodactyla includes all of the even-toed hooved mammals. Living members of the order have elongated legs and have the functional axis of the leg passing between the second and third toes.

CHARACTERISTICS

The limbs are adapted for unguligrade locomotion, with the weight borne on an axis passing between the third and fourth digits. The middle digits (III and IV) are always equally developed. The lateral digits are reduced or rudimentary. The median metacarpals and metatarsals tend to fuse into a "cannon bone." The teeth are selenodont or bunodont. The upper premolars and molars are not similar in size and shape. A diastema is present between the front teeth and the cheek teeth. Postcranial features include the presence of nineteen dorsolumbar vertebrae and the absence of a clavicle in living forms. Features of the soft anatomy include a complex, two- to four-chambered stomach. The caecum is usually smooth. External features may include horns (or antlers). If present, they are usually on the frontal bone (but sometimes on parietal or nasal bone) and always paired.

RANGE

Artiodactyls are native throughout the world except in Australia and New Zealand, where they have been introduced. Geologically the order ranges from the Lower Eocene to the Recent.

SUBORDER SUIFORMES

In this suborder the dentition is varied but upper incisors are always present. The molars are bunodont, having two pairs of rounded cusps. The limbs are short and primitive. The third and fourth metacarpals and metatarsals are not completely fused. Usually four well-developed digits are present on each foot. In the soft anatomy the stomach is simple for artiodactyls. External features include a skin which is either nearly naked or covered with sparse bristly hairs. Horns and antlers are absent. This suborder includes three families: the Suidae, or pigs; the Tayassuidae, or javelina; and the Hippopotamidae, or hippopotamus.

Family SUIDAE

Pigs

STRUCTURE

The dentition consists of the following teeth: I $^{1, 2, \text{ or } 3}/_3$, C $\frac{1}{1}$, P $^{2, 3, \text{ or } 4}/_{2 \text{ or } 4}$, M $\frac{3}{3}$ = 34 to 44. The middle upper incisors are largest; the lateral ones are progressively reduced. The upper canines are recurved and are visible externally as tusks. The skull has a prominently elevated occipital crest which slopes backward. The frontals are broad and flat, and the postorbital processes are small. A peculiar prenasal bone is developed at the anterior end of the mesethmoid. The palate extends behind the last molar. The limbs have four toes on each foot (lateral ones do not touch the ground). In

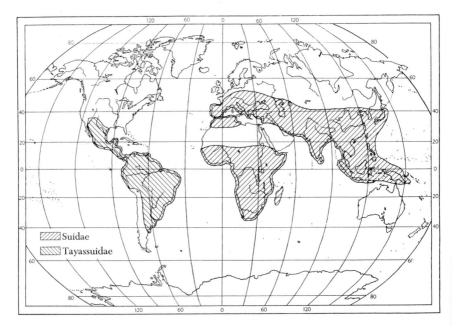

Fig. 25–1. The distribution of families Suidae and Tayassuidae.

the soft anatomy the stomach is simple and a caecum is present. External features include the nostrils that are terminal in location. The snout is elongated and mobile, with an expanded flat and nearly terminal surface.

NATURAL HISTORY

The range of this family was formerly Europe, Asia, and Africa, now introduced worldwide (Fig. 25–1). The Family Suidae, with five genera, includes the well-known pig. Wild species of suids are not gregarious, and the males associate with the females only during

Fig. 25–2. A babirussa *(Babyrousa alfurus)*. (Ernest P. Walker.)

the mating season. Typically, they are forest-dwellers, where they spend the daytime in moist, shady retreats and become active at night. They are primarily herbivorous, feeding on various roots, herbs, fungi, and some grubs. The well-developed tusks and the flat noses are used in rooting out food from the ground (Fig. 25–2). After a gestation period of 120 to 175 days, depending upon the species, four to eight young are born. At birth, all are dark brown, with pale longitudinal stripes. Domestic swine have a gestation period of 112 to 115 days, and the young are not usually the color of those of their wild relatives.

RECENT GENERA

Total, 5.

Potamochoerus Gray. African water hogs, Af.
Sus Linnaeus. Pigs or hogs, Eu., As., (worldwide, domestic).
Phacochoerus Cuvier. Wart hogs, Af.
Hylochoerus Thomas. Forest hogs, Af.
Babyrousa Perry. Barbirussa, E.Indies.

Family TAYASSUIDAE

Peccaries

STRUCTURE

The dentition consists of the following teeth: I ⅔, C ¼, P ⅔, M ⅔ = 38. The upper canines are not recurved and are triangular in cross-section. The molars and premolars are bunodont, with two pairs of cusps, and with small accessory conules. A long diastema exists between the cheek teeth and the canines. The last molar is molariform. The limbs have the third and fourth metatarsals fused at their proximal ends. There are four toes on the forefeet and three on the hind feet. Soft anatomy features include a complex stomach approaching that of the ruminants, and the presence of a cutaneous gland, opening on the rump, that gives off an offensive odor. External features include terminal nostrils, as in the pigs, and the absence of any external evidence of a tail. The body is well covered with stiff bristly hairs.

NATURAL HISTORY

The Family Tayassuidae includes but a single living genus. The peccaries, or javelinas, as they are often called, are restricted to the New World (Fig. 25–1). Javelinas usually run in herds, sometimes numbering as many as 100 individuals, and are often somewhat pugnacious. They are omnivorous, feeding on roots, fallen fruits, cactus, insects, worms, and carrion. Primarily nocturnal in habits, they feed in small groups. The scent gland has been assumed to be a means of communication and recognition between individuals in a band. A litter of one to four young are born, apparently in almost any month of the year. At birth, the collared peccary weighs approximately a pound. Adult females weigh up to 54 pounds.

ONE RECENT GENUS

Tayassu Fischer. Peccaries, javelinas, N.A., S.A.

Family HIPPOPOTAMIDAE

Hippopotami

STRUCTURE

The dentition consists of I $^{2\text{ or }3}\!/_{1\text{ or }3}$, C $\frac{1}{1}$, P $\frac{4}{4}$, M $\frac{3}{3}$ = 38 to 44. The incisors and canines grow throughout life. The canines may reach an enormous size. One canine measured 30 inches along the curve, had a basal circumference of 9 inches and weighed 17.5 pounds. The molars and premolars are completely bunodont. The skull has the facial portion much elongated. The orbits are tubular and very prominent. The limbs have four digits, all of which touch the ground in walking. The terminal phalanges have a nail-like hoof. The metacarpals and metatarsals are unfused. Soft anatomy features include the complex, two-chambered stomach and the absence of a caecum. External features include the nostrils on the upper surface of the skull and a broad, rounded muzzle. The thick skin is essentially bare.

NATURAL HISTORY

The range is restricted to Africa (Fig. 25–3). This family includes only two living genera, the *Hippopotamus* and *Choeropsis*,

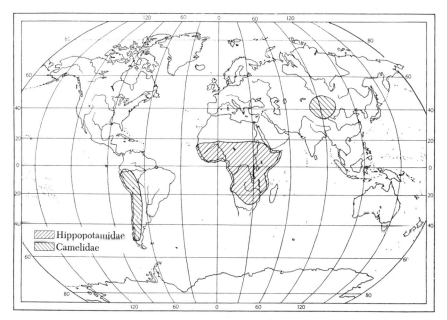

Fig. 25–3. The distribution of families Hippopotamidae and Camelidae.

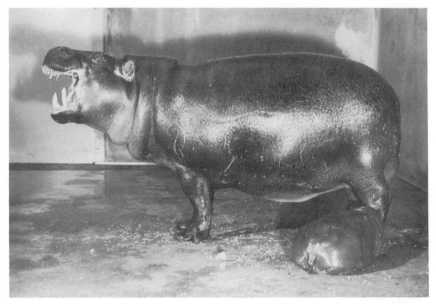

Fig. 25–4. Pigmy hippopotamus *(Choeropsis liberiensis).* (Ernest P. Walker.)

the pygmy hippopotamus. The hippopotamus is a large, heavy animal that is adapted for an aquatic and terrestrial life. Adule males may attain weights in excess of 4 tons and lengths in excess of 12 feet. The lower canines are used as weapons during the mating season. They live in herds of twenty to forty individuals, usually near water. They are expert swimmers and can remain submerged up to 8 minutes. Food consists of a variety of soft vegetation. A single young is born after a gestation period of approximately 238 days. The pygmy hippopotamus (Fig. 25–4) reaches a length of about 6 feet. It is quite limited in distribution.

RECENT GENERA

Total, 2.

Hippopotamus Linnaeus. Hippopotami, Af.
Choeropsis Leidy. Pygmy hippopotami, Af.

SUBORDER TYLOPODA

The dentition consists of I $\frac{1}{3}$, C $\frac{1}{1}$, P $^{2\,or}\frac{3}{2}$, M $\frac{3}{3} = 32$ or 34. The anterior teeth form a graded-size series. The lower incisors and canines are small, procumbent, and spatulate. The cheek teeth are selenodont. The anterior premolars are reduced or absent. The limbs have the fibula reduced and the radius and ulna fused proximally. The metacarpals and metatarsals are fused in living forms into a distinct cannon bone. The feet are digitigrade, with the spreading toes set nearly flat on the ground. The toes have nails and are protected by heavy ventral pads. Soft anatomical features include complex, ovoid, red blood cells, and the absence of a gall bladder. External features include long limbs, elongate neck, and cleft upper lip. Horns and antlers are absent. This suborder includes but a single living family, the Camelidae.

Family CAMELIDAE

Camels

STRUCTURE

The structure of this family is as outlined above in the description of the suborder.

NATURAL HISTORY

The range of wild species is restricted to the Gobi Desert region of Asia and the Andes mountains of South America (Fig. 25–3). Camels are known from two living genera. The living species are indicated in Table 25–1. The camels, *Camelus*, of the Gobi Desert

TABLE 25–1
Living Species of Camels

Camelus dromedarius [1]	Arabian dromedary	Asia
Camelus bactrianus	Camel	Asia
Lama huanacus	Guanaco	South America
Lama vicugna	Vicuña	South America
Lama glama [1]	Llama	South America
Lama pecos [1]	Alpaca	South America

[1] Known only in domestication.

region, are most active during the midday. Groups, known as droves, consist of one or two males and three to five females. Camels sleep at night in open spaces and, during the day, range over great distances during their feeding on grasses, brushwood, and shrubs. They migrate to the northern part of the range in the spring and return southward in autumn. Mating usually takes place in January or February.

The South American camelids, *Lama*, live in a variety of habits ranging from cool, open plains to high montane areas of permanent snow. The vicuña (*L. vicugna*) is diurnal and lives in bands of ten to thirty females led by a male. Each band has its own feeding territory. After a gestation period of about 10 months, a single young (occasionally two) is born. Sexual maturity is attained at 1 year and at this time the young males are expelled from the band.

RECENT GENERA

Total, 2.

Camelus Linnaeus. Camels, As.
Lama Cuvier. Llamas, alpacas, vicuñas, S.A.

SUBORDER RUMINANTIA

The dentition is varied. The upper incisors are absent in living forms. The upper canine may be present or absent. When present, it may develop into a normal or weak tusk, and be shed early. The lower canine is incisiform. The limbs are functionally didactyl in all living forms. Cannon bones are well developed. Soft anatomy features include a complex stomach, with three or four chambers. External features are varied. The skin is usually covered with hair or wool. Horns or antlers may be present or absent. Living members of this suborder are divided into two infraorders: Tragulidae and Pecora and include five families.

INFRAORDER TRAGULIDAE

The dentition consists of the following teeth: I $\frac{0}{3}$, C $\frac{1}{1}$, P $\frac{3}{3}$, M $\frac{3}{3} = 34$. In males, the upper canine is much enlarged and protrudes below the lips. The skull is without horns or antlers. The limbs have the carpals and tarsals partially fused and the median metapodials much stouter than the lateral ones. Features of the soft anatomy include a stomach with three chambers and the presence of a gall bladder. External features include the absence of horns or antlers and a small size, graceful appearance, and short tail. The nostrils are narrow and slitlike. A single living family is in this infraorder.

Family TRAGULIDAE

Chevrotains

NATURAL HISTORY

Two genera are in this family, *Hyemoschus*, or water chevrotains; and *Tragulus*, or mouse-deer. The mouse-deer is restricted to southern Asia (Fig. 25–5). *Tragulus javanicus* (Fig. 25–6) reaches a total length of about 2½ feet (of which the tail comprises about 5 inches) and a height of about 1 foot at the shoulders. They are herbivorous

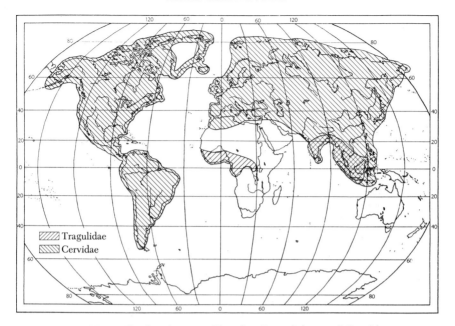

Fig. 25–5. The distribution of families Tragulidae and Cervidae.

Fig. 25–6. A mouse deer *(Tragulus javanicus)*. (Ernest P. Walker.)

and crepuscular. Two young are born at the close of the rainy season after a gestation period of 120 days.

The water chevrotains, *Hyemoschus,* are restricted to the equatorial forest zone of Africa. They are sedentary and herbivorous, feeding on green vegetation, roots, and tubers. They are generally found in pairs and are active at dusk, spending the daytime resting in shady retreats. As indicated by the common name, they are generally found only along rivers and streams and are excellent swimmers and divers.

RECENT GENERA

Total, 2.

Hyemoschus Gray. Water chevrotains, Af.
Tragulus Brisson. Chevrotains, mouse-deer, As.

INFRAORDER PECORA

The dentition is I $\frac{0}{3}$, C $^{0 \text{ or}} \frac{1}{1}$, P $\frac{3}{3}$, M $\frac{3}{3}$ = 32 or 34. The upper canine is absent in most species. The limbs have the outer toes small ("dew claws"), vestigial, or absent. Features of the soft anatomy include a complex stomach with four chambers. External features of most species include the presence of horns or antlers, at least in the males. This infraorder includes four families: Cervidae, or deer; Giraffidae, or giraffes; Antilocapridae, or pronghorn; and Bovidae, or cows and allies.

Family CERVIDAE

Deer and Allies

STRUCTURE

The dentition is I $\frac{0}{3}$, C $^{0 \text{ or}} \frac{1}{1}$, P $\frac{3}{3}$, M $\frac{3}{3}$ = 32 or 34. The upper canines are present in both sexes of seven genera; in males only, of three genera; occasionally present in seven genera; and absent in two genera. The limbs have the tarsals and carpals partially fused and the principal metapodials fused into a cannon bone. External features include deciduous antlers present except in the aberrant musk deer (*Moschus*) and water deer (*Hydropotes*), both of which have enlarged canines.

NATURAL HISTORY

The Family Cervidae is widely distributed in both the Old World and New World (Fig. 25–5). It is divided into four subfamilies: Moschinae, Muntiacinae, Cervinae, and Odocoileinae.

The Moschinae, or musk deer, with but a single genus, is restricted to Asia, mainly in the high Himalayan Mountains from 8000 to 12,000 feet in elevation. This group is considered to be the most primitive of the living cervids. Antlers are absent in both sexes, and the upper canines are present and strongly developed. A peculiar preputial musk gland is on the abdomen of the males. This gland, in great demand by the perfume trade, has resulted in the extinction of the musk deer in much of its former range. Musk deer are small, standing 20 to 24 inches high at the shoulder. The ears are large, the tail is extremely reduced, and the pelage consists of a thick covering of long, coarse hairs. They are solitary and crepuscular in habit and, after a gestation period of about 5 months, produce a single spotted fawn. The young are sexually mature during the first year and life expectancy is only about 3 years.

The Muntiacinae, or muntjaks, with two genera, are also restricted to Asia. The muntjaks, or barking deer (*Muntiacus*), are small deer with the antlers carried on a long, bony, hair-covered pedicel. The upper canines are well developed as tusks. The Indian muntjaks, *Muntiacus muntjak,* are about 20 inches high at the shoulder and weigh about 35 pounds. When excited they give a series of loud staccato barks, similar to those of a dog. Generally solitary and crepuscular in habits, they are quite pugnacious during courtship, when the males fight fiercely with antlers, tusks, and voice. After a gestation period of about 6 months, one or two spotted fawns are born. The Tibetan muntjaks, *Elaphodus,* have reduced antlers that are hidden in tufts of hair on the forehead. The upper canines are developed as tusks. These deer are always associated with water and are common in reeds bordering rivers.

The Cervinae, with four genera, are found in Eurasia and North America. It includes the well-known *Cervus*, which in Europe is known as the red deer, and in North America as the elk or wapiti.

The Subfamily Odocoileini, having ten genera, is the most widely distributed group. One of the smallest of the subfamily and perhaps the smallest in the family is the South American pudu, *Pudu pudu.* It stands only 12 inches high at the shoulders. It lives high in the Andes during the summer months and migrates down to the surrounding plains for the winter. The Chinese water deer, *Hydropotes,* are less than 2 feet in height. They lack antlers, and live in reeds bordering rivers and lakes in Korea and northwestern China. Unlike most other deer, they give birth to large litters of three to six or more fawns at a time.

RECENT GENERA

Total, 17.

Subfamily Moschinae. Musk deer.
    Moschus Linnaeus. Musk deer, As.

Subfamily Muntiacinae. Muntjaks.
 Muntiacus Rafinesque. Muntjaks, As.
 Elaphodus Milne Edwards. Tibetan muntjaks, As.
Subfamily Cervinae.
 Dama Frisch. Fallow deer, Eu., As.
 Axis Smith. Axis deer, As.
 Cervus Linnaeus. Red deer, wapiti (or elk in N.A.), Eu., As., N.A.
 Elaphurus Milne Edwards. Père David's deer, As. (surviving as domestic).
Subfamily Odocoileinae.
 Odocoileus Rafinesque. White-tailed or mule deer, N.A., S.A.
 Blastocerus Gray. Swamp or marsh deer, S.A.
 Blastoceros Fitzinger. Pampas deer, S.A.
 Hippocamelus Leuckart. Andean deer, C.A., S.A.
 Mazama Rafinesque. Brocket deer, C.A., S.A.
 Pudu Gray. Pudus, S.A.
 Alces Gray. Moose (elk in Europe), Eu., As., N.A.
 Rangifer Smith. Caribou, reindeer, Eu., As., N.A.
 Hydropotes Swinhoe. Chinese water deer, As.
 Capreolus Gray. Roe-deer, Eu., As.

Family GIRAFFIDAE

Giraffes

STRUCTURE

The dentition includes cheek teeth that are heavy and rugose, and a dental formula of I $\frac{0}{3}$, C $\frac{0}{1}$, P $\frac{3}{3}$, M $\frac{3}{3} = 32$. The skull may or may not have horn cores. The bones of the cranial roof are pneumatic. The limbs have the lateral metapodials and digits atrophied, and the limb elements elongated. External features include its large size and peculiar proportions. Horns may be present or absent; the ears are large; and the pelage is thick, short, and spotted or partially striped.

NATURAL HISTORY

The range of this family is restricted to Africa (Fig. 25–7). Two monotypic living genera are in the Family Giraffidae: *Giraffa* and *Okapia*. Giraffes (Fig. 25–8) are browsing animals that feed on the leaves, flowers, fruits, and shoots of various trees and shrubs. They generally feed during early morning and late afternoons, and occur in small herds, although bulls are sometimes solitary. A large giraffe stands between 17 and 18 feet in height, about 12 feet at the shoulders, and weighs about 2000 pounds. The females are slightly smaller. After a gestation period of 14 to 15 months, a single young is born. At birth the young stands about 5.5 feet high. The okapis

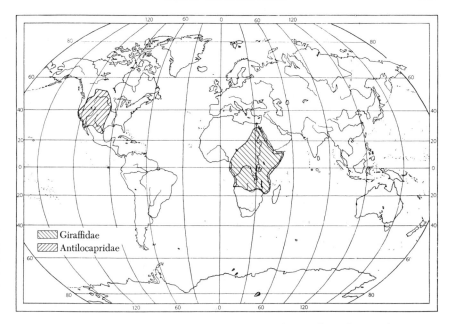

Fig. 25–7. The distribution of families Giraffidae and Antilocapridae.

have the neck and limbs less elongated and are inhabitants of the dense forest.

RECENT GENERA

Total, 2.

Giraffa Brisson. Giraffes, Af.
Okapia Lankester. Okapis, Af.

Family ANTILOCAPRIDAE

Pronghorn

STRUCTURE

The dentition consists of I %3, C %1, P %3, M %3 = 32. The cheek teeth are strongly hypsodont and P3 is greatly elongated. The limbs show no vestige of the second or fifth digit. External features include branched horns, present in both sexes (smaller in the females). These are shed annually, but the unbranched horn cores are not shed. The ears are long, the tail short. The pelage consists of stiff, coarse hairs that are erectile on the rump.

Fig. 25–8. Nubian giraffe (*Giraffa camelopardals*). (Ernest P. Walker.)

NATURAL HISTORY

The pronghorn (*Antilocapra americana*) is the only living species in this family. Its range is restricted to North America (Fig. 25–7). External measurements of a large adult are approximately: total length, 1450 mm.; tail, 170 mm.; hind foot, 410 mm. Weight is up to 140 pounds. Females are slightly smaller than males. Pronghorns are swift agile runners that are chiefly browsers, feeding on sagebrush and other shrubs. They feed in herds of fifty to a hundred individuals and formerly, before their numbers were reduced by man, in herds of up to 1000 individuals. The herds migrate to more protected areas during the winter months. During the mating season the herds break up and bucks maintain small harems of one to perhaps fifteen females. After a gestation period of 230 to 240 days, two young are born in May or June.

ONE RECENT GENUS

Antilocapra Ord. Pronghorn antelope, N.A.

Family BOVIDAE

Hollow-horned Ruminants

STRUCTURE

The dentition is I $\frac{0}{3}$, C $\frac{0}{1}$, P $\frac{3}{3}$, M $\frac{3}{3}$ = 32. The cheek teeth are selenodont and may be either brachyodont or hypsodont. The limbs have the carpals and tarsals partially co-osified; a cannon bone present, and the lateral digits either present or absent, but always reduced. External features include one pair (rarely, two pairs) of horns, usually in both sexes. The horns are unshed and form around a single, unbranched, bony core which may be compressed, twisted, or curved.

NATURAL HISTORY

The range of this family is worldwide except Australia and New Zealand (Fig. 25–9). The bovids are the most numerous and diverse of the Artiodactyla. The family, with 49 genera, is divided into five subfamilies: Bovinae, Cephalophinae, Hippotraginae, Antilopinae, and Caprinae.

The Subfamily Bovinae, with ten genera, includes the more or less cowlike or buffalo-like animals of Eurasia, Africa, and North America. The North American bison (*Bison bison*), which formerly ranged by the millions in the Great Plains of the central part of the continent, is characteristic of the group. The males, larger than the females, reach weights of up to 4000 pounds. They are grazing animals, feeding almost entirely on grass. After a gestation period of approximately 9 months, a single young is born. The gaur (Fig. 25–10) is a typical African species.

The Subfamily Cephalophinae, with two genera, are the duikers of Africa. External measurements of a large male *Sylvicapra grimmia* are: total length 1175 mm.; tail, 150 mm.; hind foot, 295 mm.; ear,

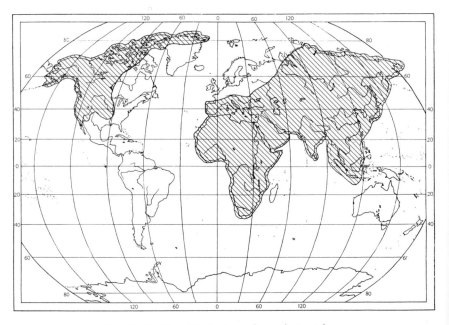

Fig. 25–9. The distribution of Family Bovidae.

130 mm. They stand about 2 feet high at the shoulders and weigh 30 to 40 pounds. Duikers live in thick, brushy areas, usually in pairs. They are crepuscular or nocturnal in habit. In their feeding trips, they form and use beaten pathways.

The Subfamily Hippotraginae, with ten genera, are the reed-bucks and relatives that occur mainly in Africa, although a few are known from the adjacent parts of Asia. The reed-bucks, *Redunca arundinum*, are medium-sized bovids. External measurements of an adult male are: total length, 1850 mm.; tail, 290 mm.; hind foot, 500 mm.; ear, 175 mm. They weigh up to 200 pounds. They live in small groups, usually in reeds and tall grasses.

The Subfamily Antilopinae are the true antelopes and gazelles. All but three of the fourteen genera in this subfamily occur only in Africa; two occur only in Asia and one occurs in Africa and Asia. One of the smallest members of the group is the tiny dik-dik, *Madoqua*, with a total length of 746 mm.; tail, 56 mm.; hind foot, 212 mm.; ear, 84 mm.; and weight of 5 to 6 pounds. Dik-diks occur singly or in groups of two or three individuals, usually on flat out-

Fig. 25–10. A gaur (*Bibos gaurus*). (Ernest P. Walker.)

crops of limestone. They are mainly browsers, feeding on the shoots and branches of many small bushes. The impala, *Aepyceros*, is one of the larger antelopes, reaching weights up to 180 pounds and standing about 40 inches high at the shoulders. Impalas are highly gregarious and formerly occurred, in the dry season, in herds of 500 to 1000 or more individuals. In recent years their numbers have been drastically reduced.

The Subfamily Caprinae, with thirteen genera, are the sheep and goats. They are usually distributed in Eurasia, North America, and northern Africa. Members of two genera have been domesticated and are the well-known sheep (*Ovis*) and goats (*Capra*).

RECENT GENERA

Total, 49.

Subfamily Bovinae.
    Tribe Strepsicerotini.
        Tragelaphus Blainville. Bushbacks, Af.
        Taurotragus Wagner. Elands, Af.
    Tribe Boselaphini.
        Boselaphus Blainville. Bushcows, bluebucks, As.
        Tetracerus Leach. Four-horned antelope, As.
    Tribe Bovini.
        Bubalus Smith. Water buffalo, As.
        Anoa Smith. Anoas, As.
        Bos Linnaeus. True cattle, Eu., As., worldwide domestic.
        Bibos Hodgson. Gaurs, As.
        Syncerus Hodgson. African buffalo, Af.
        Bison Smith. American bison, European wisent, N.A., Eu.
Subfamily Cephalophinae. Duikers.
        Cephalophus Smith. Duikers, Af.
        Sylvicapra Ogilby. Forest duikers, Af.
Subfamily Hippotraginae.
    Tribe Reduncini.
        Kobus Smith. Water bucks, Af.
        Redunca Smith. Reed-bucks, Af.
        Pelea Gray. Rheboks, Af.
    Tribe Hippotragini.
        Hippotragus Sundevall. Sable and roan antelopes, Af.
        Oryx Blainville. Oryx, Af., Arabia.
        Addax Rafinesque. Addax, N.Af., SW.As.
    Tribe Alcelaphini.
        Damaliscus Sclater and Thomas. Topis, blesboks, Af.
        Alcelaphus Blainville. Hartebeestes, Af.
        Beatragus Heller. Hunter's antelope, Af.
        Connochaetes Lichenstein. Gnus or wildebeestes, Af.
Subfamily Antilopinae. True antelopes and gazelles.
    Tribe Neotragini.
        Oreotragus Smith. Klipspringers, Af.
        Ourebia Laurillard. Orbis, Af.
        Raphicerus Smith. Steinboks, Af.
        Nesotragus Duben. Zanzibar "antelope," Af.
        Neotragus Smith. Pygmy and dwarf "antelope," Af.
        Madoqua Ogilby. Dik-diks, Af.
        Dorcatragus Noack. Beiras, Af.
    Tribe Antilopini.
        Antilope Pallas. Blackbucks, As.
        Aepyceros Sundevall. Impalas, Af.
        Ammodorcas Thomas. Dibatags, Af.
        Litocranius Kohl. Gerenuks, Af.
        Gazella Blainville. Gazelles, As., Af.

Antidorcas Sundevall. Springbucks, Af.

Procapra Hodgson. Goa, black-tailed gazelle, As.

Subfamily Caprinae. Sheep and goats.

Tribe Saigini.

Pantholops Hodgson. Chirus, As.

Saiga Gray. Saigas, Eu., As.

Tribe Rupicaprini.

Naemorphedus Smith. Gorals, As.

Capricornis Ogilby. Serows, As.

Oreamnos Rafinesque. Mountain goat, N.A.

Rupicapra Blainville. Chamois, Eu., SW.As.

Tribe Ovibovini.

Budorcas Hodgson. Takins, As.

Ovibos Blainville. Musk oxen, Eu., As., N.A.

Tribe Caprini.

Hemitragus Hodgson. Tahrs, As.

Capra Linnaeus. Goats, ibex, markhors, Eu., As., N.Af. (worldwide domestic).

Pseudois Hodgson. Burrels, bharals, As.

Ammotragus Blyth. Barbary sheep, Af.

Ovis Linnaeus. Sheep, mountain sheep, As., N.A., S.Eu., N.Af. (domestic worldwide).

Bibliography

General

BREHM, A. 1912–16. Brehms Tierleben. Die Saugetiere. 5th ed. rev. by L. Hack and M. Hilzheimer. Leipzig. 4 vols.

CABRERA, A. 1922. Manual de mastozoologie. Madrid, Barcelona. 440 + 12 pp.

ELLERMAN, J. R. 1940–49. The families and genera of living rodents. London. 3 vol.

GRASSE, P. P. (ed.). 1955. Traite de zoologie. Vol. XVII. Mammifères systématique. Masson et Cie., Paris.

KRUMBIEGEL, I. 1954–55. Biologie der Saugetiere. Krefeld Agis Verlag. 2 vol., 844 pp., illus., maps.

SIMPSON, G. G. 1945. The principles of classification and a classification of mammals. Bull. Am. Mus. Nat. Hist. 85: xvi + 350 pp.

WEBER, M. 1927–28. Die Saugetiere. 2d ed. Jena. Vol. I, xv + 444 pp., Morphology with H. M. de Burlet; vol. II, xxiv + 898 pp., Systematics with O. Abel.

Area Works of Larger Scope

Europe

BAUMANN, F. 1949. Die freilebenden Saugetiere der Schweiz. Hans Huber, Bern. xiv + 492 pp.

CABRERA, A. 1914. Mamiferos. Fauna iberica. Madrid. xviii + 441 pp., 12 pls.

IJESSLING, M. A., and A. SCHEYGROND. 1950. De zoogdieren van Nederland. 2d ed. rev. Zutphen, Thieme. viii + 544 pp., 87 pls., 301 figs.

MATTHEWS, L. H. 1952. British mammals. Collins, London.

MILLER, G. S. 1912. Catalogue of the mammals of western Europe. British Museum, London. xv + 1019 pp., 213 figs.

Asia

ALLEN, G. M. 1938–40. The mammals of China and Mongolia. Am. Mus. Nat. Hist., New York. 2 vols.

ELLERMAN, J. R., and T. C. S. MORRISON-SCOTT. 1951. Checklist of Palaearctic and Indian mammals, 1758–1945. British Museum, London. 810 pp.

OGNEV, S. I. 1928–50. The mammals of eastern Europe and northern Asia. Moscow. 7 vols.

TATE, G. H. H. 1947. Mammals of eastern Asia. The Macmillan Co., New York. xiv + 366 pp.

Africa

ALLEN, G. M. 1939. A checklist of African mammals. Bull. Mus. Comp. Zool. 83, 763 pp.

ELLERMAN, J. R., T. C. S. MORRISON-SCOTT, and R. W. HAYMAN. 1953. Southern African mammals, 1758–1951. A reclassification. British Museum, London. 363 pp.

HILL, J. E., and T. D. CARTER. 1941. The mammals of Angola, Africa. Bull. Am. Mus. Nat. Hist. 78: 1–211, pls. 1–17.

MALBRANT, R., and A. MACLATCHY. 1949. Faune de l'Équateur Africain Français. Tome 2. Mammifères. Lechevalier, Paris. 323 pp., 28 pls.

ROBERTS, A. 1951. The mammals of South Africa. Capetown. xlviii + 700 pp., 78 pls.

SHORTRIDGE, G. C. 1934. The mammals of southwest Africa. Wm. Heinemann Ltd., London. Vol. I, pp. xxv + 1–437; vol. II, pp. ix + 439–770.

Australia, Indonesia, and Pacific

CARTER, T. D., J. E. HILL, and G. H. H. TATE. 1946. Mammals of the Pacific world. The Macmillan Co., New York. xvi + 227 pp.

LAURIE, E. M. O., and J. E. HILL. 1954. List of land mammals of New Guinea, Celebes and the adjacent islands, 1758–1952. British Museum, London. 175 pp.

TROUGHTON, E. 1947. Furred animals of Australia. Charles Scribner's Sons, New York. xxvii + 374 pp., 25 colored pls.

North America

BURT, W. H., and R. P. GROSSENHEIDER. 1952. A field guide to the mammals, giving field marks of all the species found north of the Mexican boundary. Houghton Mifflin Co., Boston. xxi + 200 pp., 32 pls., range maps, and text figures.

COCKRUM, E. LENDELL. 1962. Manual for introduction to mammalogy. The Ronald Press Co., New York. See the bibliography of regional mammal studies in the appendix.

ENDERS, R. K. 1935. Mammalian life histories from Barro Colorado Island, Panama. Bull. Mus. Comp. Zool. 78: 385–502, 5 pls.

GOLDMAN, E. A. 1920. Mammals of Panama. Smithsonian Inst. Misc. Coll. 69(5): 309 pp., pl.

GOODWIN, G. G. 1945. Mammals of Costa Rica. Bull. Am. Mus. Nat. Hist. 87: 271–474, 50 figs.•

HALL, E. R., and K. R. KELSON. 1959. The mammals of North America. The Ronald Press Co., New York. Vol. I, pp. xxx + 1–546 + 1–79, Figs. 1–312, Maps 1–320; Vol. II, pp. viii + 547–1083 + 1–79, Figs. 313–553, Maps 321–500.

HAMILTON, W. J., JR. 1939. American mammals: Their lives, habits and economic relations. McGraw-Hill Book Co., Inc., New York. xii + 434 pp.

———. 1943. The mammals of eastern United States: an account of recent land mammals occurring east of the Mississippi. Comstock Publ. Assoc., Ithaca, N. Y.

MILLER, G. S., JR., and R. KELLOGG. 1955. List of North American recent mammals. Washington, D.C. U.S. Nat. Mus. Bull. 205, xii + 954 pp.

PALMER, R. S. 1954. The mammal guide. Mammals of North America, north of Mexico. Doubleday & Co., Inc., New York. 384 pp., 40 colored pls., range maps.

South America

CABRERA, A., and J. YEPES. 1940. Mamiferos sud-americanos (vida, costrumbres y descripción). Comp. Argentina de Editores, Buenos Aires. 370 pp., 78 colored pl.

OSGOOD, W. H. 1943. The mammals of Chile. Field Mus. Nat. Hist. Publ. Zool. 30: 268 pp.

PEARSON, O. P. 1951. Mammals in the highlands of southern Peru. Bull. Mus. Comp. Zool. 106: 117–176, 8 pls.

Literature Cited

ALDOUS, C. M. 1937. Notes on the life history of the snowshoe hare. J. Mammal. 18: 46–57.

ALDOUS, SHALER E. 1930. A silky pocket mouse in captivity. J. Mammal. 11: 80–81.

ALLEE, W. C., A. A. EMERSON, O. PARK, T. PARK, and K. P. SCHMIDT. 1949. Principles of animal ecology. W. B. Saunders Co., Philadelphia. xii + 837 pp.

ALLEN, D. L. 1939. Michigan cottontails in winter. J. Wildl. Mgmt. 3: 307–322.

———. 1943. Michigan fox squirrel management. Mich. Conserv. Dept., Game Div. Publ. 100, 404 pp.

ALLEN, G. M. 1938. The mammals of China and Mongolia. Am. Mus. Nat. Hist. 2 vols.; I, pp. 1–620; II, pp. 621–1350.

———. 1939. Bats. Harvard Univ. Press, Cambridge, Mass. x + 368 pp.

ALLEN, J. A. 1908. Notes on *Solenodon paradoxus* Brandt. Bull. Am. Mus. Nat. Hist. 24: 505–517.

AMEGHINO, F. 1899. On the primitive type of the plexodont molars of mammals. Proc. Zool. Soc. London for 1899; pp. 555–571.

ANGULO, L. N. 1945. Some anatomical characteristics of the *Hutia conga*. J. Mammal. 26: 425–430.

ANONYMOUS. 1958a. Leptospirosis in Ohio wildlife. J. Am. Vet. Med. Assoc. 133(2): 104.

———. 1958b. Mice spur waterfowl migration. Outdoor News Bull. 12(2): 2.

ANTHONY, H. E. 1926. Mammals of Porto Rico, living and extinct. N. Y. Acad. Sci. 9(2): 97–241.

AREY, LESLIE BRAINERD. 1952. Developmental anatomy. 6th ed. W. B. Saunders Co., Philadelphia and London. xi + 680 pp.

ARLTON, A. V. 1936. An ecological study of the mole. J. Mammal. 17: 349–371.

ASDELL, S. A. 1946. Patterns of mammalian reproduction. Comstock Publ. Assoc., Ithaca, N.Y. xi + 437 pp.

ASHBROOK, FRANK G., compiler. 1952. Annual fur catch of the United States. U.S. Fish and Wildlife Serv. leaflet 340, pp. 1–24.

BAILEY V. 1913. Life zones and crop zones of New Mexico. North Am. Fauna 35: 1–100.

BALPH, DAVID F. 1961. Underground concealment as a method of predation. J. Mammal. 42: 423–424.

BANFIELD, A. 1951. The Barren Ground caribou. Canada Dept. of Resour. & Dev., Ottawa. 56 pp.

BARTHOLOMEW, GEORGE A., and TOM J. CADE. 1957. Temperature regulation, hibernation and aestivation in the little pocket mouse, *Perognathus longimembris*. J. Mammal. 38: 60–72.

BAUMANN, F. 1949. Die freilebenden Saugetiere der Schweiz. Hans Huber, Bern. xiv + 492 pp.

BAUMGARTNER, LUTHER L. 1943. Fox squirrels in Ohio. J. Wildl. Mgt. 7: 193–202.

BEE, JAMES W., and E. RAYMOND HALL. 1956. Mammals of northern Alaska. Univ. Kansas Publs. Misc. Publ. 8: 1–309.

BEER, JAMES R., LOUIS D. FRENZEL, and CHARLES F. MACLEOD. 1958. Sex ratios of some Minnesota rodents. Am. Midland Naturalist 59(2): 518–524.

BERLAND, BJORN. 1958. The head of the hooded seal, *Cystophora cristata* Erxleben. Nature 182(4632): 408–409.

BERNSTEIN, M. E. 1948. Recent changes in the secondary sex ratio of upper social strata. Human Biol. 20: 182–194.

BISONETTE, T. H., and E. E. BISONETTE. 1944. Experimental modification and control of molts and changes of coat color in weasels by controlled lighting. Ann. N.Y. Acad. Sci., 45: 221–260.

BLAIR, W. FRANK. 1936. The Florida marsh rabbit. J. Mammal. 17: 197–207.

———. 1939. Some observed effects of stream-valley flooding on mammalian populations in eastern Oklahoma. J. Mammal., 20: 304–306.

———. 1940a. Home ranges and populations of the meadow vole in southern Michigan. J. Wildl. Mgt. 4: 149–161.

———. 1940b. Notes on home ranges and populations of the short-tailed shrew. Ecology 21: 284–288.

———. 1941a. Techniques for the study of mammal populations. J. Mammal. 22: 148–157.

————. 1941b. Some data on the home ranges and general life history of the short-tailed shrew, red-backed vole, and woodland jumping mouse in northern Michigan. Am. Midland Naturalist 25: 681–685.

————. 1942. Size of home range and notes on the life history of the woodland deer-mouse and eastern chipmunk in northern Michigan. J. Mammal. 23: 27–36.

————. 1943. Populations of the deer-mouse and associated small mammals in the mesquite association of southern New Mexico. Contrib. Lab. Vertebrate Biol. 21: 1–40.

————. 1951. Evolutionary significance of geographic variation in population density. Texas J. Sci. 1951(1): 53–57.

————. 1953. Population dynamics of rodents and other small mammals. Advances in Genet. 5: 1–41.

BLOEDEL, PENTRICE. 1955. Hunting methods of fish-eating bats, particularly *Noctilio leporinus*. J. Mammal. 36: 390–399.

BODENHEIMER, F. S. 1949. Problems of vole populations in the Middle East. Report on the population dynamics of the Levant vole (*Microtus guentheri* D. and A.). Research Council of Israel, Jerusalem. 77 pp.

BOLE, B. P., JR. 1939. The quadrat method of studying small mammal populations. Sci. Publ. Cleveland Mus. Nat. Hist. 5: 15–77.

BOLE, B. P., JR., and P. N. MOULTHROP. 1942. The Ohio Recent mammal collection in the Cleveland Museum of Natural History. Sci. Publ. Cleveland Mus. Nat. Hist. 5(6): 83–181.

BOLK, L. 1921–1922. Odontological essays. J. Anat. (London) 55: 138; 56: 107; 57: 55.

BOOTH, Y. SPENCER. 1956. Shrews (*Crocidura cassiteridum*) on the Scilly Isles. Proc. Zool. Soc. London 126: 167–170.

BOURLIÈRE, FRANÇOIS. 1954. The natural history of mammals. Alfred A. Knopf, Inc., New York. xxi + 363 + xi pp.

BRADSHAW, GORDON. 1956. Kansas small mammal census: A five-year study, with attempts to determine factors in population fluctuations. Master's thesis manuscript. Library, Kansas State College of Agr. and Appl. Sci., Manhattan, Kan.

BRADT, GLENN W. 1938. A study of beaver colonies in Michigan. J. Mammal. 19: 139–162.

BROWN, C. EMERSON. 1925. Longevity of mammals in the Philadelphia zoological garden. J. Mammal. 6: 264–267.

BROWN, DAVID H., and KENNETH S. NORRIS. 1956. Observations of captive and wild cetaceans. J. Mammal. 37: 311–326.

BUCKNER, C. H. 1957. Home range of *Synaptomys cooperi*. J. Mammal. 38: 132.

BUECHNER, HELMUT K. 1942. Interrelationships between the pocket gopher and land use. J. Mammal. 23: 346–348.

BULL, P. C. 1956. Some facts and theories on the ecology of the wild rabbit. New Zealand Sci. Rev. 14(5): 51–57.

BURNS, EUGENE. 1957. Is that so? (column in newspaper). Arizona Republic (Phoenix). April 9: p. 21.

BURT, WILLIAM H. 1930. Notes on the habits of the Mohave ground squirrel. J. Mammal. 17: 221–224.

————. 1940. Territorial behavior and populations of some small mammals of southern Michigan. Misc. Publs., Univ. Mich. Mus. Zool. 45: 1–58.

————. 1943. Territoriality and home range concepts as applied to mammals. J. Mammal. 24: 346–352.

CABRERA, ANGEL. 1925. General mammalium: Insectivora Gateopithecia. Madrid. Pp. 1–232.

CARPENTER, C. R. 1934. A field study of the behavior and social relations of the howling monkeys. Comp. Psychol. Monographs 10(2), 168 pp.

————. 1935. Behavior of red spider monkeys in Panama. J. Mammal. 16: 171–180.

————. 1940. A field study in Siam of the behavior and social relations of the gibbon (*Hylobates lar*). Comp. Psychol. Monographs 16(5), 212 pp.

————. 1942. Societies of monkeys and apes. Biol. Symposia 8: 177–204.

CARPENTER, C. R. 1950. Social behavior of non-human primates. Structure et physiologie des sociétés animales. Paris.

CARTER, T. DONALD. 1955. Remarkable age attained by a bobcat. J. Mammal. 36: 290.

CARTER, T. D., J. E. HILL, and G. H. H. TATE. 1946. Mammals of the Pacific world. The Macmillan Co., New York. xvi + 227 pp.

CHAPMAN, A. B., L. E. CASIDA, and A. COTE. 1938. Sex ratios of fetal calves. Proc. Am. Soc. Animal Production. Pp. 303–304.

CHAPSKIY, K. K. 1936. The walrus of the Kara Sea. Trans. Arctic Inst. Leningrad 67: 111 pp. (in Russian, résumé in English, pp. 112–124).

CHARLES, W. N. 1956. The effects of a vole plague in the Carron Valley, Stirlingshire. Scot. Forestry 10: 201–204.

CHRISTIAN, JOHN J. 1950. The adreno-pituitary system and population cycles in mammals. J. Mammal. 31: 247–259.

———. 1953. A natural history of a summer aggregation of *Eptesicus fuscus fuscus*. Memorandum Report 53–16. Naval Med. Research Inst., National Naval Medical Center, Bethesda, Md.

CHRISTIAN, JOHN J., and DAVID E. DAVIS. 1956. The relationship between adrenal weight and population status of urban Norway rats. J. Mammal. 37(4): 475–486.

CLARK, H. W. 1937. Association types in the north coast ranges of California. Ecology 18: 214–230.

CLARKE, JOHN R. 1953. The hippopotamus in Gambia, West Africa. J. Mammal. 34: 299–315.

CLEMENTS, F. E., and V. E. SHELFORD. 1939. Bioecology. John Wiley & Sons, Inc., New York.

COCKRUM, E. LENDELL. 1952. Mammals of Kansas. Univ. Kansas Publs., Mus. Nat. Hist. 7: 1–303.

———. 1954. Non-geographic variation in cranial measurements of wild-taken *Peromyscus leucopus novebracensis*. J. Mammal. 35: 367–376.

———. 1960. The mammals of Arizona, their taxonomy and distribution. Univ. of Ariz. Press, Tucson, Ariz.

COLE, LAMONT C. 1951. Population cycles and random oscillations. J. Wildl. Mgt. 15: 233–252.

COMFORT, ALEX. 1956. Maximum ages reached by domestic cats. J. Mammal. 37: 118–119.

CONAWAY, C. H. 1958. Maintenance, reproduction and growth of the least shrew in captivity. J. Mammal. 39: 507–512.

CONSTANTINE, DENNY G. 1957. Color variation and molt in *Tadarida brasiliensis* and *Myotis velifer*. J. Mammal. 38: 461–466.

COPE, E. D. 1878. On the mechanical genesis of tooth forms. Proc. Philadelphia Acad. Nat. Sci. for 1878.

COTT, H. B. 1940. Adaptive coloration in animals. Methuen & Co., Ltd., London. xxxii + 508 pp.

COWAN, I. McT. 1940. Distribution and variation in the native sheep of North America. Am. Midland Naturalist 24: 505–580.

COWLES, R. B. 1940. Additional implication of reptilian sensitivity to high temperature. Am. Naturalist 74: 542–561.

CRABB, WILFRED D. 1948. The ecology and management of the prairie spotted skunk in Iowa. Ecol. Monographs 18: 201–232.

CROWCROFT, PETER. 1957. Life of the shrew. Stellar Press, M. Reinhardt, London. 166 pp.

CROWCROFT, PETER, and F. P. ROWE. 1957. The growth of confined colonies of the wild house mouse (*Mus musculus* L.). Proc. Zool. Soc. London 129(3.): 359–370.

DALMAT, H. T. 1944. Parathyroid infection in the northern white-footed mouse in central Iowa. Amer. Midland Naturalist 31(1): 179–181.

DALQUEST, WALTER W. 1953. Mammals of the Mexican state of San Luis Potosi. Louisiana State Univ. Stud., Biol. Sci. Ser. 1: 1–229.

————. 1957. Observations on the sharp-nosed bat, *Rhynchiscus nasio* (Maximilian). Texas J. Sci. 9(2): 218–226.

DALQUEST, WALTER W., and DONALD F. HOFFMEISTER. 1948. Mountain sheep from the state of Washington in the collection of the University of Arizona. Trans. Kansas Acad. Sci. 51: 224–234.

DAUBENMIRE, R. F. 1938. Merriam's life zones of North America. Quart. Rev. Biol. 13: 327–332.

DAVIS, DAVID E., and JOHN J. CHRISTIAN. 1957. Relation of adrenal weight to social rank of mice. Proc. Soc. Exptl. Biol. Med. 94(4): 728–731.

DAVIS, W. B. 1938. Relation of size of pocket gophers to soil and altitude. J. Mammal. 19: 338–342.

————. 1939. The Recent mammals of Idaho. Caxton Printers, Ltd., Caldwell, Idaho. Pp. 1–400.

DAVIS, W. B., R. R. RAMSEY, and J. M. ARENDALE, JR. 1938. Distribution of pocket gophers (*Geomys breviceps*) in relation to soils. J. Mammal. 19: 412–418.

DAWSON, JANET. 1956. Splenic hypertrophy in voles. Nature 178(4543): 1183–1184.

DE CUNHA VIEIRA, C. 1955. Lista remissiva dos mamiferos do Brasil. Arquiv. Zool. estado São Paulo 8: 341–474.

DEGERBØL, M. 1940. Mammalia, *in* Zoology of the Faroes. 3(2) fasc. 65: 1–133.

DEGERBØL, M., and U. MOHL-HANSEN. 1943. Remarks on the breeding conditions and moulting of the collared lemming (*Dicrostonyx*). Medd. om Grönland 131(11): 1–40.

DE VOS, ANTON. 1958. Summer observations on moose behavior in Ontario. J. Mammal. 39: 128–139.

DICE, LEE R. 1933. Longevity in *Peromyscus maniculatus gracilis*. J. Mammal. 14: 147–148.

————. 1943. The biotic provinces of North America. Univ. Mich. Press, Ann Arbor, Mich. viii + 78 pp., 1 map.

————. 1947. Effectiveness of selection by owls on deer mice (*Peromyscus maniculatus*) which contrast in color with their background. Contrib. Lab. Vertebrate Biol. 34: 1–20.

DINGLE, RICHARD WM. 1956. Pocket gophers as a cause of mortality in eastern Washington pine plantations. J. Forestry 54(12): 832–839.

DITMARS, R. L., and A. M. GREENHALL. 1935. The vampire bat. Zoologica 19: 53–76.

DOW, SUMNER A. 1952. Antelope ageing studies in Montana. Montana Coop. Wildl. Research Unit, Spec. Report 3, pp. 1–5.

DOZIER, HUBERT, and ROBERT W. ALLEN. 1942. Color, sex ratios and weights of Maryland muskrat. J. Wildl. Mgmt. 6(4): 294–300.

DUKES, H. H. 1955. The physiology of domestic animals. 7th ed. Comstock Publ. Assoc., Ithaca, N.Y. xii + 1020 pp.

DURRANT, S. D. 1952. Mammals of Utah. Univ. Kansas Publs., Mus. Nat. Hist. 6: 1–549.

EADIE, W. ROBERT, and W. J. HAMILTON, JR. 1956. Notes on the reproduction of the star-nosed mole. J. Mammal. 37: 223–231.

ECKE, DEAN H., and ALVA R. KINNEY. 1956. Ageing meadow mice, *Microtus californicus*, by observation of molt progression. J. Mammal. 37: 249–254.

EDWARDS, R. YORKE, and RALPH W. RITCEY. 1956. The migration of a moose herd. J. Mammal. 37: 486–494.

EDWARDS, ROBERT L. 1946. Some notes on the life history of the Mexican ground squirrel in Texas. J. Mammal. 27: 105–115.

EGOSCUE, HAROLD, JR. 1956. Preliminary studies of the kit fox in Utah. J. Mammal. 37: 351–357.

EINARSEN, ARTHUR S. 1956. The deer of North America. W. P. Taylor (ed.). Stackpole Co., Harrisburg, Pa. Pp. 363–390.

ELDER, W. H. 1951. The baculum as an age criterion in minks. J. Mammal. 32: 43–50.

ELLERMAN, JOHN R. 1940–1941. The families and genera of living rodents. London Brit. Mus. Nat. Hist. Vol. 1, 689 pp.; Vol. 2, 690 pp.

ELOFF, G. 1951a. Orientation in the mole-rat, *Cryptomys*. Brit. J. Psychol. 42: 134–145.

———. 1951b. Adaptation in rodent moles and insectivorous moles and the theories of convergence. Nature 168: 1001.

———. 1953. The free state mole (*Cryptomys*). Farming in S. Africa 28(327): 203–205.

———. 1958. The function and structural degeneration of the eye of South African rodent moles, *Cryptomys bigalkei* and *Bathyergus maritimus*. S. African J. Sci. 54: 293–301.

ELTON, CHARLESS. 1942. Voles, mice and lemmings; problems in population dynamics. Clarendon Press, Oxford. Pp. 1–496.

ELTON, C., E. B. FORD, J. R. BAKER, and A. D. GARDNER. 1931. The health and parasites of a wild mouse population. Proc. Zool. Soc. London for 1931: pp. 657–721.

ERICKSON, ARNOLD B. 1949. Summer populations and movements of the cotton rat and other rodents on the Savannah River Refuge. J. Mammal. 30: 133–140.

ERRINGTON, P. L. 1951. Concerning fluctuations in populations of the prolific and widely distributed muskrat. Am. Naturalist 85: 273–292.

ERUS, N. (ed.). 1960. Production yearbook, 1959, Food and Agriculture Organization of the United Nations. Vol. 13. Statistics Div., United Nations, Rome.

EVANS, C. 1938. Observations on hibernating bats with special reference to reproduction and splenic adaptations. Am. Naturalist 72: 480–484.

EVANS, F. C., and R. HOLDENREID. 1943. A population study of the Beechey ground squirrel in central California. J. Mammal. 24: 231–260.

FAY, FRANCIS H. 1954. Quantitative experiments on the food consumption of *Parascalops breweri*. J. Mammal. 35: 107–109.

FELTEN, HEINZ. 1955. Fledermause (Mammalia, Chiroptera) aus El Salvador. Teil 2. Senck Biol. 37(½): 69–86.

FISHER, H. D., and B. A. MACKENZIE. 1954. Rapid preparation of tooth sections for age determinations. J. Wildl. Mgt. 18(4): 535–537.

FITCH, HENRY S. 1947. Ecology of a cottontail rabbit (*Sylvilagus auduboni*) population in central California. Calif. Fish Game 33: 159–184.

———. 1948. Ecology of the California ground squirrel on grazing lands. Amer. Midland Naturalist 39: 513–596.

FITCH, HENRY S., PHIL GOODRUM, and COLEMAN NEWMAN. 1952. The armadillo in the southeastern United States. J. Mammal. 33: 21–37.

FITCH, HENRY S., and L. L. SANDIGE. 1953. Ecology of the opossum on a natural area in northeastern Kansas. Univ. Kansas Publs., Mus. Nat. Hist. 7: 305–338.

FOUCH, WILLIAM R. 1958. Longevity records for the fox squirrel. J. Mammal. 39: 154–155.

FRANK, FRITZ. 1957. The causality of microtine cycles in Germany. J. Wildl. Mgt. 21: 113–121.

FRIANT, MADELEINE. 1933. Contribution à l'étude de la différenciation des dents jugales chez les mammifères. Essai d'une théorie de la dentition. Preface de R. Anthony. Publications du Muséum National d'Histoire Naturelle 1, pp. 1–132, 71 figs.

FRIEDMAN, MAURICE H. 1938. Gonadotropic extracts from the leaves of young oat plants. Proc. Soc. Exptl. Biol. Med. 37(4): 645–646.

FRIEDMAN, MAURICE H., and GERTRUDE S. FRIEDMAN. 1934. A gonad stimulating extract from alfalfa meal. Proc. Soc. Exptl. Biol. Med. 31(7): 842–843 (preliminary paper).

FRILEY, C. E., JR. 1949. Use of the baculum in age determination of Michigan beaver. J. Mammal. 30: 261–267.

GASHWILER, JAY S. 1959. Small mammal study in west-central Oregon. J. Mammal. 40: 128–139.

GENTRY, JOHN B., and EUGENE P. ODUM. 1957. The effect of weather on the winter activity of old field rodents. J. Mammal. 38: 72–77.

GERVAIS, P. 1854. Histoire naturelle des mammifères. Paris.

GLASS, BRYAN. 1958. Returns of Mexican freetail bats banded in Oklahoma. J. Mammal. 39: 435–437.

GOLDMAN, E. A. 1920. Mammals of Panama. Smithsonian Inst. Misc. Coll. 69(5): 309 pp.

———. 1937. The Colorado River as a barrier to mammalian distribution. J. Mammal. 18: 427–435.

GOLLEY, FRANK B. 1957. Gestation period, breeding and fawning behavior of Columbian black-tailed deer. J. Mammal. 38: 116–120.

GOODWIN, G. G. 1946. Mammals of Costa Rica. Bull. Am. Mus. Nat. Hist. 87(5): 275–473.

GORDON, KENNETH. 1936. Territorial behavior and social dominance among Sciuridae. J. Mammal. 17: 171–172.

GRAF, WILLIAM. 1956. Territorialism in deer. J. Mammal. 37: 165–170.

GREGORY, WILLIAM K. 1922. On the "habitus" and "heritage" of Caenolestes. J. Mammal. 3:106–114.

GRIFFIN, D. R. 1940. Notes on the life histories of New England cave bats. J. Mammal. 21: 181–187.

GRIM, JOHN NORMAN. 1958. Feeding habits of the southern California mole. J. Mammal. 39: 265–268.

GRINNELL, J. 1914. An account of the mammals and birds of the Lower Colorado Valley, with special reference to the distributional problems presented. Univ. Calif. Publ. Zool. 12: 51–294.

———. 1923. The burrowing rodents of California as agents of soil formation. J. Mammal. 4: 137–149.

———. 1933. Review of the Recent mammal fauna of California. Univ. Calif. Publ. Zool. 40: 71–234.

———. 1939. Effects of a wet year on mammalian population. J. Mammal. 20: 62–64.

GRINNELL, J., and H. S. SWARTH. 1913. An account of the birds and mammals of the San Jacinto area of southern California with remarks on the behavior of geographic races on the margins of their habitats. Univ. Calif. Publ. Zool., 10: 197–466.

GRZIMEK, BERNHARD. 1943. Weitere Vergleichsversuche mit Wolf und Hund. Zeits. fur Tierpsychol. 5: 59–73.

GUILER, ERIC R. 1958. Observations on a population of small marsupials in Tasmania. J. Mammal. 39: 44–58.

GUPTA, B. B. 1961. Investigations of the rolling mechanism in the Indian hedgehog. J. Mammal. 42: 365–371.

HAGAN, BRIGITTE. 1955. Eine neue Methode der Alterbestimmung von Kleinsaugen. Bonner Zool. Beitr. 6(½): 1–7.

HALE, JAMES B. 1949. Aging cottontail rabbits by bone growth. J. Wildl. Mgt. 13(2): 216–225.

HALL, E. RAYMOND. 1927. An outbreak of house mice in Kern County, California. Univ. Calif. Publ. Zool. 30: 189–203.

———. 1946. Mammals of Nevada. Univ. Calif. Press, Berkeley, Calif. xi + 710 pp.

———. 1951. American weasels. Univ. Kansas Publs. Mus. Nat. Hist. 4: 1–466.

HALL, E. RAYMOND, and KEITH R. KELSON. 1959. The Mammals of North America. The Ronald Press Co., New York. Vol. 1, pp. xxx + 1–546 + 1–79, Figs. 1–312, Maps 1–320; Vol. 2, pp. viii + 547–1083 + 1–79, Figs. 313–553, Maps 321–500.

HALL, H. M., and J. GRINNELL. 1919. Life-zone indicators in California. Proc. Calif. Acad. Sci. Ser. 4, 9: 37–67.

HAMILTON, W. J., JR. 1939a. Activity of Brewer's mole (Parascalops breweri). J. Mammal. 20: 307–310.

———. 1939b. American mammals. McGraw-Hill Book Co., Inc., New York. xii + 434 pp.

———. 1958. Life history and economic relations of the opossum (Didelphis marsupialis virginiana) in New York State. Cornell Univ. Agri. Expt. Sta. Mem. 354, pp. 1–48.

HARDY, R. 1945. The influence of types of soil upon the local distribution of some mammals in southwestern Utah. Ecol. Monographs. 15: 71–108, 19 figs.

HARPER, FRANCIS. 1945. Extinct and vanishing mammals of the Old World. Am. Comm. for Intern. Wildl. Protect. N. Y. Zool. Park, Spec. Publ. 12, xv + 850 pp.

HARRIS, VAN T. 1956. The nutria as a wild fur animal in Louisiana. Trans. 21st N. Am. Wildl. Conf. pp. 474–485.

HARRISON, JOHN L., and ROBERT TRAUB. 1950. Rodents and insectivores from Selangor, Malaya. J. Mammal. 31: 337–345.

HARTMAN, CARL G. 1923. Breeding habits, development and birth of the opossum. Smithsonian Inst. Rep. for 1921, Publ. 2689, pp. 347–363.

HAUGEN, ARNOLD G. 1942. Home range of cottontail rabbit. Ecology 23: 354–367.

HAUGEN, ORLAND L. 1954. Longevity of the raccoon in the wild. J. Mammal. 35: 439.

HAWBECKER, ALBERT C. 1944. The giant kangaroo rat and sheep forage. J. Wildl. Mgt. 8: 161–165.

———. 1958. Survival and home range in the Nelson antelope ground squirrel. J. Mammal. 39: 207–215.

HAWLEY, VERNON D., and FLETCHER E. NEWBY. 1957. Marten home ranges and population fluctuations. J. Mammal. 38: 174–184.

HAYNE, D. W. 1949a. Calculation of size of home range. J. Mammal. 30: 1–18.

———. 1949b. Two methods for estimating population from trapping records. J. Mammal. 30: 399–411.

———. 1950. Apparent home range of Microtus in relation to distance between traps. J. Mammal. 31: 26–39.

HEAPE, W. J., JR. 1931. Migration, emigration and nomadism. Heffer, Cambridge, England. Pp. 1–100.

HENDERSON, JUNIUS, and ELBERTA L. CRAIG. 1932. Economic mammalogy. Charles C Thomas, Publishers, Springfield, Ill. x + 397 pp.

HESSEE, R., W. C. ALLEE, and K. P. SCHMIDT. 1951. Ecological animal geography. John Wiley & Sons, Inc., New York. xiii + 715 pp.

HIRASAKA, K. 1954. Basking habit of the Japanese bear. J. Mammal. 35: 128.

HOCK, RAYMOND J. 1951. The metabolic rates and body temperatures of bats. Biol. Bull. 101(3): 289–299.

HOLLISTER, N. 1919. East African mammals in the United States National Museum. Part II. U.S. Nat. Museum Bull. 99(2): x + 175.

———. 1924. East African mammals in the United States National Museum. Part III. Primates, Artiodactyla, Perissodactyla, Proboscidea and Hyracoidea. U. S. Nat. Museum Bull. 99: viii + 164.

HOLMES, CHARLES H. 1939. Australia's patchwork creature, the platypus. Nat. Geog. Mag. 76: 273–282.

HOOPER, EMMET T. 1956. Longevity of captive kangaroo rats, Dipodomys. J. Mammal. 37: 124–125.

HOWELL, JOSEPH C. 1954. Populations and home ranges of small mammals on an overgrown field. J. Mammal. 35: 177–186.

HUEY, LAURENCE M. 1936. Some habits of a gray shrew in captivity. J. Mammal. 17: 143–145.

———. 1941. Mammalian invasion via the highway. J. Mammal. 22: 383–385.

INGLES, LLOYD G. 1953. Observations on Barro Colorado Island mammals. J. Mammal. 34: 266–268.

———. 1959. A quantitative study of mountain beaver activity. Am. Midland Naturalist 61: 419–423.

———. 1961. Reingestion in the mountain beaver. J. Mammal. 42: 411–412.

JOHNSON, G. E. 1931. Hibernation of mammals. Quart. Rev. Biol. 6: 439–461.

JONES, J. KNOX, and ALBERT A. BARBER. 1957. Home ranges and populations of small mammals in central Korea. J. Mammal. 38: 377–392.

JORDAN, JAMES S. 1948. A midsummer study of the southern flying squirrel. J. Mammal. 29: 44–48.

KAHMANN, H., and K. OSTERMANN. 1951. Wahrnehmen and Hervobringen höher Töne bei kleinen Saugetieren. Experientia 7: 268–269.

KALELA, OLAVI. 1957. Regulation of reproduction rate in subarctic populations of the vole Clethrionomys rufocanus (Sund). Ann. Acad. Sci. Fennicae Ser. A., Sect. IV (Biol.) 34, pp. 1–60.

KARTMAN, L., K. F. MURRAY, F. M. PRINCE, S. F. QUAN, and M. A. HOLMES. 1958. Public health implications of the Microtus outbreak in Oregon and California during 1957–1958. Calif. Vector Views 5(4): 19–24, April.

KATZ, I. 1949. Behavioral interactions in a herd of Barbary sheep (Ammotragus lervia). Zoologica 34: 9–18.

KEITH, L. B., and J. D. WARING. 1956. Evidence of orientation and homing in snowshoe hares. Can. J. Zool. 34: 579–581.

KELLOGG, R. 1933. Whales, giants of the sea. Nat. Geog. Mag. (3): 35–90.

———. 1939. Annotated list of Tennessee mammals. Proc. U. S. Nat. Museum 86: 245–303.

KENDEIGH, S. C. 1932. A study of Merriam's temperature laws. Wilson Bull. 44: 129–143.

KENYON, KARL W., and FORD WILKE. 1953. Migration of the northern fur seal, Callorhinus ursinus. J. Mammal. 34: 86–97.

KILHAM, LAWRENCE. 1954. Territorial behavior of red squirrel. J. Mammal. 35: 252–253.

———. 1958. Territorial behavior in pikas. J. Mammal. 39: 307.

KING, JOHN A. 1955. Social behavior, social organization, and population dynamics in a black-tailed prairie dog town in the Black Hills of South Dakota. Contrib. Lab. Vertebrate Biol., Univ. Mich. 67: 1–123.

KIRKPATRICK, RALPH, and L. SOWLS. 1962. Age determination of the collared peccary (Pecari tajacu) by the tooth replacement pattern. J. Wildl. Mgt. (In press.)

KOFORD, CARL B. 1957. The vicuña and the puma. Ecol. Monographs 27: 153–219.

KORSCHAGEN, LeROY J. 1958. December food habits of mink in Missouri. J. Mammal. 39: 521–527.

KRIZAT, G. 1940. Die Orientierung in Raume bei Talpa europaea. 2 Morph. Tiere Berlin 36: 512–556.

KUKENTHAL, W. 1891. Einige Bemerkungen über die Saugetierbezahnung. Anat. Anz. 6: 364–370.

LAMPIO, TEPPO. 1957. Migrations of squirrels. Soumen Riista 11: 48–58 (in Finnish with English summary).

LANG, H. 1923. Caudal and pectoral glands of African elephant shrews (Elephantulus). J. Mammal. 4: 261–263.

LATHAM, ROGER M. 1950. The food of predaceous animals in northeastern United States. Pa. Game Comm., final rep., P-R Project 36-R, pp. 1–69.

———. 1953. Simple method for identification of least weasel. J. Mammal. 34: 385.

LAURIE, E. O. M. 1946. The reproduction of the house mouse (Mus musculus) living in different environments. Proc. Roy. Soc. Biol. 133: 248–281.

LAWS, R. M. 1952. A new method of age determination for mammals. Nature 169(4310): 972–973.

———. 1953. The elephant seal (Mirounga leonina, Linn). Part I: Growth and age. Falkland Islands Depend. Surv., Sci. Rep. 8: 1–62.

LAYNE, JAMES N. 1957. Homing behavior of chipmunks in central New York. J. Mammal. 38: 519–520.

———. 1958. Observations on fresh water dolphins in the upper Amazon. J. Mammal. 39: 1–22.

LAYNE, JAMES N., and ALLEN H. BENTON. 1954. Some speeds of small mammals. J. Mammal. 35: 103–104.

LECHLEITNER, R. R. 1954. Age criteria in mink, Mustela vison. J. Mammal. 35: 496–503.

———. 1957. Reingestion in the black-tailed jack rabbit. J. Mammal. 38: 481–485.

Leslie, P. H., and D. Chitty. 1951. The estimation of population parameters from data obtained by means of the capture-recapture method. Biometrika 38(3–4): 269–292.

Leslie, P. H., and R. M. Ranson. 1940. The mortality, fertility and rate of natural increase of the vole (*Microtus agrestis*) as observed in the laboratory. J. Animal Ecol. 9: 27–52.

LeSouef, A. S., and H. Burrell. 1926. Wild animals of Australia. George H. Harrap & Co., Ltd., London. Pp. 1–388.

Liers, Emil E. 1958. Early breeding in the river otter. J. Mammal. 39: 438–439.

Lincoln, F. C. 1930. Calculating waterfowl abundance on the basis of banding returns. U. S. Dept. Agri. cir. 118: 1–4.

Liu, C. 1937. Notes on the food of the Chinese hedgehogs. J. Mammal. 18: 355–357.

Louch, Charles D. 1958. Adreno-cortical activity in two meadow vole populations. J. Mammal. 39: 109–116.

Lowe, Charles E. 1958. Ecology of the swamp rabbit in Georgia. J. Mammal. 39: 116–127.

Lyman, Charles P. 1943. Control of coat color in the varying hare, *Lepus americanus* Erxleben. Bull. Mus. Comp. Zool. 93: 393–461.

———. 1954. Activity, food consumption and hoarding in hibernators. J. Mammal. 35: 545–552.

McCarley, Howard. 1958. Ecology, behavior and population dynamics of *Peromyscus nuttalli* in eastern Texas. Texas J. Sci. 10(2): 147–169.

McKeever, Sturgis, J. H. Schubart, and M. D. Moody. 1958. Natural occurrence of tularemia in marsupials, carnivores, lagomorphs and large. rodents in southwestern Georgia and northwestern Florida. J. Infectious Diseases 103(2): 120–126.

Manville, Richard H. 1949. Techniques for capture and marking of mammals. J. Mammal. 30: 27–33.

———. 1953. Longevity in the coyote. J. Mammal. 34: 390.

———. 1957. Longevity of captive mammals. J. Mammal. 38: 279–280.

Mather, K., and B. J. Harrison. 1949. The manifold effect of selection. Heredity 3: 1–52, 131–162.

Matheson, Colin. 1957. Potential longevity in some mammals. J. Mammal. 38: 280.

Matthews, L. Harrison. 1952. British Mammals. William Collins Sons & Co., Ltd., London. xii + 410 pp.

Mayr, E. 1942. Systematics and the origin of the species. Columbia Univ. Press, New York. xiv. + 344 pp.

Mayr, E., E. G. Linsley, and R. L. Usinger. 1953. Methods and principles of systematic zoology. McGraw-Hill Book Co., Inc., New York. ix + 328 pp.

Merriam, C. Hart. 1890. Results of a biological survey of the San Francisco region and desert of the Little Colorado, Arizona. N. Am. Fauna 3: 1–136.

———. 1894. The geographic distribution of animals and plants in North America. U. S. Dept. Agri. Yearbook for 1894. Pp. 203–214.

———. 1899a. Life zones and crop zones of the U. S. Bull. Biol. Surv. 10: 9–79.

———. 1899b. Results of a biological survey of Mt. Shasta, California. N. Am. Fauna 16: 1–179.

Miller, Milton A. 1957. Burrows of the Sacramento Valley pocket gophers in flood-irrigated alfalfa fields. Hilgardia 26(3): 431–452.

Miller, Richard S. 1958. A study of a wood mouse population in Wytham Woods, Berkshire. J. Mammal. 39: 477–493.

Miller, W. C. 1932. A preliminary report upon the sex ratio of Scottish red deer. Proc. Roy. Phys. Soc. 22: 99–101.

Mohr, C. O. 1947. Table of equivalent population of North American small mammals. Am. Midland Naturalist 37: 223–249.

Morris, R. F. 1955. Population studies on some small forest mammals in eastern Canada. J. Mammal. 36: 21–35.

MORRISON, PETER R., FRED A. RYSER, and ROBERT L. STRECKER. 1954. Growth and the development of temperature regulation in the tundra redback vole. J. Mammal. 35: 376–386.

MOSSMAN, H. W. 1953. The genital system and the fetal membranes as criteria for mammalian phylogeny and taxonomy. J. Mammal. 34: 289–298.

MUELLER, H. C., and J. T. EMLEN, JR. 1957. Homing in bats. Science 126: 307–308.

MURIE, ADOLPH. 1944. The wolves of Mt. McKinley. U. S. Dept. Interior Nat. Park Serv., Fauna Ser. 5, xix + 238 pp.

MURIE, O. J. 1951. The elk of North America. Stackpole Co., Harrisburg, Pa. xix + 238 pp.

MYERS, K. F., and K. MATSUMURA. 1927. Incidence of carriers of B. aertyke (B. pestis Caviae) and B. enteritis in wild rats of San Francisco. J. Infectious Diseases 41: 395–404.

MYKYTOWYCZ, R. 1958. Social behaviour of an experimental colony of wild rabbits. Oryctolagus cunniculus (L.). Part I: Establishment of the colony. C.S.I.R.O. Wildl. Research 3(1): 7–25.

NALBANDOV, A. V. 1958. Reproductive physiology. W. H. Freeman & Co., Publishers, San Francisco. xi + 271 pp.

NEGUS, NORMAN C. 1958. Pelage stages in the cottontail rabbit. J. Mammal. 39: 246–252.

NELSEN, O. E. 1953. Comparative embryology of the vertebrates. Blakiston Div., McGraw-Hill Book Co., Inc., New York. xxiii + 982 pp.

NEW, JOHN G. 1958. Dyes for studying the movements of small mammals. J. Mammal. 39: 416–429.

NOBACK, C. R. 1951. Morphology and phylogeny of hair. Ann. N. Y. Acad. Sci. 53: 476–492.

NOVIKOV, B. G., and G. I. BLAGODATSKA. 1948. Mechanism of development of protective seasonal colorations. Doklady Akad. Nauk Tadzhik S.S.R. 61: 577–580 (in Russian).

OGNEV, S. I. 1928-50. The mammals of eastern Europe and northern Asia. Moscow. 7 vol., still unfinished.

OSBORN, HENRY FAIRFIELD. 1907. Evolution of mammalian molar teeth. The Macmillan Co., New York.

OSGOOD, WILFRED H. 1914. Mammals of an expedition across northern Peru. Field Mus. Publ. 176, Zool. Ser. 10(12), pp. 143–185.

———. 1943. The mammals of Chile. Zool. Ser., Field Mus. Nat. Hist. (Chicago) 30: 1–268.

PARKES, A. S. 1924. The factors governing mammalian sex ratio. Sci. Prog. 18: 426–435.

PEARSON, O. P. 1942. On the cause and nature of a poisonous action produced by the bite of a shrew (Blarina brevicauda). J. Mammal. 23: 159–166.

———. 1948. Life history of mountain viscachas in Peru. J. Mammal. 29: 345–374.

———. 1951. Mammals in the highlands of southern Peru. Bull. Mus. Comp. Zool., Harvard Univ. 106: 117–176.

PEDERSEN, CARSTEN. 1957. Cycles in Danish vole populations. Danish Rev. Game Biol. 3(2): 1–18.

PETERSEN, A. 1950. Encounters with musk oxen. Kosmos 52(1): 16–21.

PETERSON, R. L. 1955. North American moose. Univ. Toronto Press, Toronto, Canada. 280 pp.

PETRIDES, GEORGE A. 1949a. Viewpoints on the analysis of open season sex and age ratios. Trans. 14th N. Am. Wildl. Conf., pp. 391–410.

———. 1949b. Sex and age determination in the opossum. J. Mammal. 30(4): 364–378.

———. 1950. The determination of sex and age ratios in fur animals. Amer. Midland Naturalist 43(2): 355–382.

Petrides, George A. 1951. The determination of sex and age ratios in the cottontail rabbit. Am. Midland Naturalist 46(2):312–336.

Piper, S. E. 1909. The Nevada mouse plague of 1907–1908. U.S. Dept. Agri. Farmers Bull. 352: 1–23.

———. 1928. The mouse infestation of Buena Vista Lake Basin, California. Calif. Dept. Agri. Bull. 17(10): 538–560.

Pitelka, F. A. 1941. Distribution of buds in relation to major biotic communities. Am. Midland Naturalist 25: 113–137.

Po-chedley, Donald S., and Albert R. Shadle. 1955. Pelage of the porcupine, Erethizon dorsatum dorsatum. J. Mammal. 36: 84–94.

Popov, V. A. 1943. A new age index in Mustelidae. C. R. Acad. Sci. U.S.S.R. 38: 258–260.

Prakas, Ishwar. 1960. Breeding of mammals in Rajasthan Desert, India. J. Mammal. 41: 386–389.

Progulska, Donald R., and Thomas S. Baskett. 1958. Mobility of Missouri deer and their harassment by dogs. J. Wildl. Mgt. 22: 184–192.

Pruitt, William, Jr. 1957. A survey of the mammalian Family Soricidae (shrews). Sonderdruck aus Saugetier kundliche Mitteilungen 5(1): 18–27.

Quimby, Don C., and J. E. Gaab. 1957. Mandibular dentition as an age indicator in Rocky Mountain elk. J. Wildl. Mgt. 21(4): 435–451.

Rand, A. L. 1935. On the habits of some Madagascar mammals. J. Mammal. 16: 89–104.

Rasmussen, A. T. 1916. Theories of hibernation. Am. Naturalist 50: 609–625.

Rayner, G. W. 1940. Whale marking. Progress and results to December, 1939. Discovery Rep. 19: 245–284.

Reed, Charles A. 1958. Observations on the burrowing rodent Spalax in Iraq. J. Mammal. 39: 386–389.

Reuther, Ronald T. 1961. Breeding notes on mammals in captivity. J. Mammal. 42: 427–428.

Rice, Dale W. 1957. Sexual behavior of tassel-eared squirrels. J. Mammal. 38: 129.

Robinette, W. Leslie, Jay S. Gashwiler, Jessop B. Low, and Dale A. Jones. 1957. Differential mortality by sex and age among mule deer. J. Wildl. Mgt. 21(1): 1–16.

Rood, John P. 1958. Habits of the short-tailed shrew in captivity. J. Mammal. 39: 499–507.

Rose, C. 1892. Über die Entstehung und Formabanderungen der Menschlichen Molaren. Anat. Anz. 7: 392–421.

Russell, C. P. 1932. Seasonal migration of mule deer. Ecol. Monographs 2: 1–46.

Ruud, J. T. 1940. The surface structure of the baleen as a possible clue to age in whales. Hvalrådets Skrifter no. 23.

———. 1945. Further studies on the structure of the baleen plates and their application to age determination. Norske Videnskaps-Akad. Oslo. Hvalrådets Skrifter no. 29, p. 69.

Ryberg, O. 1947. Studies on bats and bat parasites. Svensk Natur., Stockholm. xvi + 330 pp.

Sanderson, Ivan T. 1937. Animal treasure. The Viking Press, Inc., New York. Pp. 1–325.

Sather, J. Henry. 1958. Biology of the Great Plains muskrat in Nebraska. Wildl. Monographs 2, pp. 1–35.

Scheffer, T. H. 1908. The pocket gopher. Kansas State Coll. Expt. Sta. Bull. 152: 111–145.

———. 1940. Excavation of a runway of the pocket gopher (Geomys bursarius). Trans. Kansas Acad. Sci. 43: 473–478.

Scheffer, V. S. 1950. Growth layers on the teeth of Pinnipedia as an indication of age. Science 112: 309–311.

Schein, M. W. 1950. The relation of sex ratio to physiological age in the wild brown rat. Am. Naturalist 84: 489–496.

SCHEINFELD, A. 1943. Factors influencing the sex ratio. Human Fertility 8: 33–42.

SCHENK, E. T., and J. H. McMASTERS. 1936. Procedures in taxonomy. Stanford Univ. Press, Stanford, Calif.

SCHENKEL, R. 1947. Ausdrucks-Studien an Wölfen. Behaviour 1: 81–129.

SCHOLANDER, P. F. 1940. Experimental investigations on the respiratory function in living mammals and birds. Hvalrådets Skrifter no. 22, pp. 1–131.

SCHRAMM, PETER. 1961. Copulation and gestation in the pocket gophers. J. Mammal. 42: 167–170.

SCOTT, W. B. 1892. The evolution of the premolar teeth in the mammals. Proc. Acad. Nat. Sci., Phila. Pp. 405–444.

SETON, E. T. 1909. Life histories of northern animals. An account of the mammals of Manitoba, vol. 1. Charles Scribner's Sons, New York. 673 pp.

SEVERINGHAUS, C. W. 1949. Tooth development and wear as criteria of age in white-tailed deer. J. Wildl. Mgt. 13: 195–216.

SHARP, WARD M. 1958. Ageing gray squirrels by use of tail-pelage characteristics. J. Wildl. Mgt. 22(1): 29–34.

SHARP, WARD M., and LOUISE H. SHARP. 1956. Nocturnal movements and behavior of wild raccoons at a winter feeding station. J. Mammal. 37: 170–177.

SHELFORD, V. E. 1932. Life zones, modern ecology and the failure of temperature. Wilson Bull. 57: 248–252.

――――. 1954. The antelope population and solar radiation. J. Mammal. 35: 533–538.

SHERMAN, H. B. 1952. A list and bibliography of the mammals of Florida, living and extinct. Quart. J. Florida Acad. Sci. 15(2): 86–126.

SHORTRIDGE, G. C. 1934. The mammals of Southwest Africa. Wm. Heinemann, Ltd., London. Vol. I, pp. xxv + 437; Vol. II, pp. ix + 439–770.

SIIVONEN, LAURI. 1956. The correlation between the fluctuations of partridge and European hare populations and the climatic conditions of winters in southwest Finland during the last thirty years. Papers on Game Research (Finnish Game Foundation) no. 17, 1–30.

SIMPSON, G. G. 1945. The principles of classification and a classification of mammals. Bull. Am. Mus. Nat. Hist., 85: xvi + 350.

SMITH, R. W. 1940. The land mammals of Nova Scotia. Am. Midland Naturalist 24: 213–241.

SOPER, J. DEWEY. 1921. Notes on the snowshoe rabbit. J. Mammal. 2: 101–108.

SOUTHERN, H. N. 1948. Sexual and aggressive behavior in the wild rabbit. Behaviour 1: 173–194.

SOWLS, LYLE K. 1961. Gestation period of the collared peccary. J. Mammal. 42: 425–426.

SOWLS, LYLE K., VEARL R. SMITH, ROBERT JENNESS, ROBERT E. SLOAN, and EDNA REGEBER. 1961. Chemical composition and physical properties of the milk of the collared peccary. J. Mammal. 42: 245–251.

SPECTOR, WILLIAM S. (ed.) 1956. Handbook of biological data. W. B. Saunders Co., Philadelphia. xxxvi + 584 pp.

SPENCER, DONALD A. (compiler). 1958a. Preliminary investigations of the northwestern Microtus irruption. U. S. Fish Wildlife Serv., Denver Wildl. Research Lab., Spec. Rep. 13 pp., mimeo.

――――. 1958b. Biological aspects of the 1957 1958 meadow mouse irruption in the Pacific Northwest. U.S. Fish Wildlife Serv., Wildlife Research Lab., Spec. Rep. 9 pp., mimeo.

SPERBER, I. 1948. On the growth of the rootless molars, particularly in the field vole (Microtus agrestis L.). Arch. Zool. 40A: 1–12.

STAINS, HOWARD J., and F. S. BARKALOW, JR. 1951. The value of North Carolina's game and fish. Game Div., N. Carolina Wildl. Resources Comm., pp. 1–32.

STICKEL, LUCILLE F. 1946a. Experimental analysis of methods for measuring small mammal populations. J. Wildl. Mgt. 10: 150–159.

――――. 1946b. The source of animals moving into a depopulated area. J. Mammal. 27: 301–307.

STICKEL, LUCILLE F. 1949. An experiment on *Peromyscus* homing. Am. Midland Naturalist 41: 659–664.

———. 1954. A comparison of certain methods of measuring ranges of small mammals. J. Mammal. 35: 1–15.

STICKEL, LUCILLE F., and WILLIAM H. STICKEL. 1949. A *Sigmodon* and *Baiomys* population in ungrazed and unburned Texas prairie. J. Mammal. 30: 141–150.

STONE, WALTER D. 1957. The gestation period of the two-toed sloth. J. Mammal. 38: 419.

STORER, I. I., F. C. EVANS, and F. G. PALMER. 1944. Some rodent populations in the Sierra Nevada of California. Ecol. Monographs 14: 165–192.

STORER, I. I., and P. W. GREGORY. 1934. Color aberrations in the pocket gopher and their probable genetic explanation. J. Mammal. 15: 300–312.

STUERWE, FREDERICK W. 1943. Raccoons, their habits and management in Michigan. Ecol. Monographs 13: 203–258.

SUTHERLAND, A. 1897. The temperature of reptiles, monotremes and marsupials. Proc. Roy. Soc. Victoria, N. S. 9: 57–67.

SVIHLA, ARTHUR. 1958. Subfreezing body temperatures in formant ground squirrels. J. Mammal. 39: 296–297.

TAMAKA, RYO. 1958. A change in outbreaking populations of the brown rat under pressure of frequent poisoning operations. Bull. Kochi Women's Univ., vol. 6, Ser. of Nat. Sci. no. 2, pp. 1–6.

TAMAKA, RYO, and SEIYU TERAMURA. 1953. A population of the Japanese field vole infested with Tsutsugamushi disease. J. Mammal. 34: 345–352.

TAPPER, DONALD T. 1941. Natural history of the tulare kangaroo rat. J. Mammal. 22: 117–148.

TATE, G. H. H. 1931. Random observations on habits of South American mammals. J. Mammal. 12: 248–256.

———. 1947. Mammals of eastern Asia. The Macmillan Co., New York. xiv + 366 pp.

TAYLOR, W. P. 1934. Significance of extreme or intermittent conditions in distribution of species and management of natural resources, with a restatement of Liebigs' law of minimum. Ecology, 15: 374–379.

TESTER, JOHN R. 1953. Fall food habits of the raccoon in the South Platte Valley of northeastern Colorado. J. Mammal. 34: 500–502.

THOMPSON, DANIEL Q. 1952. Travel, range and food habits of timber wolves in Wisconsin. J. Mammal. 33: 429–442.

TROUGHTON, ELLIS. 1943. Furred animals of Australia. 2d ed. Angus & Robertson, Ltd., Sydney, Australia. xxvii + 374 pp.

———. 1947. Furred animals of Australia. Charles Scribner's Sons, New York. xxvii + 374 pp.

UECKERMANN, E. 1956. Studies on the cause of debarking by red deer. Z. Jagawissensch. 2: 123–131 (in German).

VANDER HORST, C. J. 1946. Some remarks on the biology of reproduction in the female *Elephatulus*. Trans. Roy. Soc. S. Africa 31(2): 181–199, 7 figs.

VILLA, BERNARDO, and E. L. COCKRUM. 1962. Migration in the guano bat, *Tadarida brasiliensis mexicana* (Saussure). J. Mammal. 43: 43–64.

WATSON, GEORGE E., III. 1961. Behavioral and ecological notes on *Spalax leucodon*. J. Mammal. 42: 359–365.

WEAVER, J. E., and F. E. CLEMENTS. 1938. Plant ecology. 2d ed. McGraw-Hill Book Co., Inc., New York.

WEBER, MAX. 1927–1928. Die Saugetiere. Vol. I, xv + 444 pp.; Vol. II, xxiv + 898 pp.

WHARTON, CHARLES H. 1950. Notes on the life history of the flying lemur. J. Mammal. 31: 269–273.

WHITE, JOHN A. 1953. The baculum in the chipmunks of western North America. Univ. Kansas Publs., Mus. Nat. Hist. 5: 611–631.

WILKE, FORD. 1954. Seals of northern Hokkaido. J. Mammal. 35: 218–224.

WINGE, HERLUF (translation). 1941. The interrelationships of the mammalian genera. C. A. Reitzels Forlang, Copenhagen. 3 vol.

WOOD, JOHN E. 1958. Age structure and productivity of a gray fox population. J. Mammal. 39: 74–86.

WRIGHT, P. L. 1950. Development of the baculum of the long-tailed weasel. Proc. Soc. Expt. Biol. Med. 75: 820–822.

WRIGHT, S. 1931. Evolution of Mendelian populations. Genetics, 16: 97–159.

YERGER, RALPH W. 1953. Home range, territoriality, and populations of the chipmunk in central New York. J. Mammal. 34: 448–458.

YOUNGMAN, PHILLIP M. 1956. A population of the striped field mouse *Apodemus agrarius coreae*, in central Korea. J. Mammal. 37: 1–10.

ZIPPIN, CALVIN. 1956. An evaluation of the removal method of estimating animal population. Biometrics 12(2): 163–189.

Index

Page references in italics, e.g. *192*, refer to a map or illustration. Page references in boldface, e.g. **192**, refer to a definition or a taxonomic listing.